D1078881

Microsoft® ADO.NET 2.0
Step by Step

Rebecca M. Riordan

PUBLISHED BY
Microsoft Press
A Division of Microsoft Corporation
One Microsoft Way
Redmond, Washington 98052-6399

Library of Congress Control Number 2005934152

Printed and bound in the United States of America.

1 2 3 4 5 6 7 8 9   QWT   8 7 6 5

Distributed in Canada by H.B. Fenn and Company Ltd.

A CIP catalogue record for this book is available from the British Library.

Microsoft Press books are available through booksellers and distributors worldwide. For further information about international editions, contact your local Microsoft Corporation office or contact Microsoft Press International directly at fax (425) 936-7329. Visit our Web site at www.microsoft.com/mspress. Send comments to mspinput@microsoft.com.

Microsoft, ActiveX, IntelliSense, Microsoft Press, MSDN, Visual Basic, Visual C#, Visual Studio, Visual Web Developer, Windows, and Windows Server are either registered trademarks or trademarks of Microsoft Corporation in the United States and/or other countries. Other product and company names mentioned herein may be the trademarks of their respective owners.

The example companies, organizations, products, domain names, e-mail addresses, logos, people, places, and events depicted herein are fictitious. No association with any real company, organization, product, domain name, e-mail address, logo, person, place, or event is intended or should be inferred.

This book expresses the author's views and opinions. The information contained in this book is provided without any express, statutory, or implied warranties. Neither the authors, Microsoft Corporation, nor its resellers, or distributors will be held liable for any damages caused or alleged to be caused either directly or indirectly by this book.

Acquisitions Editor: Ben Ryan
Project Editor: Devon Musgrave

Body Part No. X11-50256

Contents at a Glance

Table of Contents

Part V   ADO.NET and Other Types of Data

What do you think of this book? We want to hear from you!

Microsoft is interested in hearing your feedback about this publication so we can continually improve our books and learning resources for you. To participate in a brief online survey, please visit: *www.microsoft.com/learning/booksurvey/*

Introduction

Welcome to *Microsoft ADO.NET 2.0 Step by Step*. ADO.NET is the data access component of the Microsoft .NET Framework development platform. The exercises in this book will introduce you to the ADO.NET object model and show you how to use that model in developing data-bound Windows Forms and Web Forms. In later topics, we'll look at how ADO.NET interacts with Extensible Markup Language (XML) and how to access older versions of ADO from the .NET environment.

An exhaustive treatment of data handling would be, well, exhausting, so this book is necessarily limited in scope. My goal is to provide you with an understanding of the ADO.NET data objects—what they are and how they work together. So fair warning: This book *will not* make you an expert in ADO.NET. (How I wish it were that simple!)

What this book *will* do is give you a road map—a fundamental understanding of the environment—from which you will be able to build expertise. You'll know what you need to do to start building data applications. The rest will come with time and experience. This book is intended as a starting point. If I've done my job, it will give you the big picture of a complex set of interacting objects, but it's up to you to fill in the details that you'll need in your own work.

Who Is This Book For?

This book is intended for developers new to using ADO.NET. To keep the book within manageable proportions, I've assumed that you already have a basic understanding of the .NET Framework and Microsoft Visual Studio 2005 and are reasonably competent in your chosen programming language—either Microsoft Visual Basic or Microsoft Visual C#. If you're completely new to the .NET environment, you might want to start with *Microsoft Visual Basic 2005 Step by Step* by Michael Halvorson (Microsoft Press, 2005) or *Microsoft Visual C# 2005 Step by Step* by John Sharp (Microsoft Press, 2005), depending on your language of choice.

I've also assumed that you have a basic understanding of relational databases and how they're structured, and that you have at least a basic understanding of the SQL syntax of your chosen database engine. If you're new to database design, you might want to start with *An Introduction to Database Systems* by C.J. Date (Addison-Wesley, 2003) or my own *Designing Effective Database Systems* (Addison-Wesley, 2005).

The Organization of This Book

This book is divided into five sections that concentrate on different aspects of using ADO.NET in a .NET Framework application. Part I gives you a brief overview of the ADO.NET environment. Part II concentrates on the data provider objects that handle the low-level communication between a database engine and a .NET Framework application. Part III explores the

ADO.NET objects that model relational data in an application, while Part IV examines the process of binding Windows Forms and Web Forms to ADO.NET data objects. Finally, Part V examines the interaction between ADO.NET and other data environments, discussing ADO.NET and XML data, as well as the use of legacy ADO and ADOX objects from within a .NET Framework application.

Finding Your Best Starting Point in This Book

This book is designed to help you build skills in a number of essential areas. You can use this book if you are new to programming or you are switching from another programming language such as C, C++, Sun Microsystems' Java, or Microsoft Visual Basic 6.0. Use the following table to find your best starting point.

If you are	Follow these steps
New to database programming in the .NET Framework	Install the code samples as described in the "Code Samples" section of this Introduction.
	Complete Parts I, II and III and Chapter 10 in Part IV.
	Complete the remaining chapters of Parts IV and V as your interest dictates.
Migrating from ADO.NET version 1	Install the code samples as described in the "Code Samples" section of this Introduction.
	Skim Parts I through III, concentrating on Chapter 8, to learn about new objects, methods and properties.
	For information on the new Windows Form data-binding architecture, read Chapters 12 and 13.
	For information on the new Web Form data-binding architecture, read Chapters 15 and 16.
Switching from ADO	Install the code samples as described in the "Code Samples" section of this Introduction.
	Complete Parts I through III and Chapter 10 sequentially.
	Complete the remaining chapters in Parts IV and V depending on your interest.

Conventions and Features in This Book

This book presents information using conventions designed to make the information readable and easy to follow.

- Separate exercises are given for Visual Basic programmers and Visual C# programmers. You can skip the exercises that do not apply to you.

- Each exercise is a series of tasks. Each task is presented as a series of numbered steps (1, 2, and so on). A round bullet (•) indicates an exercise that has only one step.

- Boxed elements labeled "Tip" or "Note" provide additional information or alternative methods for completing a step successfully.

- Boxed elements labeled "Important" alert you to information you need to check before continuing.

- Text that you type appears in bold.

- A plus sign (+) between two key names means that you must press those keys at the same time. For example, "Press Alt+Tab" means that you hold down the Alt key while you press the Tab key.

System Requirements

You'll need the following hardware and software to complete the practice exercises in this book:

- Microsoft Windows XP with Service Pack 2, Microsoft Windows Server 2003 with Service Pack 1, or Microsoft Windows 2000 with Service Pack 4

- Microsoft Visual Studio 2005 Standard Edition or Microsoft Visual Studio 2005 Professional Edition

> **Note**   The Visual Studio 2005 software is **not** included with this book. The CD packaged in the back of this book contains the code samples needed to complete the exercises. The Visual Studio 2005 software must be purchased separately.

- Microsoft SQL Server 2005 Express Edition (included with Visual Studio 2005)
- 600 MHz Pentium or compatible processor (1 GHz Pentium recommended)
- 192 MB RAM (256 MB or more recommended)
- Video (800 × 600 or higher resolution) monitor with at least 256 colors (1024 × 768 High Color 16-bit recommended)
- CD-ROM or DVD-ROM drive
- Microsoft Mouse or compatible pointing device

Code Samples

The companion CD packaged in the back of this book contains the code samples that you'll use as you perform the exercises. By using the code samples, you won't waste time creating files that aren't relevant to the exercise. The files and the step-by-step instructions in the exercises also let you learn by doing, which is an easy and effective way to acquire and remember new skills.

> **Important**   This book and code samples have been designed for use with a default installation of Microsoft SQL Server 2005 Express Edition, which has an instance name of SQLEXPRESS. If you want to use this book with a different SQL Server instance name or with the full version of SQL Server, the book's exercise steps and connection strings will have to be adjusted accordingly.

Installing the Code Samples

Follow these steps to install the code samples on your computer so that you can use them with the exercises in this book.

1. Remove the companion CD from the package inside this book, and insert it into your CD-ROM drive.

    An end user license agreement appears on your screen.

> **Note**   If the end user license agreement does not appear, open My Computer from the desktop or Start menu, double-click the icon for your CD-ROM drive, and then double-click StartCD.exe.

2. Review the end user license agreement. If you accept the terms, select the accept option, and then click Next.

    A menu appears with options related to the book.

3. Click Install Code Samples.

4. Follow the instructions that appear.

    The code samples are installed to the following location on your computer:

    C:\Microsoft Press\ADO.NET 2.0 Step by Step

Attaching the AdoStepByStep Database

After you have installed the code samples on your computer, you need to attach the AdoStep-ByStep SQL Server database.

> **Important**   To successfully attach the AdoStepByStep database, SQL Server 2005 Express Edition must be installed and you must have administrative privileges.

1. Open the C:\Microsoft Press\ADO.NET 2.0 Step by Step\SampleDBs folder.

2. Double-click ConfigDB.exe.

3. Click Attach.

   After a few moments, a dialog box appears, indicating whether the attachment was successful.

Using the Code Samples

Each exercise in this book explains when and how to use any code samples necessary for that exercise. When it's time to use a code sample, you will be told how to open the file. The chapters are built around scenarios that simulate real programming projects so that you can easily apply the skills you learn to your own work. In addition, each project has a solution project. These solutions are stored in folders with "Finish" appended to the name.

Uninstalling the Code Samples—Read!

Follow these steps to remove the code samples from your computer:

1. Open the C:\Microsoft Press\ADO.NET 2.0 Step by Step\SampleDBs folder.

2. Double-click ConfigDB.exe.

3. Click Detach.

   After a few moments, a dialog box appears indicating whether the detachment was successful.

4. In Control Panel, open Add Or Remove Programs.

5. From the list of Currently Installed Programs, select Microsoft ADO.NET 2.0 Step by Step.

6. Click Remove.

7. Follow the instructions that appear to remove the code samples.

Prerelease Software

This book was reviewed and tested against the August 2005 Community Technical Preview (CTP) of Visual Studio 2005. The August CTP was the last preview before the final release of Visual Studio 2005. This book is expected to be fully compatible with the final release of Visual Studio 2005. If there are any changes or corrections for this book, they will be collected and added to a Microsoft Knowledge Base article. See the "Support for This Book" section in this Introduction for more information.

Online Companion Content

Content and links related to this book can be found on its online companion content page, which is published on the Microsoft Web site. The online companion content page for this book can be found at:

http://www.microsoft.com/mspress/companion/0-7356-2164-0/

This page includes a link to the Microsoft Press Technology Updates Web page. As technologies related to this book are updated, links to additional information will be added to the Microsoft Press Technology Updates Web page. Visit the page periodically for updates on Visual Studio 2005 and other technologies.

> **Note**   Code samples for this book are on the CD packaged with the book, not on the online companion content page.

Support for This Book

Every effort has been made to ensure the accuracy of this book and the contents of the companion CD. As corrections or changes are collected, they will be added to a Microsoft Knowledge Base article. To see the list of known corrections for this book, you can view the article at:

http://support.microsoft.com/kb/905037/

Microsoft Press provides support for books and companion CDs at the following Web site:

http://www.microsoft.com/learning/support/books/

Questions and Comments

If you have comments, questions or ideas regarding this book or its companion CD, or questions that are not answered by visiting the sites above, please send them to Microsoft Press via e-mail to *mspinput@microsoft.com* or via postal mail to:

Microsoft Press
Attn: Developer Step by Step Series Editor
One Microsoft Way
Redmond, WA 98052-6399

Please note that Microsoft software product support is not offered through the above addresses.

Part I
Getting Started with ADO.NET

Chapter 1
Getting Started with ADO.NET

After completing this chapter, you will be able to:

- Identify the primary objects that make up Microsoft ADO.NET and how they interact.
- Create a data source by using the Data Source Configuration Wizard.
- Create a simple data-bound form by using the Data Source window.

Like other components of the Microsoft .NET Framework, Microsoft ADO.NET consists of a set of .NET objects that interact to provide the required functionality. Unfortunately, this interaction can make learning to use the object model frustrating—it's easy to start thinking that you need to learn all of it before you can understand any of it.

The solution to this problem is to start by building a conceptual framework. In other words, before you try to learn the details of how any particular object functions, you need to have a general understanding of what each object does and how the objects interact.

That's what we'll do in this chapter. We'll start by looking at the main ADO.NET objects and how they work together to get data from a physical data store to the user and back again.

On the Fundamental Interconnectedness of All Things

Microsoft Visual Studio 2005 and Microsoft .NET Framework 2.0 make it much easier to create simple data-bound forms. It's now possible to create a Microsoft Windows Form that provides the basic data manipulation functionality displaying and editing data items, moving through the rows in a table, adding new rows and deleting existing ones—without writing a single line of code. We'll see an example of this later in this chapter.

A margin note like this points you to the discussion of a property or method that hasn't yet been introduced. In later chapters, we'll examine each object in the ADO.NET object model in turn. At least, in theory. In reality, because the objects are so closely interlinked, it's impossible to look at any single object in isolation. When it's necessary to use a method or property that we haven't yet examined, I'll use margin notes, like the one to the left, to point you to the chapter where it's discussed.

The ADO.NET Object Model

The following figure shows a simplified view of the primary objects in the ADO.NET object model. Of course, the reality of the class library is more complicated, but we'll deal with the intricacies later. For now, it's enough to understand what the primary objects are and how they typically interact.

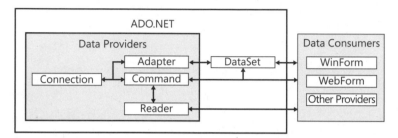

The ADO.NET classes are divided into two components: the Data Providers (sometimes called Managed Providers), which handle communication with a physical data store, and the DataSet, which represents the actual data. Either component can communicate with data consumers such as WebForms and WinForms.

Data Providers

The Data Provider components are specific to a data source. The .NET Framework includes four Data Providers:

1.   A generic provider that can communicate with any OLE DB data source

2.   A SQL Server provider, customized for Microsoft SQL Server 7.0 and later

3.   An ODBC provider that has been optimized for ODBC data sources

4.   An Oracle provider optimized for Oracle databases

You can also write your own data provider. (You might be relieved to know that we won't be covering the creation of data providers in this book.)

The Data Providers included in the .NET Framework contain the same objects, although their names and some of their properties and methods are different. For example, the SQL Server version of a database connection is the SqlConnection, while the OLE DB version is an OleDbConnection.

Connections are discussed in detail in Chapter 2.

The Connection object represents the physical connection to a data source. Its properties determine the data provider (in the case of the OLE DB Data Provider), the data source and the database to which it will connect, and the string to be used during connecting. Its methods are fairly simple: You can open and close the connection, change the database and manage transactions.

We'll discuss Command objects in detail in Chapter 3.

The Command object represents a SQL statement or stored procedure to be executed at the data source. Command objects can be created and executed independently against a Connection object, and they are used by DataAdapter and TableAdapter objects to handle communications between a DataSet and a data source. Command objects can support SQL statements and stored procedures that return single values, one or more sets of rows, or no values at all.

DataReaders are the subject of Chapter 4.

A DataReader is a fast, low-overhead object for obtaining a forward-only, read-only stream of data from a data source. DataReaders cannot be created directly in code; they are created only by calling the ExecuteReader method of a Command object.

We'll discuss adapters in Chapters 5 and 8.

ADO.NET 1.0 provides only a single type of adapter, the DataAdapter, while ADO.NET 2.0 provides two. The DataAdapter is still supported, and a new object, the TableAdapter, has been added.

The DataAdapter is functionally the most complex object in a Data Provider. It provides the bridge between a Connection and a DataSet. The DataAdapter contains four Command objects: SelectCommand, UpdateCommand, InsertCommand and DeleteCommand. As you might expect, the DataAdapter uses the SelectCommand to fill a DataSet and the remaining three Commands to transmit changes back to the data source as required.

Although it won't do to push the analogy too far, you can think of TableAdapters as strongly typed DataAdapters. You can manipulate the SelectCommand property of a DataAdapter at run time to retrieve data from any table in the database specified by its Connection, but a TableAdapter is specific to a DataTable in a typed DataSet.

In fact, a TableAdapter contains both a DataAdapter object and a Connection object as private properties, and it adds some additional functionality that makes connecting to a data source both simpler and more powerful.

Microsoft ActiveX Data Objects (ADO)

In functional terms, the Connection and Command objects are roughly equivalent to their ADO counterparts, while the DataReader functions like a firehose cursor. The DataAdapter, TableAdapter and DataSet have no real equivalent in ADO.

DataSets

DataSets and their component collections are the subject of Chapters 7 and 8.

The DataSet is a memory-resident representation of data. Its structure is shown in the following figure. The DataSet can be considered a somewhat simplified relational database, modeling tables and the relationships between them. It's important to understand, however, that the DataSet is always disconnected from the data source—it doesn't "know" where the data it contains is from, and in fact, it can contain data from multiple sources.

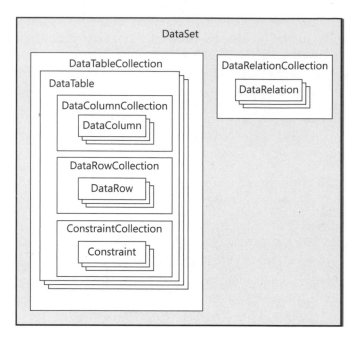

The DataSet is composed of two primary objects: the DataTableCollection, accessed through the Tables property, and the DataRelationCollection, accessed through the Relations property. The DataTableCollection contains zero or more DataTable objects, which are in turn made up of three collections: DataColumnCollection, DataRowCollection, and Constraint-Collection. The DataRelationCollection contains zero or more DataRelation objects.

The DataTableCollection Object

We'll discuss DataColumns in Chapter 7.

The DataColumnCollection of a DataTable defines the columns that compose the DataTable. In addition to the ColumnName and DataType properties, you can use DataColumn properties to define such things as whether or not a column allows nulls (AllowDBNull), its maximum length (MaxLength), and even an expression that is used to calculate its value (Expression).

We'll discuss DataRows in Chapter 8.

The DataRowCollection of a Data Table, which might be empty, contains the actual data contained by the table, as defined by the DataColumnCollection. For each DataRow, the DataTable maintains its original, current and proposed values. As we'll see, this greatly simplifies certain kinds of programming tasks, such as allowing users to discard the changes they have made to a DataRow.

ADO

The ADO.NET DataTable corresponds to the ADO Recordset object, although it plays a very different role in the object model.

We'll discuss
Constraints in
Chapter 7.
The ConstraintCollection of a DataTable contains zero or more Constraints. Just as in a relational database, Constraints are used to maintain the integrity of the data. ADO.NET supports two types of constraints: ForeignKey and Unique. ForeignKeyConstraints maintain relational integrity; that is, they ensure that a child row in a DataTable cannot be orphaned. UniqueConstraints maintain data integrity; that is, they ensure that duplicate rows cannot be added to the DataTable. (The PrimaryKey property of the DataTable is used to ensure entity integrity; that is, it enforces the uniqueness of each row.)

The DataRelationCollection Object

We'll discuss
DataRelations
in Chapter 7.
The DataRelationCollection of the DataSet contains zero or more DataRelations. DataRelations provide a simple programmatic interface for navigating from a master row in one table to the related rows in another. For example, given a DataSet containing an Order DataTable, you can use DataRelations to easily extract the related rows from the OrderDetails DataTable. A DataRelation by itself, however, won't enforce relational integrity. As we've seen, a ForeignKeyConstraint is used for that purpose.

Creating a Simple Data-Bound Form

The process of connecting data to the controls on a form is called *data binding*. Data binding can be performed in code, but the Microsoft Visual Studio integrated development environment (IDE) and the new TableAdapter object make the process very simple. In this section, we'll use the designers and wizards that Visual Studio provides to quickly create a simple data-bound Windows Form.

Important   If you have not yet installed the book's code samples, work through the "Code Samples" section in the Introduction before returning to this chapter.

Configuring a Data Source

The first step in binding data to a form is to create a data source for your project. Visual Studio provides the Data Source Configuration Wizard, which makes this process very simple.

Add a Data Source to a Project

1. Start an instance of Visual Studio.

2. Open the Chapter 01 – Start project, and if necessary, double-click Employees.vb (or EmployeesForm.cs if you're using C#) to open the form.

   Visual Studio opens and displays the form.

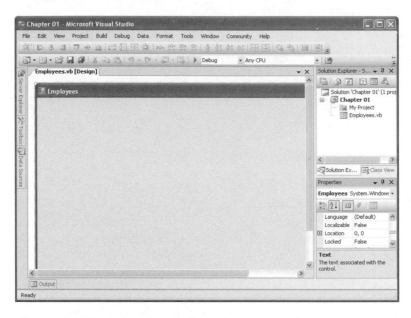

3. Choose Add New Data Source from the Data menu.

    Visual Studio opens the Data Source Configuration Wizard.

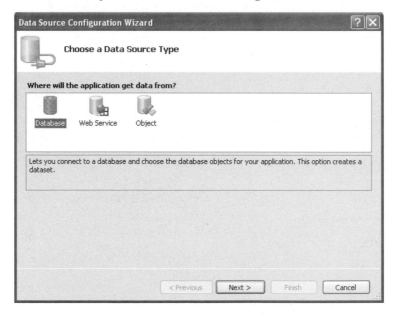

> **Tip**   You can also choose Add New Data Source from the Data Sources window. To open the Data Sources window, choose Show Data Sources from the Data menu.

4. Accept the default selection of Database as the data source type, and then click Next.

The Data Source Configuration Wizard displays a page asking you to choose a connection.

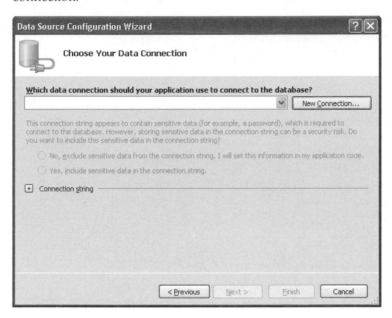

5. Click New Connection.

The Choose Data Source dialog box appears.

Tip   If the Add Connection dialog box appears, click Change to open the Change Data Source dialog box.

6. Choose Microsoft SQL Server, clear the Always Use This Selection check box, and then click Continue.

The Add Connection dialog box appears.

7. In the Server Name box, type **(local)\SQLEXPRESS**.

The (local) portion indicates the local computer, and SQLEXPRESS is the SQL Server instance name.

> **Important**   This book and code samples have been designed for use with a default installation of Microsoft SQL Server 2005 Express Edition, which has an instance name of SQLEXPRESS. If you want to use this book with a different SQL Server instance name or with the full version of SQL Server, you will have to adjust the exercise steps and connection strings accordingly.

8. In the Select Or Enter A Database Name drop-down list, select the AdoStepByStep database.

> **Important**   If the AdoStepByStep database name does not appear in the list, make sure you followed all of the code sample installation instructions in the Introduction.

9. Click OK in the Add Connection dialog box, and then click Next on the Data Source Configuration Wizard page.

   The Data Source Configuration Wizard displays a page offering to save the connection string to the application file.

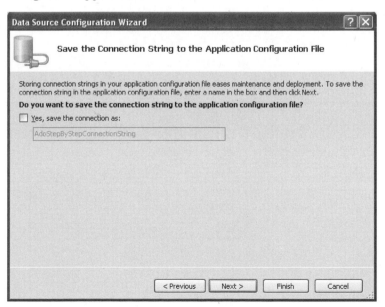

10. Be sure the Yes, Save The Connection As check box is cleared, and then click Next.

    After a few moments, the Data Source Configuration Wizard displays the objects in the database.

11. Expand the Tables node, and select Employees.

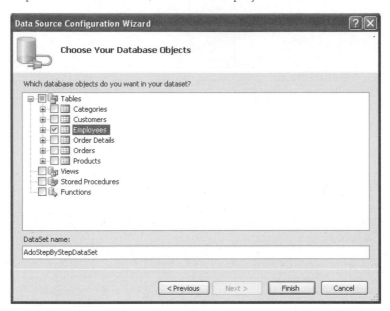

12. Click Finish.

The Data Source Configuration Wizard adds the new data source to the Data Sources window.

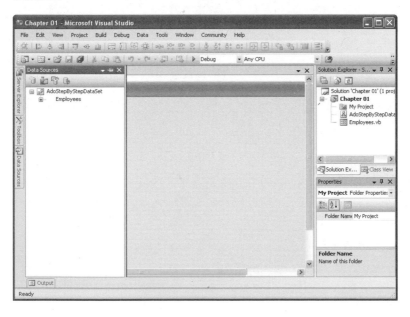

> **Tip**　If the Data Sources window is not open, choose Show Data Sources from the Data menu to display the Data Sources window.

Using the Data Sources Window

After a data source has been established, the Data Sources window allows you to preview data and add data-bound controls to your form by simply dragging a table or column onto the form's design surface. You can specify the type of control created by selecting either the table or column name and dropping down a list of available control types.

Preview the Contents of a Table

1. Double-click AdoStepByStepDataSet.xsd in the Solution Explorer.

   Visual Studio displays the DataSet in the DataSet Designer.

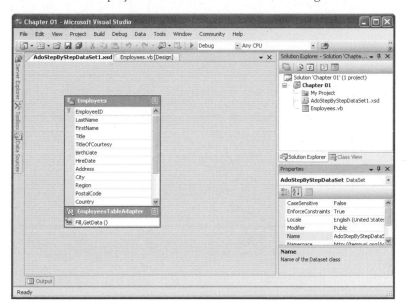

2. Right-click the Employees table, and choose Preview Data from the context menu.

   Visual Studio displays the Preview Data dialog box.

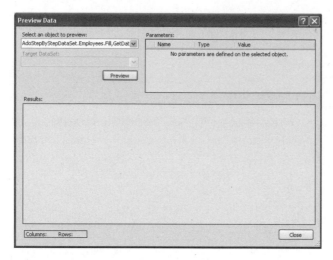

3. Click the Preview button.

   Visual Studio displays the contents of the table.

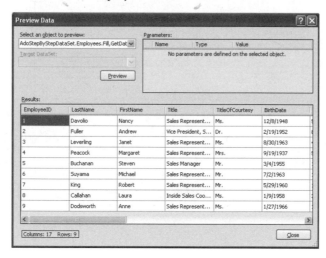

4. Close the dialog box.

Change the Default Control Type of a Column

1. Switch back to the Employees form by double-clicking Employees.vb [Design] (or Employees.cs [Design] if you're using C#).

2. In the Data Sources window, expand the Employees table node, select EmployeeID, and expand the drop down box.

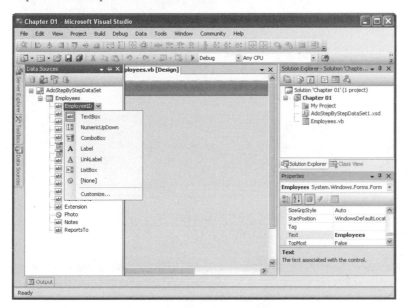

3. Select Label from the list.

   Visual Studio changes the default control type for the column.

> **Tip** You can change the default control for all columns of a given data type in the Options dialog box available from the Visual Studio Tools menu.

Add a Data-Bound Control to a Form

1. Drag the EmployeeID column to the upper-right corner of the form.

We'll discuss the Binding-Navigator in Chapter 13.

   Visual Studio adds a label control, a BindingNavigator control and several components to the form.

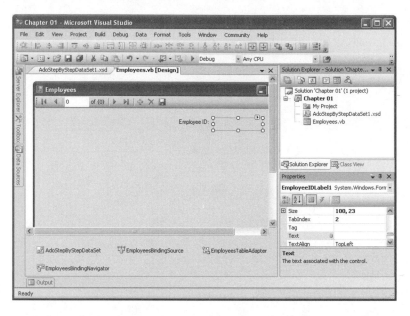

2. Drag the Title, First Name, Last Name, Hire Date and Notes columns to the form, and arrange them as shown in the following figure.

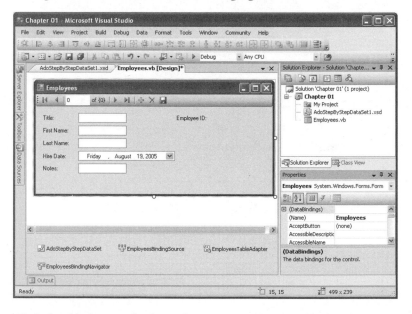

3. Click the Smart Tag glyph on the Notes text box, and select the MultiLine check box on the context menu.

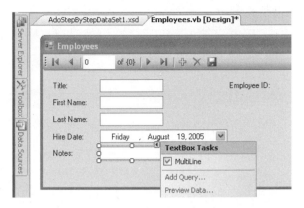

4. Move and enlarge the control as shown in the following figure.

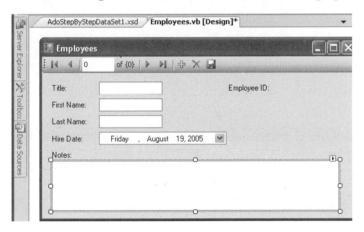

5. Press F5 to run the application.

Visual Studio compiles the application and displays the data in the Employees table in the controls on the form.

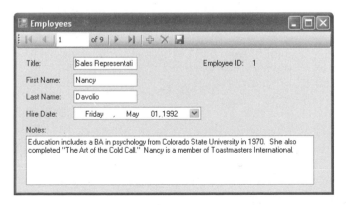

6. Use the navigation button controls on the BindingNavigator control at the top of the form to move through the table. When you finish, close the application.

Summary

In this chapter, we saw how easy it is to build a simple data-bound Windows Form in Microsoft Visual Studio 2005. In the remainder of the book, we'll examine each of the ADO.NET and related classes in detail, beginning with the Connection object, which handles communication between a .NET Framework application and a data source.

Part II
Data Provider Objects

Chapter 2

Using Connections

After completing this chapter, you will be able to:

- Add an instance of a Connection to a Windows Form.
- Create a Connection using code.
- Use Connection properties.
- Use an intermediary variable to reference multiple types of Connections.
- Bind Connection properties to form controls.
- Open and close Connections.
- Respond to a Connection.StateChange event.

In this chapter, we'll begin our detailed examination of the Microsoft ADO.NET object model with the object at the lowest level, the Connection.

Understanding Connections

Connections are responsible for handling the physical communication between a data store and a .NET application. The Connection object is part of a Data Provider, and each Data Provider implements its own version. For example, the OleDb Data Provider implements the OleDbConnection class in the System.Data.Odbc namespace, and the SQL Server Data Provider implements the SqlConnection class in the System.Data.SqlClient namespace.

> **Note** It's important to understand that if you're using a Connection object implemented by another data provider, the properties, methods and events might vary from those described here.

As we saw in Chapter 1, "Getting Started with ADO.NET," Microsoft ADO.NET 2.0 implements a new object, the TableAdapter, which greatly simplifies the process of binding data to a form. One of the things that the TableAdapter does is encapsulate a Connection object of the appropriate type for the data source.

The TableAdapter exposes its Connection through the Connection property. As we'll see in this section, you can also create an independent Connection object at design time or run time.

Creating Connections

With the inclusion of the TableAdapter in ADO.NET 2.0, it's no longer necessary to explicitly create Connection objects, but there remain situations in which they are useful—the Table-Adapter is a wonderful object, but it isn't appropriate to all situations.

> **Important**   If you have not yet installed the book's code samples, work through the "Code Samples" section in the Introduction before returning to this chapter.

Creating Connections at Design Time

The Connection object is no longer included by default in Microsoft Visual Studio 2005, but it is still available. After you've added the Connection object to the Toolbox, adding a Connection to a form is a simple matter of dragging it onto the form design surface.

Add a Connection to the Toolbox

1. Open the Chapter 02 – Start project in Visual Studio and, if necessary, double-click Connections.vb (or Connections.cs if you're using C#) in the Solution Explorer to open the form.

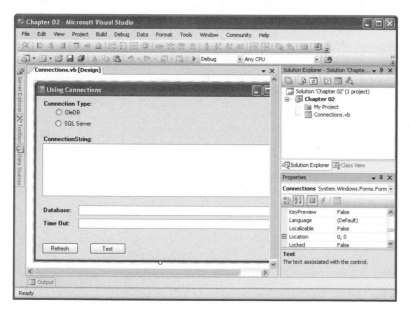

2. Open the Toolbox, and right-click the Data tab.

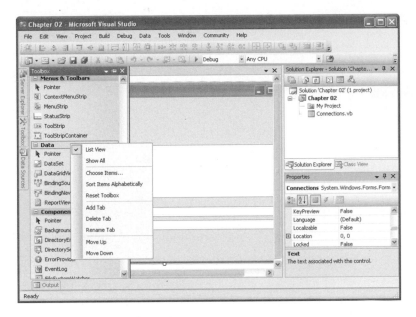

3. Select Choose Items from the context menu.

    After a few moments, Visual Studio displays the Choose Toolbox Items dialog box.

4. Select the SqlConnection check box.

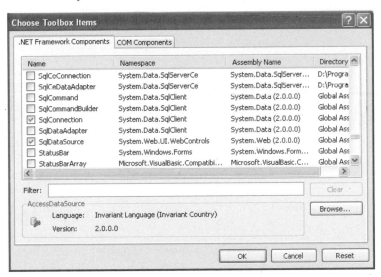

5. Click OK.

    Visual Studio adds the SqlConnection control to the Toolbox.

Add a Connection to a Form

1. In the Form Designer, drag the SqlConnection control onto the form surface.

   Visual Studio adds the appropriate control to the component tray.

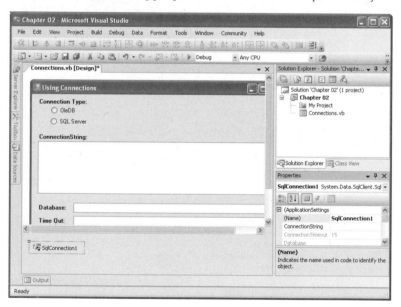

2. In the Properties window, change the name of the object to **cnSql**.

> **Note** If the Properties window is not currently displayed, click the View menu, and then click Properties Window.

3. Expand the ConnectionString property combo box, and choose the Connection you set up in the last chapter.

Creating Connections at Run Time

When you're working in Visual Studio, you'll usually use the Designer to create Connection objects, but sometimes it's useful to create a Connection that isn't attached to a form. When this happens, you can create one at run time in code.

As shown in Table 2-1, the Connection object provides two overloaded versions of its constructor, giving you the option of passing in the ConnectionString or setting it later.

Table 2-1   Connection Constructors

Method	Description
New()	Creates a Connection with the ConnectionString property set to an empty string.
New(connectionString)	Creates a Connection with the connectionString property specified.

The ConnectionString property, as you might expect, is used by the Connection object to connect to the data source. We'll explore it in detail in the next section of this chapter.

Create a Connection in Code: Visual Basic

1. Display the code for the Connections form by pressing F7.

2. Add the following line, which creates a new Connection object using the default values inside the Class declaration, before the New procedure:

```
Dim cnOleDb As OleDbConnection
```

3. Add the following line inside the New constructor, where indicated:

```
cnOleDb = New OleDbConnection()
```

The beginning of your class file should now be:

```
Imports System.Data
Imports System.Data.OleDb
Imports System.Data.SqlClient
Public Class Connections
    Dim cnOleDb As OleDbConnection

    Public Sub New()

        ' This call is required by the Windows Form Designer.
        InitializeComponent()

        ' Add exercise code here:
        cnOleDb = New OleDbConnection()

    End Sub
```

Create a Connection in Code: Visual C#

1. Display the code for the Connections form by pressing F7.

2. Add the following line, which creates a new Connection using the default values, after the opening bracket of the class declaration. For the time being, ignore the warning that the variable is never used. (We'll set the properties of the Connection in later exercises.)

```
private OleDbConnection cnOleDb;
```

3. Add the following line to the bottom of the class constructor, where indicated:

```
cnOleDb = new OleDbConnection();
```

The beginning of your class file should now be:

```
using System;
using System.Collections.Generic;
using System.ComponentModel;
using System.Data;
using System.Data.OleDb;
using System.Data.SqlClient;
using System.Drawing;
using System.Text;
using System.Windows.Forms;

namespace Chapter_02
{
    public partial class Connections : Form
    {
        private OleDbConnection cnOleDb;

        public Connections()
        {
            InitializeComponent();
```

```
        //Add exercise code here:
        cnOleDb = new OleDbConnection();
    }
```

Configuring Connections

The significant properties of the Connection objects implemented by the Microsoft .NET Framework Data Providers are shown in Table 2-2 through Table 2-5.

Table 2-2   OleDbConnection Properties

Property	Meaning	Default
ConnectionString	The string that is used to connect to the data source when the Open method is executed.	Empty
ConnectionTimeout	The maximum time the Connection object attempts to make the connection before throwing an exception.	15 seconds
Database	The name of the database to be opened after the connection is opened.	Empty
DataSource	The location and file containing the database.	Empty
Provider	The name of the OLE DB Data Provider.	Empty
ServerVersion	The version of the server, as provided by the OLE DB Data Provider.	Empty
State	A ConnectionState value indicating the current state of the Connection.	Closed

Table 2-3   SqlConnection Properties

Property	Meaning	Default
ConnectionString	The string used to connect to the data source when the Open method is executed.	Empty
ConnectionTimeout	The maximum time the Connection object attempts to make the connection before throwing an exception.	15 seconds
Database	The name of the database to be opened after the connection is opened.	Empty
DataSource	The location and file containing the database.	Empty

Table 2-3   **SqlConnection Properties**

Property	Meaning	Default
PacketSize	The size of network packets used to communicate with SQL Server.	8192 bytes
ServerVersion	The version of SQL Server being used.	Empty
State	A ConnectionState value indicating the current state of the Connection.	Closed
WorkStationID	A string identifying the database client. Or, if that is not specified, the name of the workstation.	Empty

Table 2-4   **OdbcConnection Properties**

Property	Meaning	Default
ConnectionString	The string used to connect to the data source when the Open method is executed.	Empty
ConnectionTimeout	The maximum time the Connection object attempts to make the connection before throwing an exception.	15 seconds
Database	The name of the database to be opened after the connection is opened.	Empty
DataSource	The location and file containing the database.	Empty
Driver	The name of the ODBC data provider.	Empty
ServerVersion	The version of the server, as provided by the ODBC data provider.	Empty
State	A ConnectionState value indicating the current state of the Connection.	Closed

Table 2-5   **OracleConnection Properties**

Property	Meaning	Default
ConnectionString	The string used to connect to the data source when the Open method is executed.	Empty
ConnectionTimeout	The maximum time the Connection object attempts to make the connection before throwing an exception.	15 seconds
Database	The name of the database to be opened after the connection is opened.	Empty

Table 2-5   OracleConnection Properties

Property	Meaning	Default
DataSource	The location and file containing the database.	Empty
ServerVersion	The version of the server, as provided by the Oracle data provider.	Empty
State	A ConnectionState value that indicates the current state of the Connection.	Closed

As you can see, the various versions of the Connection object expose a slightly different set of properties. To make matters worse, not all OLE DB Data Providers support all of the OleDb-Connection properties, and if you're working with a custom data provider, all bets are off.

What this means in real terms is that we still can't quite write code that is completely data source-independent unless we're prepared to give up the optimizations provided by specific data providers. However the problem isn't as bad as it might at first seem because the .NET Framework provides a number of ways to accommodate run-time configuration. And in reality, the issue simply doesn't arise as frequently as one might expect.

The ConnectionString Property

The ConnectionString is the most important property of any Connection object. In fact, the remaining properties are read-only and set by the Connection based on the value provided for the ConnectionString.

All ConnectionStrings have the same basic format. They consist of sets of keywords and values, with the pairs separated by semicolons. The whole string is delimited by either single or double quotes:

```
"keyword = value; keyword = value; keyword = value"
```

Keyword names are case-insensitive, but the values might not be, depending on the data source. The use of single or double quotes follows the normal rules for strings. For example, if the database name is Becca's Data, then the ConnectionString must be delimited by double quotes: *"Database=Becca's Data"*. Using *'Database=Becca's Data'* would cause an error.

If you use the same keyword multiple times, the last instance is used. For example, given the ConnectionString *"database=Becca's data;database=Northwind"*, the initial database is set to Northwind. The use of multiple instances of a keyword is perfectly legal (if somewhat confusing), so no syntax error is generated.

Unfortunately, the format of the ConnectionString is the easy part. It's determining the contents that can be difficult, because they will always be unique to the Data Provider. The valid keywords for the .NET Framework Data Providers are documented in MSDN Help. And remember, you can always cheat (a little) by creating a design-time Connection and then copying the values.

The ConnectionString can be set only when the Connection is closed. When it is set, the Connection object checks the syntax of the string and then sets the remaining properties (which you'll remember are read-only), but the ConnectionString is fully validated only when the connection is opened. If the Connection detects an invalid or unsupported property, it generates an exception. The type depends on the type of Connection object being used. A SqlConnection, for example, generates a SqlDbException.

In this exercise, we'll set the ConnectionString for the OleDbConnection that we created in the previous exercise. We'll connect to a Microsoft Access database file.

Set a ConnectionString Property: Visual Basic

1. Add the following line to the New procedure after the line that we added in the previous exercise (be sure to put the connection string on a single line):

```
cnOleDb.ConnectionString = "Provider=Microsoft.Jet.OLEDB.4.0;
Data Source='C:\Microsoft Press\ADO.NET 2.0 Step by Step\
SampleDBs\AdoStepByStep.mdb'"
```

> **Tip** If your Access database is in a different location, you will need to adjust the Data Source path accordingly.

Your New procedure should now be:

```
Public Sub New()

    ' This call is required by the Windows Form Designer.
    InitializeComponent()

    ' Add exercise code here:
    cnOleDb = New OleDbConnection()
    cnOleDb.ConnectionString = "Provider=Microsoft.Jet.OLEDB.4.0;
Data Source='C:\Microsoft Press\ADO.NET 2.0 Step by Step\
SampleDBs\AdoStepByStep.mdb'"

End Sub
```

Set a ConnectionString Property: Visual C#

1. Add the following lines to the procedure after the after the line we added in the previous exercise (be sure to put the connection string on a single line):

```
cnOleDb.ConnectionString = "Provider=Microsoft.Jet.OLEDB.4.0;
Data Source='C:\\Microsoft Press\\ADO.NET 2.0 Step by Step\\
SampleDBs\\AdoStepByStep.mdb'";
```

> **Tip**   If your Access database is in a different location, you will need to adjust the Data
> Source path accordingly.

Your constructor should now be:

```
public Connections()
{
    InitializeComponent();

    //Add exercise code here:
    cnOleDb = new OleDbConnection();
    cnOleDb.ConnectionString = "Provider=Microsoft.Jet.OLEDB.4.0;
Data Source='C:\\Microsoft Press\\ADO.NET 2.0 Step by Step\\
SampleDBs\\AdoStepByStep.mdb'";
}
```

Storing the ConnectionString in the Application Configuration File

The ConnectionString properties we set in the previous exercises are hard-coded. That's not a
problem for our little exercises, but in the real world, the location of a database is almost certain to change. That makes the ConnectionString a perfect candidate for storing the application configuration file (conventionally named app.config).

Visual Studio provides a settings designer that is available from the project properties dialog
box. (Select <Project Name> Properties from the Project menu, and then click the Settings
tab.) You can also access the file at run time by using the My.Setting class in Visual Basic or the
Settings class in C#. In this section, we'll use the Properties window to store the Connection-
String property in the application configuration file directly.

Store a ConnectionString in the Application Configuration File

1. In the Form Designer, select the cnSql control in the component tray.

2. In the Properties window, select the ConnectionString property, and press Ctrl+X to cut
   the property to the clipboard.

3. Expand the (ApplicationSettings) section, click (Property Binding), and then click the
   ellipsis button after (Property Binding).

   Visual Studio displays the Application Settings dialog box.

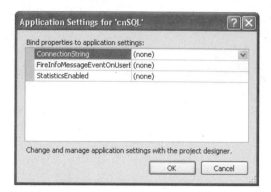

4. Display the ConnectionString list box, and then click (New...)

   Visual Studio displays the New Application Setting dialog box.

5. Select the DefaultValue cell, and press Ctrl+V to paste the ConnectionString.

6. Select the Name cell, and name the setting **SqlConnectionString**.

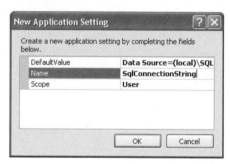

7. Click OK in the New Application Setting dialog box and in the Application Settings dialog box.

   Visual Studio displays the bound property in the Properties window.

Using Other Connection Properties

With the Connection objects in place, we can now add the code to display the Connection properties on the sample form. But first we need to use a little bit of object-oriented sleight of hand to accommodate the two types of objects.

One method is to write conditional code. In Visual Basic, this type of code looks like this:

```
If Me.rbOleChecked then
  Me.txtConnectionString.Text = Me.OleDbConnection1.ConnectionString
  Me.txtDatabase.Text = Me.OleDbConnection1.Database.String
  Me.txtTimeOut.Text = Me.OleDbConnection1.ConnectionTimeout
Else
  Me.txtConnectionString.Text = Me.SqlConnection1.ConnectionString
  Me.txtDatabase.Text = Me.SqlConnection1.Database.String
  Me.txtTimeOut.Text = Me.SqlConnection1.ConnectionTimeout
End If
```

Another option is to use compiler constants to conditionally compile code. Again, in Visual Basic:

```
#Const SqlVersion

#If SqlVersion Then
  Me.txtConnectionString.Text = Me.SqlConnection1.ConnectionString
  Me.txtDatabase.Text = Me.SqlConnection1.Database.String
  Me.txtTimeOut.Text = Me.SqlConnection1.ConnectionTimeout
#Else
  Me.txtConnectionString.Text = Me.OleDbConnection1.ConnectionString
  Me.txtDatabase.Text = Me.OleDbConnection1.Database.String
  Me.txtTimeOut.Text = Me.OleDbConnection1.ConnectionTimeout
#End If
```

Either option requires a lot of typing in a lot of places, and it can become a maintenance nightmare. If you need to access only the ConnectionString, Database and TimeOut properties (and these are the most common), there's an easier way.

The majority of classes in the .NET Framework Data Providers, including the Connection classes, inherit from the System.Data.Common namespace. That makes them, in effect, siblings in the .NET Framework class hierarchy.

By declaring a variable as a DbConnection, we can use it as an intermediary to access many of the shared properties of the various connection objects.

Create an Intermediary Variable: Visual Basic

1. In the Code Editor, declare the variable by adding the following line of code at the beginning of the class module, under the Connection declaration we added previously:

```
Dim myConnection As Data.Common.DbConnection
```

Your class module should now be:

```
Imports System.Data
Imports System.Data.OleDb
Imports System.Data.SqlClient
Public Class Connections
    Dim cnOleDb As OleDbConnection
    Dim myConnection As Data.Common.DbConnection

Public Sub New()
    …
```

2. Add the following assignment statement to the rbOleDbConnection_CheckedChanged procedure:

```
myConnection = cnOleDb
```

3. Add the following assignment statement to the rbSQLConnection_CheckedChanged procedure:

```
myConnection = cnSql
```

Create an Intermediary Variable: Visual C#

1. Declare the variable by adding the following line of code at the beginning of the class module, under the Connection declaration we added previously:

```
private System.Data.Common.DbConnection myConnection;
```

The beginning of your class file should now be:

```
using System;
using System.Collections.Generic;
using System.ComponentModel;
using System.Data;
using System.Data.OleDb;
using System.Data.SqlClient;
using System.Drawing;
using System.Text;
using System.Windows.Forms;

namespace Chapter_02
{
    public partial class Connections : Form
    {
        private OleDbConnection cnOleDb;
        private System.Data.Common.DbConnection myConnection;

        public Connections()
        …
```

2. Add the following line to the rbOleDBConnection_CheckedChanged event handler:

```
myConnection = cnOleDb;
```

3. Add the following line to the rbSQLConnection_CheckedChanged event handler:

```
myConnection = cnSql;
```

Binding Connection Properties to Form Controls

Now that the intermediary variable is in place, we can add the code to display the Connection properties (or rather, the DbConnection properties) in the form control.

Bind Connection Properties to Form Controls: Visual Basic

1. Add the following procedure to the class module:

```
Private Sub RefreshValues()
  txtConnectionString.Text = myConnection.ConnectionString
  txtDatabase.Text = myConnection.Database
  txtTimeOut.Text = myConnection.ConnectionTimeOut
End Sub
```

2. Add a call to the RefreshValues procedure at the end of each CheckedChanged event handler.

   The code should now be:

```
Private Sub rbOleDBConnection_CheckedChanged(ByVal sender As Object,
ByVal e As System.EventArgs) Handles rbOleDBConnection.CheckedChanged
  myConnection = cnOleDb
  RefreshValues()
End Sub

Private Sub rbSQLConnection_CheckedChanged(ByVal sender As Object,
ByVal e As System.EventArgs) Handles rbSQLConnection.CheckedChanged
  myConnection = cnSql
  RefreshValues()
End Sub
```

3. Save and run the program by pressing F5.

4. Choose each of the connection radio buttons in turn to confirm that their properties are displayed in the appropriate text boxes.

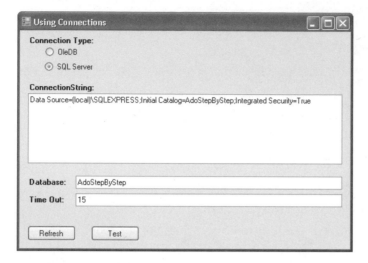

5. Close the application.

Bind Connection Properties to Form Controls: Visual C#

1. Add the following procedure to the class module below the CheckChanged event handlers:

```
private void RefreshValues()
{
  txtConnectionString.Text = myConnection.ConnectionString;
  txtDatabase.Text = myConnection.Database;
  txtTimeOut.Text = myConnection.ConnectionTimeout.ToString();
}
```

2. Add a call to the RefreshValues procedure at the end of each CheckedChanged event handler.

   The code should now be:

```
void rbOleDBConnection_CheckedChanged(object sender, EventArgs e)
{
  myConnection = cnOleDb;
  RefreshValues();
}

void rbSQLConnection_CheckedChanged(object sender, EventArgs e)
{
  myConnection = cnSql;
  RefreshValues();
}
```

3. Save and run the program by pressing F5.

4. Choose each Connection in turn to confirm that its properties are displayed in the appropriate text boxes.

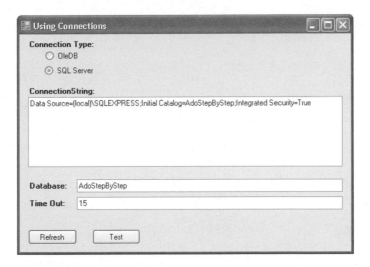

5. Close the application.

Connection Methods

The DbConnection class defined in the Data.Common namespace exposes the set of methods shown in Table 2-6. All the corresponding Connection objects exposed by Data Providers support this set, although some of them expose additional methods.

Table 2-6 DbConnection Methods

Method	Description
BeginTransaction	Begins a database transaction.
ChangeDatabase	Changes the current database on an open Connection.
Close	Closes the connection to the data source.
CreateCommand	Creates and returns a Command object associated with the Connection.
GetSchema	Retrieves schema information from the database.
Open	Establishes a connection to the data source.

We'll examine transaction processing in Chapter 6.

The Connection methods that you will use most often are the Open method and the Close method, which do exactly what you would expect—open and close the connection to the data source. The BeginTransaction method begins transaction processing for a Connection.

We'll examine Data Commands in Chapter 3.

The other methods also do what you'd expect them to do. Using the ChangeDatabase method, you can connect to a different database while the connection is open. Using the CreateCommand method, you can create an ADO.NET Data Command object. Finally, the GetSchema method returns information about the structure of the database.

Opening and Closing Connections

The Open and Close methods are invoked automatically by the three objects that use a Connection: the DataAdapter, TableAdapter and Data Command. You can also invoke them explicitly in code, if required.

We'll examine the Data-Adapter in Chapter 4 and the Table-Adapter in Chapter 8. If you call the Open method on a Connection that is already open, it is closed and re-opened. If the Open method is invoked on a Connection by one of the objects that use it, such as a Data Command, these objects leave the Connection in the state in which they find it. If the Connection is open when a DataAdapter.Fill method is invoked, for example, it remains open when the Fill operation is complete. On the other hand, if the Connection is closed when the Fill method is invoked, the DataAdapter closes it upon completion.

If you invoke the Open method explicitly, the connection remains open until it is explicitly closed. It does not close automatically, even if the Connection object goes out of scope. (Calling the Dispose method of the Connection object, however, closes the connection.)

> **Important**   You must *always* explicitly invoke a Close method when you have finished using a Connection object, and for scalability and performance purposes, you should call Close as soon as possible after you've completed the operations on the Connection.

Open and Close a Connection: Visual Basic

1. Add the following lines to the btnTest_Click event handler to open the connection, display its status in a message box, and then close the connection:

    ```
    myConnection.Open()
    MessageBox.Show(myConnection.State.ToString())
    myConnection.Close()
    ```

2. Press F5 to save and run the application.

3. Change the Connection Type, and then click the Test button.

    The application displays the Connection state.

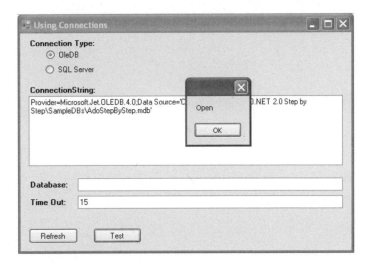

> **Tip**   If you receive a "NullReferenceException was unhandled" error, you forgot to select a connection before clicking Test. This is why, in the real world, you should always wrap a Connection.Open call in a Try/Catch error handler.

4. Close the application.

Open and Close a Connection: Visual C#

1. Add the following code to the btnTest_Click event handler:

```
myConnection.Open();
MessageBox.Show(myConnection.State.ToString());
myConnection.Close();
```

2. Press F5 to save and run the application.

3. Change the Connection Type, and then click the Test button.

   The application displays the Connection type.

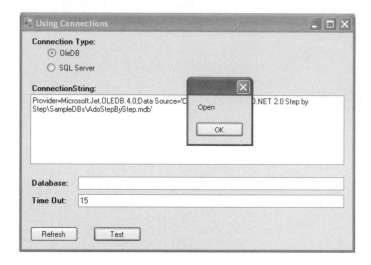

> **Tip**   If you receive a "NullReferenceException was unhandled" error, you forgot to select a connection before clicking Test. This is why, in the real world, you should always wrap a Connection.Open call in a Try/Catch error handler.

4. Close the application.

Controlling Connection Pooling

The Open and Close methods of the Connection object are expensive procedures. Although it's easiest to think of the Open and Close methods as discrete operations, in fact the .NET Framework, by default, pools connections to improve performance.

A *connection pool* is simply a group of connections that are available for any bit of code that requires them. If, while a Connection is in the pool, another request is made to open a Connection with the same ConnectionString, the pooled Connection is provided to the calling procedure, saving the processing expense of creating and opening a new connection to the data source.

If the Connection is not reused within a certain time (which varies depending on the Data Provider and the data source), the Connection will be closed and the Connection object will be made available to the garbage collector.

You don't need to do anything to turn on connection pooling, because ADO.NET always uses it by default. You will rarely need to turn off connection pooling, since its cost is low compared to that of reopening connections, but should you need to do so, you can. The mechanism for turning off connection pooling is determined by the Data Provider and the data source.

To turn off connection pooling with the OleDbConnection class, you add the keyword *OLE DB Services*=-4 to the connection string. Connection pooling that uses the OdbcConnection class is determined by the data source, while the OracleConnection and SqlConnection classes both support the Pooling keyword, which, if false, turns off connection pooling. In addition, the OracleConnection and SqlConnection classes support the additional pooling-related keywords shown in Tables 2-7 and 2-8, respectively.

Table 2-7   SqlConnection Pooling-Related Connection String Keywords

Name	Default	Description
Connection Lifetime	0	Determines the age of a pooled connection; if the connection has been open longer than the time specified (in seconds), it will not be pooled; the default value of 0 disables this functionality.
Connection Reset	true	Determines whether the connection is reset when removed from the pool; resetting the connection requires a round-trip to the server, but ensures a "clean" connection.
Enlist	true	Determines whether the connection will be enlisted in the current transaction context after it's removed from the pool.
Load Balance Timeout	0	The minimum time the connection can live in the pool before being destroyed.
Max Pool Size	100	The maximum number of connections maintained in the pool.
Min Pool Size	0	The minimum number of connections maintained in the pool.
Pooling	true	Determines whether the connection can be drawn from the current pool; a value of false forces a new connection to be created.

Table 2-8   OracleConnection Pooling-Related Connection String Keywords

Name	Default	Description
Connection Lifetime	0	Determines the age of a pooled connection; if the connection has been open longer than the time specified (in seconds), it will not be pooled; the default value of 0 disables this functionality.
Enlist	true	Determines whether the connection will be enlisted in the current transaction context when it is removed from the pool.
Max Pool Size	100	The maximum number of connections maintained in the pool.
Min Pool Size	0	The minimum number of connections maintained in the pool.
Pooling	true	Determines whether the connection can be drawn from the current pool; a value of false forces a new connection to be created.

Connection Events

The DbConnection object exposes only a single event, StateChange, but all of the .NET Framework Connection objects expose an additional one: InfoMessage.

StateChange Events

Not surprisingly, the StateChange event fires whenever the state of the Connection object changes. The event passes a StateChangeEventArts object to its handler, which, in turn, has two properties: OriginalState and CurrentState. The possible values for OriginalState and CurrentState are shown in Table 2-9.

Table 2-9   Connection States

State	Meaning
Broken	The Connection is open, but not functional. It can be closed and re-opened.
Closed	The Connection is closed.
Connecting	The Connection is the process of connecting, but has not yet done so.
Executing	The Connection is executing a command.
Fetching	The Connection is retrieving data.
Open	The Connection is open.

Respond to a StateChange Event: Visual Basic

1. Add a StateChange event handler by selecting cnSql in the Code Editor object list box and StateChange in the event list box.

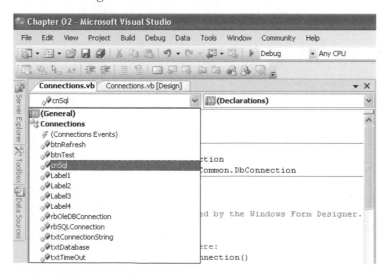

2. To display the previous and current Connection states, add the following code to the cnSql_StateChange event handler:

```
Dim theMessage As String
theMessage = "The Connection has changed from " & _
        e.OriginalState.ToString() & _
        " to " & e.CurrentState.ToString()
MessageBox.Show(theMessage)
```

3. Press F5 to save and run the program.

4. Select the SQL Server radio button, and then click the Test button.

   The application displays message boxes when the Connection is opened and closed.

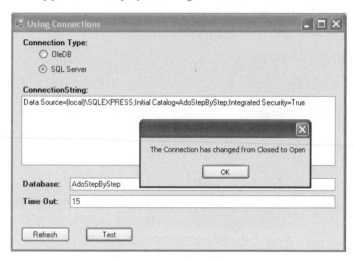

5. Close the application.

Respond to a StateChange Event: Visual C#

1. In the Form Designer, select the cnSql control in the components tray.

2. In the Properties window, click the Events button to display the events for the cnSql control.

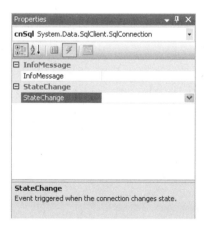

3. Select the StateChange event, and press the Enter key to add the cnSql_StateChange event handler and switch to code view.

4. To Connection states, add the following display the previous and current Connection states, add the following code to the cnSql_StateChange event handler:

```
string theMessage;
theMessage = "The Connection State has changed from " +
        e.OriginalState.ToString() +
        " to " + e.CurrentState.ToString();
MessageBox.Show(theMessage);
```

5. Press F5 to save and run the program.

6. Select the SQL Server radio button, and then click the Test button.

   The application displays two message boxes as the Connection is opened and closed.

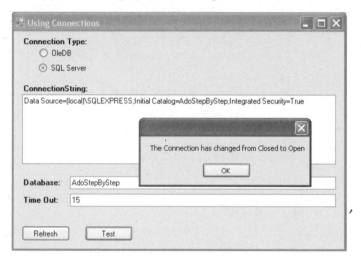

7. Close the application.

InfoMessage Events

The InfoMessage event is triggered when the data source returns warnings. The information passed to the event handler depends on the data provider. In SQL Server, for example, these messages are sent to the client by using the PRINT command or the RAISERROR command with a severity level set to 10 or less. For details, see MSDN Help for the Data Provider you're using.

Summary

In this chapter we examined the Connection object that handles communication between a .NET Framework application and a data source. We saw how to create a provider-specific Connection at design time and run time, and also how to use the dbConnection to provide a generic interface. We looked at the properties of the Connection, the most important of which is the ConnectionString, and at the events exposed by all of the versions of the class.

Chapter 3
Using Data Commands and DataReaders

After completing this chapter, you will be able to:

- Create a Data Command at design time and at run time.
- Configure a Data Command in Microsoft Visual Studio and at run time.
- Configure the Parameters collection in Visual Studio.
- Create and configure a Parameter at run time.
- Set Parameter values.
- Execute a command by using a Data Command.
- Create a DataReader at run time.
- Retrieve DataReader properties.
- Execute the methods of the DataReader.

The Connection object that we examined in Chapter 2, "Using Connections," represents the physical connection to a data source, the conduit for exchanging information between an application and the data source. Two Microsoft .NET Framework objects work in conjunction to actually retrieve the data:

- The Data Command, which, in the context of the .NET Framework, encapsulates the SQL language commands to be executed by the database server.
- The DataReader, which is used to retrieve rows from those Data Commands that return them. (As we'll see, not all Data Commands return data.)

In this chapter we'll look at creating independent Data Commands. They are also encapsulated in other .NET Framework data controls, such as the DataAdapter that we'll examine in the next chapter.

Understanding Data Commands

Essentially, a Microsoft ADO.NET Data Command is simply a SQL statement or a reference to a stored procedure that is executed against a Connection object. The most common use of a Data Command is to execute commands, such as SELECT or DELETE, from the database server's data manipulation language (DML), but in fact any command that is supported by the database server can be executed by using a Data Command.

In addition to DML, you can use a Data Command to call stored procedures on the database server. You can also execute SQL statements that return no rows, such as commands that form part of the database server's data definition language (DDL) that changes the structure of the data source.

Data Commands are part of the .NET Framework Data Providers, and each Data Provider implements a slightly different version—for example, the OleDBCommand in the System.Data.OleDb namespace and the SqlCommand in the System.Data.SqlClient namespace. But as with the Connection object we looked at in the previous chapter, the System.Data.Common namespace implements a generic command, the DbCommand object, which can be used to simplify accessing data from multiple data sources.

You must be aware, however, that every database server supports a slightly different dialect of the SQL language, and in practice this makes generic Data Commands rather less useful than generic Connections. In particular, as we'll see later in this chapter, the syntax for specifying query parameters tends to vary between servers, and in real-world applications, most queries require parameters.

> **Note**   It's important to understand that if you're using a Command object implemented by a different Data Provider, the properties, methods and events might vary from those described here.

We'll discuss DataAdapters in Chapter 4 and Table-Adapters in Chapter 8. Data Commands that execute DML statements—those that retrieve and update rows of data—are most often used as part of either a DataAdapter or TableAdapter, but you can also create Data Commands independently when you need to do something that isn't supported (or isn't easy) with either of the Adapter objects. When you want to execute some other type of SQL statement, you'll almost always need an independent Data Command.

Creating Data Commands

Like most of the objects that can exist at the form level, Data Commands can be created and configured either at design time in Visual Studio or at run time with code.

Creating Data Commands at Design Time

Like the Connection objects we examined in Chapter 2, Data Commands aren't included by default in the Visual Studio Toolbox, but you can easily add them from the Choose Toolbox Items dialog box.

Add a Design-Time Command to the Toolbox

1. Open the Chapter 3 – Start project in Visual Studio, and if necessary, double-click CommandsAndReaders.vb (or CommandsAndReaders.cs if you're using C#) in the Solution Explorer to open the form.

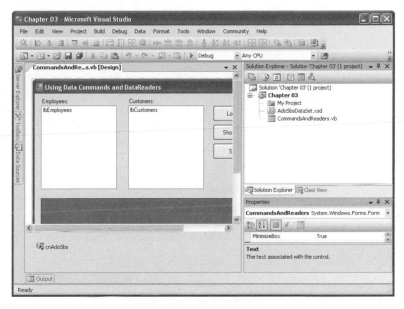

2. Open the Toolbox, and right-click the Data tab.

3. Select Choose Items from the context menu.

   After a few moments, Visual Studio displays the Choose Toolbox Items dialog box.

4. Select the SqlCommand check box.

5. Click OK.

   Visual Studio adds the SqlCommand control to the Toolbox.

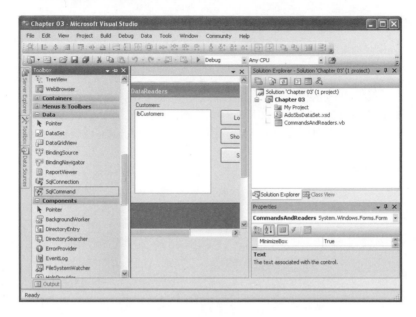

Add an Instance of a Design-Time Command to a Form

1. With the CommandsAndReaders form open in the Form Designer, drag the SqlCommand control onto the form surface.

   Visual Studio adds the control to the component tray.

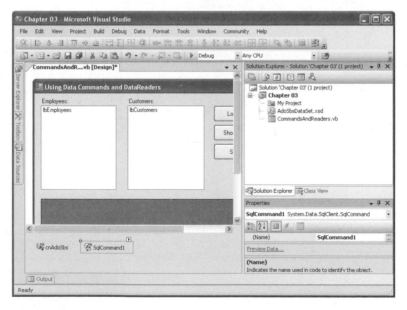

2. In the Properties window, change the name of the Command from SqlCommand1 to **cmdGetEmployees**.

Creating Connections at Run Time

We'll discuss the version of the Data Command constructor that supports transactions in Chapter 7.

The Data Command exposes four versions of its constructor, as shown in Table 3-1. The New() constructor sets all the properties of the Data Command to their default values. The other versions allow you to set properties of the Data Command during creation. Whichever version you choose, of course, you can set or change property values after the Data Command has been created.

Exercise Scaffolding

Because of the nature of the ADO.NET object model and the way that various objects interrelate, the project for this exercise, and for most of the exercises in the book, contain code that isn't discussed. The "unmentioned" code falls into four categories:

- Code that uses objects we haven't yet discussed
- Code we've discussed in earlier chapters
- Code that repeats exercises in the current chapter
- Standard .NET Framework code that's outside the scope of this book

The first two categories have comments referring you to the appropriate chapter. In all cases, try not to let the scaffolding bother you. It's just that—scaffolding—and not anything to worry about.

Table 3-1   Data Command Constructors

Method	Description
New()	Creates a new, default instance of the Data Command.
New(command)	Creates a new Data Command with the CommandText property set to the string specified by command.
New(command, connection)	Creates a new Data Command with the CommandText property set to the string specified by command and the Connection property set to the Connection object specified by connection.
New(command, connection, transaction)	Creates a new Data Command with the CommandText property set to the string specified by command, the Connection property set to the Connection object specified by connection, and the Transaction property set to the Transaction object specified by transaction.

Create a Command in Code: Visual Basic

1. Press F7 to display the Code Editor.

2. Add the following lines, which declare two Command variables, inside the Class declaration, after the declaration of dsAdoSbs:

```
Friend WithEvents cmdGetCustomers As SqlCommand
Friend WithEvents cmdGetOrders As SqlCommand
```

3. In the New procedure, add the following line after the call to InitializeComponent and before the call to CreateScaffolding:

```
cmdGetCustomers = New SqlCommand("SELECT * FROM Customers", cnAdoSbs)
```

This line instantiates the Command object, passing the CommandText and Connection object in the constructor. The beginning of your class file should now be:

```
Imports System.Data
Imports System.Data.SqlClient
Public Class CommandsAndReaders
    Dim dsAdoSbs As AdoSbsDataSet
    Friend WithEvents cmdGetCustomers As SqlCommand
    Friend WithEvents cmdGetOrders As SqlCommand

    Public Sub New()

        ' This call is required by the Windows Form Designer.
        InitializeComponent()

        ' Add exercise code here:
        cmdGetCustomers = New SqlCommand("SELECT * FROM Customers", cnAdoSbs)

        ' This call supports the exercise:
        CreateScaffolding()
    End Sub
```

Create a Command in Code: Visual C#

1. Press F7 to display the Code Editor.

2. Add the following lines, which declare two Command variables, inside the class declaration, after the declaration of dsAdoSbs.

```
internal SqlCommand cmdGetCustomers;
internal SqlCommand cmdGetOrders;
```

3. Add the following line after the call to InitializeComponent and before the call to CreateScaffolding:

```
cmdGetCustomers = new SqlCommand("SELECT * FROM Customers",
    cnAdoSbs);
```

This line instantiates the Command object, passing the CommandText and Connection object to the constructor. The beginning of your class file should now be:

```
using System;
using System.Collections.Generic;
using System.ComponentModel;
using System.Data;
using System.Data.SqlClient;
using System.Drawing;
using System.Text;
using System.Windows.Forms;

namespace Chapter_03
{
    public partial class CommandsAndReaders : Form
    {
        AdoSbsDataSet dsAdoSbs;
        internal SqlCommand cmdGetCustomers;
        internal SqlCommand cmdGetOrders;

        public CommandsAndReaders()
        {
            InitializeComponent();

            //Add exercise code here:
            cmdGetCustomers = new SqlCommand("SELECT * FROM Customers", cnAdoSbs);

            //This call supports the exercise:
            CreateScaffolding();
        }
```

Obtain a Reference to a Command from a Connection: Visual Basic

1. Add the following line, which obtains a new Data Command from the existing Connection object, to the end of the New procedure, after the instantiation of cmdGetCustomers:

```
cmdGetOrders = cnAdoSbs.CreateCommand()
```

Your New procedure should now be:

```
Public Sub New()

    ' This call is required by the Windows Form Designer.
    InitializeComponent()

    ' Add exercise code here:
    cmdGetCustomers = New SqlCommand("SELECT * FROM Customers", cnAdoSbs)
    cmdGetOrders = cnAdoSbs.CreateCommand()

    ' This call supports the exercise:
    CreateScaffolding()
End Sub
```

Obtain a Reference to a Command from a Connection: Visual C#

1. Add the following line, which obtains a new Data Command from the existing Connection object, to the end of the constructor, after the instantiation of cmdGetCustomers:

```
cmdGetOrders = cnAdoSbs.CreateCommand();
```

The class constructor should now be:

```
public CommandsAndReaders()
{
    InitializeComponent();

    //Add exercise code here:
    cmdGetCustomers = new SqlCommand("SELECT * FROM Customers", cnAdoSbs);
    cmdGetOrders = cnAdoSbs.CreateCommand();

    //This call supports the exercise:
    CreateScaffolding();
}
```

Configuring Data Commands

The properties exposed by the Data Command object are shown in Table 3-2. These properties are checked for syntax errors only when they are set. Final validation occurs only when the Data Command is executed by a data source.

Table 3-2   Data Command Properties

Property	Description
CommandText	The SQL statement or stored procedure to execute.
CommandTimeout	The time (in seconds) to wait for a response from the data source.
CommandType	Indicates how the CommandText property is to be interpreted; defaults to Text.
Connection	The Connection object on which the command is to be executed.
Parameters	The Parameters Collection.
Transaction	The Transaction in which the command executes.
UpdatedRowSource	Determines how results are applied to a DataRow when the Command is used by the Update method of a DataAdapter or TableAdapter.

We'll discuss the Transaction property in Chapter 7.

The CommandText property, which is a String, contains either the actual text of the command to be executed or the name of a stored procedure in the data source. At design time, either you can enter a SQL statement directly into the Properties window, or you can use the Query Builder to design a query interactively.

If you've ever used the Microsoft SQL Server Enterprise Manager, the Query Builder in Visual Studio will look familiar to you. It provides several mechanisms for developing a SQL query statement. You can select the check boxes next to column names in the Diagram Pane, and the

Query Builder adds them to the Grid Pane and to the SQL statement. You can use the Grid Pane to set criteria and sort orders, or you can type the statement directly into the SQL Pane.

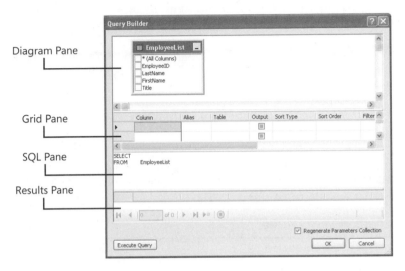

After you have entered a SQL statement by using any combination of these methods, clicking the Execute Query button displays the results in the Results Pane (or displays an error message, if you don't yet have things quite right).

The CommandTimeout property determines the time that the Data Command waits for a response from the server before it generates an error. Note that this is the wait time before the Data Command begins receiving results, not the time it takes the command to execute. The data source might take several minutes to return all the rows of a large table, but if the first row is received within the specified CommandTimeout period, no error is generated.

The CommandType property tells the Data Command how to interpret the contents of the CommandText property. The possible values are shown in Table 3-3.

Table 3-3   CommandType Values

Value	Description
StoredProcedure	Indicates that the CommandText property contains the name of a stored procedure to be executed.
TableDirect	Indicates that the CommandText property contains the name of a table from which all columns and rows will be retrieved.
Text	Indicates that the CommandText property contains a SQL statement to be executed.

Text is the default value of the CommandType property, and it's also the most commonly used. Note that TableDirect is only supported by the OLE DB Data Provider.

The Connection property contains a reference to the Connection object against which the Data Command will execute. The Connection object must belong to the same namespace as the Data Command; that is, a SqlCommand must contain a reference to a SqlConnection, and an OracleCommand must contain a reference to an OracleConnection.

The Parameters property contains a collection of Parameters for the SQL command or stored procedure specified in the CommandText property. We'll examine this collection in some detail later in this chapter.

See Chapter 7 for more information. The Transaction property contains a reference to a Transaction object and serves to enroll the Data Command in that Transaction.

We'll examine the Data-Adapter in Chapter 5 and the DataRow in Chapter 7. The UpdatedRowSource property determines how results are applied to a DataRow when the Data Command is executed by the Update method of a DataAdapter. The possible values for the UpdatedRowSource property are shown in Table 3-4.

Table 3-4   UpdatedRowSource Values

Value	Description
Both	Both the output parameters and the first row returned by the Command are mapped to the changed row.
FirstReturnedRecord	The first row returned by the Command is mapped to the changed row.
None	Any returned parameters or rows are discarded.
OutputParameters	Only the output parameters of the Command are mapped to the changed row.

If Visual Studio generates the Data Command automatically, the default value of the Updated-RowSource property is set to None. If the Data Command is generated at run time or created by the user at design time, the default value is Both.

Setting Command Properties at Design Time

As might be expected, the properties of a Command object created in Visual Studio are set by using the Properties window. When specifying the CommandText property, you can either type the value directly or use the Query Builder to generate the required SQL statement. You must specify the Connection property before you attempt to set the CommandText property; otherwise, Visual Studio displays an error message.

Set Command Properties in Visual Studio

1. In the Form Designer, select cmdGetEmployees in the component tray.
2. In the Properties window, select the Connection property, click the down arrow, expand the Existing node in the list, and then click cnAdoSbs.

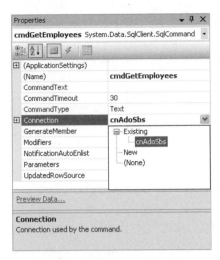

3. Select the CommandText property, and then click the ellipsis button.

The Query Builder opens, and the Add Table dialog box appears automatically.

4. Click EmployeeList.

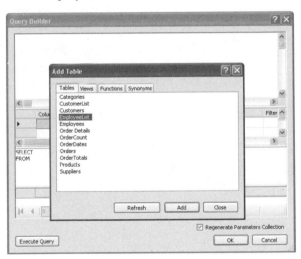

5. Click Add to add EmployeeList to the Query Builder, and then click Close.

The EmployeeList table is added to the Query Builder.

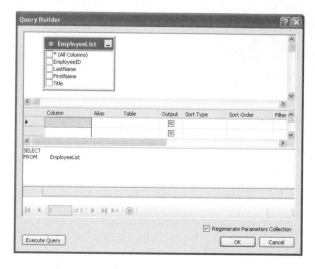

6. In the Grid Pane, type the following expression in the first cell in the column labeled Column:

```
LastName + ' ' + FirstName
```

7. Press Tab to move to the Alias column.

> **Tip** An N prefix might be added automatically to the single quoted space. The N prefix indicates that the string is Unicode, which can become important when you work with languages other than English.

8. Change the Alias column from Expr1 to **FullName**.

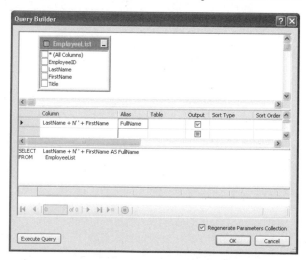

9. In the Diagram Pane, select the EmployeeID, LastName and FirstName check boxes.

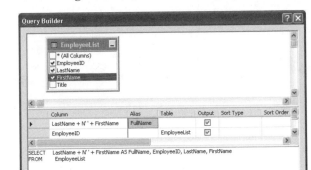

10. Click OK.

Visual Studio generates the SQL command and sets the CommandText property in the Properties window.

Setting Command Properties at Run Time

The majority of the properties of the Command object can be set by using simple assignment statements. The exception is the Parameters collection, which (because it is a collection) uses the Add method. We'll discuss the Parameters collection in the next section.

Set Command Properties in Code: Visual Basic

1. In the Code Editor, add the following line to the New procedure after the instantiation of the cmdGetOrders Data Command:

```
cmdGetOrders.CommandText = "SELECT * FROM OrderTotals WHERE " & _
   "EmployeeID = @empID AND CustomerID = @custID"
```

This line specifies the command to be executed—a parameterized query for which the EmployeeID and CustomerID values are to be provided at run time. Your New procedure should now be:

```
Public Sub New()

   ' This call is required by the Windows Form Designer.
   InitializeComponent()

   ' Add exercise code here:
   cmdGetCustomers = New SqlCommand("SELECT * FROM Customers", cnAdoSbs)
   cmdGetOrders = cnAdoSbs.CreateCommand()
```

```
        cmdGetOrders.CommandText = "SELECT * FROM OrderTotals WHERE " & _
            "EmployeeID = @empID AND CustomerID = @custID"

        ' This call supports the exercise:
        CreateScaffolding()
    End Sub
```

Set Command Properties in Code: Visual C#

1. In the Code Editor, add the following line to the class constructor after the instantiation of the cmdGetOrders Data Command:

```
cmdGetOrders.CommandText = "SELECT * FROM OrderTotals WHERE " +
    "EmployeeID = @empID AND CustomerID = @custID";
```

This line specifies the command to be executed—a parameterized query for which the EmployeeID and CustomerID values are to be provided at run time. Your constructor should now be:

```
public CommandsAndReaders()
{
    InitializeComponent();

    //Add exercise code here:
    cmdGetCustomers = new SqlCommand("SELECT * FROM Customers", cnAdoSbs);
    cmdGetOrders = cnAdoSbs.CreateCommand();
    cmdGetOrders.CommandText = "SELECT * FROM OrderTotals WHERE " +
        "EmployeeID = @empID AND CustomerID = @custID";

    //This call supports the exercise:
    CreateScaffolding();
}
```

Using the Parameters Collection

There are three steps to using parameters in queries and stored procedures in a Data Command:

1. Specify the parameters in the text of the query or stored procedure.

2. Add the parameters to the Parameters collection of the Data Command.

3. Set the parameter values.

If you're using a stored procedure, the syntax for specifying parameters is determined by the data source when the stored procedure is created. If you are using parameters in a SQL command specified in the CommandText property of the Command object, the syntax requirement is determined by the .NET Data Provider.

Unfortunately, the Data Providers supported by the .NET Framework use different syntax. The ODBC and OleDB Data Providers use a question mark as a placeholder for a parameter:

```
SELECT * FROM Customers WHERE CustomerID = ?
```

The SqlCommand object uses named providers prefixed with the at (@) character:

```
SELECT * FROM Customers WHERE CustomerID = @ID
```

Finally, the OracleCommand object uses named providers prefixed with the colon (:) character:

```
SELECT * FROM Customers WHERE CustomerID = :ID
```

Having used the correct syntax to create the stored procedure or SQL command, you must then add each parameter to the Parameters collection of the Command object. Again, if you use Visual Studio, it configures the collection for you, but if you create or reconfigure the Command object at run time, you must use the Add method of the Parameters collection to create a Parameter object for each parameter in the query or stored procedure.

The Parameters collection provides a number of methods for configuring the collection at run time. The most useful of these are shown in Table 3-5. Note that because the OleDb and ODBC Data Providers don't support named parameters, the parameters are substituted in the order they are found in the Parameters collection. Because of this, it is important that you configure the items in the collection correctly. (Incorrect configuration can be a very difficult bug to track, and yes, this is the voice of experience.)

Table 3-5   Parameters Collection Methods

Method	Description
Add(parameter)	Adds the specified parameter to the end of the collection.
Add(name, type)	Creates a new Parameter of the specified type that has the name specified in the name string, and then adds the Parameter to the end of the collection.
Add(name, type, size)	Creates a new Parameter of the specified type and size that has the name specified in the name string, and then adds the Parameter to the end of the collection.
Add(name, type, size, sourceColumn)	Creates a new Parameter of the specified type and size that has the name specified in the name string, adds the Parameter to the end of the collection, and then maps it to the DataTable column specified in the sourceColumn string.
AddWithValue(name, value)	Creates a new Parameter that has the name specified in the name string and the specified value, and then adds the Parameter to the end of the collection.
Clear	Removes all Parameters from the collection.
Insert(index, value)	Creates a new Parameter that has the specified value, and then adds the Parameter to the collection at the specified (zero-index) index position.
Insert(index, parameter)	Adds the specified parameter to the collection at the specified (zero-index) index position.
Remove(value)	Removes the Parameter that has the specified value from the collection.

Table 3-5   **Parameters Collection Methods**

Method	Description
Remove(parameter)	Removes the specified parameter from the collection.
RemoveAt(index)	Removes the Parameter at the specified (zero-index) index position from the collection.
RemoveAt(name)	Removes the Parameter with the specified name from the collection.

Configuring the Parameters Collection at Design Time

Visual Studio configures parameters for Command objects created at design time when the CommandText property is set. Note, however, that the operation is not reciprocal: Adding a parameter to the CommandText property adds a Parameter to the Parameters collection of the Data Command but does not update the CommandText property.

Visual Studio also provides a Parameter Collection Editor for configuring parameters.

Configure the Parameters Collection in Visual Studio

1. In the Form Designer, drag a SqlCommand object from the Toolbox onto the form.

    Visual Studio adds a new command to the component tray.

2. In the Properties window, change the name of the new Command from SqlCommand1 to **cmdCountOrders**.

3. In the Properties window, select the Connection property, click the down arrow, expand the Existing node in the list, and then click cnAdoSbs.

4. Set the CommandText property as follows:

    ```
    SELECT OrderCount
    FROM OrderCount
    WHERE (EmployeeID = @empID) AND (CustomerID = @custID)
    ```

 Tip   you can type the command directly in the Properties window or use the Query Builder.

5. If a dialog box appears asking if you want to apply the new parameter configuration or if you want to regenerate the Parameters collection, click Yes.

6. In the Properties window, select the Parameters property, and then click the ellipsis button.

    Visual Studio displays the SqlParameter Collection Editor. Because the Query Builder generated the parameters for us, there is nothing to do this time, but you can add, change or remove parameters as necessary.

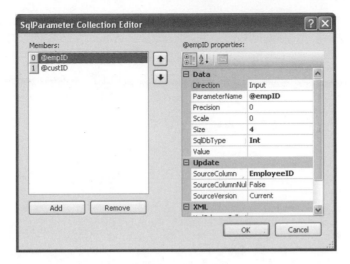

7. Click OK.

Adding and Configuring Parameters at Run Time

Parameters can be added to a Command object's Parameters collection at run time by using one of the Add methods shown previously in Table 3-5.

Add and Configure a Parameter in Code: Visual Basic

1. In the Code Editor, add the following lines to the New procedure, just before the call to CreateScaffolding:

```
cmdGetOrders.Parameters.Add("@empID", SqlDbType.Int)
cmdGetOrders.Parameters.Add("@custID", SqlDbType.VarChar)
```

Your New procedure should now be:

```
Public Sub New()

    ' This call is required by the Windows Form Designer.
    InitializeComponent()

    ' Add exercise code here:
    cmdGetCustomers = New SqlCommand("SELECT * FROM Customers", cnAdoSbs)
    cmdGetOrders = cnAdoSbs.CreateCommand()
    cmdGetOrders.CommandText = "SELECT * FROM OrderTotals WHERE " & _
        "EmployeeID = @empID AND CustomerID = @custID"
    cmdGetOrders.Parameters.Add("@empID", SqlDbType.Int)
    cmdGetOrders.Parameters.Add("@custID", SqlDbType.VarChar)

    ' This call supports the exercise:
    CreateScaffolding()
End Sub
```

Add and Configure a Parameter in Code: Visual C#

1. In the Code Editor, add the following lines to the CommandsAndReaders constructor, just before the call to CreateScaffolding:

```
cmdGetOrders.Parameters.Add("@empID", SqlDbType.Int);
cmdGetOrders.Parameters.Add("@custID", SqlDbType.VarChar);
```

Your class constructor should now be:

```
public CommandsAndReaders()
{
    InitializeComponent();

    //Add exercise code here:
    cmdGetCustomers = new SqlCommand("SELECT * FROM Customers", cnAdoSbs);
    cmdGetOrders = cnAdoSbs.CreateCommand();
    cmdGetOrders.Connection = cnAdoSbs;
    cmdGetOrders.CommandText = "SELECT * FROM OrderTotals WHERE " +
        "EmployeeID = @empID AND CustomerID = @custID";
    cmdGetOrders.Parameters.Add("@empID", SqlDbType.Int);
    cmdGetOrders.Parameters.Add("@custID", SqlDbType.VarChar);

    //This call supports the exercise:
    CreateScaffolding();
}
```

Setting Parameter Values

After you establish the Parameters collection and before you execute the command, you must set the values for each of the Parameters. As we've seen, this can be done when the Parameter is created; or it can be done at run time by using a simple assignment statement.

Set Parameter Values in Code: Visual Basic

1. Add the following code to the btnOrderCount_Click event handler:

```
cmdCountOrders.Parameters(0).Value = 8
cmdCountOrders.Parameters(1).Value = "BONAP"
```

This code sets the value of each parameter in the cmdCountOrders.Parameters collection to arbitrary (but valid) values.

Set Parameter Values in Code: Visual C#

1. Add the following code to the btnOrderCount_Click event handler:

```
cmdCountOrders.Parameters[0].Value = 8;
cmdCountOrders.Parameters[1].Value = "BONAP";
```

This code sets the value of each parameter in the cmdCountOrders.Parameters collection to arbitrary (but valid) values.

Command Methods

The methods exposed by the Command object are shown in Table 3-6. Of these, the most important are the four Execute methods: ExecuteNonQuery, ExecuteReader, ExecuteScalar and ExecuteXmlReader.

Table 3-6   Data Command Methods

Method	Description
Cancel	Cancels the execution of the command.
CreateParameter	Creates a new Parameter.
ExecuteNonQuery	Executes a command and returns the number of rows affected.
ExecuteReader	Executes the command and returns a DataReader.
ExecuteScalar	Executes the command and returns the first column of the first row of the result set.
ExecuteXmlReader	Executes the command and builds an XMLReader.
Prepare	Creates a prepared (compiled) version of the command on the data source.
ResetCommandTimeout	Resets the CommandTimeout property to its default value.

The ExecuteNonQuery method is used when the SQL command or stored procedure to be executed returns no rows. DDL commands would, for example, typically return no rows, and therefore would be executed by using ExecuteNonQuery.

ExecuteScalar is used for SQL commands and stored procedures that return a single value. The most common example of this sort of command is one that returns a count of rows:

```
SELECT COUNT(*) FROM Customers
```

We'll discuss DataReaders in Chapter 4 and XML-Readers in Chapter 18.

The ExecuteReader and ExecuteXMLReader methods are used for commands and stored procedures that return multiple rows.

The ExecuteReader method can be executed with no parameters, or you can supply a CommandBehavior value to control precisely how the command will be executed. The possible CommandBehavior values are shown in Table 3-7.

Table 3-7   CommandBehavior Values

Value	Description
CloseConnection	Closes the Connection referenced by the Connection property when the DataReader is closed.
KeyInfo	Indicates that the query returns column and primary key information.
SchemaOnly	Returns the database schema only, without affecting any rows in the data source.
SequentialAccess	The results of each column of each row are accessed sequentially.
SingleResult	Returns only a single value.
SingleRow	Returns only a single row.

Most CommandBehavior values are self-explanatory. Both KeyInfo and SchemaOnly are useful if you cannot determine the structure of the command's result set prior to run time.

The SequentialAccess behavior allows the application to read large binary column values by using the GetBytes or GetChars methods of the DataReader, while the SingleResult and SingleRow behaviors can be optimized by the data source.

Executing Commands

The methods of the Command object are straightforward, but you must be careful that the return value to which you assign the method call corresponds to the settings of the CommandBehavior property.

Execute a Command in Code: Visual Basic

1. Add the following lines to the end of the btnOrderCount_Click procedure:

```
Dim cnt As Int16
Dim strMsg As String

cnAdoSbs.Open()
cnt = cmdCountOrders.ExecuteScalar()
strMsg = "Employee 8 has " & cnt & " orders."
MessageBox.Show(strMsg)

cnAdoSbs.Close()
```

The added snippet first declares a couple of variables, and then opens the cnAdoSbs Connection. It then calls the ExecuteScalar method of cmdCountOrders and stores the result in the integer variable cnt. The remaining lines display the result in a message box and then close the connection. The event handler should now be:

```
Private Sub btnOrderCount_Click(ByVal sender As System.Object, _
    ByVal e As System.EventArgs) Handles btnOrderCount.Click

    cmdCountOrders.Parameters(0).Value = 8
    cmdCountOrders.Parameters(1).Value = "BONAP"

    Dim cnt As Int16
    Dim strMsg As String

    cnAdoSbs.Open()

    cnt = cmdCountOrders.ExecuteScalar()
    strMsg = "Employee 8 has " & cnt & " orders."
    MessageBox.Show(strMsg)

    cnAdoSbs.Close()
End Sub
```

2. Press F5 to run the application, and click the Show Order Count button.

Visual Studio displays a message box showing the number of orders for the parameters supplied.

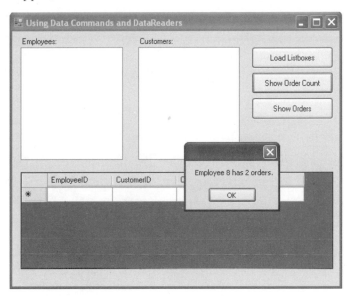

3. Close the application.

Execute a Command in Code: Visual C#

1. Add the following lines to the end of the btnOrderCount_Click procedure:

```
int cnt;
string strMsg;

cnAdoSbs.Open();

cnt = (int)cmdCountOrders.ExecuteScalar();
strMsg = "Employee 8 has " + cnt.ToString() + " orders.";
MessageBox.Show(strMsg);

cnAdoSbs.Close();
```

The added snippet first declares a couple of variables and then opens the cnAdoSbs connection. It then calls the ExecuteScalar method of cmdCountOrders and stores the result in the short variable cnt. The remaining lines display the result in a message box and then close the connection. The event handler should now be:

```
private void btnOrderCount_Click(object sender, EventArgs e)
{
    cmdCountOrders.Parameters[0].Value = 8;
    cmdCountOrders.Parameters[1].Value = "BONAP";
```

```
    int cnt;
    string strMsg;

    cnAdoSbs.Open();

    cnt = (int)cmdCountOrders.ExecuteScalar();
    strMsg = "Employee 8 has " + cnt.ToString() + " orders.";
    MessageBox.Show(strMsg);

    cnAdoSbs.Close();
}
```

2. Press F5 to run the application, and click the Show Order Count button.

   Visual Studio displays a message box showing the number of orders for the parameters supplied.

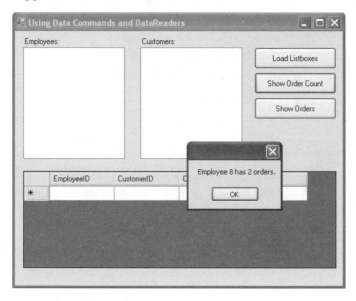

3. Close the application.

Understanding DataReaders

The DataReader object returns a read-only, forward-only stream of data from the Data Command. Traditional database developers call this a *fire hose cursor*—a fast, narrow stream of data like water in a fire hose. Because only a single row of data is in memory at a time (unlike a DataSet, which stores the entire result set, as we'll see in Chapter 6, "Modeling a Database Using DataSets and DataRelations"), a DataReader requires very little overhead. Even with the DataSet optimizations in ADO.NET 2.0, a DataReader is still significantly faster, provided you're using a row once and then discarding it.

The Read method of the DataReader is used to retrieve a row, and the Get<Type> methods (where Type is a system data type, such as GetString to return a data string) are used to return individual columns within the current row.

Like Data Connections and Data Commands, DataReaders are part of a Data Provider and are therefore specific to a data source. As with the other objects we've examined, in practice you use a DataReader object that is specific to the namespace of the Data Provider you are using—SqlDataReader, for example. But like the other objects, the System.Data.Common namespace provides a generic object, the DbDataReader, which you can use in those rare instances in which you need to create provider-independent code.

We'll discuss DataSets in Chapter 6.

A DataReader is almost always used in conjunction with a Data Command. The only exception, as we'll see in Chapter 6, is the TableReader object, a variation of the DataReader that is used with the DataSet.

DataReaders are appropriate whenever you don't need cached data access to data. DataReaders aren't used often in Microsoft Windows applications, but they are useful when you're processing rows individually and then discarding them. Report generators, for example, might see a performance benefit from DataReaders.

Creating DataReaders

Unlike the other ADO.NET objects we've examined, DataReaders are only created at run time—Visual Studio does not expose a Toolbox control that you can manipulate at design time.

Creating DataReaders at Run Time

Although the generic DbDataReader class exposes a constructor, the DataReaders exposed by Data Providers, such as the SqlDataReader that we'll use in this chapter, do not. This isn't a design flaw—the sole purpose of a DataReader is to retrieve the rows returned by a Data Command, so you can use the ExecuteReader method of a Data Command to acquire a reference to a DataReader.

Create a DataReader in Code: Visual Basic

1. Add the following line to the top of the class declaration, below the declaration of cmdGetOrders:

   ```
   Dim drOrders As SqlDataReader
   ```

2. Add the following lines to the bottom of the btnShowOrders_Click event handler, where indicated:

   ```
   cnAdoSbs.Open()
   drOrders = cmdGetOrders.ExecuteReader()

   drOrders.Close()
   cnAdoSbs.Close()
   ```

The first line opens the Connection object, and the second line creates the DataReader. The final two lines close both objects. (We'll be adding code to actually use the DataReader in the next two exercises.)

Your event handler should now be:

```
Private Sub btnShowOrders_Click(ByVal sender As System.Object, _
    ByVal e As System.EventArgs) Handles btnShowOrders.Click
    Dim dr As DataRow
    cmdGetOrders.Parameters(0).Value = lbEmployees.SelectedItem(0)
    cmdGetOrders.Parameters(1).Value = lbCustomers.SelectedItem(0)
    dsAdoSbs.OrderTotals.Clear()

    'Insert exercise code here:
    cnAdoSbs.Open()
    drOrders = cmdGetOrders.ExecuteReader()

    drOrders.Close()
    cnAdoSbs.Close()
End Sub
```

Create a DataReader in Code: Visual C#

1. Add the following line to the top of the class declaration, below the declaration of cmdGetOrders:

    ```
    SqlDataReader drOrders;
    ```

2. Add the following lines to the bottom of the btnShowOrders_Click event handler, where indicated:

    ```
    cnAdoSbs.Open();
    drOrders = cmdGetOrders.ExecuteReader();

    drOrders.Close();
    cnAdoSbs.Close();
    ```

    The first line opens the Connection object, and the second line creates the DataReader. The final two lines close both objects. (We'll be adding code to actually use the DataReader in the next two exercises.)

    Your event handler should now be:

    ```
    private void btnShowOrders_Click(object sender, EventArgs e)
    {
        DataRow dr;
        cmdGetOrders.Parameters[0].Value =
            ((DataRowView)lbEmployees.SelectedItem)[0];
        cmdGetOrders.Parameters[1].Value =
            ((DataRowView)lbCustomers.SelectedItem)[0];
        dsAdoSbs.OrderTotals.Clear();

        //Insert exercise code here:
        cnAdoSbs.Open();
    ```

```
drOrders = cmdGetOrders.ExecuteReader();

drOrders.Close();
cnAdoSbs.Close();
}
```

DataReader Properties

The properties of the DataReader are shown in Table 3-8.

Table 3-8   DataReader Properties

Property	Description
Depth	The depth of nesting for the current row in hierarchical result sets. SQL Server always returns zero.
FieldCount	The number of columns in the current row.
HasRows	Returns a Boolean indicating whether the DataReader contains rows of data.
IsClosed	Indicates whether the DataReader is closed.
Item	The value of a column.
RecordsAffected	The number of rows changed, deleted or inserted.

Most of the properties are self-explanatory. The Item property supports two versions:

- Item(name), which takes a string specifying the name of the column as a parameter
- Item(index), which takes an Int32 as an index of the columns collection. As with all collections in the .NET Framework, the collection index is zero-based.

Retrieving DataReader Properties

All properties of the DataReader are read-only. They are accessed in the same way that you access the properties of any ADO.NET object.

Retrieve a DataReader Property: Visual Basic

1. Add the following lines between the ExecuteReader and Close statements in the btnShowOrders_Click event handler:

```
With drOrders
  If .HasRows Then
  Else
   MessageBox.Show("This employee placed no orders for this customer.")
  End If
End With
```

This added snippet displays a message box if there are no orders for the Employee and Customer selected in the form's two list boxes. (The code that sets the Command Parameters to these values has already been added to the project.)

Your event handler should now be:

```
Private Sub btnShowOrders_Click(ByVal sender As System.Object, _
    ByVal e As System.EventArgs) Handles btnShowOrders.Click
    Dim dr As DataRow
    cmdGetOrders.Parameters(0).Value = lbEmployees.SelectedItem(0)
    cmdGetOrders.Parameters(1).Value = lbCustomers.SelectedItem(0)
    dsAdoSbs.OrderTotals.Clear()

    'Insert exercise code here:
    cnAdoSbs.Open()
    drOrders = cmdGetOrders.ExecuteReader()
    With drOrders
      If .HasRows Then
      Else
        MessageBox.Show("This employee placed no orders for this customer.")
      End If
    End With

    drOrders.Close()
    cnAdoSbs.Close()
End Sub
```

Retrieve a DataReader Property: Visual C#

1. Add the following lines between the ExecuteReader and Close statements in the btnShowOrders_Click event handler:

```
if (drOrders.HasRows)
{
}
else
{
  MessageBox.Show("This employee placed no orders for this customer.");
};
```

This snippet displays a message box if no orders for the Employee and Customer are selected in the form's two list boxes. (The code that sets the Command Parameters to these values has already been added to the project.)

Your event handler should now be:

```
private void btnShowOrders_Click(object sender, EventArgs e)
{
    DataRow dr;
    cmdGetOrders.Parameters[0].Value =
        ((DataRowView)lbEmployees.SelectedItem)[0];
    cmdGetOrders.Parameters[1].Value =
        ((DataRowView)lbCustomers.SelectedItem)[0];
    dsAdoSbs.OrderTotals.Clear();

    //Insert exercise code here:
    cnAdoSbs.Open();
    drOrders = cmdGetOrders.ExecuteReader();
```

```
       if (drOrders.HasRows)
       {
       }
       else
       {
          MessageBox.Show("This employee placed no orders for this customer.");
       };

       drOrders.Close();
       cnAdoSbs.Close();
    }
```

DataReader Methods

The methods exposed by the DataReader are shown in Table 3-9.

Table 3-9   DataReader Methods

Method	Description
Close	Closes the DataReader.
Get<Type>	Gets the value of the specified column as the specified type, where <Type> is the name of a system Type, as shown in Table 3-10.
GetDataTypeName	Gets the name of the data source type.
GetFieldType	Returns the system type of the specified column.
GetName	Gets the name of the specified column.
GetOrdinal	Gets the ordinal position of the specified column.
GetProviderSpecificFieldType	Returns the data type of the specified column.
GetSchemaTable	Returns a DataTable that describes the structure of the DataReader.
GetValue	Gets the value of the specified column as its native type.
GetValues	Gets all the columns in the current row.
IsDbNull	Indicates whether the column contains a nonexistent value.
NextResult	Advances the DataReader to the next result.
Read	Advances the DataReader to the next row.

The Close method closes the DataReader and, if the CloseConnection behavior has been specified, closes the associated Connection object as well.

Using the GetDataTypeName, GetFieldType, GetName, GetOrdinal and IsDbNull methods, you can determine at run time the properties of a specified column. Note that IsDbNull is the only way to check for a null value, because the .NET Framework doesn't have an intrinsic Null data type.

The NextResult method is used when a SQL command or stored procedure returns multiple result sets. It positions the DataReader at the beginning of the next result set. Again, the

DataReader is positioned before the first row, not at the first row, and you must call Read before accessing any results.

The GetValues method returns all of the columns in the current row as an object array, while the GetValue method returns a single value as one of the .NET Framework types. However, if you know the data type of the value to be returned in advance, it is more efficient to use one of the Get<Type> methods shown in Table 3-10.

> **Important**   The SqlDataReader object supports additional Get<Type> methods for values of System.Data.SqlType. They are detailed in MSDN Help.

Table 3-10   GetType Methods

GetBoolean	GetDateTime	GetInt16
GetByte	GetDecimal	GetInt32
GetBytes	GetDouble	GetInt64
GetChar	GetFloat	GetString
GetChars	GetGuid	

The Read Method

The most important method of the DataReader is Read. The Read method retrieves the next row of the result set. When the DataReader is first opened, it is positioned at the beginning of the file, before the first row, not at the first row. You must call Read before the first row of the result set is returned.

Retrieve Data by Using a DataReader: Visual Basic

1. Finish the btnShowOrders_Click event handler by adding the following lines inside the True part of the If .HasRows statement:

```
While .Read
  dr = dsAdoSbs.OrderTotals.NewRow
  dr("EmployeeID") = .GetInt32(0)
  dr("CustomerID") = .GetString(1)
  dr("OrderID") = .GetInt32(2)
  dr("Total") = .GetDecimal(3)
  dsAdoSbs.OrderTotals.AddOrderTotalsRow(dr)
End While
```

The complete handler is now:

```
Dim dr As DataRow
cmdGetOrders.Parameters(0).Value = lbEmployees.SelectedItem(0)
cmdGetOrders.Parameters(1).Value = lbCustomers.SelectedItem(0)
dsNwind.OrderTotals.Clear()
```

```
'Insert exercise code here:
cnAdoSbs.Open()
drOrders = cmdGetOrders.ExecuteReader()
With drOrders
  If .HasRows Then
    While .Read
      dr = dsAdoSbs.OrderTotals.NewRow
      dr("EmployeeID") = .GetInt32(0)
      dr("CustomerID") = .GetString(1)
      dr("OrderID") = .GetInt32(2)
      dr("Total") = .GetDecimal(3)
      dsAdoSbs.OrderTotals.AddOrderTotalsRow(dr)
    End While
  Else
    MessageBox.Show("This employee placed no orders for this customer.")
  End If
End With

drOrders.Close()
cnAdoSbs.Close()
```

2. Press F5 to run the application.

3. Click the Load Listboxes button, select an Employee and Customer in the list boxes, and then click the Show Orders button.

   Visual Studio displays the orders in the DataGridView at the bottom of the form, or displays a message box if there are no orders.

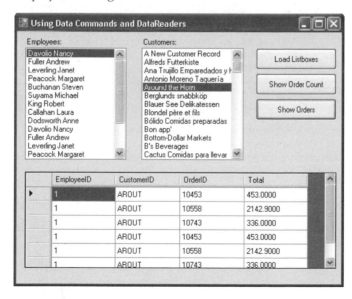

4. Close the application.

Retrieve Data by Using a DataReader: Visual C#

1. Finish the btnShowOrders_Click event handler by adding the following lines inside the true part of the if (drOrders.HasRows) statement:

```
while (drOrders.Read())
{
  dr = dsAdoSbs.OrderTotals.NewRow();
  dr["EmployeeID"] = drOrders.GetInt32(0);
  dr["CustomerID"] = drOrders.GetString(1);
  dr["OrderID"] = drOrders.GetInt32(2);
  dr["Total"] = drOrders.GetDecimal(3);
  dsAdoSbs.OrderTotals.AddOrderTotalsRow((AdoSbsDataSet.OrderTotalsRow)dr);
}
```

The complete handler is now:

```
private void btnShowOrders_Click(object sender, EventArgs e)
{
    DataRow dr;
    cmdGetOrders.Parameters[0].Value =
        ((DataRowView)lbEmployees.SelectedItem)[0];
    cmdGetOrders.Parameters[1].Value =
        ((DataRowView)lbCustomers.SelectedItem)[0];
    dsAdoSbs.OrderTotals.Clear();

    //Insert exercise code here:
    cnAdoSbs.Open();
    drOrders = cmdGetOrders.ExecuteReader();

    if (drOrders.HasRows)
    {
        while (drOrders.Read())
        {
          dr = dsAdoSbs.OrderTotals.NewRow();
          dr["EmployeeID"] = drOrders.GetInt32(0);
          dr["CustomerID"] = drOrders.GetString(1);
          dr["OrderID"] = drOrders.GetInt32(2);
          dr["Total"] = drOrders.GetDecimal(3);
         dsAdoSbs.OrderTotals.AddOrderTotalsRow((AdoSbsDataSet.OrderTotalsRow)dr);
        }
    }
    else
    {
        MessageBox.Show("This employee placed no orders for this customer.");
    };

    drOrders.Close();
    cnAdoSbs.Close();
}
```

2. Press F5 to run the application.

3. Click the Load Listboxes button, select an Employee and Customer in the list boxes, and then click the Show Orders button.

Visual Studio displays the orders in the DataGridView at the bottom of the form, or displays a message box if there are no orders.

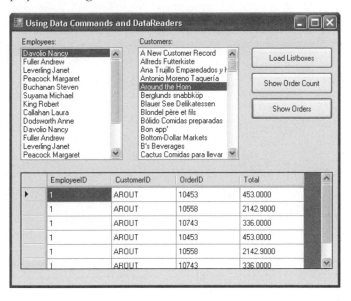

4. Close the application.

Summary

In this chapter we looked at Data Commands and the DataReader object. Data Commands represent SQL commands to be executed by the server and are specific to a Data Provider. DataReaders, which are also Data Provider-specific, return data one row and column at a time. We saw how to create Data Commands at design time and run time, and how to create DataReaders independently and by using the ExecuteReader method of the Data Command. We also saw examples of creating command parameters, how to set those values at run time, and finally how to return results from a Data Command by using a DataReader.

Chapter 4

Using DataAdapters

After completing this chapter, you will be able to:

- Create a DataAdapter.
- Preview the results of a DataAdapter.
- Configure a DataAdapter.
- Use the Table Mappings dialog box.
- Use the methods of a DataAdapter.
- Respond to DataAdapter events.

In this chapter we'll examine the DataAdapter, the Microsoft ADO.NET object that sits between the Connection we looked at in Chapter 2, "Using Connections," and the DataSet that we'll examine in Chapter 7, "Using DataTables."

Understanding DataAdapters

Like the Connection and Command objects, the DataAdapter is part of a Data Provider, and there is a version specific to each Data Provider as well as a generic version in the System.Data.Common namespace.

We'll discuss DataSets in detail in Chapter 6.

DataAdapters act as the "glue" between a data source and the DataSet object. We haven't yet discussed DataSets in detail, but for right now all you need to understand is that a DataSet is an in-memory cache of data that is structured just like a relational database with related tables, rows and columns.

In very abstract terms, the DataAdapter receives the data from the Connection objects and passes it to the DataSet. It also passes changes back from the DataSet to the Connections to update the data in a data source. (Remember that the data source can be any kind of structured data, not just a database.)

Tip Typically there is a one-to-one relationship between a DataAdapter and a DataTable within a DataSet, but this isn't necessarily the case—a DataAdapter can link to multiple tables within a single DataSet.

We'll discuss
TableAdapters
in Chapter 8. To perform updates on the data source, DataAdapters encapsulate four Data Commands, one for each possible action. These are exposed as the SelectCommand, UpdateCommand, Insert-Command and DeleteCommand properties of the DataAdapter.

Microsoft ADO.NET 2.0 adds a new object, the TableAdapter, which encapsulates the Data-Adapter and adds some additional functionality. However, when the extra functionality of the TableAdapter is unnecessary, you will want to use a DataAdapter independently to avoid unnecessary overhead.

Creating DataAdapters

Microsoft Visual Studio 2005 provides several methods for creating DataAdapters interactively, and we'll examine two in this section. Of course, if you need to, you can create a Data-Adapter manually in code, and we'll look at that method in this section, as well.

Creating DataAdapters at Design Time

The TableAdapter has become the default adapter object in much of Visual Studio. For example, if you drag a table, query or stored procedure from the Data Sources window, Visual Studio now adds a TableAdapter to the form rather than a DataAdapter. But you can still create a DataAdapter at design time if you add it to the Visual Studio Toolbox. (Like other basic ADO.NET objects, DataAdapters are no longer available in the Toolbox by default.)

When you drag a DataAdapter from the Toolbox onto the form design surface, Visual Studio starts the DataAdapter Configuration Wizard. If you want to configure the DataAdapter manually, you can simply cancel the wizard and set the DataAdapter's properties in code or in the Properties window. We'll examine the DataAdapter's properties and how to set them manually later in this chapter.

Add a Design-Time DataAdapter to the Toolbox

1. Start an instance of Visual Studio, open the Chapter 04 – Start project, and if necessary, double-click DataAdapters.vb (or DataAdapters.cs if you're using C#) in the Solution Explorer to open the form.

2. Open the Toolbox, and right-click the Data tab.

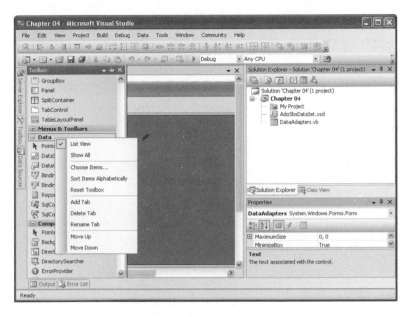

3. Select Choose Items on the context menu.

   After a few moments, Visual Studio displays the Choose Toolbox Items dialog box.

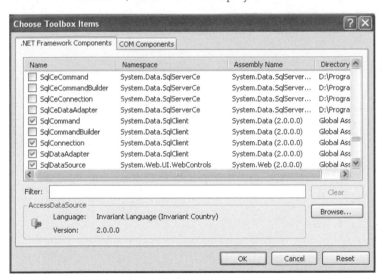

4. Scroll down, and select the SqlDataAdapter check box.

5. Click OK.

Visual Studio adds the SqlDataAdapter control to the Data section of the Toolbox.

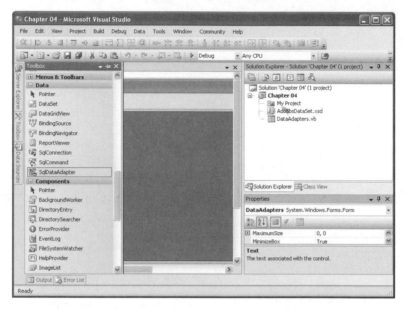

Create a DataAdapter by Using the DataAdapter Configuration Wizard

1. Drag a SqlDataAdapter control onto the form design surface from the Toolbox.

   Visual Studio starts the DataAdapter Configuration Wizard.

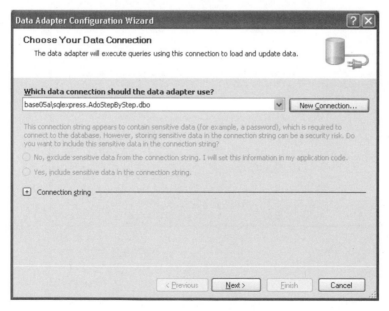

2. Visual Studio probably suggests the location of the sample databases we've been using. If it doesn't, click New Connection. In the Add Connection dialog box, make sure Data

Source is set to Microsoft SQL Server. In the Server Name box, type **(local)\SQLEX-PRESS**. In the Log On To The Server section, select the Use Windows Authentication option. In the Connect To A Database section, select the Select Or Enter A Database Name option. Click the down arrow, and select the AdoStepByStep database. When finished, click OK.

3. When the correct location is displayed on the Choose Your Data Connection page, click Next.

Visual Studio displays the Choose A Command Type page.

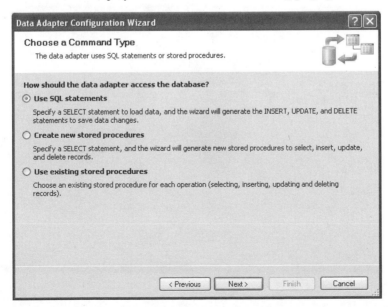

4.   Accept the default of Use SQL Statements, and click Next.

Visual Studio displays the Generate The SQL Statements page.

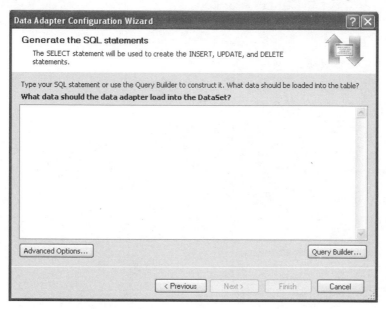

5.   Click the Query Builder button.

Visual Studio displays the Query Builder and the Add Table dialog box.

6.   Select the Categories table, click Add, and then click Close.

Visual Studio adds the table to the Query Builder.

7.   In the Grid Pane, click the * (All Columns) check box.

The Query Builder generates the SQL statement.

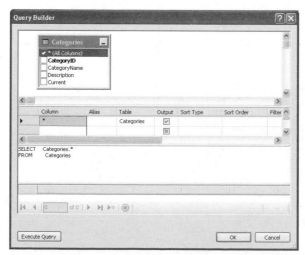

8. Click OK in the Query Builder, and then click Finish on the Generate The SQL Statements page.

    Visual Studio adds a DataAdapter and a Connection to the form's component tray.

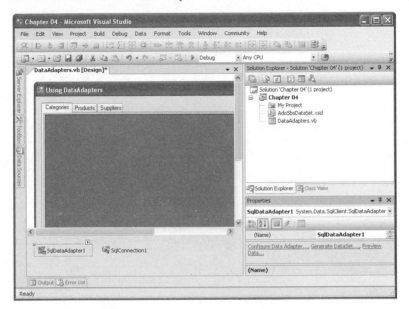

9. Select SqlDataAdapter1 in the component tray, and then in the Properties window, rename the control **daCategories**.

10. Select SqlConnection1 in the component tray, and then in the Properties window, rename the control **cnAdoSbs**.

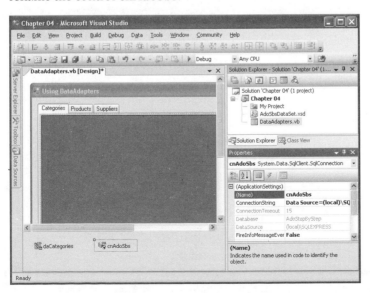

Create a DataAdapter Manually

1. Drag a SqlDataAdapter control onto the form design surface from the Toolbox.

   Visual Studio starts the DataAdapter Configuration Wizard

2. Click Cancel.

   Visual Studio closes the wizard and adds the DataAdapter to the form's component tray.

3. Select the new DataAdapter, and then in the Properties window, change its name to **daProducts**.

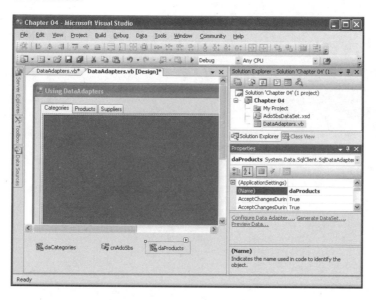

Creating DataAdapters at Run Time

When we created ADO.NET objects in code in previous chapters, we first declared them and then initialized them. The process of creating a DataAdapter is essentially the same but with a little twist: Because the DataAdapter references four Command objects, you must declare and instantiate each of the Commands and then set the DataAdapter Command properties to reference them.

Create a DataAdapter at Run Time: Visual Basic

1. Press F7 to display the code for the DataAdapter form in the Code Editor.

2. Add the following lines inside the Class declaration, after the declaration of dsAdoSbs:

```
Friend WithEvents cmdSelectSuppliers As New SqlCommand()
Friend WithEvents cmdInsertSuppliers As New SqlCommand()
Friend WithEvents cmdUpdateSuppliers As New SqlCommand()
Friend WithEvents cmdDeleteSuppliers As New SqlCommand()
Friend WithEvents daSuppliers As New SqlDataAdapter()
```

This snippet declares and creates four Data Commands and a DataAdapter.

The beginning of the code file should now be:

```
Imports System.Data
Imports System.Data.SqlClient
Public Class DataAdapters
    Dim dsAdoSbs As AdoSbsDataSet
    Friend WithEvents cmdSelectSuppliers As New SqlCommand ()
    Friend WithEvents cmdInsertSuppliers As New SqlCommand ()
    Friend WithEvents cmdUpdateSuppliers As New SqlCommand ()
    Friend WithEvents cmdDeleteSuppliers As New SqlCommand ()

    Friend WithEvents daSuppliers As New SqlDataAdapter()

    Public Sub New()
...
```

3. Add the following lines, which assign the four Data Command objects to the Data-Adapter, to the New procedure, where indicated after the call to InitializeComponent:

```
daSuppliers.SelectCommand = cmdSelectSuppliers
daSuppliers.InsertCommand = cmdInsertSuppliers
daSuppliers.UpdateCommand = cmdUpdateSuppliers
daSuppliers.DeleteCommand = cmdDeleteSuppliers
```

The procedure should now be:

```
Public Sub New()

    ' This call is required by the Windows Form Designer.
    InitializeComponent()

    ' Add exercise code here:
    daSuppliers.SelectCommand = cmdSelectSuppliers
    daSuppliers.InsertCommand = cmdInsertSuppliers
    daSuppliers.UpdateCommand = cmdUpdateSuppliers
    daSuppliers.DeleteCommand = cmdDeleteSuppliers

    ' This call supports the exercise
    CreateScaffolding()
End Sub
```

Create a DataAdapter at Run Time: Visual C#

1. Press F7 to display the code for the DataAdapter form in the Code Editor.

2. Add the following lines, which declare and create four Data Commands and a Data-Adapter, inside the class declaration, after the declaration of dsAdoSbs:

```
SqlCommand cmdSelectSuppliers;
SqlCommand cmdInsertSuppliers;
SqlCommand cmdUpdateSuppliers;
SqlCommand cmdDeleteSuppliers;
SqlDataAdapter daSuppliers;
```

The beginning of your class file should now be:

```
using System;
using System.Collections.Generic;
using System.ComponentModel;
using System.Data;
using System.Data.SqlClient;
using System.Drawing;
using System.Text;
using System.Windows.Forms;

namespace DataAdapters
{
    public partial class DataAdapters : Form
    {
        AdoSbsDataSet dsAdoSbs;
        SqlCommand cmdSelectSuppliers;
        SqlCommand cmdInsertSuppliers;
        SqlCommand cmdUpdateSuppliers;
        SqlCommand cmdDeleteSuppliers;
        SqlDataAdapter daSuppliers;

        public DataAdapters()
        {
...
```

3. Add the following lines, which instantiate the objects declared in the previous step, to the class constructor after the call to InitializeComponent, where indicated:

```
cmdSelectSuppliers = new SqlCommand();
cmdInsertSuppliers = new SqlCommand ();
cmdUpdateSuppliers = new SqlCommand ();
cmdDeleteSuppliers = new SqlCommand();
daSuppliers = new SqlDataAdapter();
```

Your constructor should now be:

```
public DataAdapters()
{
    InitializeComponent();

    //Insert exercise code here:
    cmdSelectSuppliers = new SqlCommand();
    cmdInsertSuppliers = new SqlCommand ();
    cmdUpdateSuppliers = new SqlCommand();
    cmdDeleteSuppliers = new SqlCommand ();
    daSuppliers = new SqlDataAdapter();   //This call supports the exercise:
    CreateScaffolding();
}
```

4. Now below the code we just added, add the commands that assign the Data Command objects to the DataAdapter:

```
daSuppliers.SelectCommand = cmdSelectSuppliers;
daSuppliers.InsertCommand = cmdInsertSuppliers;
daSuppliers.UpdateCommand = cmdUpdateSuppliers;
daSuppliers.DeleteCommand = cmdDeleteSuppliers;
```

Your constructor should now be:

```
public DataAdapters()
{
    InitializeComponent();

    //Insert exercise code here:
    cmdSelectSuppliers = new SqlCommand();
    cmdInsertSuppliers = new SqlCommand();
    cmdUpdateSuppliers = new SqlCommand();
    cmdDeleteSuppliers = new SqlCommand();
    daSuppliers = new SqlDataAdapter();
    daSuppliers.SelectCommand = cmdSelectSuppliers;
    daSuppliers.InsertCommand = cmdInsertSuppliers;
    daSuppliers.UpdateCommand = cmdUpdateSuppliers;
    daSuppliers.DeleteCommand = cmdDeleteSuppliers;

    //This call supports the exercise:
    CreateScaffolding();
}
```

Previewing Results

When you're creating a DataAdapter at design time, it's useful to quickly check the configuration. Visual Studio provides a quick and easy method to check the configuration of a form-level DataAdapter: the DataAdapter Preview dialog box. The Visual Studio Form Designer provides access to the DataAdapter Preview dialog box through the Smart Tag displayed when the control is selected in the component tray.

Preview the Results of a DataAdapter

1. Press F7 to display the Form Designer.

2. Select daCategories in the component tray.

3. Click the small arrow displayed in the upper-right corner of the control to display the smart tag menu.

4. Click Preview Data.

   Visual Studio displays the Preview Data dialog box.

5. Click Preview.

   Visual Studio displays the data retrieved by the DataAdapter.

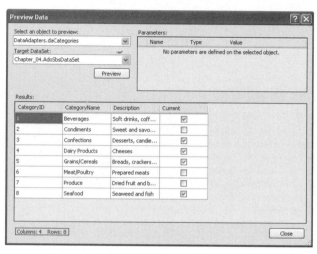

6. Close the Preview Data dialog box.

Configuring DataAdapters

The properties exposed by the DataAdapter are shown in Table 4-1. The majority of the properties exposed by the DataAdapter control how updated data is handled in the DataSet. They are included here for completeness, but we won't examine them until later chapters.

Table 4-1   DataAdapter Properties

Property	Description
AcceptChangesDuringFill	Determines whether AcceptChanges is called on a DataRow after it is added to the DataTable.
AcceptChangesDuringUpdate	Determines whether AcceptChanges is called on a DataRow after it is updated.
ContinueUpdateOnError	Determines whether the DataAdapter generates an exception when an error is encountered during an Update operation.
DeleteCommand	The Data Command used to delete rows in the data source.
FillLoadOption	Determines how version information is handled in the DataSet.
InsertCommand	The Data Command used to insert rows in the data source.

Table 4-1   **DataAdapter Properties**

Property	Description
MissingMappingAction	Determines the action taken when incoming data cannot be matched to an existing table or column.
MissingSchemaAction	Determines the action taken when incoming data does not match the schema of an existing DataSet.
SelectCommand	The Data Command used to retrieve rows from the data source.
TableMappings	A collection of DataTableMapping objects that determine the relationship between the columns in a DataSet and the data source.
UpdateBatchSize	Determines batch processing support, and specifies the number of commands that can be executed in a batch.
UpdateCommand	The Data Command used to update rows in the data source.

We'll examine the Accept-Changes method in Chapter 10. The AcceptChangesDuringFill and AcceptChangesDuringUpdate properties determine whether the AcceptChanges method is called for each row of a DataSet that is added or updated, respectively, by the DataAdapter. The default value is True.

We'll examine DataRows in Chapter 7 and the RowError property in Chapter 10. The ContinueUpdateOnError property determines how the DataAdapter behaves if an error is encountered during an update. If this property is set to True, the DataAdapter throws an exception and stops the update. If it is set to False, the update to that DataRow is skipped, the error is placed in its RowError property, and processing continues with the next row.

The four command properties, DeleteCommand, InsertCommand, UpdateCommand and SelectCommand, encapsulate Data Command objects. We'll examine these properties in detail later in this chapter.

We'll examine DataRows in Chapter 7 and the FillLoad-Option in Chapter 10. The FillLoadOption determines how version information is handled during an update. The possible values are shown in Table 4-2. The default is OverwriteChanges.

Table 4-2   **LoadOption Enumeration**

Value	Description
OverwriteChanges	The incoming values for this row are written to both the current value and the original value versions of the data for each column.
PreserveChanges	The incoming values for this row are written to the original value version of the data for each column.
Upsert	The incoming values for this row are written to the current value version of the data for each column and the original values are maintained.

The MissingMappingAction property determines how the system reacts when a Select-Command returns columns or tables that are not found in the DataSet. The possible values are shown in Table 4-3. The default value is Passthrough.

Table 4-3   MissingMappingAction Enumeration

Value	Description
Error	Throws a SystemException.
Ignore	Ignores any columns or tables not found in the DataSet.
Passthrough	The missing column or table is added to the DataSet, using its name in the data source.

Similarly, the MissingSchemaAction property determines how the system responds if a column is missing in the DataSet. The MissingSchemaAction property is referenced only if the MissingMappingAction property is set to its default value of Passthrough. The possible values for MissingSchemaAction are shown in Table 4-4. The default is Add.

Table 4-4   MissingSchemaAction Enumeration

Value	Description
Add	Adds the necessary columns to the DataSet.
AddWithKey	Adds both the necessary columns and tables and PrimaryKey constraints.
Error	Throws a SystemException.
Ignore	Ignores the extra columns.

The TableMappings property determines how tables and columns in the data source are mapped to tables and columns in the DataSet. We'll examine TableMappings in detail later in this chapter.

Finally, the UpdateBatchSize property controls batch processing. The exact behavior of this property is determined by the Data Provider and is detailed in MSDN Help.

When working in the Visual Studio Form Designer, you can rerun the DataAdapter Configuration Wizard at any time from the DataAdapter's smart tag menu, or you can set individual properties in the Properties window.

You can also set the properties of DataAdapters in code, using the same techniques you use for any property: Simply assign the new value.

DataAdapter Commands

As we've seen, each DataAdapter contains references to four Command objects, each of which has a CommandText property that contains the actual SQL statement to be executed.

If you create a DataAdapter by using the DataAdapter Configuration Wizard, Visual Studio attempts to automatically generate the CommandText property for each Command. You can also edit the SQL statement in the Properties window, although you must first associate the Command with a Connection object. (You might recall that this was also true when working with independent Data Commands.)

> **Tip**   Every DataAdapter Command is associated with a Connection. In the majority of cases, you use a single Connection for all of the Commands, but this isn't a requirement. You can associate a different Connection with each Command, if necessary.

You must specify the CommandText property for the SelectCommand object, but the Microsoft .NET Framework can generate the CommandText for the remaining Data Commands on the fly if necessary.

Internally, Visual Studio uses the CommandBuilder object to generate the SQL statements for each Command. You can instantiate a CommandBuilder object in code and use it to generate Commands as required, but you must be aware of the CommandBuilder's limitations. For example, it cannot handle parameterized stored procedures. Although the CommandBuilder technique is useful in certain rare cases, it's usually better to control the CommandText property of each of the Command objects directly, if you need more than read-only access to the data.

Set the CommandText Property of a DataAdapter in Visual Studio

1. In the Form Designer, select the daProducts DataAdapter, and then in the Properties window, expand the SelectCommand property.

2. Select the Connection property, click the down arrow, expand the Existing node in the list, and then click cnAdoSbs.

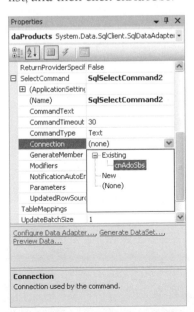

3. Select the CommandText property, and then click the ellipsis button.

    Visual Studio opens the Query Builder and displays the Add Table dialog box.

4. Select the Products table, click Add, and then click Close.

    Visual Studio closes the Add Table dialog box and adds the table to the Query Builder.

5. Add all of the columns in the table to the query by selecting the * (All Columns) check box in the Grid Pane.

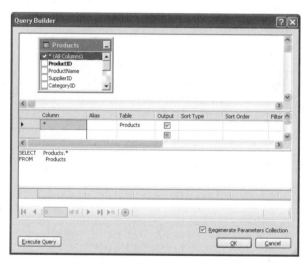

6. Click OK.

    Visual Studio generates the CommandText property.

Set the CommandText Property of a DataAdapter at Run Time: Visual Basic

1. Press F7 to display the Code Editor.

2. Add the following lines to the New procedure, before the call to CreateScaffolding():

    ```
    cmdSelectSuppliers.CommandText = "SELECT * FROM Suppliers"
    cmdSelectSuppliers.Connection = cnAdoSbs
    ```

    Your New procedure should now be:

    ```
    Public Sub New()

        ' This call is required by the Windows Form Designer.
        InitializeComponent()

        ' Add exercise code here:
        daSuppliers.SelectCommand = cmdSelectSuppliers
        daSuppliers.InsertCommand = cmdInsertSuppliers
        daSuppliers.UpdateCommand = cmdUpdateSuppliers
        daSuppliers.DeleteCommand = cmdDeleteSuppliers
        cmdSelectSuppliers.CommandText = "SELECT * FROM Suppliers"
        cmdSelectSuppliers.Connection = cnAdoSbs
    ```

```
    ' This call supports the exercise
    CreateScaffolding()
End Sub
```

Set the CommandText Property of a DataAdapter at Run Time: Visual C#

1. Press F7 to display the Code Editor.

2. Add the following lines to the constructor, before the call to CreateScaffolding():

```
cmdSelectSuppliers.CommandText = "SELECT * FROM Suppliers";
cmdSelectSuppliers.Connection = cnAdoSbs;
```

Your constructor should now be:

```
public DataAdapters()
{
    InitializeComponent();

    //Insert exercise code here:
    cmdSelectSuppliers = new SqlCommand();
    cmdInsertSuppliers = new SqlCommand();
    cmdUpdateSuppliers = new SqlCommand();
    cmdDeleteSuppliers = new SqlCommand();
    daSuppliers = new SqlDataAdapter();
    daSuppliers.SelectCommand = cmdSelectSuppliers;
    daSuppliers.InsertCommand = cmdInsertSuppliers;
    daSuppliers.UpdateCommand = cmdUpdateSuppliers;
    daSuppliers.DeleteCommand = cmdDeleteSuppliers;
    cmdSelectSuppliers.CommandText = "SELECT * FROM Suppliers";
    cmdSelectSuppliers.Connection = cnAdoSbs;

    //This call supports the exercise:
    CreateScaffolding();
}
```

The DataTableMappingCollection

A DataSet has no knowledge of where the data it contains originates, and a Connection has no knowledge of what happens to the data it retrieves. The primary job of the DataAdapter is to maintain the link between the two. It does this by using the DataTableMappingCollection.

The structure of the DataTableMappingCollection is shown in the following figure. At the highest level, the DataTableMappingCollection contains one or more DataTableMapping objects. Typically, there is only one DataTableMapping object, because most DataAdapters return only a single record set. However, if a DataAdapter manages multiple record sets, as might be the case when the data source is a stored procedure that returns multiple result sets, there is a DataTableMapping object for each record set.

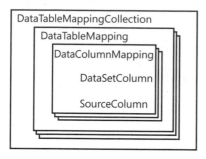

The DataTableMapping object is itself a collection that contains one or more DataColumn-Mapping objects. Each DataColumnMapping object has two properties: the DataSetColumn, which is the case-*in*sensitive name of the column in the DataSet, and the SourceColumn, which is the case-sensitive name of the column in the underlying data source. There is a Data-ColumnMapping object for each column managed by the DataAdapter.

By default, the .NET Framework creates a DataTableMappingCollection with the Data-SetColumn name of each column in the DataSet set to the SourceColumn name. There are times, however, when this setting isn't what you want. For example, you might want to change the mappings for programming convenience (as when there are spaces in the column names of the data source) or because you're working with a pre-existing DataSet with column names that are different from those of the data source.

Change a DataSet Column Name by Using the Table Mappings Dialog Box

1. Press F7 to display the Form Designer.

2. Select the daCategories DataAdapter in the component tray.

3. In the Properties window, select the TableMappings property.

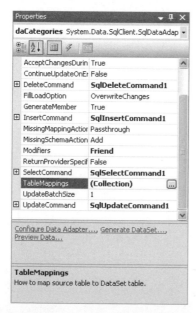

4. Click the ellipsis button.

   Visual Studio displays the Table Mappings dialog box.

5. Select the Use A DataSet To Suggest Table And Column Names check box.

   Visual Studio correlates the column names between the source table and the DataSet.

6. Click OK to close the dialog box.

Using DataAdapter Methods

The DataAdapter supports two important methods: Fill, which loads data from the data source into the DataSet; and Update, which transfers the data in the other direction, from the DataSet to the data source. We'll examine both methods in this set of exercises.

The Fill Method

The Fill method loads data from a data source into one or more tables of a DataSet by using the command specified in the CommandText of the DataAdapter's SelectCommand. The DbDataAdapter object, from which the Data Provider-specific DataAdapters are inherited, supports several variations of the Fill method. The most commonly used Fill methods are shown in Table 4-5.

> **Tip**   Several of the Data Provider-specific DataAdapters support additional versions. MSDN Help contains details.

Table 4-5   DbDataAdapter Fill Methods

Method	Description
Fill(dataSet)	Creates a DataTable named Table and populates it with the rows returned from the data source.
Fill(dataTable)	Fills the specified DataTable with the rows returned from the data source.
Fill(dataSet, tableName)	Fills the DataTable named in the tableName string, within the specified DataSet, with the rows returned from the data source.
Fill(dataTable, dataReader)	Fills the specified DataTable by using the specified DataReader.
Fill(dataTable, command, commandBehavior)	Fills the specified DataTable by using the SQL string passed in the command parameter and the specified CommandBehavior.
Fill(dataSet, startRecord, maxRecords, tableName)	Fills the DataTable specified in the tableName string, in the specified DataSet, beginning at the zero-based startRecord and continuing for maxRecords or until the end of the result set.
Fill(dataSet, tableName, dataReader, startRecord, maxRecords)	Fills the DataTable specified in the tableName string, in the specified DataSet, beginning at the zero-based startRecord and continuing for maxRecords or until the end of the result set, using the specified DataReader.
Fill(dataSet, startRecord, maxRecords, tableName, command, commandBehavior)	Fills the DataTable specified in the tableName string, in the specified DataSet, beginning at the zero-based startRecord and continuing for maxRecords or until the end of the result set, using the SQL text contained in the Command parameter and the specified CommandBehavior.

Fill a DataSet from a DataAdapter: Visual Basic

1. Press F7 to display the Code Editor.

2. Add the following lines to the bottom of the btnFill_Click event handler:

```
daCategories.Fill(dsAdoSbs.Categories)
daProducts.Fill(dsAdoSbs.Products)
daSuppliers.Fill(dsAdoSbs.Suppliers)
```

The event handler should now be:

```
Private Sub btnFill_Click(ByVal sender As System.Object, _
   ByVal e As System.EventArgs) Handles btnFill.Click

   'The following lines clear the DataSet
   dsAdoSbs.Categories.Clear()
   dsAdoSbs.Products.Clear()
   dsAdoSbs.Suppliers.Clear()

   'Add exercise code here:
   daCategories.Fill(dsAdoSbs.Categories)
  daProducts.Fill(dsAdoSbs.Products)
   daSuppliers.Fill(dsAdoSbs.Suppliers)
End Sub
```

3. Press F5 to run the application, and then click Fill.

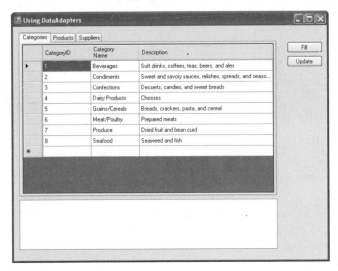

4. Verify that each of the data grids has been filled correctly, and then close the application.

Fill a DataSet from a DataAdapter: Visual C#

1. Press F7 to display the Code Editor.

2. Add the following lines to the btnFill_Click event handler:

```
daCategories.Fill(dsAdoSbs.Categories);
daProducts.Fill(dsAdoSbs.Products);
daSuppliers.Fill(dsAdoSbs.Suppliers);
```

The event handler should now be:

```
void btnFill_Click(object sender, EventArgs e)
{
    //The following lines clear the dataset
    dsAdoSbs.Categories.Clear();
    dsAdoSbs.Products.Clear();
    dsAdoSbs.Suppliers.Clear();

    //Add exercise code here:
    daCategories.Fill(dsAdoSbs.Categories);
    daProducts.Fill(dsAdoSbs.Products);
    daSuppliers.Fill(dsAdoSbs.Suppliers);
}
```

3. Press F5 to run the application, and then click Fill.

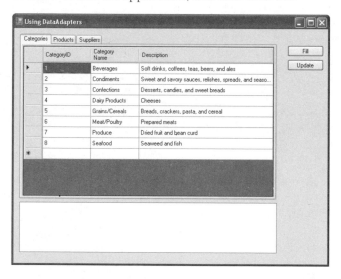

4. Verify that each of the data grids has been filled correctly, and then close the application.

The Update Method

Remember that the DataSet doesn't retain any knowledge about the source of the data it contains, and that because ADO.NET uses a disconnected architecture, the changes you make to DataSet rows aren't automatically propagated back to the data source. You must use the DataAdapter's Update method to do this. The Update method calls the DataAdapter's Insert-Command, DeleteCommand or UpdateCommand, as appropriate, for each row in a DataSet that has changed.

There are several versions of the Update method, as shown in Table 4-6. The DataAdapters exposed by each Data Provider support all of these versions, and none of the Data Providers included in the .NET Framework expose any additional versions.

Table 4-6 DataAdapter Update Methods

Method	Description
Update(dataSet)	Updates the data source from a DataTable named Table in the specified DataSet.
Update(dataRows)	Updates the data source from the specified array of DataRows.
Update(dataTable)	Updates the data source from the specified DataTable.
Update(dataRows, dataTableMapping)	Updates the data source from the specified array of DataRows, using the specified DataTableMapping.
Update(dataSet, sourceTable)	Updates the data source from the DataTable specified in the sourceTable string in the specified DataSet.

Update a Data Source by Using a DataAdapter: Visual Basic

1. In the Code Editor, add the following code to the btnUpdate_Click event handler:

```
daCategories.Update(dsAdoSbs.Categories)
daProducts.Update(dsAdoSbs.Products)
daSuppliers.Update(dsAdoSbs.Suppliers)
```

   This code block updates the underlying data source with the changes made to each of the DataTables in dsAdoSbs.

2. Press F5 to run the application.

3. Click the Fill button.

   The application fills the data grids.

4. Click the Category Name cell of the first row, and change its value from Beverages to Old Beverages.

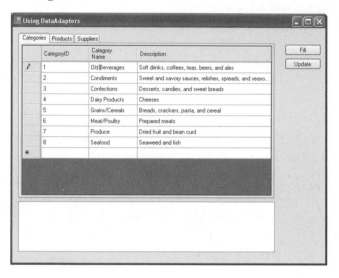

5. Click Update.

   The application updates the data source.

6. Click Fill to ensure that the change has been propagated to the data source.

7. Close the application.

Update a Data Source by Using a DataAdapter: Visual C#

1. In the Code Editor, add the following code to the btnUpdate_Click event handler:

   ```
   daCategories.Update(dsAdoSbs.Categories);
   daProducts.Update(dsAdoSbs.Products);
   daSuppliers.Update(dsAdoSbs.Suppliers);
   ```

   This code block updates the underlying data source with the changes made to each of the DataTables in dsAdoSbs.

2. Press F5 to run the application.

3. Click the Fill button.

   The application fills the data grids.

4. Click the Category Name cell of the first row, and change its value from Beverages to **Old Beverages**.

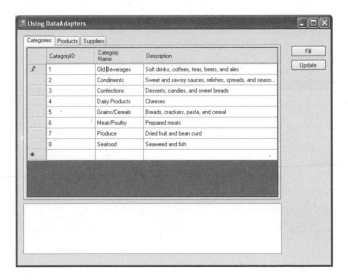

5. Click Update.

    The application updates the data source.

6. Click Fill to ensure that the change has been propagated to the data source.

7. Close the application.

Responding to DataAdapter Events

In addition to events caused by errors, the DataAdapter exposes two events: RowUpdating and RowUpdated. The RowUpdating event occurs before the actual DataSet update, and the RowUpdated event occurs after it, providing fine control of the process.

The RowUpdating Event

The RowUpdating event is fired after the Update method has set the parameter values of the command to be executed but before the update actually occurs.

The event handler for this event receives an argument whose properties provide essential information about the command that is about to be executed. The argument is specific to the Data Provider, but all Data Providers expose the same properties. The most commonly used properties are shown in Table 4-7.

Table 4-7   RowUpdating and RowUpdated Argument Properties

Property	Description
Command	A reference to the Data Command to be executed.
Row	A reference to the DataReader being updated.

Table 4-7   RowUpdating and RowUpdated Argument Properties

Property	Description
StatementType	The type of SQL statement to be executed.
TableMapping	The DataTableMapping used by the update.

The event argument's Command property contains a reference to the actual Data Command that is used to update the data source. Using this reference, you can, for example, examine the Command's CommandText property to determine the SQL statement that will be executed (and change it if necessary).

The StatementType property defines the action to be performed. This property is an enumeration containing the members Select, Insert, Update and Delete. The StatementType is read-only, so you cannot use it to change the type of action to be performed.

The Row property contains a read-only reference to the DataReader to be propagated to the data source, while the TableMappings property contains a reference to the DataTableMapping that is being used for the update.

Respond to a RowUpdating Event: Visual Basic

1. In the Code Editor, add an event handler to the RowUpdating event of the daCategories DataAdapter by selecting daCategories in the object list and RowUpdating in the event list.

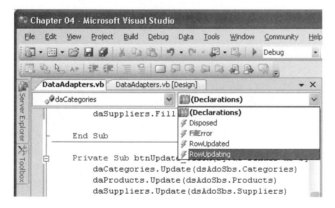

2. Add the following code to the daCategories_RowUpdating event handler:

```
txtMessages.Text &= vbCrLf & "Beginning Update..."
txtMessages.Text &= vbCrLf & "Executing a command of type " & _
    e.StatementType.ToString()
```

3. Press F5 to run the application, and then click Fill to fill the data grids.

4. Change the Category Name for CategoryID 1 back to **Beverages**.

   Recall that we changed this name to Old Beverages in the previous exercise.

5. Click Update.

   The application updates the data source and the text in the message box at the bottom of the DataAdapters window.

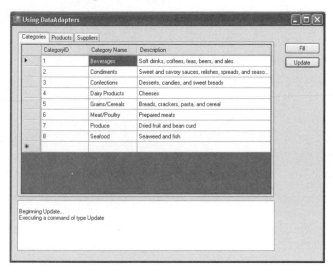

6. Close the application.

Respond to a RowUpdating Event: Visual C#

1. Make sure the form is displayed in design view.

2. Select the daCategories DataAdatper in the component tray.

3. In the Properties window, click the Events button.

4. Select the RowUpdating property, and press the Enter key.

   Visual Studio adds the daCategories_RowUpdating event handler and displays it in the Code Editor.

5. Add the following code to the daCategories_RowUpdating event handler:

```
txtMessages.Text += "\r\nBeginning Update...";
txtMessages.Text += "\r\nExecuting a command of type " +
    e.StatementType.ToString();
```

6. Press F5 to run the application, and then click Fill to fill the data grids.

7. Change the Category Name for CategoryID 1 back to **Beverages**.

   Recall that we changed this name to Old Beverages in the previous exercise.

8. Click Update.

   The application updates the data source and the text in the message box.

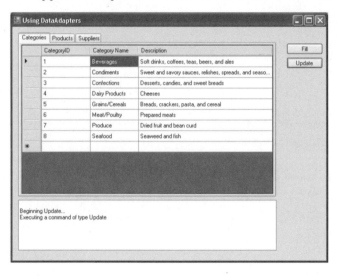

9. Close the application.

The RowUpdated Event

The RowUpdated event is fired after the Update method executes the appropriate command against the data source. The event handler for this event is passed a Data Provider–specific argument that exposes the same properties as the RowUpdating event shown in Table 4-7. The RowUpdated event argument also exposes one additional property, RecordsEffected, which is a read-only value that indicates the number of rows that were changed, inserted or deleted by the SQL command that was executed.

Summary

In this chapter, we examined the DataAdapter object, which acts as an intermediary between a Connection and a DataSet. The DataAdapter encapsulates one or more Data Command objects that control how data is selected, inserted, updated and deleted.

Chapter 5

Transaction Processing in ADO.NET

After completing this chapter, you will be able to:

- Create a Transaction.
- Create a Nested Transaction.
- Commit a Transaction.
- Roll back a Transaction.

In the last few chapters, we've seen how Microsoft ADO.NET Data Provider objects interact in the process of editing and updating data. In this chapter, we'll complete our examination of ADO.NET Data Providers with an exploration of transaction processing.

Understanding Transactions

A transaction is a series of actions that must be treated as a single unit of work—either all the actions succeed, or they all fail. The classic example of a transaction is the transfer of funds from one bank account to another. To transfer an amount of, say, $100, the funds are withdrawn from one account and deposited in another. If the withdrawal succeeds but the deposit fails, money is lost in cyberspace. If the withdrawal fails but the deposit succeeds, money is invented. Clearly, if either action fails, they both fail.

ADO.NET models transactions by using the Transaction object. Transactions are created, as we'll see, by using the BeginTransaction method of a Connection. Transactions are tied to the Connection used to create them; although they expose a Connection property, it cannot be changed. In order for a Command to be part of the transaction ("enrolled" in the transaction), its Transaction property must be set to the Transaction object.

 Note While the Transaction is pending, only Commands that are enrolled in the Transaction can be executed. Attempting to execute any other Command generates an error.

Unfortunately, Commands won't be enrolled in a transaction automatically. You must explicitly set the Transaction property of the Data Command to reference the Transaction. After the transaction is either committed (changes saved) or rolled back (changes discarded), however, the Transaction reference in any Data Command is reset to a null reference, so it isn't necessary to perform this step manually.

Using Transactions

The Transaction object is implemented as part of the Data Provider, and there are versions in each Data Provider namespace, as well as in the System.Data.Common namespace.

The Transaction object mediates between your Microsoft.NET Framework code and the underlying data source. Although it's theoretically possible to use Data Commands to execute BEGIN TRANSACTION SQL statements on the data source, executing such statements can be dangerous because the application and database engine transactions can easily get out of sync.

There are three steps to using a transaction after it is created. First it is assigned to the commands that participate in it. Second, the commands are executed. Finally, the transaction is closed by either committing it or rolling it back.

Creating Transactions

Transactions are created by calling the BeginTransaction method of the Connection object, which returns a reference to a new Transaction object. BeginTransaction is overloaded, allowing an IsolationLevel to optionally be specified, as shown in Table 5-1. The Connection must be valid and open when the BeginTransaction method is called.

Table 5-1 Connection BeginTransaction Methods

Method	Description
BeginTransaction()	Begins a transaction.
BeginTransaction(isolationLevel)	Begins a transaction at the specified IsolationLevel.

Because Microsoft SQL Server supports named transactions, the SqlClient Data Provider exposes two additional versions of BeginTransaction, as shown in Table 5-2.

Table 5-2 Additional SqlClient BeginTransaction Methods

Method	Description
BeginTransaction(transactionName)	Begins a transaction with the name specified in the transactionName string.
BeginTransaction(isolationLevel, transactionName)	Begins a transaction at the specified IsolationLevel with the name specified in the transactionName string.

The optional IsolationLevel parameter of the BeginTransaction method specifies the locking behavior of the Connection. The possible values for the IsolationLevel are shown in Table 5-3. The default value, if the parameter is not specified, is ReadCommitted.

Table 5-3   IsolationLevel Enumeration

Value	Description
Chaos	Pending changes from more highly ranked transaction cannot be overwritten.
ReadCommitted	Shared locks are held while the data is being read, but data can be changed before the end of the transaction.
ReadUncommitted	No shared locks are issued, and no exclusive locks are honored.
RepeatableRead	Exclusive locks are placed on all data used in the query.
Serializable	A range lock is placed on the DataSet.
Unspecified	An existing isolation level cannot be determined.

Creating Transactions at Run Time

Because you can create a Transaction only through a call to the Data Command's BeginTransaction method, it must be created in code.

Create a New Transaction: Visual Basic

1. Open the Chapter 05 – Start project in Microsoft Visual Studio, and if necessary, double-click Transactions.vb in the Solution Explorer to display the form in the Form Designer.

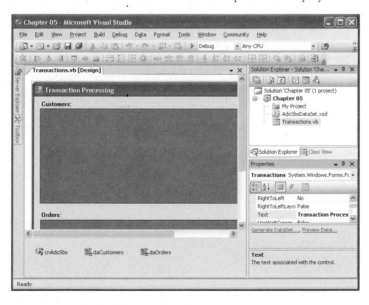

2. Press F7 to display the Code Editor.

3. Add the following lines to the btnCreate_Click event:

```
Dim strMsg As String
Dim trnNew As SqlTransaction

cnAdoSbs.Open()
trnNew = cnAdoSbs.BeginTransaction()
strMsg = "  Isolation Level: "
strMsg &= trnNew.IsolationLevel.ToString()
MessageBox.Show(strMsg)
cnAdoSbs.Close()
```

This code block creates a new Transaction using the default constructor and displays its IsolationLevel in a message box.

4. Press F5 to run the application.

5. Click Load Data.

    The application fills the DataSet and displays the DataRow values in the Customers and Orders list boxes.

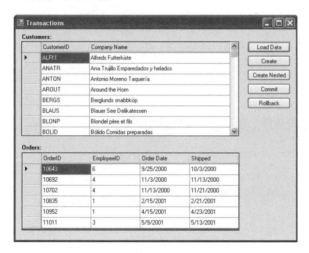

6. Click Create.

    The application displays the transaction's IsolationLevel in a message box.

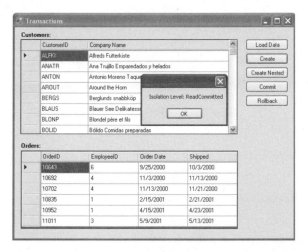

7. Click OK in the message box, and then close the application.

Create a New Transaction: Visual C#

1. Open the Chapter 05 – Start project in Visual Studio and if necessary, double-click Transaction.cs in the Solution Explorer to display the form in the Form Designer.

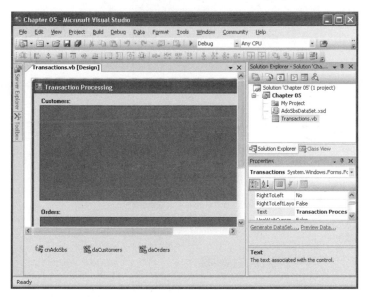

2. Press F7 to display the Code Editor.

3. Add the following lines to the btnCreate_Click event handler:

```
string strMsg;
SqlTransaction trnNew;
```

```
cnAdoSbs.Open();
trnNew = cnAdoSbs.BeginTransaction();
strMsg = " Isolation Level: " ;
strMsg += trnNew.IsolationLevel.ToString();
MessageBox.Show(strMsg);
cnAdoSbs.Close();
```

This code block creates a new Transaction using the default constructor and displays its IsolationLevel in a message box.

4. Press F5 to run the application.

5. Click Load Data.

The application fills the DataSet and displays the DataRow values in the Customers and Orders list boxes.

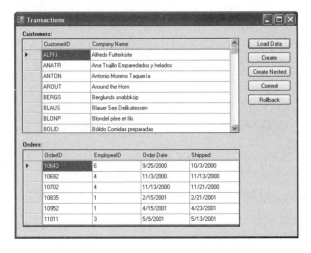

6. Click Create.

The application displays the transaction's IsolationLevel in a message box.

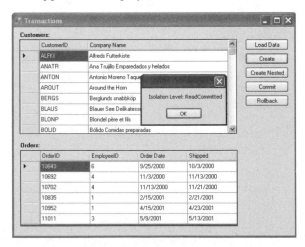

7. Click OK in the message box, and then close the application.

Creating Nested Transactions

Although it isn't possible to assign two transactions to a single Command, the OleDbTransaction object supports nested transactions. (They aren't supported by SQL Server and aren't available when using the SqlTransaction).

> **ADO**
>
> Multiple transactions on a single Connection, which were supported in ADO, are not supported in ADO.NET.

The syntax for creating a nested transaction is the same as the syntax for creating a top-level transaction. The difference is that the nested transaction is created by calling the Begin method of the Transaction object itself, not the BeginTransaction method of the Connection.

All nested transactions must be finalized (either committed or rolled back) before the transaction containing them is committed. However, if the parent transaction is rolled back, the nested transactions are also rolled back even if they were previously committed.

Committing and Rolling Back Transactions

After the Transaction object has been created, the next step is to assign it to the Transaction property of one or more Data Commands and then execute them. This is done by using a simple .NET Framework assignment statement:

Visual Basic
```
myCommand.Transaction = myTransaction
```

C#
```
myCommand.Transaction = myTransaction;
```

The final step in transaction processing is to either commit or roll back the changes that were made by the Data Commands participating in the transaction. If the Transaction is committed, all changes are accepted in the data source. If the Transaction is rolled back, all changes are discarded, and the data source is returned to the state it was in before the transaction began.

> **ADO**
>
> Unlike ADO, the ADO.NET Commit and Rollback methods are exposed on the Transaction object, not the Command object.

As you might expect, Transactions are committed by using the Transaction's Commit method and rolled back by using the Transaction's Rollback method, neither of which accepts parameters.

It's customary to wrap the commands that are executed within a transaction in a Try...Catch...Finally structure. If the Commands succeed, the Try block commits them, but if they fail, the Catch block rolls them back. In either case, the Finally block closes the Connection.

Commit a Transaction: Visual Basic

1. In the Code Editor, add the following lines to the btnCommit_Click event handler:

```
Dim trnNew As SqlTransaction

AddRows("AAA" & Convert.ToString(System.DateTime.Now.Second))

cnAdoSbs.Open()
trnNew = cnAdoSbs.BeginTransaction()
daCustomers.InsertCommand.Transaction = trnNew
daOrders.InsertCommand.Transaction = trnNew
Try
    daCustomers.Update(dsAdoSbs.Customers)
    daOrders.Update(dsAdoSbs.Orders)
    trnNew.Commit()
    MessageBox.Show("Transaction Committed")
Catch ex as SqlException
    trnNew.Rollback()
    MessageBox.Show(ex.Message.ToString())
Finally
    cnAdoSbs.Close()
End Try
```

This code block adds a row to the DataSet using the scaffolding procedure AddRows, and then opens a Connection, creates a Transaction, and attempts to Update the underlying data source. Note that the calls to the Update method are wrapped in a Try Catch block.

2. Press F5 to run the application.

3. Click Load Data.

4. Click Commit.

The application displays a message box confirming the updates.

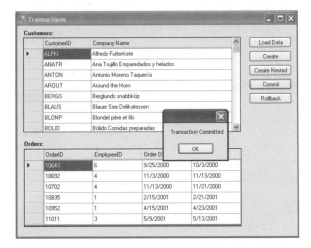

5. Click OK in the message box.

6. Locate the new AAAxx customer that was added.

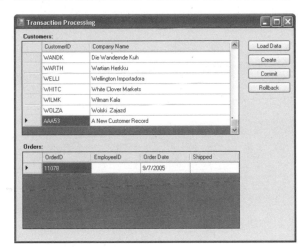

7. Close the application.

Commit a Transaction: Visual C#

1. In the Code Editor, add the following lines to the btnCommit_Click event handler:

```
SqlTransaction trnNew;

AddRows("AAA" + Convert.ToString(System.DateTime.Now.Second));

cnAdoSbs.Open();
trnNew = cnAdoSbs.BeginTransaction();
daCustomers.InsertCommand.Transaction = trnNew;
daOrders.InsertCommand.Transaction = trnNew;
```

```
try
{
    daCustomers.Update(dsAdoSbs.Customers);
    daOrders.Update(dsAdoSbs.Orders);
    trnNew.Commit();
    MessageBox.Show("Transaction Committed");
}
catch (SqlException ex)
{
    trnNew.Rollback();
    MessageBox.Show(ex.Message.ToString());
}
finally
{
    cnAdoSbs.Close();
}
```

This code block adds a row to the DataSet using the scaffolding procedure AddRows, and then opens a Connection, creates a Transaction, and attempts to Update the underlying data source. Note that the calls to the Update method are wrapped in a Try Catch block.

2. Press F5 to run the application.

3. Click Load Data.

4. Click Commit.

The application displays a message box confirming the updates.

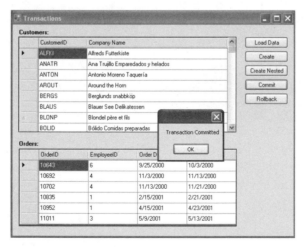

5. Click OK in the message box.

6. Locate the new AAAxx customer that was added.

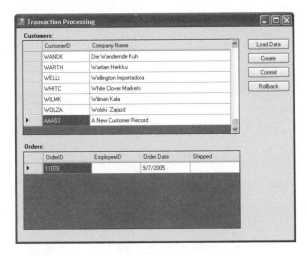

7. Close the application.

Roll Back a Transaction: Visual Basic

1. Add the following lines to the btnRollback_Click event handler:

```
Dim trnNew As SqlTransaction

AddRows("AAA" & Convert.ToString(System.DateTime.Now.Second))

cnAdoSbs.Open()
trnNew = cnAdoSbs.BeginTransaction()
daCustomers.InsertCommand.Transaction = trnNew
daOrders.InsertCommand.Transaction = trnNew
Try
    daOrders.Update(dsAdoSbs.Orders)
    daCustomers.Update(dsAdoSbs.Customers)
    trnNew.Commit()
    MessageBox.Show("Transaction Committed" )
Catch ex as SqlException
    trnNew.Rollback()
    MessageBox.Show(ex.Message.ToString())
Finally
    cnAdoSbs.Close()
End Try
```

This procedure is almost identical to the Commit procedure in the previous exercise. However, because the order of the Updates is reversed so that the Orders DataTable is updated before the Customers DataTable, the first Update will fail and a message box will display the error.

2. Press F5 to run the application.

3. Click Load Data.

4. Click Rollback.

The application displays a message box explaining the error.

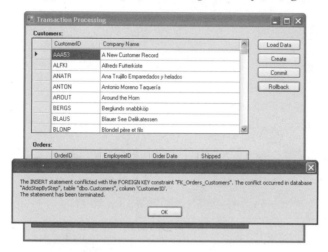

5. Click OK to close the message box.

6. Locate and select the new row that attempted to be added.

   The Orders list displays an exclamation icon indicating an error.

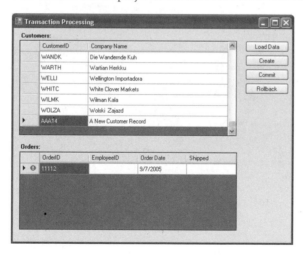

7. Close and restart the application to confirm that the row was not added.

8. Close the application.

Roll Back a Transaction: Visual C#

1. In the Code Editor, add the following lines to the btnRollback_Click event handler:

```
SqlTransaction trnNew;

AddRows("AAA" + Convert.ToString(System.DateTime.Now.Second));
```

```
cnAdoSbs.Open();
trnNew = cnAdoSbs.BeginTransaction();
daCustomers.InsertCommand.Transaction = trnNew;
daOrders.InsertCommand.Transaction = trnNew;
try
{
   daOrders.Update(dsAdoSbs.Orders);
   daCustomers.Update(dsAdoSbs.Customers);
   trnNew.Commit();
   MessageBox.Show("Transaction Committed");
}
catch (SqlException ex)
{
   trnNew.Rollback();
   MessageBox.Show(ex.Message.ToString());
}
finally
{
   cnAdoSbs.Close();
}
```

This procedure is almost identical to the Commit procedure in the previous exercise. However, because the order of the Updates is reversed so that the Orders DataTable is updated before the Customers DataTable, the first Update will fail and a message box will display the error.

2. Press F5 to run the application.

3. Click Load Data.

4. Click Rollback.

The application displays a message box explaining the error.

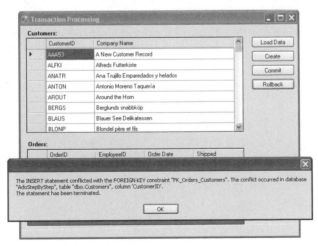

5. Click OK in the message box.

6. Locate and select the new row that attempted to be added. The Orders list should display an exclamation icon indicating an error.

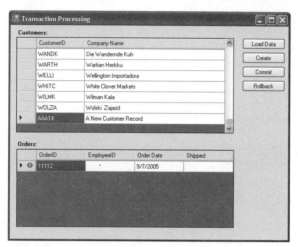

7. Close and restart the application to confirm that the row was not added.

8. Close the application.

Summary

In this chapter, we examined the surprisingly simple process of wrapping changes to a data source in a transaction by using the .NET Framework Transaction object. Transactions are first created by using the BeginTransaction method of a Connection, or in the case of nested transactions, the Begin method of a Transaction. After the transaction is created, it is assigned to the Transaction property of the Data Commands that will participate in it. When this step is complete, the transaction is controlled by using the Commit and Rollback methods of the Transaction.

Part III
Data Provider Objects

Chapter 6

Modeling a Database by Using DataSets and DataRelations

After completing this chapter, you will be able to:

- Create Typed and Untyped DataSets.
- Add DataTables to DataSets.
- Add DataRelations to DataSets.
- Clone and copy DataSets.

Beginning with this chapter, we'll move away from the Microsoft ADO.NET Data Providers to examine the objects that support the manipulation of data in your applications. We'll start with the DataSet, the memory-resident structure that represents relational data.

Understanding DataSets

In the Microsoft .NET Framework, a DataSet is an in-memory cache of data. The structure of the DataSet is essentially the same as that of a relational database, as shown in the following figure.

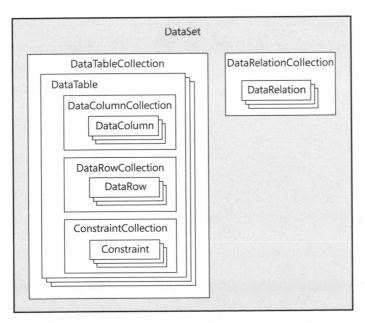

ADO.NET supports two distinct kinds of DataSets: Typed and Untyped. Architecturally, an Untyped DataSet is a direct instantiation of the System.Data.DataSet object, while a Typed DataSet is an instantiation of a class that inherits from System.Data.DataSet.

In functional terms, a Typed DataSet defines a specific schema that exposes its tables, and the columns within them, as object properties. This makes manipulating the DataSet far simpler syntactically because you can reference tables and columns directly by their names.

For example, given a Typed DataSet called dsOrders that contains a DataTable called Order-Headers, you can reference the value of the OrderID column as

> We'll discuss DataTables, DataRows and DataColumns in detail in Chapter 7.

```
dsOrders.OrderHeaders(x).OrderID
```

where x is the DataRow. If you were working with an Untyped DataSet with the same structure, however, you would need to reference the OrderHeaders DataTable and OrderID Column by using the Tables, Rows, and Item properties, respectively, as in

```
dsOrders.Tables("OrderHeader").Rows(x).Item("OrderID")
```

When you're working in Microsoft Visual Studio 2005, the Code Editor supports the tables and columns of a Typed DataSet by using IntelliSense, which makes the reference even easier. (Remember, every time you type something you have another opportunity to make a typographical error.)

The Typed DataSet provides another important benefit: It allows compile-time checking of data values. For example, assuming that OrderTotal is numeric, the compiler generates an error on the following line:

```
dsOrders.OrderHeader.Rows(0).OrderTotal = "Hello, World!"
```

But if you were working with an Untyped DataSet, the following line would compile without error:

```
dsOrders.Tables("OrderHeader").Rows(0).Item("OrderTotal") = "Hello, World!"
```

Despite the advantages of the Typed DataSet, there are times when you'll need an Untyped DataSet. This most often occurs when you don't know the structure of the DataSet until run time, which might be the case, for example, if your application receives a DataSet from a middle-tier component or a Web service. Or you might need to reconfigure a DataSet's schema at run time, in which case regenerating a Typed DataSet is an unnecessary overhead.

Regenerating the Typed DataSet is necessary whenever the portion of the underlying database on which it is based changes. If your database schema is at all volatile, you'll want to think carefully about using a Typed DataSet.

Unlike the stream of data returned from a DataReader, the DataSet is an in-memory cache of data. All of the rows of data in a DataSet are available at all times.

> **ADO**
>
> Unlike an ADO DataSet, the ADO.NET DataSet presents its data as an array of rows and there is no concept of a "current record."

Because all data is stored in memory, a DataSet does have more overhead than a DataReader, but it is the most efficient method for manipulating data that will be edited, and the only effective means of allowing a user to navigate through rows of data.

In Microsoft ADO.NET 2.0, you can treat a DataSet as a DataReader by using the CreateData-Reader method, which returns a DataTableReader object. We'll discuss DataTableReader objects later in this chapter.

Creating DataSets

Like most other ADO.NET objects, and indeed, most .NET Framework objects, DataSets can be created at design time or run time. Design-time support for creating and editing DataSets is provided by a specialized Visual Studio tool, the DataSet Designer.

We'll discuss TableAdapters in detail in Chapter 8. Visual Studio 2005 introduces a new object to the ADO.NET data model, the TableAdapter. TableAdapters are closely related to a Type DataSet, but they are separate objects. They are created and updated as part of a Typed DataSet in the DataSet Designer and are created by default when you generate DataSets interactively in Visual Studio. For now, you can simply think of them as Typed DataAdapters.

Creating Typed DataSets

In Chapter 1, "Getting Started with ADO.NET," we created a Typed DataSet by using the Data Source Configuration Wizard. Whenever you add a Data Source to a Visual Studio project, the Data Source Configuration Wizard creates the DataSet automatically.

In this chapter, we'll look at two additional methods for creating Typed DataSets: generating a DataSet from a DataAdapter, and creating and editing Typed DataSets in the DataSet Designer.

> **Note**   Although it is theoretically possible to create a Typed DataSet in code, it is extraordinarily tedious. If for some reason you need to do this, I suggest you look at a Typed DataSet code file created by Visual Studio for an example of the structure. In Visual Studio 2005, these files are named <DataSetName>.Designer.vb or <DataSetName>.Designer.cs.

Create a Typed DataSet by Using the DataSet Designer

1. Open the Chapter 06 – Start project in Visual Studio, and if necessary, double-click
   DataSets.vb (or DataSets.cs if you're using C#) in the Solution Explorer to open the
   form in the Form Designer.

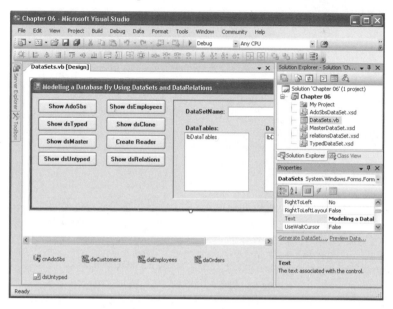

2. Select Add New Item from the Project menu.

   Visual Studio displays the Add New Item dialog box.

3. Select DataSet from the list, and change the name to **TypedDataSet.xsd**.

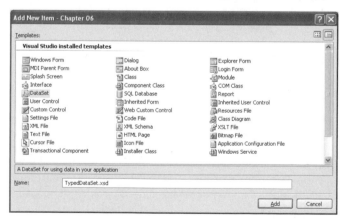

4. Click Add.

   Visual Studio adds a new DataSet to the project and opens the DataSet Designer.

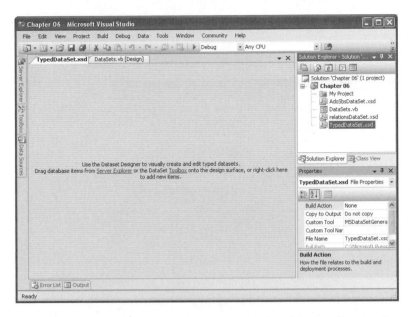

5. Drag a DataTable control from the DataSet tab of the Toolbox to the DataSet Designer.

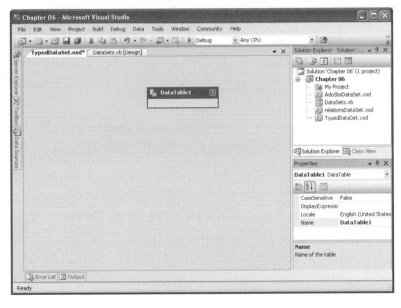

6. In the Properties window, change the name of the DataTable to **firstDataTable**.

Tip   You can also change the DataTable name by double-clicking it in the title bar of the DataTable. If you double-click the design surface itself, you'll open the Typed DataSet in the Code Editor. Simply close the file without saving it to return to the DataSet Designer.

7. Right-click the title bar of the DataTable in the DataSet Designer, choose Add, and then choose Column.

The DataSet Designer adds a DataColumn to the DataTable.

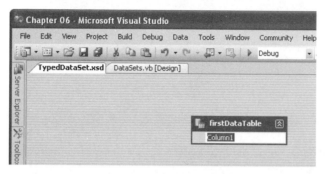

8. Change the DataColumn's name to **RowID** by typing the new value in the cell or in the Properties window.

9. Repeat steps 8 and 9 to add a second DataColumn, named **Description**, to the DataTable.

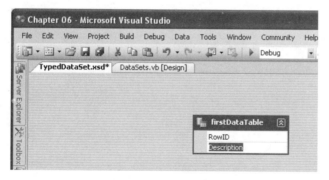

10. Save the DataSet and close the DataSet Designer.

11. Press F7 to display the Code Editor for DataSets.vb (or DataSets.cs).

12. Uncomment the code for the btnDsTyped_Click event handler, which is simply a call to a scaffolding procedure.

13. Press F5 to run the application.

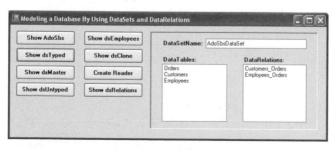

14. Click the Show dsTyped button.

    The application displays information about the new DataSet in the form panel.

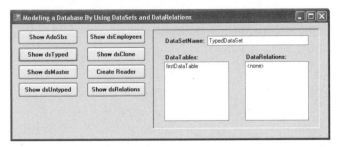

15. Close the application.

Create a Typed DataSet from a DataAdapter

1. In the Form Designer, select daCustomers in the component tray.

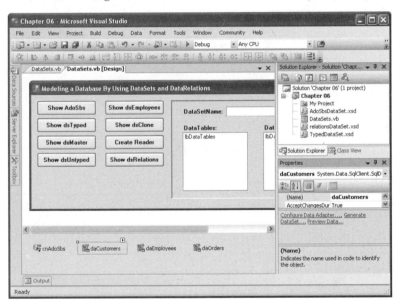

2. Choose Generate Dataset from the Data menu.

    Visual Studio displays the Generate Dataset dialog box.

> **Tip** The Generate Dataset command is also available from the component's Smart Tag menu.

3. Select the New option, and name the DataSet **MasterDataSet**.

4. Clear the Add This Dataset To The Designer check box.

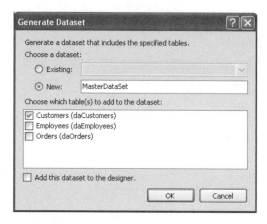

5. Click OK.

   Visual Studio adds the new DataSet to the project.

6. Press F7 to display the Code Editor.

7. Uncomment the code for the btnDsMaster_Click event handler, which simply contains a call to a procedure in the exercise scaffolding.

8. Press F5 to run the application, and then click the Show dsMaster button.

   The application displays the DataSet properties on the form.

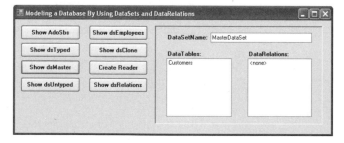

9. Close the application.

10. Double-click MasterDataSet.xsd in the Solution Explorer.

    Visual Studio opens the DataSet in the DataSet Designer.

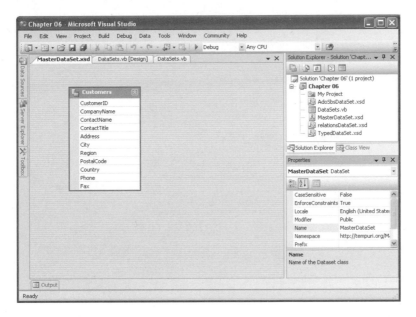

11. Close the DataSet Designer.

Creating Untyped DataSets

You can create Untyped DataSets both interactively in Visual Studio and at run time in code.

The DataSet object supports three versions of the usual New constructor to create an Untyped DataSet in code, as shown in Table 6-1. Typically, only the first two constructors are used in application programs.

Table 6-1   DataSet Constructors

Method	Description
New()	Creates an Untyped DataSet with the default name NewDataSet.
New(dsName)	Creates an Untyped DataSet with the name specified in the dsName string.
New(serializationInfo, streamingContext)	Used internally by the .NET Framework.

Create an Untyped DataSet in Visual Studio

1. In the Form Designer, drag a DataSet control from the Data tab of the Toolbox onto the component tray.

   Visual Studio displays the Add Dataset dialog box.

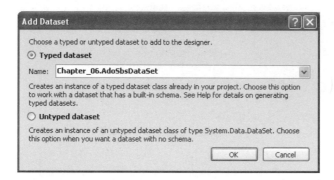

2. Click Untyped Dataset, and then click OK.

    Visual Studio adds an Untyped DataSet to the component tray.

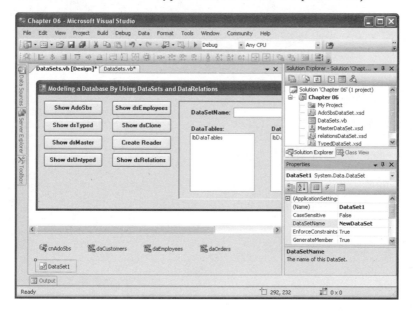

3. In the Properties window, set the DataSet name to **dsUntyped**.

4. Press F7 to display the Code Editor.

5. Uncomment the btnUntyped_Click event handler code, which simply calls the Show-DataSet scaffolding procedure.

6. Press F5 to run the application.

7. Click the Show dsUntyped button.

    The application displays the Untyped DataSet's properties (no tables and no relations).

8. Close the application.

Create an Untyped DataSet at Run Time: Visual Basic

1. Add the following line to the class declaration, below the declaration of dsAdoSbs:

```
Dim dsEmployees As DataSet
```

2. In the New procedure, add the following lines above the call to CreateScaffolding:

```
dsEmployees = New DataSet("dsEmployees")
```

The beginning of the class file should now be:

```
Imports System.Data
Imports System.Data.SqlClient
Public Class DataSets
   Dim dsAdoSbs As AdoSbsDataSet   Dim dsEmployees As DataSet

Public Sub New()
   'This call is required by the Windows Form Designer
   InitializeComponent()

   'Add exercise code here:
   dsEmployees = New DataSet("dsEmployees")

   'This call supports the exercise
   CreateScaffolding()
End Sub
```

3. Uncomment the btnEmployees_Click event handler, which calls the ShowDataSet scaffolding procedure.

4. Press F5 to run the application.

5. Click the Show dsEmployees button.

   The application displays the DataSet properties.

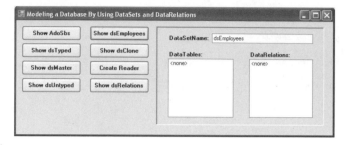

6. Close the application.

Create an Untyped DataSet at Run Time: Visual C#

1. Add the following line to the class declaration, below the declaration of dsAdoSbs:

```
DataSet dsEmployees;
```

2. In the DataSets constructor, add the following line after InitializeComponent and before the call to CreateScaffolding:

```
dsEmployees = new DataSet("dsEmployees");
```

The beginning of your class file should now be:

```
using System;
using System.Collections.Generic;
using System.ComponentModel;
using System.Data;
using System.Data.SqlClient;
using System.Drawing;
using System.Text;
using System.Windows.Forms;

namespace Chapter_06
{
   public class DataSets: Form
   {
      AdoSbsDataSet dsAdoSbs;
      DataSet dsEmployees;

      public DataSets()
      {
         InitializeComponent();

         //Add exercise code here:
         dsEmployees = new DataSet("dsEmployees");

         //This call supports the exercise:
         CreateScaffolding();
      }
```

3. Uncomment the btnEmployees_Click event handler code.

4. Press F5 to run the application.

5. Click the Show dsEmployees button.

   The application displays the DataSet properties.

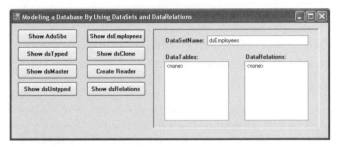

6. Close the application.

Configuring DataSets

The properties exposed by the DataSet are shown in Table 6-2.

Table 6-2   DataSet Properties

Property	Value
CaseSensitive	Determines whether comparisons are case-sensitive.
DataSetName	The name used to reference the DataSet in code.
DefaultViewManager	Defines the default filtering and sorting order of the DataSet.
EnforceConstraints	Determines whether constraint rules are followed during changes.
ExtendedProperties	Custom user information.
HasErrors	Indicates whether any of the DataRelations in the DataSet contain errors.
IsInitialized	Indicates whether the DataSet is initialized.
Locale	The locale information to be used when comparing strings.
Namespace	The namespace used when reading or writing an XML document.
Prefix	An XML prefix used as an alias for the namespace.
Relations	A collection of DataRelation objects that define the relationship of the DataTables within the DataSet.
RemotingFormat	Determines the Serialization format of the DataSet.
SchemaSerializationMode	Determines whether the DataSet schema is included during serialization.
Tables	The collection of DataTables contained in the DataSet.

We'll examine the DataSet's XML-related methods in Chapter 19.

The majority of the properties supported by the DataSet are related to its interaction with XML. Of the non-XML properties, the two most important are the Tables and Relations collections, which contain and define the data maintained within the DataSet.

The DataSet Tables Collection

For Typed DataSets, the contents of the Tables collection are defined the by DataSet schema, which you can edit in the DataSet Designer. For Untyped DataSets, you can create tables and their columns either by using the DataSet Designer or programmatically.

> **Note**   We'll add DataTables to Untyped DataSets in Chapter 7.

Add a DataTable to a Typed DataSet in Visual Studio

1. In the Form Designer, select daEmployees in the component tray.

2. Choose Generate Dataset from the Data menu.

   Visual Studio displays the Generate Dataset dialog box.

3. Choose Chapter_06.MasterDataSet as the DataSet to which you want to add the table, and clear the Add This Dataset To The Designer check box.

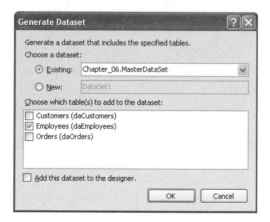

4. Click OK.

   Visual Studio adds the DataTable to the DataSet.

Add a DataTable to a Typed DataSet by Using the DataSet Designer

1. Double-click MasterDataSet.xsd in the Solution Explorer.

   Visual Studio opens the DataSet in the DataSet Designer.

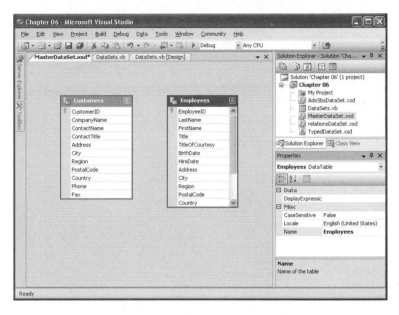

2.   Open the Server Explorer window, and verify that the connection to the AdoStepByStep database is displayed. If the AdoStepByStep database is not displayed, click the Connect To Database toolbar button, and specify a connection to a SQL Server data source. Set Server Name to (local)\SQLEXPRESS, select Use Windows Authentication, and select the AdoStepByStep database.

3. In the Server Explorer window, expand the AdoStepByStep database, and expand the Tables node.

4. Drag the Orders table onto the DataSet Designer.

   The DataSet Designer adds the Orders table to the DataSet.

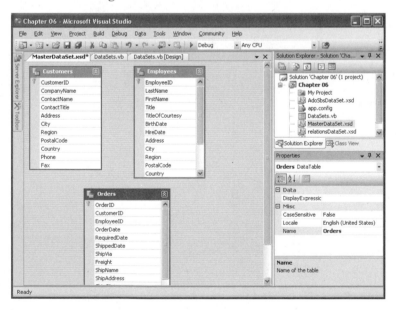

5. Save the DataSet, and close the DataSet Designer.

6. Press F5 to run the application.

7. Click the Show dsMaster button.

   The application displays the revised properties.

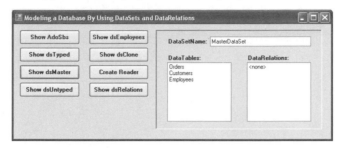

8. Close the application.

Using DataSet Methods

The primary methods supported by the DataSet object are listed in Table 6-3.

Table 6-3   **Methods of the DataSet**

Method	Description
AcceptChanges	Commits all pending changes to the DataSet.
Clear	Empties all the tables in the DataSet.
Clone	Copies the structure of the DataSet.
Copy	Copies the structure and contents of the DataSet.
CreateDataReader	Returns a DataTableReader from the DataSet.
GetChanges	Returns a DataSet containing only those DataRows that have been changed.
GetObjectData	Provides a SerializationInfo object containing the information required to serialize the DataSet.
GetXml	Returns an XML representation of the DataSet.
GetXmlSchema	Returns an XSD representation of the DataSet's schema.
HasChanges	Returns a Boolean value indicating whether the DataSet has pending changes.
InferXmlSchema	Infers a schema from an XML TextReader or a file.
Merge	Combines two DataSets.
ReadXml	Reads an XML schema and data into a DataSet.
ReadXmlSchema	Reads an XML schema into the DataSet.
RejectChanges	Rolls back all changes pending in the DataSet.
Reset	Returns the DataSet to its original state.
WriteXml	Writes an XML schema and data from the DataSet.
WriteXmlSchema	Writes the DataSet structure as an XML schema.

Like its properties, the majority of the DataSet's methods are related to its interaction with XML, which will be examined in Part V, "ADO.NET and XML."

We'll examine the methods used to update data in Chapter 10. The HasChanges, GetChanges, AcceptChanges, RejectChanges and Merge methods are used when updating the DataSet's Tables collection.

The GetObjectData method populates a SerializationInfo object that is used when serializing the DataSet. Used in conjunction with the RemotingFormat and SchemaSerializationMode properties, this method allows you to efficiently transfer and store DataSet data. (For more details on Serialization and the RemotingFormat property, please refer to Visual Studio online help.)

The CreateDataReader returns a DataTableReader from the DataSet, allowing you read-only, forward-only access to the data. The DataTableReader is functionally identical to the Data-Reader.

The three remaining methods are Clear, which empties the DataSet; Clone, which creates an empty copy of the DataSet; and Copy, which creates a complete copy of the DataSet and its data.

Cloning a DataSet

The Clone method creates an exact duplicate of a DataSet, including its DataTables, DataRelations and Constraints, but not its data.

Clone a DataSet: Visual Basic

1. Press F7 to display the Code Editor.

2. Add the following line to the class declaration, below the declaration of dsEmployees:

```
Dim dsClone As DataSet
```

3. Add the following lines to the New procedure, before the call to CreateScaffolding:

```
dsClone = dsEmployees.Clone()
```

The beginning of your class file should now be:

```
Imports System.Data
Imports System.Data.SqlClient
Public Class DataSets
    Dim dsAdoSbs As AdoSbsDataSet
    Dim dsEmployees As DataSet
    Dim dsClone As DataSet

Public Sub New()
    'This call is required by the Windows Form Designer
```

```
InitializeComponent()

'Add exercise code here:
dsEmployees = New DataSet("dsEmployees")
dsClone = dsEmployees.Clone()

'This call supports the exercise:
CreateScaffolding()
End Sub
```

4. Uncomment the code for the btnClone_Click event handler, which calls the Show-DataSet exercise scaffolding.

5. Press F5 to run the application.

6. Click the Show dsClone button.

   The application displays the DataSet properties.

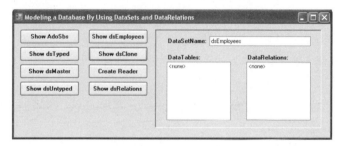

7. Close the application.

Clone a DataSet: Visual C#

1. Press F7 to display the Code Editor.

2. Add the following line to the class declaration, below the declaration of dsEmployees:

   ```
   DataSet dsClone;
   ```

3. Add the following lines to the DataSets constructor, before the call to CreateScaffolding:

   ```
   dsClone = dsEmployees.Clone();
   ```

   The beginning of your class file should be:

   ```
   using System;
   using System.Collections.Generic;
   using System.ComponentModel;
   using System.Data;
   using System.Data.SqlClient;
   using System.Drawing;
   using System.Text;
   using System.Windows.Forms;
   ```

```
namespace Chapter_06
{
  public class DataSets: Form
  {

    AdoSbsDataSet dsAdoSbs;
    DataSet dsEmployees;
    DataSet dsClone;

    public DataSets()
    {
      InitializeComponent();

      //Add exercise code here:
      dsEmployees = new DataSet("dsEmployees");
      dsClone = dsEmployees.Clone();

      //This call supports the exercise:
      CreateScaffolding();
    }
```

4. Uncomment the code for the btnClone_Click event handler;

5. Press F5 to run the application.

6. Click the Show dsClone button.

   The application displays the DataSet properties.

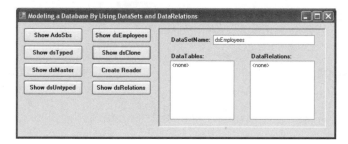

7. Close the application.

Creating DataTableReaders

The CreateDataReader method of the DataSet returns a DataTableReader. There are two versions of DataSet.CreateDataReader: CreateDataReader(), which returns a DataTableReader with multiple result sets, one for each DataTable in the DataSet; and CreateDataReader-(DataTable()), which takes an array of DataTables as a parameter that returns result sets for only those DataTables specified.

> **Tip** If you want a DataTableReader that returns data from a single DataTable, you can use the CreateDataReader method of the DataTable rather than the DataSet.

With both forms of the DataSet.CreateDataReader method call, the result sets are returned in the order the DataTables are declared in the Tables collection of the DataSet. The columns within each result set are in the same order as the DataColumns of the corresponding Data-Table.

A DataTableReader exposes precisely the same properties and methods as a DataReader, but it isn't part of a Data Provider. This means that the DataTableReader is defined as part of the System.Data namespace, and you don't need to work with different versions of the object depending on your Data Provider. More importantly, it means that DataTableReaders work with disconnected data—you don't need an open Connection to the data source when using a DataTableReader.

Create a DataTableReader: Visual Basic

1. In the Code Editor, add the following lines to the end of the btnReader_Click event handler, where indicated:

```
dr = dsAdoSbs.CreateDataReader(dsAdoSbs.Employees)
MessageBox.Show("The DataTableReader has " & dr.FieldCount.ToString() & _
    " rows")
```

The procedure should now be:

```
Private Sub btnReader_Click(ByVal sender As System.Object, _
    ByVal e as System.EventArgs) Handles btnReader.Click

    Dim dr as DataTableReader
    dsAdoSbs = New AdoSbsDataSet
    daEmployees.Fill(dsAdoSbs, "Employees")

    'Add exercise code here:
    dr = dsAdoSbs.CreateDataReader(dsAdoSbs.Employees)
    MessageBox.Show("The DataTableReader has " & dr.FieldCount.ToString() &
        " rows")
End Sub
```

2. Press F5 to run the application.

3. Click the Create Reader button.

   The application displays the number of rows in the DataTable.

4. Close the application.

Create a DataTableReader: Visual C#

1. In the Code Editor, add the following lines to the end of the btnReader_Click event handler:

```
dr = dsAdoSbs.CreateDataReader(dsAdoSbs.Employees);
MessageBox.Show("The DataTableReader has " + dr.FieldCount.ToString() +
    " rows");
```

The procedure should now be:

```
private void btnReader_Click(object sender, EventArgs e)
{
    DataTableReader dr;
    dsAdoSbs new AdoSbsDataSet();
    daEmployees.Fill(dsAdoSbs, "Employees");

    //Add exercise code here:
    dr = dsAdoSbs.CreateDataReader(dsAdoSbs.Employees);
    MessageBox.Show("The DataTableReader has " + dr.FieldCount.ToString() +
        " rows");
}
```

2. Press F5 to run the application.

3. Click the Create Reader button.

The application displays the number of rows in the DataTable.

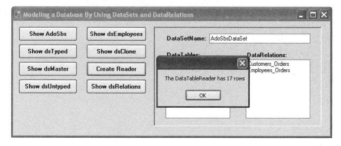

4. Close the application.

Understanding DataRelations

While the DataSet's Tables collection defines the structure of the data stored in a DataSet, the Relations collection defines the relationships between the DataTables. The Relations collection contains zero or more DataRelation objects, each one representing the relationship between two tables.

DataRelations also provide a mechanism for enforcing relational integrity through their Child-KeyConstraint and ParentKeyConstraint properties. However, it's important to understand that the constraints are enforced only if the DataSet's EnforceConstraints property is set to True, which is the default.

As we'll see in the next chapter, the DataRelation object allows you to easily move between parent and child rows. Given a parent, you can find all the related children; given a child, you can find its parent row.

Creating DataRelations

Like other components of a DataSet, DataRelations can be created in the DataSet Designer or at run time in code.

Add a DataRelation to a DataSet by Using the DataSet Designer

1. Double-click relationsDataSet.xsd in the Solution Explorer.

   Visual Studio opens the DataSet in the DataSet Designer.

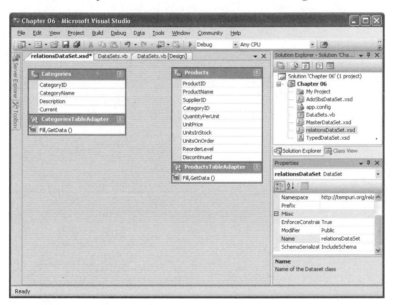

2. Drag a Relation control from the DataSet tab of the Toolbox onto the Categories table.

   The DataSet Designer displays the Relation dialog box.

3. Change the Relation name to **Product_Categories**, set Parent Table to Products, set Child Table to Categories, set Key Columns to CategoryID, and set Foreign Key Columns to Category ID.

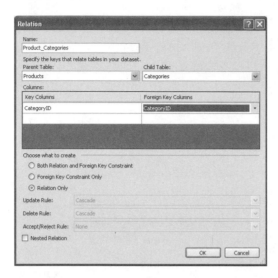

4. Click OK.

    The DataSet Designer adds the DataRelation to the DataSet.

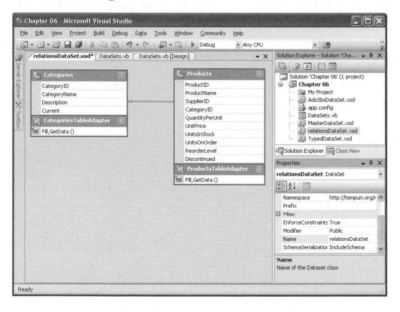

> **Tip**   In the DataSet Designer, you can display the names of a Relation by right-clicking the Relation line and choosing Show Relation Labels.

5. Save the DataSet, and close the DataSet Designer.

6. Press F5 to run the application.

7. Click the Show dsRelations button.

The application displays the DataSet properties.

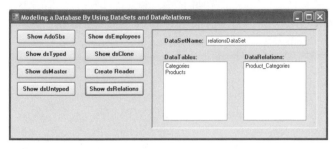

8.   Close the application

Configuring DataRelations

The properties of the DataRelation are shown in Table 6-4.

Table 6-4   DataRelation Properties

Property	Description
ChildColumns	Returns an array of DataColumns that define the many side of the relationship.
ChildKeyConstraint	Returns the ForeignKeyConstraint that controls this DataRelation.
ChildTable	Returns a reference to the DataTable on the many side of the relationship.
DataSet	Returns a reference to the DataSet of which this DataRelation forms a part.
ExtendedProperties	A collection of custom properties.
Nested	Determines whether or not this DataRelation defines a hierarchical relationship.
ParentColumns	Returns an array of DataColumns that define the one side of the relationship.
ParentKeyConstraint	Returns the UniqueConstraint that controls this DataRelation.
ParentTable	Returns a reference to the DataTable on the one side of the relationship.
RelationName	Determines the name of the DataRelation.

The majority of these properties are read-only, set when the DataRelation is created. You can, however, change the values in the DataSet Designer, which re-creates the DataRelation in the background.

The three exceptions to this read-only rule include the RelationName, which can be changed at any time; the Nested property, which is used with hierarchical data; and the ExtendedProperties property, which is used to define properties that are unique to your application. (We won't be discussing extended properties in this book.)

We'll discuss XML in Chapters 18 and 19. The Nested property, False by default, doesn't affect the structure of the DataSet, which always behaves like a relational database. It does, however, affect how the data is written as XML data or synchronized with an XmlDataDocument—when the property is True, child rows are nested within the parent rows.

Summary

In this chapter, we examined the DataSet object, which models the structure of a relational database, and the DataRelation object, which models relationships between DataTables. We examined the two types of DataSets, Typed and Untyped, and how to create each one. We briefly examined the properties of the DataSet and then turned our attention to how to add a DataTable to a Typed DataSet. Next, we examined DataSet methods and saw an example of cloning a DataSet and creating a DataTableReader.

We then looked at DataRelations, which model one-to-one and one-to-many relationships between DataTables, and saw how to create them using the DataSet Designer. Finally, we examined the properties of the DataRelation, but we deferred detailed discussion of them until Chapters 18 and 19.

Chapter 7
Using DataTables

After completing this chapter, you will be able to:

- Create DataTables by using the DataSet Designer.
- Create DataTables at run time.
- Add a DataTable to a DataSet at run time.
- Configure DataTables.
- Add and configure DataColumns.
- Create DataTable Constraints.
- Create and configure DataRows.
- Use DataTable and DataRow methods.

We've been working with DataTables in the last few chapters without really examining them. In this chapter we'll finally take a detailed look at their structure, properties and methods.

Understanding DataTables

In Chapter 6, "Modeling a Database by Using DataSets and DataRelations," we defined a DataSet as an in-memory representation of relational data. DataTables contain the actual data within the DataSet. However, DataTables don't exist only within DataSets—they can also exist independently.

As we'll see, although the DataTable has properties of its own, it functions primarily as a container for three collections:

- The Columns property is a collection of DataColumn objects that defines the schema of the table—the order of the columns and their structure.
- The Rows property is a collection of DataRow objects—the actual data maintained by the DataTable.
- The Constraints property is a collection of Constraint objects that works in conjunction with the DataTable's PrimaryKey property to enforce integrity rules on the data.

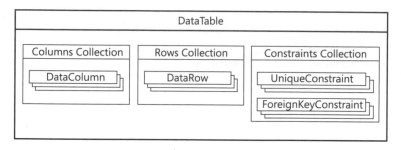

As we saw in the last chapter, DataSets function primarily as containers for DataTables, which in turn are containers (through their Rows collection) for the actual data.

However, although DataTables are most often used as part of a DataSet, they can be created independently. You might want to create an independent DataTable, for example, to provide data for a bound control or simply to allow the DataTable to be configured before being added to the DataSet.

Creating DataTables

Like most other Microsoft ADO.NET objects, DataTables can be created at design time or run time. You can create them as part of a Typed DataSet by using the Data Source Configuration Wizard, you can add them to a new or existing DataSet by using the DataSet Designer, or you can create them explicitly at run time by using the DataTable constructor or implicitly by using the Fill method of a DataAdapter.

Creating DataTables by Using the DataSet Designer

We'll examine TableAdapters in Chapter 8.

The DataSet Designer is the primary mechanism for creating Typed DataSets in Microsoft Visual Studio 2005. As we saw in the previous chapter, when you create a Typed DataSet indirectly by using the Data Source Configuration Wizard, Visual Studio in fact creates a TableAdapter that combines both a DataTable and certain basic functionality (primarily Fill and Update methods). In most cases, a TableAdapter will suit your needs, but by working directly with the DataSet Designer, you can create DataTables without the added functionality (and overhead) provided by a TableAdapter.

Add a DataTable to a Typed DataSet by Using the DataSet Designer

1. Open the Chapter 07 – Start project in Visual Studio and, if necessary, double-click DataTables.vb (or DataTables.cs if you're using C#) in the Solution Explorer to display the form in the Form Designer.

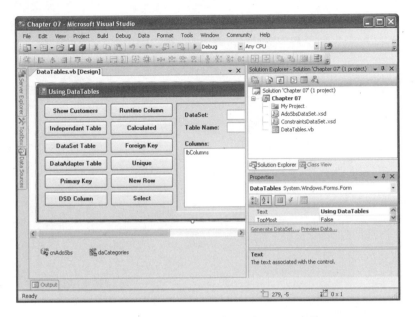

2. Double-click AdoSbsDataSet.xsd in the Solution Explorer.

   Visual Studio opens the DataSet in the DataSet Designer. Notice that because the DataSet was generated by the Data Source Configuration Wizard, the Orders and Employees tables in the data source are represented by TableAdapters rather than by DataTables. (The TableAdapter functionality is shown at the bottom of the table object.)

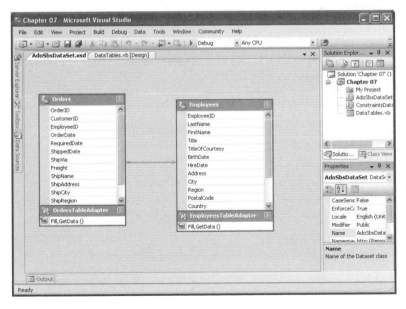

3. Drag a DataTable control from the Toolbox onto the DataSet Designer.

Visual Studio adds the table to the DataSet.

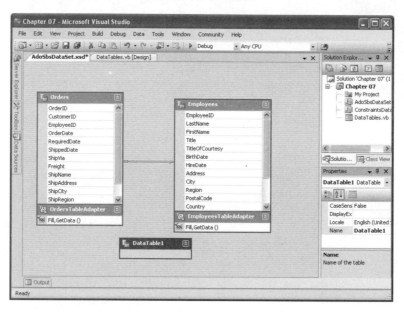

4. Click the new DataTable in the DataSet Designer, and in the Properties window, change the name of the DataTable to **Customers**.

5. Save the DataSet, and close the DataSet Designer.

6. Press F7 to display the Code Editor.

7. Uncomment the code in the btnCustomers_Click event handler.

8. Press F5 to run the application.

9. Click the Show Customers button.

    The application displays the details of the DataTable.

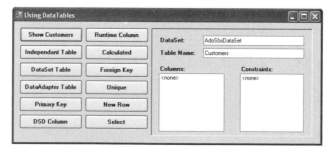

10. Close the application.

Creating Independent DataTables at Run Time

Independent DataTables are created using the standard Microsoft NET Framework syntax. The four versions of the DataTable's New constructor are shown in Table 7-1.

Table 7-1   DataTable Constructors

Method	Description
New()	Creates a new DataTable.
New(tableName)	Creates a new DataTable with the name specified in the tableName string.
New(tableName, namespace)	Creates a new DataTable with the name specified in the tableName string, belonging to the specified XML namespace.
New(serializableInfo, streamingContext)	Used internally by the .NET Framework.

Create an Independent DataTable in Code: Visual Basic

1. In the Code Editor, add the following lines to the btnAddTable_Click event handler:

```
Dim dtNew As DataTable

dtNew = New DataTable("NewTable")
ShowDetails(dtNew)
```

These lines create a DataTable and display its details on the application's form using the ShowDetails scaffolding procedure.

2. Press F5 to run the application.

3. Click Independent Table.

The application displays the details of the new table.

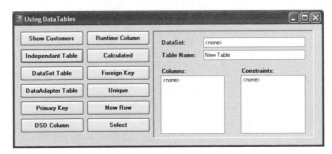

4. Close the application.

Create an Independent DataTable in Code: Visual C#

1. In the Code Editor, add the following lines to the btnAddTable_Click event handler:

    ```
    DataTable dtNew;

    dtNew = new DataTable("New Table");
    ShowDetails(dtNew);
    ```

    These lines create a DataTable and display its details on the application's form using the ShowDetails scaffolding procedure.

2. Press F5 to run the application.

3. Click Independent Table.

    The application displays the details of the new table.

4. Close the application.

Creating DataSet DataTables at Run Time

The four methods that can be used to explicitly add a DataTable to the DataSet's Tables collection are shown in Table 7-2. Note that these methods are called on the Tables collection, not on the DataSet itself. For example, you would call myDataSet.Tables.Add(), not myDataSet.Add().

Table 7-2   DataSet Add Table Methods

Method	Description
Add()	Creates a new DataTable with the name TableN, where N is a sequential number within the DataSet.
Add(tableName)	Creates a new DataTable with the name specified in the tableName string.
Add(tableName, tableNamespace)	Creates a new DataTable with the name specified in the tableName string and in the specified namespace.
Add(dataTable)	Adds the specified DataTable to the DataSet.
AddRange(tableArray)	Adds the DataTables in the tableArray to the DataSet.

The first version of the Add method creates a DataTable with the name TableN, where N is a sequential number. Note that this behavior is different from creating an independent Data-Table without passing a table name to the constructor. In the latter case, the TableName property is an empty string.

The second version of the Add method, Add(tableName), creates the new DataTable and sets its TableName property to the string supplied. The third version of the Add method also creates a new DataTable and allows you to specify a namespace for the table. (A namespace is a logical grouping of items.)

You can add an independent DataTable that you've created at run time to a DataSet by using the Add(dataTable) version of the constructor. You can also use this version to add a Data-Table that belongs to a different DataSet.

The AddRange version allows you to add an array of DataTables. This version is particularly convenient if you're moving DataTables from one DataSet to another.

Add a DataTable to an Untyped DataSet in Code: Visual Basic

1. In the Code Editor, add the following code, to the btnDataSet_Click event handler:

```
Dim ds As DataSet
Dim dt As DataTable

ds = New DataSet()
dt = ds.Tables.Add("DataSet Table")

ShowDetails(dt)
```

This code creates a new DataSet with a DataTable inside it and displays its details on the application's form using the ShowDetails scaffolding procedure.

2. Press F5 to run the application.

3. Click the DataSet Table button.

The application displays the details of the new DataSet and DataTable.

4. Close the application.

Add a DataTable to an Untyped DataSet in Code: Visual C#

1. In the Code Editor, add the following code to the btnDataSet_Click event handler:

```csharp
DataSet ds;
DataTable dt;

ds = new DataSet();
dt = ds.Tables.Add("DataSet Table");

ShowDetails(dt);
```

This code creates a new DataSet with a DataTable inside it and displays its details on the application's form using the ShowDetails scaffolding procedure.

2. Press F5 to run the application.

3. Click the DataSet Table button.

The application displays the details of new DataSet and DataTable.

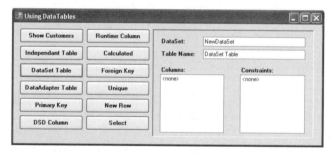

4. Close the application.

Creating DataTables by Using a DataAdapter

We examined the DataAdapter object in Chapter 4, "Using DataAdapters." At that time, we saw that it exposes two methods, Fill and FillSchema, which can be used to load data from a data source. As a by-product, either of these methods will create DataTables if they don't exist when the method is called.

Create a DataTable by Using a DataAdapter: Visual Basic

1. In the Code Editor, add the following lines to the btnDataAdapter_Click event handler:

```vb
Dim ds As DataSet

ds = New DataSet("DataAdapter DataSet")
daCategories.FillSchema(ds, SchemaType.Source)
ShowDetails(ds.Tables(0))
```

These lines create a DataSet and then use a DataAdapter to create a new table.

2. Press F5 to run the application.

3. Click the DataAdapter Table button.

    The application displays the details of the new table.

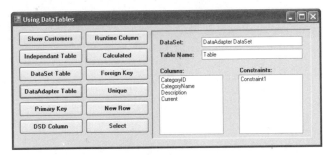

4. Close the application.

Create a DataTable by Using a DataAdapter: Visual C#

1. In the Code Editor, add the following lines to the btnDataAdapter_Click event handler:

```
DataSet ds;

ds = new DataSet();
daCategories.FillSchema(ds, SchemaType.Source);
ShowDetails(ds.Tables[0]);
```

These lines create a DataSet and then use a DataAdapter to create a new table.

2. Press F5 to run the application.

3. Click the DataAdapter Table button.

    The application displays the details of the new table.

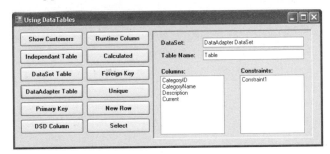

4. Close the application.

Configuring DataTables

The primary properties of the DataTable are shown in Table 7-3. The most important of these are the three properties that control the data—Columns, Rows and Constraints. We'll look at each of these in detail later in this chapter.

Table 7-3   DataTable Properties

Property	Description
CaseSensitive	Determines how string comparisons are performed.
ChildRelations	A collection of DataRelation objects for which this DataTable is the Parent table.
Columns	The collection of DataColumns that define the schema of the DataTable.
Constraints	The collection of Constraints maintained by the DataTable.
DataSet	The DataSet of which this DataTable is a member.
DefaultView	A DataView representing the DataTable.
DisplayExpression	An expression used to represent the table name in the user interface.
ExtendedProperties	A collection of custom properties.
HasErrors	Indicates whether there are errors in any of the rows belonging to the DataTable.
IsInitialized	Indicates whether the DataTable has been initialized.
MinimumCapacity	Determines the initial number of DataRows allocated for the DataTable.
Namespace	The XML namespace of the DataTable.
ParentRelationships	A collection of DataRelation objects for which this DataTable is the child table.
Prefix	The XML namespace prefix of the DataTable.
PrimaryKey	An array of columns that function as the primary key of the DataTable.
RemotingFormat	The SerializationFormat used by the DataTable.
Rows	The collection of DataRows containing the data maintained by the DataTable.
TableName	The name by which the DataTable is referenced in code.

In addition to the collection properties, the DataTable exposes a number of properties that allow you to fine-tune its behavior. Most of these are self-explanatory, but a few bear closer examination.

If the DataTable belongs to a DataSet, the CaseSensitive property defaults to the value defined for the DataSet, but it can be overridden on a table-by-table basis. For an independent Data-Table, the default value for this property is False.

The ChildRelations and ParentRelations collections contain references to DataRelations in a DataSet that reference the DataTable as a child or parent, respectively. For most independent DataTables, these collections are Null, but it is theoretically possible to manually add a DataRelation to one of these collections if, for example, the DataTable is related to itself.

We'll discuss
DataViews in
Chapter 9. The DefaultView property allows you to define default filtering and sorting for the DataTable. This property is new to Microsoft ADO.NET 2.0.

The DisplayExpression property determines how the name of the table is displayed to the user. DisplayExpression uses an expression that is calculated at run time. Because the property uses an expression rather than a simple string, you can use it, for example, to calculate the way the table name is displayed based on its contents.

The MinimumCapacity property, which is new to ADO.NET 2.0, is an Integer value representing a number of rows. The default value is 50. This property determines the amount of memory initially allocated for the DataTable, and it can provide significant performance benefits when loading data.

Most DataTable properties are set just like the properties of any other object—by simple assignment, or, if the property is a collection, by calling the Add method of the collection.

Primary Key Constraints

The most important type of integrity constraint in relational database theory is entity integrity: the rule that each row of a table (or in relational terms, each tuple of a relation) must be unique. In real terms, this means that there must be some column or combination of columns that uniquely identifies each row.

In the Microsoft .NET Framework, this fundamental principle is implemented by setting the PrimaryKey property to an array of one or more DataColumns that will be used to impose uniqueness. Note, however, that the .NET Framework doesn't impose entity integrity—the PrimaryKey property can be empty, in which case duplicate rows are allowed in the DataTable.

Display a PrimaryKey Constraint: Visual Basic

1. In the Code Editor, add the following code to the btnPrimaryKey_Click event handler:

```
Dim ca As Data.DataColumn()
Dim str As String
Dim x As Integer

ca = dsAdoSbs.Employees.PrimaryKey
Select Case ca.Length
   Case 0
      str = "There is no primary key set"
   Case 1
      str = "The primary key is " & ca(0).ColumnName.ToString()
   Case Else
      str = "The primary key columns are "
      For x = 1 To ca.Length
         str &= ca(x).ColumnName.ToString & " "
      Next
End Select

MessageBox.Show(str)
```

This code displays the PrimaryKey property in a message box.

2. Press F5 to run the application.

3. Click the Primary Key button.

    The application displays the primary key in a message box.

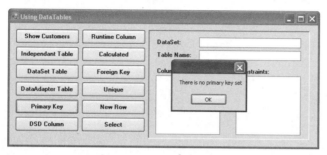

4. Close the application.

Display a PrimaryKey Constraint: Visual C#

1. In the Code Editor, add the following code to the btnPrimaryKey_Click event handler:

```
DataColumn[] ca;
string str;

ca = dsAdoSbs.Employees.PrimaryKey;

switch(ca.Length)
{
    case 0:
        str = "There is no primary key set";
        break;
    case 1:
        str = "The primary key is " + ca[0].ColumnName.ToString();
        break;
    default:
        str = "The primary key columns are ";
        for (int x = 1; x < ca.Length; x++)
            str += ca[x].ColumnName.ToString() + " ";
        break;
}
MessageBox.Show(str);
```

This code displays the PrimaryKey property in a message box.

2. Press F5 to run the application.

3. Click the Primary Key button.

   The application displays the primary key in a message box.

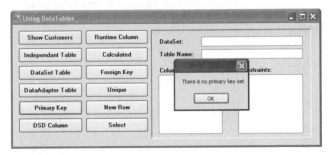

4. Close the application.

Creating DataColumns

The DataTable's Columns collection contains zero or more DataColumn objects that define the structure of the table. DataColumns are created automatically if a DataTable is created by using the Data Source Configuration Wizard or the DataAdapter's Fill or FillSchema method. You can also create them interactively in the DataSet Designer.

Creating DataColumns by Using the DataSet Designer

Whether you're working with a DataTable that you created explicitly in the DataSet Designer or with a TableAdapter that was created by Visual Studio, you can easily add a DataColumn to any DataTable.

Create a DataColumn in the DataSet Designer

1. Double-click AdoSbsDataSet.xsd in the Solution Explorer.

   Visual Studio opens the DataSet in the DataSet Designer.

2. Right-click the Customers DataTable that you added earlier, click Add, and then choose Column.

   The DataSet Designer adds a DataColumn to the DataTable.

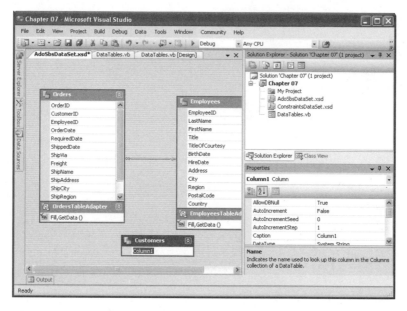

3. Change the name of the DataColumn to **firstColumn**.

4. Save and close the DataSet Designer.

5. In the Code Editor, uncomment the code in the btnNewColumn_Click event handler, which calls the ShowDetails scaffolding procedure.

6. Press F5 to run the application.

7. Click the DSD Column button.

   The application displays the DataTable details.

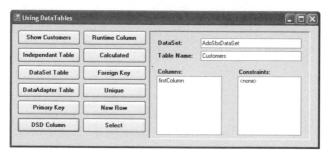

8. Close the application.

Creating DataColumns at Run Time

If you're creating a DataColumn in code, you can use one of the New constructors shown in Table 7-4.

Table 7-4   **DataColumn Constructors**

Method	Description
New()	Creates a new DataColumn with no column name or caption.
New(columnName)	Creates a new DataColumn with the specified columnName.
New(columnName, dataType)	Creates a new DataColumn with the specified columnName and the data type specified by the dataType parameter.
New(columnName, dataType, expression)	Creates a new DataColumn with the specified columnName and dataType, calculated by using the specified expression.
New(columnName, dataType, expression, mappingType)	Creates a new DataColumn with the specified columnName and dataType, calculated by using the specified expression, and mapped by using the specified column MappingType.

Create a DataColumn in Code: Visual Basic

1. In the Code Editor, add the following lines to the btnRuntimeColumn_Click event handler:

```
dsAdoSbs.Customers.Columns.Add("SecondColumn", _
    System.Type.GetType("System.String"))
ShowDetails(dsAdoSbs.Customers)
```

These lines create a new DataColumn and then display the DataTable details.

2. Press F5 to run the application.

3. Click the Runtime Column button.

The application displays the new column in the Columns list box.

4. Close the application.

Create a DataColumn in Code: Visual C#

1. In the Code Editor, add the following lines, to the btnRuntimeColumn_Click event handler:

    ```
    dsAdoSbs.Customers.Columns.Add("SecondColumn", System.Type.GetType("System.String"));
    ShowDetails(dsAdoSbs.Customers);
    ```

    These lines create a new DataColumn and then display the DataTable details.

2. Press F5 to run the application.

3. Click the Runtime Column button.

    The application displays the new column in the Columns Listbox.

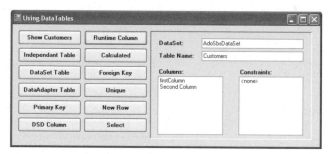

4. Close the application.

Configuring DataColumns

The primary properties of the DataColumn are shown in Table 7-5. They correspond closely to the properties of data columns in most relational databases.

Table 7-5   DataColumn Properties

Property	Description
AllowDbNull	Determines whether the DataColumn can be left empty.
AutoIncrement	Determines whether the system will automatically increment the value of the DataColumn as DataRows are added to the DataTable.
AutoIncrementSeed	The starting value of an AutoIncrement DataColumn.
AutoIncrementStep	The increment by which an AutoIncrement DataColumn increases.
Caption	The name of the column displayed in the user interface.
ColumnMapping	The MappingType of the DataColumn.
ColumnName	The name by which the DataColumn is referenced in code.
DataType	The .NET Framework data type of the DataColumn.
DateTimeMode	Determines how DateTime values are interpreted.
DefaultValue	The value of the DataColumn provided by the system if no other value is provided.
Expression	The expression used to calculate the value of the DataColumn.
ExtendedProperties	A collection of custom properties.

Table 7-5   DataColumn Properties

Property	Description
MaxLength	The maximum length of a text column.
Namespace	The XML namespace of the DataColumn.
Ordinal	The position of the DataColumn in the Columns collection.
Prefix	The XML prefix of the DataColumn.
ReadOnly	Determines whether the value of the DataColumn can be changed after the DataRow containing it has been added to the DataTable.
Table	The DataTable to which the DataColumn belongs.
Unique	Determines whether each DataRow in the DataTable must contain unique values for this DataColumn.

Creating Calculated Columns

The Expression property of the DataColumn allows you to generate column values at run time based on a simple expression syntax. You can calculate values based on other Data-Columns in the same DataTable or on other DataTables in the DataSet.

Create a Calculated DataColumn: Visual Basic

1. In the Code Editor, add the following lines to the end of the btnCalculated_Click event handler:

    ```
    Dim col As DataColumn
    col = dsAdoSbs.Employees.Columns.Add("FullName", _
       System.Type.GetType("System.String"))
    col.Expression = "FirstName + ' ' + LastName"

    MessageBox.Show(dsAdoSbs.Employees.Rows(0).Item("FullName"))
    ```

    These lines create a calculated column and then display its value in a message box. Your event handler should now be:

    ```
    Private Sub btnCalculated_Click(ByVal sender As System.Object, _
       ByVal e As System.EventArgs) Handles btnCalculated.Click

       Dim ta As AdoSbsDataSetTableAdapters.EmployeesTableAdapter
       ta = New AdoSbsDataSetTableAdapters.EmployeesTableAdapter()
       ta.Fill(dsAdoSbs.Employees)

       'Put exercise code here
       Dim col As DataColumn
       col = dsAdoSbs.Employees.Columns.Add("FullName", _
          System.Type.GetType("System.String"))
       col.Expression = "FirstName + ' ' + LastName"

        MessageBox.Show(dsAdoSbs.Employees.Rows(0).Item("FullName"))
    End Sub
    ```

2. Press F5 to run the application.

3. Click the Calculated button.

   The application displays the full name of the first employee.

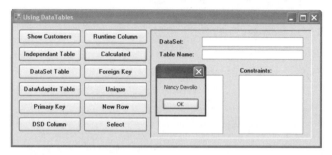

4. Close the application.

Create a Calculated DataColumn: Visual C#

1. In the Code Editor, add the following lines, to the end of the btnCalculated_Click event handler:

```
DataColumn col;
col = dsAdoSbs.Employees.Columns.Add("FullName",
    System.Type.GetType("System.String"));
col.Expression = "FirstName + ' ' + LastName";

MessageBox.Show(dsAdoSbs.Employees.Rows[0]["FullName"].ToString());
```

These lines create a calculated column and then display its value in a MessageBox. Your event handler should now be:

```
private void btnCalculated_Click(object sender, EventArgs e)
{
    AdoSbsDataSetTableAdapters.EmployeesTableAdapter ta;
    ta = new AdoSbsDataSetTableAdapters.EmployeesTableAdapter();
    ta.Fill(dsAdoSbs.Employees);

    //Put exercise code here:
    DataColumn col;
    col = dsAdoSbs.Employees.Columns.Add("FullName",
        System.Type.GetType("System.String"));
    col.Expression = "FirstName + ' ' + LastName";

     MessageBox.Show(dsAdoSbs.Employees.Rows[0]["FullName"].ToString());
}
```

2. Press F5 to run the application.

3. Click the Calculated button.

   The application displays the full name of the first employee.

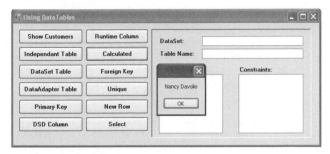

4. Close the application.

Adding Constraints

The Constraints collection is used along with the DataTable's PrimaryKey property to maintain the integrity of the data within a DataTable. ADO.NET creates several types of constraints automatically. When you create a DataRelation, for example, ADO.NET creates the corresponding ForeignKeyConstraint, and when you set the Unique property of a column to True, ADO.NET creates a UniqueConstraint.

The System.Data.Constraint object has only three properties, shown in Table 7-6.

Table 7-6   Constraint Properties

Property	Description
ConstraintName	The name of the Constraint.
ExtendedProperties	A collection of custom properties.
Table	The DataTable to which the Constraint belongs.

Obviously, an object that has only a name and a container is of little use when it comes to enforcing integrity. In real applications, you will instantiate one of the objects that inherit from Constraint: ForeignKeyConstraint or UniqueConstraint.

ForeignKeyConstraints

A ForeignKeyConstraint sets up the relationship between two DataTables or, in rare cases, between individual rows in a single table. It says, essentially, that any values found in the specified columns of the child table must be present in the parent table.

The properties of the ForeignKeyConstraint object are shown in Table 7-7. This constraint represents the rules that are enforced when a parent-child relationship exists between tables or between rows in a single table.

Table 7-7   ForeignKeyConstraint Properties

Property	Description
AcceptRejectRule	Determines the action that takes place when the AcceptChanges or RejectChanges method is called on the DataTable.
Columns	The collection of child columns for the constraint.
DeleteRule	The action that takes place when the row is deleted.
ExtendedProperties	A collection of custom properties.
RelatedColumns	The collection of parent columns for the constraint.
RelatedTable	The parent DataTable for the constraint.
Table	Overrides the Constraint.Table to return the child DataTable for the constraint.
UpdateRule	The action that takes place when the row is updated.

The actions to be taken by the constraint are determined by three properties: AcceptRejectRule, DeleteRule and UpdateRule.

The possible values of the AcceptRejectRule are Cascade or None. The DeleteRule and UpdateRule properties can be set to any of the values shown in Table 7-8. Both properties have a default value of Cascade.

Table 7-8   Action Rule Values

Value	Description
Cascade	Delete or update the related rows.
None	Take no action on the related rows.
SetDefault	Set values in the related rows to their default values.
SetNull	Set values in the related rows to Null.

ForeignKeyConstraints can be explicitly created only at run time. In the DataSet Designer, ForeignKeyConstraints are created as a by-product of the creation of a DataRelation.

At run time, you can use one of the versions of the New constructor shown in Table 7-9. (The .NET Framework exposes other versions of the constructor, but they are for internal use by Visual Studio.)

Table 7-9   ForeignKeyConstraint Constructors

Method	Description
New(parentColumn, child-Column)	Creates a new ForeignKeyConstraint with the specified parent and child DataColumns.
New(parentColumn[], childColumn[])	Creates a new ForeignKeyConstraint with the specified parent and child DataColumn arrays.
New(name, parentColumn, childColumn)	Creates a new ForeignKeyConstraint with the specified name and parent and child DataColumns.
New(name, parentColumn[], childColumn[])	Creates a new ForeignKeyConstraint with the specified name and parent and child DataColumn arrays.

Add a ForeignKeyConstraint in the DataSet Designer

1. Double-click ConstraintsDataSet.xsd in the Solution Explorer.

   Visual Studio opens the DataSet in the DataSet Designer.

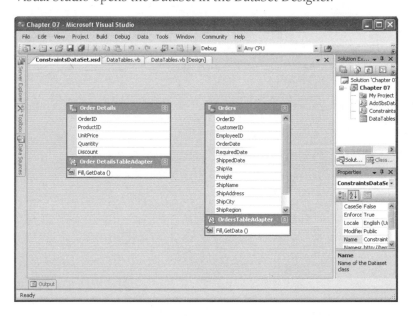

2. Drag a Relation control from the Toolbox onto the OrderDetails TableAdapter.

   The DataSet Designer opens the Relation dialog box.

3.   Select the Both Relation And Foreign Key Constraint option.

4.   Accept the default values for the Update Rule, Delete Rule, and Accept/Reject Rule, and then click OK.

The DataSet Designer creates the ForeignKeyConstraint and the DataRelation.

5.   Save the DataSet and close the DataSet Designer.

6.   Press F5 to run the application.

7.   Click the Foreign Key button.

The application displays the new constraint.

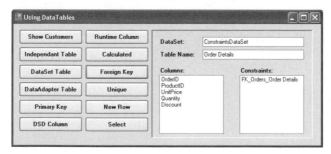

8.   Close the application.

UniqueConstraints

UniqueConstraints, as you might expect, ensure that each DataRow in a DataTable contains a unique value for the specified DataColumn or combination of DataColumns. The PrimaryKey property of the DataTable that we examined earlier creates a special kind of Unique-Constraint, the primary difference being that the PrimaryKey column(s) can be passed to a Find method.

The properties of a UniqueConstraint are shown in Table 7-10.

Table 7-10   UniqueConstraint Properties

Property	Description
Columns	The array of DataColumns being constrained.
ConstraintName	The name of the UniqueConstraint.
ExtendedProperties	A collection of custom properties.
IsPrimaryKey	Indicates whether the constraint defines the primary key of the table.
Table	The DataTable to which this constraint belongs.

Like ForeignKeyConstraints, UniqueConstraints can be created in the DataSet Designer or at run time. In the DataSet Designer, you can only create single-column UniqueConstraints, and you do so by setting the Unique property of a DataColumn.

At run time, you can use one of the versions of the UniqueConstraint constructor shown in Table 7-11.

Table 7-11   UniqueConstraint Constructors

Method	Description
New(column)	Creates a new UniqueConstraint on the specified DataColumn.
New(column[])	Creates a new UniqueConstraint on the specified DataColumn array.
New(column, isPrimaryKey)	Creates a new UniqueConstraint on the specified DataColumn and indicates whether the column is the primary key.
New(column[], isPrimaryKey)	Creates a new UniqueConstraint on the specified DataColumn array and indicates whether the column array is the primary key.
New(name, column)	Creates a new UniqueConstraint on the specified column with the specified name.
New(name, column[])	Creates a new UniqueConstraint on the specified column array with the specified name.
New(name, column, isPrimaryKey)	Creates a new UniqueConstraint on the specified column with the specified name and indicates whether the column is the primary key.
New(name, column[], isPrimaryKey)	Creates a new UniqueConstraint on the specified column array with the specified name and indicates whether the column array is the primary key.

Add a UniqueConstraint in Code: Visual Basic

1. In the Code Editor, add the following lines to the btnUnique_Click event handler:

```
Dim ucNew As UniqueConstraint

ucNew = New UniqueConstraint("MasterValue", dsAdoSbs.Orders.ShipNameColumn)
dsAdoSbs.Orders.Constraints.Add(ucNew)

ShowDetails(dsAdoSbs.Orders)
```

These lines create a new UniqueConstraint and add it to the Orders table.

2. Press F5 to run the application.

3. Click the Unique button.

The application displays the table details showing the new constraint.

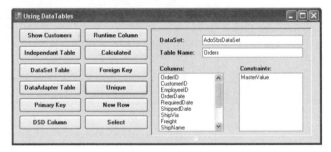

4. Close the application.

Add a UniqueConstraint in Code: Visual C#

1. In the Code Editor, add the following lines to the btnUnique_Click event handler:

```
UniqueConstraint ucNew;

ucNew = new UniqueConstraint("MasterValue", dsAdoSbs.Orders.ShipNameColumn);
dsAdoSbs.Orders.Constraints.Add(ucNew);

ShowDetails(dsAdoSbs.Orders);
```

These lines create a new UniqueConstraint and add it to the Orders table.

2. Press F5 to run the application.

3. Click the Unique button.

The application displays the table details showing the new constraint.

4. Close the application.

Creating DataRows

The DataRow object represents the actual data maintained by a DataTable. DataRows are only created at run time. Like the DataTable itself, they are primarily useful as part of a collection (in this case, the Rows collection of the DataTable), but they can be created and configured independently before being added to a DataTable.

You cannot create a generic DataRow—they are only created by calling one of the New<row-Type> methods of a DataTable object. For an Untyped DataSet, there is only one version of this method: NewRow. Typed DataSets add an additional version, New<Type>Row, where <Type> is the name of the DataTable in the DataSet class. For example, a DataTable that models the Employees table of the AdoStepByStep database would expose a method named NewEmployeesRow.

The two versions of the method return slightly different results: The NewRow method returns a generic DataRow (albeit with the schema of the DataTable), and the New<Type>Row method returns a typed DataRow. In our example, NewEmployeesRow returns an Employees-Row.

Because the Rows property of a DataRow is a collection, you can add new data to the Data-Table by using one of the two forms of the Add method shown in Table 7-12.

Table 7-12   Rows.Add Methods

Method	Description
Add(DataRow)	Adds the specified DataRow to the DataTable.
Add(dataValues[])	Creates a new DataRow in the table and sets its Item values to the values specified in the dataValues array.

Create a DataRow: Visual Basic

1. In the Code Editor, add the following lines, which create and add two DataRows, where indicated in the middle of the btnNewRow_Click event handler:

```
dr = dsAdoSbs.Employees.NewRow()
dsAdoSbs.Employees.Rows.Add(dr)

dEr = dsAdoSbs.Employees.NewEmployeesRow()
dsAdoSbs.Employees.Rows.Add(dEr)
```

Your procedure should now be:

```
Private Sub btnNewRow_Click(ByVal sender As System.Object, _
    ByVal e As System.EventArgs) Handles btnNewRow.Click


    Dim dr As Data.DataRow
    Dim dEr As AdoSbsDataSet.EmployeesRow

    Dim str As String
    str = "The Employees table has "
    str &= dsAdoSbs.Employees.Rows.Count
    str &= " rows."
    MessageBox.Show(str)

    'Add exercise code here:
    dr = dsAdoSbs.Employees.NewRow()
    dsAdoSbs.Employees.Rows.Add(dr)

    dEr = dsAdoSbs.Employees.NewEmployeesRow()
    dsAdoSbs.Employees.Rows.Add(dEr)

    str = "Now the Employees table has "
    str &= dsAdoSbs.Employees.Rows.Count
    str &= " rows."
    MessageBox.Show(str)
End Sub
```

2. Press F5 to run the application.

3. Click the New Row button.

   The application displays the number of rows before and after the two new ones are added.

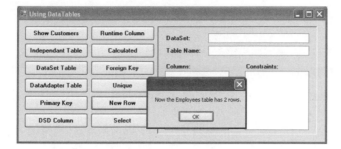

4. Close the application.

Create a DataRow: Visual C#

1. In the Code Editor, add the following lines, which create and add two DataRows, where indicated in the middle of the btnNewRow_Click event handler:

```
dr = dsAdoSbs.Employees.NewRow();
dsAdoSbs.Employees.Rows.Add(dr);

dEr = dsAdoSbs.Employees.NewEmployeesRow();
dsAdoSbs.Employees.Rows.Add(dEr);
```

Your procedure should now be:

```
private void btnNewRow_Click(object sender, EventArgs e)
{
    DataRow dr;
    AdoSbsDataSet.EmployeesRow dEr;

    string str;
    str = "The Employees table has ";
    str += dsAdoSbs.Employees.Rows.Count.ToString();
    str += " rows.";
    MessageBox.Show(str);

    //Add exercise code here:
    dr = dsAdoSbs.Employees.NewRow();
    dsAdoSbs.Employees.Rows.Add(dr);

    dEr = dsAdoSbs.Employees.NewEmployeesRow();
    dsAdoSbs.Employees.Rows.Add(dEr);

    str = "Now the Employees table has ";
    str += dsAdoSbs.Employees.Rows.Count.ToString();
    str += " rows.";
    MessageBox.Show(str);
}
```

2. Press F5 to run the application.

3. Click the New Row button.

The application displays the number of rows before and after the two new ones are added.

4.   Close the application.

Configuring DataRows

We'll discuss the RowState property in detail in Chapter 10. The properties of a DataRow are shown in Table 7-13. The majority of the properties are self-explanatory. The exception is RowState, which we'll examine briefly here and in detail in Chapter 10, "Editing and Updating Data."

Table 7-13   DataRow Properties

Property	Description
HasErrors	Indicates whether there are any errors in the DataRow.
Item	The value of a DataColumn in the DataRow.
ItemArray	The values of all DataColumns in the DataRow represented as an array.
RowError	The custom error description for a DataRow.
RowState	The DataRowState of a DataRow.
Table	The DataTable to which the DataRow belongs.

Using DataTable Methods

The primary methods supported by the DataTable are shown in Table 7-14. We'll examine most of these in Chapter 10, when we look at editing and updating data.

Table 7-14   DataTable Methods

Method	Description
AcceptChanges	Commits the pending changes to all DataRows.
BeginInit	Begins the initialization of a DataTable.
BeginLoadData	Turns off notifications, index maintenance, and constraint enforcement while a bulk data load is being performed; used in conjunction with the Load-DataRow and EndLoadData methods.
Clear	Removes all DataRows from the DataTable.
Clone	Copies the structure of a DataTable.

Table 7-14   **DataTable Methods**

Method	Description
Compute	Performs an aggregate operation on the DataTable.
Copy	Copies the structure of and data in a DataTable.
CreateDataReader	Returns a DataTableReader corresponding to the DataRows in the DataTable.
EndInit	Ends the initialization of a DataTable.
EndLoadData	Reinstates notifications, index maintenance and constraint enforcement after a bulk data load has been performed.
GetChanges	Returns a copy of the DataTable containing all DataRows that have been changed.
GetErrors	Gets an array of DataRows containing errors.
GetObjectData	Returns a SerializationInfo object with the information required to serialize the DataTable.
ImportRow	Copies a DataRow, including all row values and the row state, into a DataTable.
Load	Fills a DataTable with DataRows from the specified data source.
LoadDataRow	Used during bulk updating of a DataTable to update or add a new DataRow.
Merge	Merges two DataTables.
NewRow	Creates a new DataRow that matches the DataTable schema.
NewRowArray	Returns an array of new DataRows that match the DataTable schema.
ReadXml	Reads an XML schema and data into a DataTable.
ReadXmlSchema	Reads an XML schema into a DataTable.
RejectChanges	Rolls back all pending changes on the DataTable.
Reset	Resets the DataTable to its original state.
Select	Gets an array of DataRow objects.
WriteXml	Serializes a DataTable in XML format.
WriteXmlSchema	Serializes a DataTable schema in XML format.

The Select Method

The Select method is used to obtain a subset of the data in a DataTable. The Select method doesn't affect the contents of the table. Instead, the method returns an array of DataRows that match the criteria you specified.

Note   The DataView, which we'll examine in Chapter 9, "Using DataViews," also allows you to filter and sort DataRows.

The Select method is overloaded, exposing the versions shown in Table 7-15, which allow you to optionally specify selection criteria and a sort order for the DataRows returned. Those versions of the method that do not specify a sortOrder string return the DataRows in primary key order or, if the PrimaryKey property of the DataTable hasn't been specified, in the order in which the DataRows were added to the DataTable.

Table 7-15   Select Methods

Method	Description
Select()	Returns an array of all the DataRows in the DataTable.
Select(filterString)	Returns an array of the DataRows in the DataTable that match the specified filterString criteria.
Select(filterString, sortOrder)	Returns an array of the DataRows in the DataTable that match the specified filterString criteria, in the order specified by sortOrder.
Select(filterString, sortOrder, dataViewRowState)	Returns an array of the DataRows in the DataTable that match the specified filterString and DataViewRowState criteria, in the specified sortOrder.

Display a Subset of DataRows by Using the Select Method: Visual Basic

1. In the Code Editor, add the following code where indicated at the end of the btnSelect_Click event handler:

```
Dim drFound() As AdoSbsDataSet.EmployeesRow
drFound = dsAdoSbs.Employees.Select("LastName LIKE 'D*'")

str = "There are "
str &= drFound.Length.ToString()
str &= " Employees whose surname begins with 'D'"
MessageBox.Show(str)
```

This code selects only those Employees whose last name begins with the letter D. Your procedure should now be:

```
Private Sub btnSelect_Click(ByVal sender As System.Object, _
   ByVal e As System.EventArgs) Handles btnSelect.Click

   'Fill the table
   Dim ta As AdoSbsDataSetTableAdapters.EmployeesTableAdapter
   ta = New AdoSbsDataSetTableAdapters.EmployeesTableAdapter()
   ta.Fill(dsAdoSbs.Employees)

   'Display the number of rows
   Dim str As String
   str = "The Employees DataTable has "
   str &= dsAdoSbs.Employees.Rows.Count.ToString()
   str &= " rows."
   MessageBox.Show(str)

   'Place exercise code here:
   Dim drFound() As AdoSbsDataSet.EmployeesRow
   drFound = dsAdoSbs.Employees.Select("LastName LIKE 'D*'")

   str = "There are "
   str &= drFound.Length.ToString()
```

```
    str &= " Employees whose surname begins with 'D'"
    MessageBox.Show(str)

End Sub
```

2. Press F5 to run the application.

3. Click the Select button.

   The application displays the total number of DataRows in the table and then the number of rows selected.

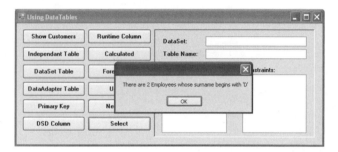

4. Close the application.

Display a Subset of DataRows by Using the Select Method: Visual C#

1. In the Code Editor, add the following code to the btnSelect_Click event handler where indicated:

```
DataRow[] drFound;
drFound = dsAdoSbs.Employees.Select("LastName LIKE 'D*'");

str = "There are ";
str += drFound.Length.ToString();
str += " Employees whose surname begins with 'D'";
MessageBox.Show(str);
```

   This code selects only those Employees whose last name begins with the letter D. Your procedure should now be:

```
private void btnSelect_Click(object sender, EventArgs e)
{
    //Fill the table
    AdoSbsDataSetTableAdapters.EmployeesTableAdapter ta;
    ta = new AdoSbsDataSetTableAdapters.EmployeesTableAdapter();
    ta.Fill(dsAdoSbs.Employees);

    //Display the number of rows
    string str;
    str = "The Employees table has ";
    str += dsAdoSbs.Employees.Rows.Count.ToString();
    str += " rows.";
    MessageBox.Show(str);
```

```
//Place exercise code here:
DataRow[] drFound;
drFound = dsAdoSbs.Employees.Select("LastName LIKE 'D*'");

str = "There are ";
str += drFound.Length.ToString();
str += " Employees whose surname begins with 'D'";
MessageBox.Show(str);
}
```

2. Press F5 to run the application.

3. Click the Select button.

    The application displays the total number of DataRows in the table and then the number of rows selected.

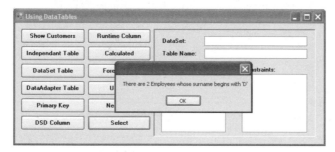

4. Close the application.

Using DataRow Methods

The methods supported by the DataRow object are shown in Table 7-16. The majority of the methods are used when editing data, and we'll look at them in detail in Chapter 10.

Table 7-16   DataRow Methods

Method	Description
AcceptChanges	Commits all pending changes to a DataRow.
BeginEdit	Begins an edit operation.
CancelEdit	Cancels an edit operation.
ClearErrors	Clears all the errors for the row.
Delete	Deletes the row.
EndEdit	Ends an edit operation.
GetChildRows	Gets all the child rows of a DataRow.
GetColumnError	Gets the error description for a specified column.

Table 7-16 DataRow Methods

Method	Description
GetColumnsInError	Returns an array of columns containing errors.
GetParentRow	Gets the parent row of a DataRow based on the specified DataRelation.
GetParentRows	Gets the parent rows of a DataRow based on the specified DataRelation.
HasVersion	Indicates whether a specified version of the DataRow exists.
IsNull	Indicates whether the specified column is empty.
RejectChanges	Rolls back all pending changes to the DataRow.
SetAdded	Changes the RowState of the DataRow to Added.
SetColumnError	Sets the error description for a column.
SetModified	Changes the RowState of the DataRow to Modified.
SetParentRow	Sets the parent row of a DataRow.

Responding to DataTable Events

The events supported by the DataTable are shown in Table 7-17. The events are useful primarily as part of the editing and data validation process, and we'll examine them in detail in Chapters 10 and 14.

Table 7-17 DataTable Events

Event	Description
ColumnChanged	Raised after a DataColumn has been changed.
ColumnChanging	Raised before a DataColumn is changed.
Initialized	Raised when a DataTable is initialized.
RowChanged	Raised after a DataRow is changed.
RowChanging	Raised before a DataRow is changed.
RowDeleted	Raised after a DataRow is deleted.
RowDeleting	Raised before a DataRow is deleted.
TableCleared	Raised after a DataTable is cleared.
TableClearing	Raised before a DataTable is cleared.
TableNewRow	Raised when a DataRow is added to the DataTable.

Summary

In this chapter we examined the DataTable, which models a table in a relational database. We saw how to create DataTables at run time and design time, and saw how to add an independent DataTable to a DataSet.

We examined the properties of the DataSet, and then turned to its collection properties, Constraints, Columns and Rows. The Constraints collection contains instances of the unique and foreign key constraints that implement data integrity. The Columns collection defines the schema of the DataTable, and the DataRows collection contains the actual data. We saw examples of creating and adding items to each of these collections.

Finally, we examined the methods exposed by the DataTable and the DataRow, and took a quick look at the DataTable events that we'll examine in detail in Chapters 10 and 14.

Chapter 8

Using TableAdapters

After completing this chapter, you will be able to:

- Create a TableAdapter class with the TableAdapter Configuration Wizard and the Server Explorer.

- Create a TableAdapter object in Visual Studio and at run time.

- Configure a TableAdapter class.

- Add a query to a TableAdapter.

- Configure a TableAdapter object.

- Execute the query methods of a TableAdapter.

In earlier chapters, you've seen the TableAdapters created by the Data Source Configuration Wizard. If you've examined the scaffolding code in some of the exercises, you've even seen them instantiated and used. In this chapter, we'll examine this new class of objects in detail.

Understanding TableAdapters

The TableAdapter is new to Microsoft ADO.NET 2.0, or more properly, to Microsoft Visual Studio 2005, because the TableAdapter class isn't technically part of ADO.NET or the Microsoft .NET Framework. Instead, TableAdapters classes are created by Visual Studio at design time as part of Typed DataSets.

TableAdapters combine the functionality of the Command and DataAdapter objects and link that functionality to the structure of a Typed DataSet. As we'll see, the link is reciprocal: When you change the SQL query that defines a TableAdapter's Fill method, the DataSet Designer alters the DataTable definition, and vice versa.

> **Tip** To see the files generated by Visual Studio for a Typed DataSet, click the Show All Files button on the Solution Explorer toolbar.

Like a DataAdapter, the primary purpose of a TableAdapter is to synchronize the data contained in a DataSet with the data in the data source. It provides one or more methods to fill the DataSet from the data source and to update the data source with changes made to the DataSet.

The class is defined inside the <DataSetName>.Designer.vb file, where <DataSetName> is, of course, the name of the Typed DataSet. TableAdapters are defined as a separate <DataSet>TableAdapters namespace at the end of the file.

> **Note**   Partial class declarations, new to Microsoft .NET Framework 2.0, allow you to split the definition of a class across multiple files. The most immediate effect of this split is that the code generated by Visual Studio can be separated from user-written code.

Each TableAdapter is defined as a separate partial class within the TableAdapters namespace. The Partial declaration means that you can easily extend the class definition in a separate code file, insulating your extensions from the actions of the DataSet Designer.

At the simplest level, you can think of TableAdapters as sophisticated DataAdapters. Because they encapsulate the Connection object, they save you a few lines of code for instantiating, opening and closing a Connection object, and their syntax is simpler. But that's only the beginning.

As we've seen, the DataAdapter exposes only four commands, Select, Update, Insert and Delete, each of which corresponds to a single SQL command. Because the TableAdapter class is generated at design time, it can support any number of SQL statements, each exposed in a simple method call, and the DataSet Designer provides a simple interactive interface for adding queries at design time.

Furthermore, because you can extend the class definition of a TableAdapter, you can add any functionality you require. In fact, TableAdapters are the first step toward turning a Typed DataSet into a complete object that combines data and functionality.

Strict object-oriented programming (OOP) methodology defines an object as a single entity, so the DataSet/TableAdapter combination doesn't quite fit the definition. However, the two object types are much more closely linked than is typical with the .NET Framework. Remember that changes made to the DataSet will update the Fill method of the TableAdapter and vice versa.

Creating TableAdapters

There are two steps to creating a TableAdapter: First, you must create the class itself (or, more often, have Visual Studio create it for you), and then you must instantiate it, as with any .NET Framework object.

Creating TableAdapter Classes

TableAdapter classes are defined by default whenever you use the Data Source Configuration Wizard to define a Typed DataSet. They can also be defined in the DataSet Designer.

Like Typed DataSets, it is theoretically possible to code a TableAdapter class from scratch, but again, it's difficult to imagine a situation in which this would be a sensible action.

Create a TableAdapter by Using the TableAdapter Configuration Wizard

1. Open the Chapter 08 – Start project in Visual Studio, and double-click AdoSbs-DataSet.xsd in the Solution Explorer.

    Visual Studio opens the DataSet in the DataSet Designer.

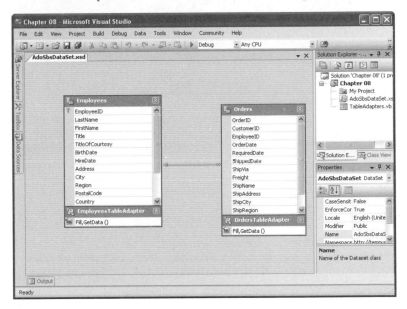

2. Drag a TableAdapter from the Toolbox onto the DataSet Designer.

    The DataSet Designer opens the TableAdapter Configuration Wizard.

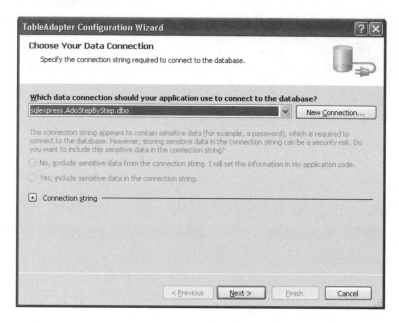

3. Make sure that the connection suggested by the wizard points to the AdoStepByStep sample database. If it doesn't, click the New Connection button, and create a new connection as described in Chapter 1, "Getting Started with ADO.Net." When you are finished, click Next.

    The wizard suggests saving the connection string to the application configuration file.

4. Clear the check box, if necessary, and then Click Next.

    The wizard displays a page requesting the command type.

5. Accept the default Use SQL Statements option, and click Next.

    The wizard displays a page requesting the SQL statement to be used to fill the table.

6. Enter the following SQL statement:

```
SELECT * FROM [Order Details]
```

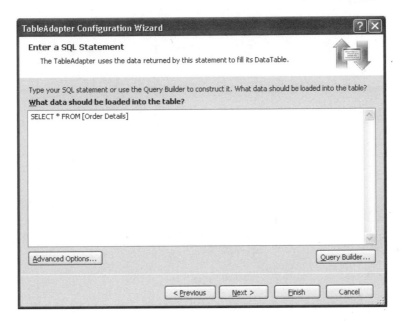

7.   Click Finish.

The TableAdapter Configuration Wizard adds the DataTable and its TableAdapter to the DataSet. Notice that it also creates the Relation between Order Details and Orders.

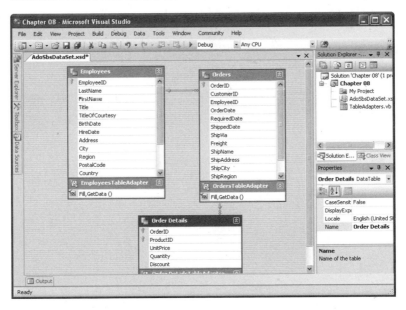

8.   Save the DataSet.

9.   Double-click TableAdapters.vb (or TableAdapters.cs if you're using C#) in the Solution Explorer.

Visual Studio opens the form in the Form Designer.

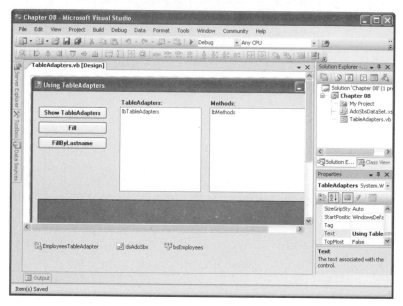

10.   Press F5 to run the application.

11.   Click the Show TableAdapters button.

The application displays the defined TableAdapters.

12.   Select one of the TableAdapters to see the methods defined for that TableAdapter.

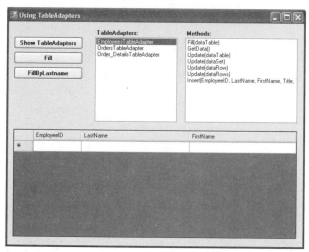

13.   Close the application.

Create a TableAdapter from the Server Explorer

1. With the AdoSbsDataSet still open in the DataSet Designer (it should still be open from the last exercise), open the Server Explorer by choosing Server Explorer from the View menu.

2. Verify that the connection to the AdoStepByStep database is displayed. If it isn't, click the Connect To Database toolbar button on the Server Explorer tab, and create a connection to the AdoStepByStep SQL Server database as described in Chapter 6, "Modeling a Database by Using DataSets and DataRelations."

3. Expand the connection to the AdoStepByStep sample database, and then expand the Tables node.

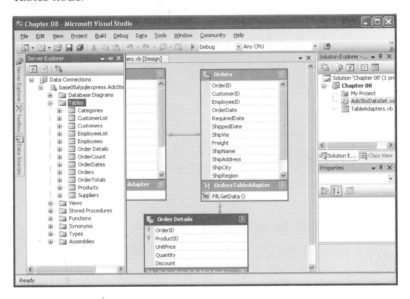

4. Drag the Customers table onto the DataSet designer.

   The DataSet Designer creates the DataTable and TableAdapter and adds them to the DataSet.

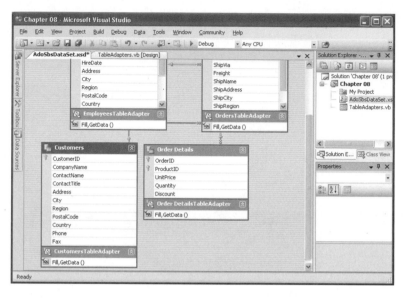

5. Save the DataSet.

6. Press F5 to run the application.

7. Click the Show TableAdapters button.

   The application shows the defined TableAdapters, including the new Customers Table-Adapter.

8. Select CustomersTableAdapters to see the defined methods.

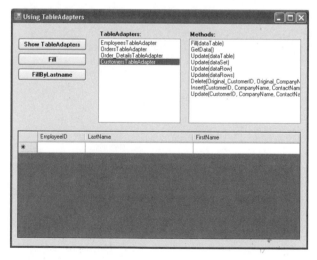

9. Close the application.

Creating TableAdapter Objects

Like any other classes in the .NET Framework, TableAdapter classes must be instantiated before use. You can create objects at design time by dragging a DataTable from the Data Sources window, or at run time by using the New constructor.

Create a TableAdapter in Visual Studio

1. Display the Form Designer, and then open the Toolbox.

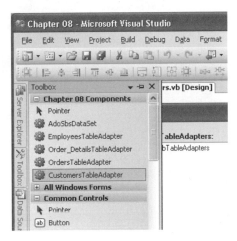

2. Drag the CustomersTableAdapter from the Chapter 08 Components section onto the Form Designer.

    Visual Studio adds an instance of the TableAdapter to the components tray.

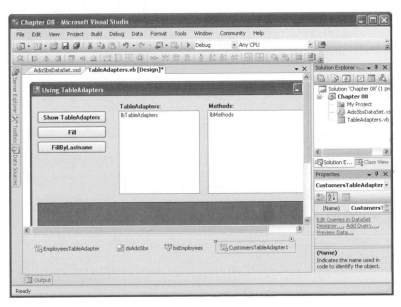

3.   In the Properties window, change the name of CustomersTableAdapter1 to **taCustomers**.

Create a TableAdapter in Code: Visual Basic

1.   Press F7 to display the Code Editor.

2.   Add the following line to the class declaration, above the New constructor:

```
Dim taEmployees As AdoSbsDataSetTableAdapters.EmployeesTableAdapter
```

3.   Add the following line where indicated at the end of New constructor:

```
taEmployees = New AdoSbsDataSetTableAdapters.EmployeesTableAdapter()
```

The beginning of your class file should now be:

```
Imports System.Data
Imports System.Data.SqlClient
Imports System.Reflection
Public Class TableAdapters

    Dim taEmployees As AdoSbsDataSetTableAdapters.EmployeesTableAdapter

    Public Sub New()

        ' This call is required by the Windows Form Designer.
        InitializeComponent()

        ' Add exercise code here:
        taEmployees = New AdoSbsDataSetTableAdapters.EmployeesTableAdapter()

    End Sub
```

Create a TableAdapter in Code: Visual C#

1.   Press F7 to display the Code Editor.

2.   Add the following line to the class declaration, above the Chapter_08 constructor:

```
AdoSbsDataSetTableAdapters.EmployeesTableAdapter taEmployees;
```

3.   Add the following line to the end of the constructor where indicated:

```
taEmployees = new AdoSbsDataSetTableAdapters.EmployeesTableAdapter();
```

The beginning of your class file should now be:

```
using System;
using System.Collections.Generic;
using System.ComponentModel;
using System.Data;
using System.Data.SqlClient;
using System.Drawing;
using System.Reflection;
```

```
using System.Text;
using System.Windows.Forms;

namespace Chapter_08
{
    public partial class TableAdapters : Form
    {
        AdoSbsDataSetTableAdapters.EmployeesTableAdapter taEmployees;

        public TableAdapters()
        {
            InitializeComponent();

            //Add exercise code here:
            taEmployees = new AdoSbsDataSetTableAdapters.EmployeesTableAdapter();
        }
    }
}
```

Configuring TableAdapters

Because the TableAdapter exposes only two simple properties, the majority of its configuration occurs at design time, when you configure the class itself.

Configuring TableAdapter Classes

The TableAdapter class properties are shown in Table 8-1. The properties fall into two categories: those that determine how the class will be defined, and those that determine how data will be manipulated by the TableAdapter.

Table 8-1   TableAdapter Class Properties

Property	Description
BaseClass	The class from which the TableAdapter inherits its functionality.
ConnectionModifier	Determines the visibility of the encapsulated Connection.
Modifier	Determines the visibility of the TableAdapter.
Name	The name of the TableAdapter.
GenerateDBDirectMethods	Determines whether the TableAdapter exposes Insert, Update and Delete methods that are sent directly to the database.
DeleteCommand	The SQL statement used to delete rows.
InsertCommand	The SQL statement used to insert rows.
SelectCommand	The SQL statement used to fill the DataTable.
UpdateCommand	The SQL statement used to update rows.

You can make the TableAdapter class properties visible in the DataSet Designer by selecting a TableAdapter at the bottom of a DataTable and then viewing the Properties window.

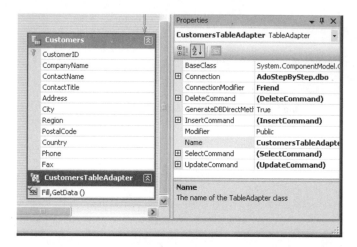

The BaseClass property determines the .NET Framework class from which the TableAdapter is derived. By default, this property is set to System.ComponentModel.Component. You can change this setting to simply extended the TableAdapter, but there is rarely a need to do so.

The ConnectionModifier property determines the visibility of the encapsulated Connection object. All of the standard visibility modifiers are available, with Friend being the default.

The Modifier property determines whether the TableAdapter exposes the DataTable itself through its GetData method. The options are Public and Friend, with Public being the default.

The Name property, as you might expect, determines the name by which the TableAdapter is referred to in code. The default is <DataTable>TableAdapter, but you can change it to any string that conforms to the rules for naming objects in the .NET Framework.

The GenerateDBDirectMethods property determines whether the TableAdapter generates Insert, Update and Delete commands that are executed directly against the Data Source, by-passing the DataTable. This property is True by default.

Finally, the four Command properties determine the SQL statements to be executed by the TableAdapter. These are similar to the corresponding Command properties in a DataAdapter, but they expose fewer Command properties. The TableAdapter commands expose only CommandText, CommandType and Parameters properties, while the commands encapsulated by a DataAdapter expose additional properties such as the CommandTimeout.

> **Important**   The smaller property set of the TableAdapter is something you need to consider when you decide whether to use a TableAdapter. If you need finer control over command behavior than is available in a TableAdapter, you must use a DataAdapter instead.

By default, a TableAdapter created by Visual Studio or the DataSet Designer exposes a single query that corresponds to the Fill and GetData methods. (We'll examine TableAdapter methods later in this chapter.) You can add additional queries by using the TableAdapter Query Configuration Wizard.

Each TableAdapter query exposes the properties shown in Table 8-2.

Table 8-2   TableAdapter Query Properties

Property	Description
FillMethodModifier	Determines the visibility of the Fill method.
FillMethodName	The name of the method.
GenerateMethods	Determines whether the TableAdapter generates Fill or GetData methods, or both.
GetMethodModifier	Determines the visibility of the GetData method.
GetMethodName	The name of the method.
CommandText	The SQL statement executed by the methods.
CommandType	The command type of the SQL statement.
ExecuteMode	The return type of the SQL statement.
Parameters	The Parameters collection of the SQL statement.

You can make the TableAdapter query properties visible in the DataSet Designer by selecting a TableAdapter at the bottom of a DataTable, selecting the TableAdapter query, and then viewing the Properties window.

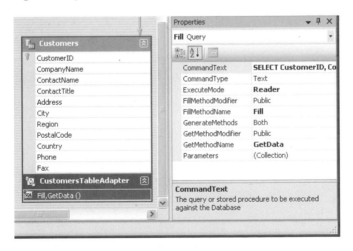

The GenerateMethods property, which can be set to Fill, Get or Both, determines what methods will be defined in the TableAdapter class. The default is Both.

For each method selected, the <method>MethodModifier property allows you to set the visibility, while the <method>MethodName property determines the method name. The Properties window exposes only the applicable properties, based on the setting of the Generate-Methods property.

The CommandText, CommandType and Parameters properties are common to all data commands in the .NET Framework.

The ExecuteMode property specifies the return type of the SQL statement. This property can be set to Reader, indicating that the statement returns DataRows; Scalar, indicating that the query returns a single value; or NonQuery, indicating that the query returns no values.

Edit the Fill Method of a TableAdapter

1. Display the DataSet Designer, and select the Fill,GetData() method of the Employees TableAdapter.

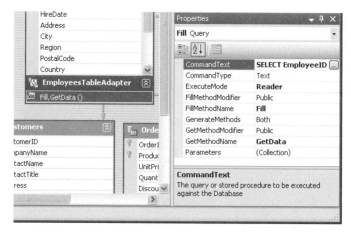

2. In the Properties window, click the ellipsis button next to the CommandText property.

    The DataSet Designer opens the Query Builder.

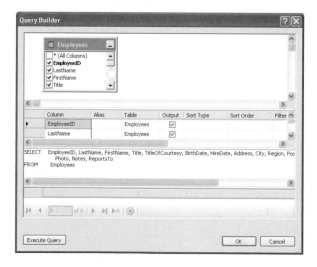

3. Change the SQL statement to:

```
SELECT EmployeeID, LastName, FirstName
FROM Employees
```

4. Click OK.

   The DataSet Designer displays a message box asking whether to regenerate updating commands.

5. Click Yes.

   The DataSet Designer updates the Fill method and the DataTable column list.

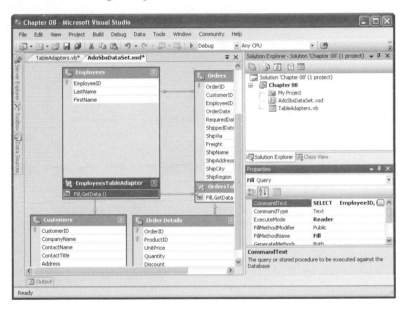

6. Save the DataSet.

Add a Query to a TableAdapter

1. In the DataSet Designer, right-click the EmployeesTableAdapter and choose Add Query.

   The DataSet Designer opens the TableAdapter Query Configuration Wizard.

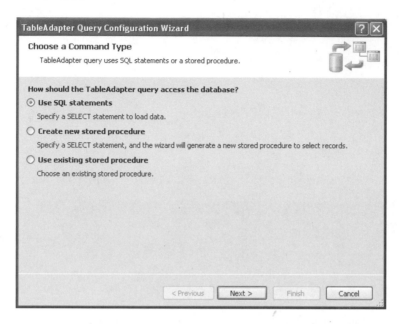

2. Accept the default command type, Use SQL Statements, and then click Next.

   The TableAdapter Query Configuration Wizard displays a page requesting the type of query.

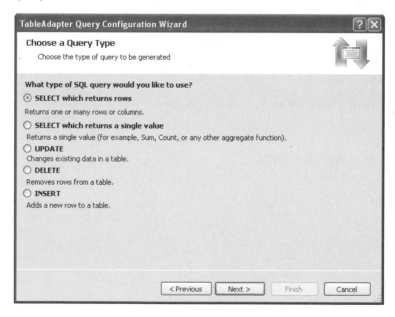

3. Accept the default of SELECT Which Returns Rows, and then click Next.

   The TableAdapter Query Configuration Wizard displays a page requesting the SQL statement.

4. Add a WHERE clause to the statement:

```
SELECT      EmployeeID, LastName, FirstName
FROM        Employees
WHERE LastName = @LastName
```

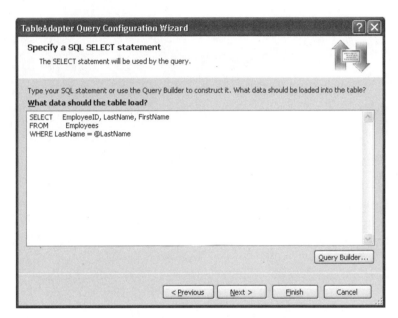

5. Click Next.

   The TableAdapter Query Configuration Wizard displays a page requesting the methods to be added.

6. Change the name of the Fill A DataTable method to **FillByLastName**, and clear the Return A DataTable check box.

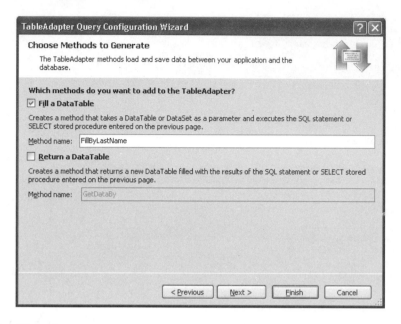

7. Click Next.

    The TableAdapter Query Configuration Wizard displays a results page indicating that the SELECT statement and the Fill method were generated.

8. Click Finish.

    The TableAdapter Query Configuration Wizard adds the new query to the Table-Adapter.

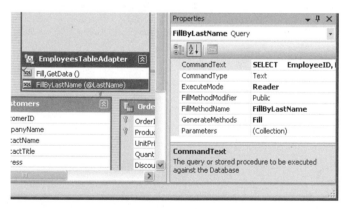

9. Save and close the DataSet.

10. Press F5 to run the application.

11. Click the Show TableAdapters button.

    The application displays the defined TableAdapter.

12.   Select EmployeesTableAdapter in the list box.

The application displays the query functions, which include FillByLastName.

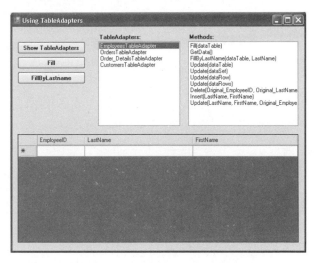

13.   Close the application.

Configuring TableAdapter Objects

After the TableAdapter class is defined, the TableAdapter object itself is very simple, exposing only the two properties shown in Table 8-3. (You can, of course, add additional properties by extending the class definition.)

Table 8-3   TableAdapter Properties

Property	Description
ClearBeforeFill	Determines whether a DataTable is emptied before data is loaded.
Connection	Returns the encapsulated Connection object.

The ClearBeforeFill property determines whether a DataTable will be emptied of DataRows before data is loaded into it.

The Connection property returns the Connection object encapsulated by the DataAdapter, allowing you to fine-tune its behavior. The visibility of this property is, however, controlled by the value of the ConnectionModifier property of the TableAdapter (set in the DataSet Designer). If the ConnectionModifier property is set to Private, for example, the Connection will not be exposed by the TableAdapter.

Using TableAdapter Methods

By default, the TableAdapter exposes the methods shown in Table 8-4. As we've seen, you can change the names of each of these methods in the DataSet Designer.

Table 8-4   Default TableAdapter Methods

Method	Description
Delete(col0...colN)	Deletes rows in the data source.
Fill(dataTable)	Loads data into the specified DataTable.
FillBy(dataTable, param0...paramN)	Loads data into the specified DataTable based on the specified parameters.
GetData	Returns a DataTable.
GetDataBy(dataTable, param0...paramN)	Returns a DataTable based on the specified parameters.
Insert(col0...colN)	Inserts rows in the data source.
Update(dataTable)	Synchronizes the specified DataTable with a data source.
Update(dataSet)	Synchronizes the DataTable in the specified DataSet with the data source.
Update(dataRow)	Synchronizes the specified DataRow with the data source.
Update(dataRows())	Synchronizes the specified array of DataRows with the data source.
Update(col0...colN)	Updates the rows in the data source.

The Delete, Insert and Update(col0...colN) methods are only available if the GenerateDB DirectMethods property of the DataAdapter class is True. They operate directly on the data source, by-passing the DataSet.

The Fill method corresponds to the Fill method of the DataAdapter, but supports only one version, Fill(dataTable).

The GetData method returns a new copy of the DataTable. Internally, this method creates the DataTable and calls the Fill method.

The FillBy and GetDataBy methods are generated only if the SELECT query has parameters. They will have a signature matching the query parameter list specified in the DataSet Designer.

Finally, the Update(dataTable) method is identical to the Update(dataTable) method of the DataAdapter.

Executing Query Methods

As we've seen, the queries that you add to the TableAdapter in the DataSet Designer are exposed as methods of the TableAdapter class. For each query, you can choose to expose a Fill method that receives a DataTable as a parameter and fills it with data (optionally clearing it first), or a Get method that returns a new DataTable, or both.

This is one of the primary advantages of the TableAdapter over the earlier Connection/Data-Adapter object combination. The TableAdapter is extensible—you can add additional queries to the TableAdapter in the DataSet Designer and expose them as methods of the TableAdapter class.

Execute a Default Query Method: Visual Basic

1. In the Code Editor, add the following line to the btnFill_Click event handler:

   ```
   taEmployees.Fill(dsAdoSbs.Employees)
   ```

   This line calls the default Fill method of the taEmployees TableAdapter we created earlier.

2. Press F5 to run the application.

3. Click the Fill button.

   The application fills the DataGridView.

4. Close the application.

Execute a Default Query Method: Visual C#

1. In the Code Editor, add the following line to the btnFill_Click event handler:

```
taEmployees.Fill(dsAdoSbs.Employees);
```

This line calls the default Fill method of the taEmployees TableAdapter we created earlier.

2. Press F5 to run the application.

3. Click the Fill button.

The application fills the DataGridView.

4. Close the application.

Execute a Parameterized Query Method: Visual Basic

1. In the Code Editor, add the following line to the btnGet_Click event handler:

```
taEmployees.FillByLastName(dsAdoSbs.Employees, "Davolio")
```

This line calls the default FillByLastName method of the taEmployees TableAdapter.

2. Press F5 to run the application.

3. Click the FillByLastName button.

The application fills the DataGridView with the matching record.

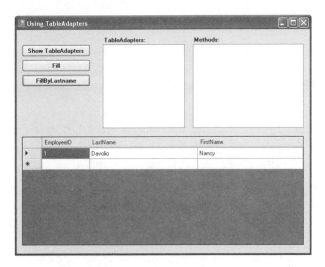

4. Close the application.

Execute a Parameterized Query Method:Visual C#

1. In the Code Editor, add the following line to the btnGet_Click event handler:

```
taEmployees.FillByLastName(dsAdoSbs.Employees, "Davolio");
```

This line calls the default FillByLastName method of the taEmployees TableAdapter.

2. Press F5 to run the application.

3. Click the FillByLastName button.

The application fills the DataGridView with the matching record.

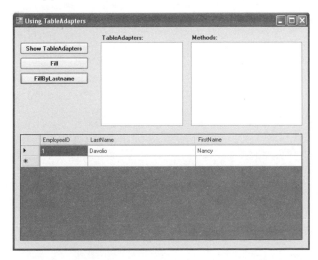

4. Close the application.

Summary

In this chapter we examined TableAdapters, which combine and extend the functionality of a DataAdapter and a Connection. TableAdapters are specific to a DataTable and are generated at design time by Visual Studio 2005.

We examined the technique for creating a TableAdapter class in the DataSet Designer and saw an example of adding a parameterized query to the TableAdapter class. We then looked at the straight-forward process of instantiating a TableAdapter at run time and calling its methods. Along the way, we examined the properties exposed by both the TableAdapter class and the instantiated TableAdapter object, which are closely related to the properties exposed by the DataAdapter and Connection objects that the TableAdapter encapsulates.

Chapter 9
Using DataViews

After completing this chapter, you will be able to:

- Add a DataView to a form.
- Create a DataView at run time.
- Create calculated columns in a DataView.
- Sort DataView rows.
- Filter DataView rows.
- Search a DataView based on a primary key value.

In Chapter 7, "Using DataTables," we looked at the Select method of the DataTable, which provides a mechanism for filtering and sorting DataRows. The DataView provides another mechanism for performing the same actions at design time.

Understanding DataViews

A DataView provides a filtered and sorted view of a single DataTable. Although the DataView provides the same functionality as the DataTable's Select method, it has a number of advantages. Because DataViews are distinct objects, they can be created and configured at both design time and run time, making them easier to implement in many situations.

We'll examine Data Binding in Chapters 12 and 14.

Furthermore, unlike the array of DataRows returned from the Select method, DataViews can be used as the data source for bound controls.

You can create multiple DataViews for any given DataTable. In fact, every DataTable encapsulates at least one DataView in its DefaultDataView property. The properties of the Default-DataView can be set at run time, but not at design time.

The rows of a DataView, although very much like DataRows, are actually DataRowView objects that reference DataRows. The properties of the DataRowView are shown in Table 9-1.

> **Note**   Only the Item property is also exposed by the DataRow; the other properties are unique to the DataView.

Table 9-1   DataRowView Properties

Property	Description
DataView	The DataView to which this DataRowView belongs.
IsEdit	Indicates whether the DataRowView is currently being edited.
IsNew	Indicates whether the DataRowView is new.
Item	The value of a column in the DataRowView.
Row	The DataRow that is being viewed.
RowVersion	The current version of the DataRowView.

DataViewManagers

Functionally, a DataViewManager is similar to a DataSet. Just as a DataSet acts as a container for DataTables, the DataViewManager acts as a container for DataViews, one for each DataTable in a DataSet.

The DataViews within the DataViewManager are accessed through the DataViewSettings collection. It's convenient to think of a DataViewSetting as existing for each DataTable in a DataSet. In reality, the DataViewSetting isn't physically created until (and unless) it is referenced in code.

DataViewManagers are most often used when the DataSet contains related tables, because they allow you to maintain sorting and filtering criteria across calls to GetChildRows. If you were to use individual DataViews on the child table, the sorting and filtering criteria would need to be reset after each call. With a DataViewManager, after the criteria are established, the rows returned by GetChildRows are sorted and filtered automatically.

In Chapter 6, "Modeling a Database by Using DataSets and DataRelations," we saw that the DataSet has a DefaultViewManager property. In reality, when you bind to a DataSet, you're actually binding to the default DataViewManager. Under most circumstances, you can ignore this technicality, but it can be useful for setting default sorting and filtering criteria at run time.

Note, however, that the DataSet's DefaultDataViewManager property is read-only—you can set its properties, but you cannot create a new DataViewManager and assign it to the DataSet as the default.

Creating DataViews

Because DataViews are independent Microsoft ADO.NET objects, you can create and configure them at design time by using Microsoft Visual Studio 2005. You can, of course, also create and configure them at run time.

Creating DataViews at Design Time

Visual Studio supports the design-time creation of DataViews through the DataView control on the Data tab of the Toolbox. As with any other control with design-time support, you simply drag the control onto a form and set its properties in the Properties window.

However, like several of the other low-level ADO.NET objects we've examined, the DataView isn't included in the Toolbox by default; you must add it by using the Choose Toolbox Items dialog box.

Create and Bind a DataView in Visual Studio

1. Open the Chapter 09 – Start project in Visual Studio, and if necessary, double-click the DataViews.vb form (or DataViews.cs if you're using C#) in the Solution Explorer to open the form in the Form Designer.

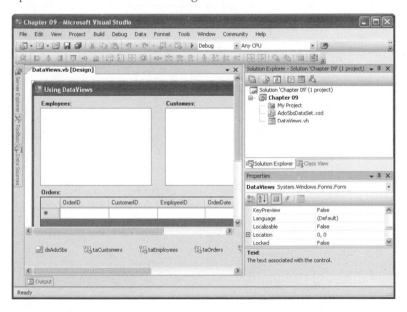

2. Add the DataView control to the Toolbox by right-clicking the Data tab, selecting Choose Items, then selecting DataView in the Choose Toolbox Items dialog box and clicking OK.

    Refer to the first exercise in Chapter 2, "Using Connections," for detailed instructions.

3. Drag a DataView control onto the Form Designer.

Visual Studio adds the control to the component tray.

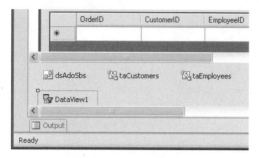

4. In the Properties window, change the DataView's name to **dvOrders**.

5. In the Properties window for dvOrders, select the Table property.

6. Click the Table down arrow, expand the dsAdoSbs node, and choose Orders.

7. In the Properties window, change the Sort property to **OrderID**.

8. On the Form Designer, select the dgvOrders DataGridView control.

9. In the Properties window, select the DataSource property.

10. Click the DataSource down arrow, expand the Other Data Sources node, expand the DataViews List Instances node, and then select dvOrders.

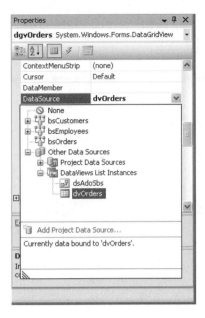

11. Press F5 to run the application.

    Visual Studio displays the information in the Orders DataGridView arranged according to the values in the OrderID column.

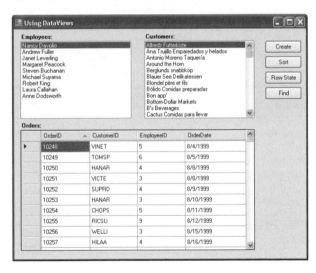

12. Close the application.

Creating DataViews at Run Time

The DataView object can be created at run time. The DataView supports the three versions of the New constructor shown in Table 9-2.

Table 9-2   DataView Constructors

Method	Description
New()	Creates a new DataView.
New(dataTable)	Creates a new DataView and sets its Table property to the specified DataTable.
New(dataTable, rowFilter, sort, rowState)	Creates a new DataView with the specified Data-Table, row filter, sort order, and DataViewRowState.

Create a DataView in Code: Visual Basic

1. Press F7 to display the Code Editor.

2. Add the following lines to the btnCreate_Click event handler:

```
Dim drCurrent As DataRow
Dim dvNew As DataView

dvNew = New DataView()
drCurrent = CType(lbCustomers.SelectedItem, DataRowView).Row

dvNew.Table = dsAdoSbs.Orders
dvNew.RowFilter = "CustomerID = '" & drCurrent(0) & "'"

dgvOrders.DataSource = dvNew
```

The code first declares a DataRow that will contain the item selected in the lbCustomers list box, and then declares and instantiates a new DataView using the default constructor. Next, drCurrent is assigned to the current selection in the list box.

The Table property of the dvNew DataView is set to the Orders table, and the RowFilter property is set to show only the orders for the selected customer. Finally, the dgvOrders DataGridView is bound to the new DataView.

3. Press F5 to run the application.

4. Select a customer in the Customers list box, and then click the Create button.

   The DataGridView displays the orders for the selected customer.

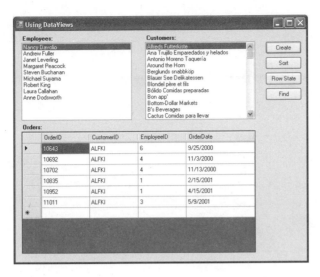

5. Close the application.

Create a DataView in Code: Visual C#

1. Press F7 to display the Code Editor.

2. Add the following lines to the btnCreate_Click event handler:

```
DataRow drCurrent;
DataView dvNew;

dvNew = new DataView();
drCurrent = ((DataRowView)lbCustomers.SelectedItem).Row;

dvNew.Table = dsAdoSbs.Orders;
dvNew.RowFilter = "CustomerID = '" + drCurrent[0] + "'";

dgvOrders.DataSource = dvNew;
```

The code first declares a DataRow that will contain the item selected in the lbCustomers list box, and then declares and instantiates a new DataView using the default constructor. Next, drCurrent is assigned to the current selection in the list box.

The Table property of the dvNew DataView is set to the Orders table, and the RowFilter property is set to show only the orders for the selected customer. Finally, the dgvOrders DataGridView is bound to the new DataView.

3. Press F5 to run the application.

4. Select a customer in the Customers list box, and then click the Create button.

    The DataGridView displays the orders for the selected customer.

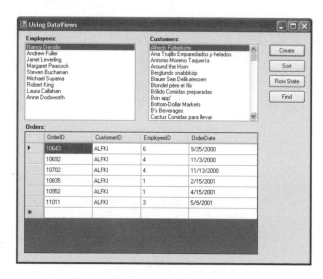

5.   Close the application.

Configuring DataViews

The properties exposed by the DataView object are shown in Table 9-3.

Table 9-3   DataView Properties

Property	Description
AllowDelete	Determines whether rows in the DataView can be deleted.
AllowEdit	Determines whether rows in the DataView can be changed.
AllowNew	Determines whether rows can be added to the DataView.
ApplyDefaultSort	Determines whether the default sort order, determined by the underlying data source, is used.
Count	The number of DataRowViews in the DataView.
DataViewManager	The DataViewManager to which this DataView belongs.
IsInitialized	Indicates whether the DataView has been initialized.
Item(index)	Returns the specified DataRowView.
RowFilter	The expression used to filter the rows contained in the DataView.
RowStateFilter	The DataViewRowState used to filter the rows contained in the DataView.
Sort	The expression used to sort the rows contained in the DataView.
Table	The DataTable that is the source of rows for the DataView.

The AllowDelete, AllowEdit and AllowNew properties determine whether the data reflected by the DataView can be changed through the DataView. (Data can always be changed by referencing the row in the underlying DataTable.)

The Count property does exactly what one might expect—it returns the number of DataRows reflected in the DataView, while the DataViewManager and Table properties connect the DataView to other objects within the application.

Finally, the RowFilter, RowStateFilter and Sort properties control which DataRows are reflected in the DataView and how those rows are ordered. We'll examine these properties later in this chapter.

DataColumn Expressions

Expressions, technically DataColumn expressions, are used by the RowFilter and Sort properties of the DataView. We saw how DataColumn expressions were used in previous chapters when we created a calculated column in a DataTable and when we set the sort and filter expressions for the DataTable Select method. Now it's time to examine them more closely.

A DataColumn expression is a string, and you can use all the standard string handling functions to build one. For example, you can use the concatenation operator (& in Visual Basic and + in C#) to join two strings into a single expression:

```
myExpression =  "CustomerID = '" & strCustID & "'"
```

Note that the value of strCustID will be surrounded by single quotation marks in the resulting text. In building DataColumn expressions, columns can be referred to directly by using the ColumnName property, but any actual text values must be enclosed in quotation marks.

In addition, certain special characters must be "escaped"; that is, wrapped in square brackets. For example, a column named Miles/Gallon would be referenced as [Miles/Gallon], as follows:

```
MyExpression = "[Miles/Gallon] > 10"
```

> **Tip**   You can find the complete list of special characters in the MSDN Help topic about the DataColumn.Expression property.

Numeric values in DataColumn expressions require no special handling, as shown in the previous example, but date values must be surrounded by hash marks (#), as follows:

```
MyExpression = "OrderDate > #01/01/2001#"
```

> **Important**   Dates in code must conform to US usage; that is, month/day/year.

As we've seen, DataRow columns are referred to by the ColumnName property. You can reference a column in a child DataRow by prepending the ColumnName with "Child," as follows:

```
myExpression = "Child.OrderTotal > 3000"
```

The syntax for referencing a parent row is identical:

```
MyExpression = "Parent.CustomerID = 'AFLKI'"
```

References to parent and child rows are frequently used along with one of the aggregate functions shown in Table 9-4. The aggregate functions can also be used directly, without reference to child or parent rows.

Table 9-4   Aggregate Functions

Function	Result
Sum	Sum
Avg	Average
Min	Minimum
Max	Maximum
Count	Count
StDev	Statistical standard deviation
Var	Statistical variance

When setting the expressions for DataViews, you will frequently be comparing values. The .NET Framework handles the usual range of comparison operators, shown in Table 9-5.

Table 9-5   Comparison Operators

Operator	Action
AND	Logical AND
OR	Logical OR
NOT	Logical NOT
<	Less than
>	Greater than
<=	Less than or equal to
>=	Greater than or equal to
<>	Not equal
IN	Determines whether the value specified is contained in a set
LIKE	Inexact match using a wildcard character

The IN operator requires the set of values to be surrounded by parentheses and the values themselves to be separated by commas, as follows:

```
MyExpression = "myColumn IN ('A', 'B', 'C')"
```

The LIKE operator treats the characters * and % as interchangeable wildcards—both replace zero or more characters. The wildcard characters can be used at the beginning or end of a string, or at both ends, but cannot be contained within a string.

DataColumn expressions also support the arithmetic operators shown in Table 9-6.

Table 9-6   Arithmetic Operators

Operator	Action
+	Addition
-	Subtraction
*	Multiplication
/	Division
%	Integer division

The addition character (+) is also used for string concatenation within a DataColumn expression, rather than the more usual ampersand character (&).

Finally, DataColumn expressions support a number of special functions, as shown in Table 9-7.

Table 9-7   Special Functions

Function	Result
Convert(expression, type)	Converts the value returned by expression to the specified .NET Framework Type.
Len(string)	Returns the number of characters in the specified string.
ISNULL(expression, replacementValue)	Determines whether expression evaluates to db-Null, and if so, returns replacement value.
IIF(expression, valueIfTrue, valueIfFalse)	Returns valueIfTrue if expression evaluates to True; otherwise, returns valueIfFalse.
TRIM(string)	Returns the string with leading and trailing space characters removed.
SUBSTRING(expression, start, length)	Returns the expression, beginning at the specified start zero-based position and extending for the specified length.

Sort Expressions

Although the DataColumn expressions used in the Sort property can be arbitrarily complex, in most cases they take the form of one or more ColumnNames separated by commas, as follows:

```
myDataView.Sort = "CustomerID, OrderID"
```

Optionally, the ColumnNames can be followed by ASC or DESC to cause the values to be sorted in ascending or descending order, respectively. The default sort order is ascending, so the ASC keyword isn't strictly necessary, but it can sometimes be useful to include it for clarity.

Change the Sort Order of a DataView: Visual Basic

1. In the Code Editor, add the following lines to the btnSort_Click event handler:

```
dvOrders.Sort = "EmployeeID, CustomerID, OrderID DESC"
dgvOrders.Refresh()
```

   The code sets the sort order of the dgvOrders DataGridView to sort first by EmployeeID, then by CustomerID and finally by OrderID in descending order.

2. Press F5 to run the application.

3. Click the Sort button.

   The application displays the sorted contents of the DataGridView.

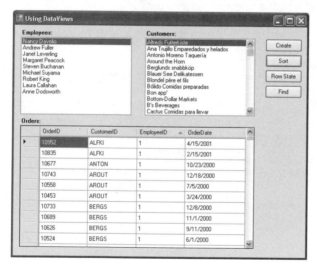

4. Close the application.

Change the Sort Order of a DataView: Visual C#

1. In the Code Editor, add the following lines to the btnSort_Click event handler:

```
dvOrders.Sort = "EmployeeID, CustomerID, OrderID DESC";
dgvOrders.Refresh();
```

   The code sets the sort order of the dgvOrders DataGridView to sort first by EmployeeID, then by CustomerID and finally by OrderID in descending order.

2. Press F5 to run the application.

3. Click the Sort button.

The application displays the sorted contents of the DataGridView.

4. Close the application.

The RowState Filter

In Chapter 7, we saw that each DataRow maintains its status in the RowState property. The DataView's RowStateFilter property can be used to limit the DataRowViews within the Data-View to those with a certain RowState. The possible values for the RowStateFilter property are shown in Table 9-8.

Table 9-8   DataViewRowState Values

Value	Description
Added	Only those rows that have been added.
CurrentRows	All current row values.
Deleted	Only those rows that have been deleted.
ModifiedCurrent	Current row values of only those rows that have been modified.
ModifiedOriginal	Original row values of only those rows that have been modified.
None	No rows.
OriginalRows	Original values of all rows.
Unchanged	Only those rows that have not been modified.

Display Only New Rows: Visual Basic

1. In the Code Editor, add the following code to the btnRowState_Click event handler:

```
Dim drNew As DataRowView

drNew = dvOrders.AddNew()
drNew("CustomerID") =  "ALFKI"
drNew("EmployeeID") = 1
drNew("OrderID") = 0

dvOrders.RowStateFilter = DataViewRowState.Added
dgvOrders.Refresh()
```

The code first creates a new DataRowView (we'll examine the AddNew method in the next section), and then sets the RowStateFilter to display only the new (added) rows. Finally, the dgvOrders DataGridView is refreshed to display the changes.

2. Press F5 to run the application.

3. Click the Row State button.

The DataGridView shows only the new order.

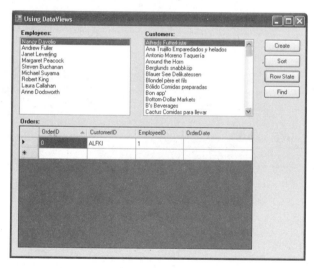

4. Close the application.

Display Only New Rows: Visual C#

1. In the Code Editor, add the following code to the btnRowState_Click event handler:

```
DataRowView drNew;

drNew = dvOrders.AddNew();
drNew["CustomerID"] = "ALFKI";
drNew["EmployeeID"] = 1;
drNew["OrderID"] = 0;

dvOrders.RowStateFilter = DataViewRowState.Added;
dgvOrders.Refresh();
```

The code first creates a new DataRowView (we'll examine the AddNew method in the next section), and then sets the RowStateFilter to display only the new (added) rows. Finally, the dgvOrders DataGridView is refreshed to display the changes.

2. Press F5 to run the application.

3. Click the Row State button.

The DataGridView shows only the new order.

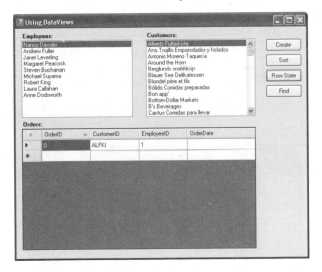

4. Close the application.

Using DataView Methods

The primary methods supported by the DataView are shown in Table 9-9. The AddNew method, which we used in the previous exercise, adds a new DataRowView to the DataView, while the Delete method deletes the row at the specified index.

Table 9-9   DataView Methods

Method	Description
AddNew	Adds a new row to a DataView.
BeginInit	Begins the initialization of a DataView.
CopyTo	Copies items into an array.
Delete	Removes a DataRowView from a DataView.
EndInit	Ends the initialization of a DataView.
Find	Returns the index position of the first DataRowView containing the sort key value(s) specified.
FindRows	Returns an array of DataRowViews containing the sort key value(s) specified.
ToTable	Creates a new DataTable based on the DataRowViews in the DataView.

The Find Method

The DataView's Find method finds rows based on the Sort expression. If you have not specified a value for this property, the ApplyDefaultSort property must be set to True, and the values specified must match the primary key of the underlying DataTable.

There are two versions of the Find method that you can use to pass either a single value or an array of values. Both versions return the zero-based index of the first DataRowView that matches the value or values specified, or -1 if no match is found.

Find a Row Based on Its Primary Key Value: Visual Basic

1. In the Code Editor, add the following code to the btnFind_Click event handler:

```
Dim idxFound As Integer
Dim strMessage As String

idxFound = dvOrders.Find(10255)

strMessage = "The OrderID is " & _
    dvOrders(idxFound).Item("OrderID")
strMessage &= vbCrLf & "The CustomerID is " & _
    dvOrders(idxFound).Item("CustomerID")
strMessage &= vbCrLf & "The Employee ID is " & _
    dvOrders(idxFound).Item("EmployeeID")
MessageBox.Show(strMessage)
```

This code uses the Find method to locate Order 10255 and then displays the results in a message box.

2. Press F5 to run the application.

3. Click the Find button.

    The application displays the results.

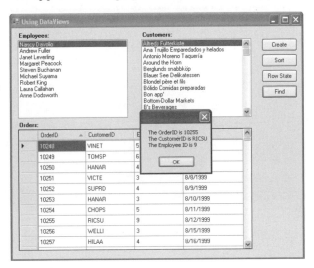

4. Click OK, and close the application.

Find a Row Based on Its Primary Key Value: Visual C#

1. In the Code Editor, add the following code to the btnFind_Click event handler:

```
int idxFound;
string strMessage;

dvOrders.ApplyDefaultSort = true;
idxFound = dvOrders.Find(10255);

strMessage =  "The OrderID is " +
    dvOrders[idxFound]["OrderID"];
strMessage += "\nThe CustomerID is " +
    dvOrders[idxFound]["CustomerID"];
strMessage += "\nThe Employee ID is " +
    dvOrders[idxFound]["EmployeeID"];
MessageBox.Show(strMessage);
```

    This code uses the Find method to locate Order 10255 and then displays the results in a message box.

2. Press F5 to run the application.

3. Click the Find button.

The application displays the results.

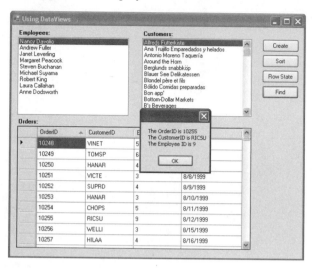

4.   Click OK, and close the application.

Summary

In this chapter we examined the DataView object. The DataView allows the contents of a DataTable to be sorted and filtered, and unlike the Sort and Filter methods of the DataTable, it can be created at design time and can serve as the data source for bound controls.

Part IV
Manipulating Data

Chapter 10
Editing and Updating Data

After completing this chapter, you will be able to:

- Use the RowState property of a DataRow.

- Retrieve a specific version of a DataRow.

- Add a DataRow to a DataTable.

- Delete a DataRow from a DataTable.

- Edit a DataRow.

- Temporarily suspend enforcement of constraints during updates.

- Accept and reject changes to data.

In the previous few chapters, we've examined each of the Microsoft ADO.NET objects in turn. Starting with this chapter, we'll look at how these objects work together to perform specific tasks. Specifically, in this chapter we'll examine the process of editing and updating data.

Understanding the Editing and Updating Process

Given e disconnected architecture of ADO.NET, there are four distinct phases to the process of editing and updating data from a data source:

1. Retrieve data from the data source.

2. Modify the in-memory copy of the data.

3. Update the data source.

4. Update the DataSet.

First, the data is retrieved from the data source, stored in memory, and possibly displayed to the user. This phase is typically done by using the Fill method of a DataAdapter or Table-Adapter to fill the tables of a DataSet. But as we've seen, data can also be retrieved by using a Data Command and a DataReader.

We'll examine data binding later in Part IV. In the second phase, the data is modified as required. Values can be changed, new rows added, and existing rows deleted. Data modification can be done under programmatic control or by way of the data binding mechanisms of Windows Forms and Web Forms. We'll explore how to make changes to data under programmatic control in this chapter. In Windows Forms, the data binding architecture handles transmitting changes from data-bound controls to the

DataSet. No other action is required. In Web Forms, any data changes must of course be submitted to the server.

If the changes made to the in-memory copy of the data are to be persisted, they must be propagated to the data source, which is the third phase of the process. If a DataSet is used for managing the in-memory data, the data source propagation can be done by using the Update method of the DataAdapter or TableAdapter. Alternatively, Command objects can be used directly to submit the changes. (Of course, as we've seen, DataAdapters and TableAdapters use Data Commands to submit data as well.)

In the fourth and final phase, the DataSet can be updated to reflect the new state of the data source. This is done by using the AcceptChanges method of the DataSet or DataTable. Both the Fill and Update methods of the DataAdapter call AcceptChanges automatically. The Table-Adapter behaves identically, performing the Fill and Update commands by using its encapsulated DataAdapter. If you execute Data Commands directly, you must call AcceptChanges explicitly to update the status of the DataSet.

Concurrency

Given the disconnected methodology used by ADO.NET, there is always a chance that a row in the data source might have been changed since it was loaded into the DataSet. This is a *concurrency violation*.

The Update method supports a DBConcurrencyException, which one might expect to be thrown if a concurrency violation occurs. In fact, the DBConcurrencyException is thrown whenever the number of rows updated by a Data Command is zero. This is typically due to a concurrency violation, but it's important to understand that this is not necessarily the case; there might simply have been no rows to update.

Understanding DataRowStates and Versions

As we saw in Chapter 7, "Using DataTables," the DataRow maintains a RowState property that indicates whether the row has been added, deleted or modified. In addition, the DataTable maintains multiple copies of each row, each reflecting a different version. We'll explore both the RowState property and row versions in this section.

The RowState Property

The RowState property of the DataRow reflects the actions that have been taken since the DataTable was created, or since the last time the AcceptChanges method was called. The possible values for RowState, as defined by the DataRowState enumeration, are shown in Table 10-1.

Table 10-1   DataRowState Enumeration

Value	Description
Added	The DataRow is new.
Deleted	The DataRow has been deleted from the DataTable.
Detached	The DataRow has not yet been added to a DataTable.
Modified	The contents of the DataRow have been changed.
Unchanged	The DataRow has not been modified.

The baseline values of the rows in a DataTable are established when the AcceptChanges method is called, either by the Fill or Update methods of the DataAdapter or TableAdapter, or explicitly by program code. At that time, all the DataRows have their RowState set to Unchanged.

Not surprisingly, if the value of any column of a DataRow is changed after AcceptChanges is called, its RowState is set to Modified. If new DataRows are added to the DataSet by using the Add method of the DataSet's Row collection, their RowState is Added. The new rows maintain the Added status even if their contents are changed before the next call to AcceptChanges.

If a DataRow is deleted by using the Delete method, it isn't actually removed from the DataSet until AcceptChanges is called. Instead, its RowState is set to Deleted, and, as we'll see, its Current values are set to Null.

DataRows don't necessarily belong to a DataTable. An independent row has a RowState of Detached until it is added to the Rows collection of a DataTable, at which time its RowState is Added.

Row Versions

A DataTable maintains multiple versions of any given DataRow, depending on the actions that have been performed on it since the last time AcceptChanges was called. The possible versions of a DataRow are shown in Table 10-2.

Table 10-2   DataRowVersion Enumeration

Version	Meaning
Current	The current values of each DataRow.
Default	The default values used for new rows.
Original	The values set when the row was created or when AcceptChanges was last called.
Proposed	The values assigned after a BeginEdit method has been called.

There will always be a Current version of every row in the DataSet. The Current version of the DataRow reflects any changes that have been made to its values since the row was created.

Rows that existed in the DataSet when AcceptChanges was last called have an Original version, which contains the initial data values. Rows that are added to the DataSet don't have an Original version until AcceptChanges is called again.

If any of the columns of a DataTable has a value assigned to its DefaultValue property, all the DataRows in the table have a Default version, with the values determined by the DefaultValue property of each column.

DataRows have a Proposed version after a call to DataRow.BeginEdit and before a call to either EndEdit or CancelEdit. Later in this chapter, we'll examine these methods, which are used to temporarily suspend data constraints.

> **Note** The example application for the following exercise displays the Original and Current values of a DataSet. The display is based on the Windows Form BindingSource object, which we won't examine until Chapter 11, "Manual Data Binding in Windows Forms," so the code to display these values is already in place.

Explore DataRowStates and DataRow Versions

1. In Microsoft Visual Studio 2005, open the Chapter 10 - Start project, and, if necessary, double-click Editing.vb (or Editing.cs if you're using C#) in the Solution Explorer.

    Visual Studio displays the form in the Form Designer.

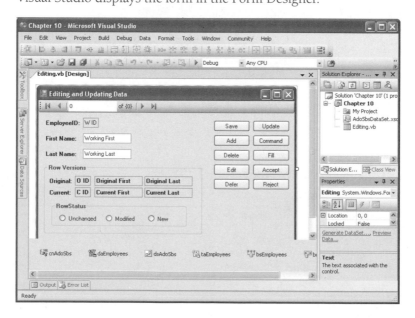

2. Press F5 to run the application.

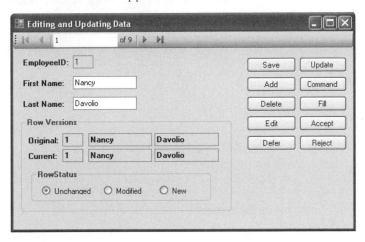

3. Use the navigation buttons at the top of the form to move through the DataSet.

    All the rows have identical Current and Original versions, and the RowStatus is Unchanged.

4. Change the value of the First Name or Last Name text box of one row, and then click Save.

    The Current version of the row is updated to reflect the name, and the RowState changes to Modified.

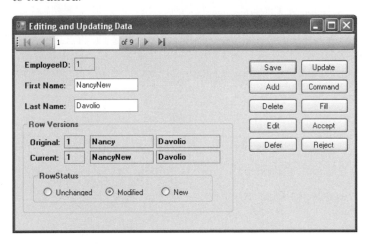

5. Close the application.

Editing Data in a DataSet Under Program Control

We'll discuss editing using data-bound controls later in Part IV. Editing data after it is loaded into a DataSet is a straightforward process of calling methods and setting property values. In this chapter, we'll concentrate on manipulating the contents of the DataSet programmatically, leaving the discussion of using Windows Form and Web Form controls to later chapters.

Adding a DataRow

There is no way to create a new DataRow directly in a DataTable. Instead, a DataRow object must be created independently and then added to the DataTable's Rows collection.

The DataTable's NewRow method returns a detached row with the same schema as the table on which it's called. The values of the row can then be set, and the new row can be appended to the DataTable.

Add a Row to the DataTable: Visual Basic

1. Press F7 to display the Code Editor.

2. Add the following code to the btnAdd_Click event handler:

```
Dim drNew As DataRow

drNew = dsAdoSbs.Employees.NewRow()
drNew.Item("FirstName") = "New First"
drNew.Item("LastName") = "New Last"
dsAdoSbs.Employees.Rows.Add(drNew)
```

   The first line declares the DataRow variable that will contain the new row. Then the NewRow method is called, instantiating the variable. Its fields are set, and it is added to the Rows collection of the Employees table.

3. Press F5 to run the application.

4. Click Add.

   The application adds a new row.

5. Move to the last row of the DataSet by clicking the Move Last button.

   The application displays the new row.

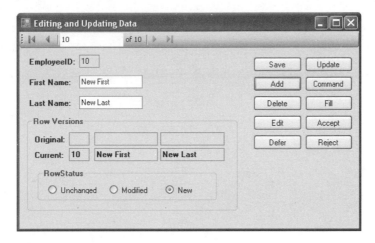

6. Close the application.

Add a Row to the DataTable: Visual C#

1. Press F7 to display the Code Editor.

2. Add the following code to the btnAdd_Click event handler:

```
DataRow drNew;

drNew = (AdoSbsDataSet.EmployeesRow)dsAdoSbs.Employees.NewRow();
drNew["FirstName"] = "New First";
drNew["LastName"] = "New Last";
dsAdoSbs.Employees.Rows.Add(drNew);
```

The first line declares the DataRow variable that will contain the new row. Then the NewRow method is called, instantiating the variable. Its fields are set, and it is added to the Rows collection of the Employees table.

3. Press F5 to run the application.

4. Click Add.

The application adds a new row.

5. Move to the last row of the DataSet by clicking the Move Last button.

The application displays the new row.

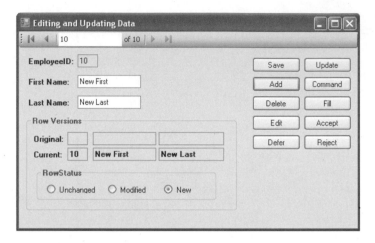

6. Close the application.

Deleting a DataRow

The DataTable's Rows collection supports three methods to remove DataRows, shown in Table 10-3. Each of these methods physically removes the DataRow from the collection.

Table 10-3   DataRowCollection Remove Methods

Method	Description
Clear()	Removes all rows from the DataTable.
Remove(dataRow)	Removes the specified DataRow.
RemoveAt(index)	Removes the DataRow at the specified position.

A row that has been physically removed from a DataTable by using one of these methods won't be deleted from the data source when the DataSet changes are persisted. If you need to delete the row from the data source as well as from the DataTable (as is the usual case), you must use the Delete method of the DataRow object instead.

The Delete method physically removes the DataRow only if it has been added to the DataTable since the last time AcceptChanges was called. Otherwise, it sets the RowState property to Deleted and sets the values of the Current version of the DataRow to Null.

> **Note**   The following exercise uses the MoveNext method of the BindingSource control, which we'll discuss in the Chapter 11. For now, you only need to know that this method makes the next DataRow in the DataTable the current row.

Delete a DataRow by Using the Delete Method: Visual Basic

1. In the Code Editor, add the following code to the btnDelete_Click event handler:

```
Dim dr As DataRow

dr = GetRow()

dr.Delete()
bsEmployees.MoveNext()
```

The GetRow procedure, which is not intrinsic to the Microsoft .NET Framework, is included in the scaffolding section of the exercise.

2. Press F5 to run the application.

3. Make sure that Nancy Davolio's data is displayed on the form.

4. Click Delete.

The application deletes the row, displays the next row, and changes the number of employees to 8.

5. Close the application.

Delete a DataRow by Using the Delete Method: Visual C#

1. In the Code Editor, add the following code to the btnDelete_Click event handler:

```
DataRow dr;

dr = GetRow();
dr.Delete();
bsEmployees.MoveNext();
UpdateDisplay();
```

The GetRow and UpdateDisplay procedures, which are not intrinsic to the .NET Framework, are included in the scaffolding section of the exercise.

2. Press F5 to run the application.

3. Make sure that Nancy Davolio's data is displayed on the form.

4. Click Delete.

    The application deletes the row, displays the next row, and changes the number of employees to 8.

5. Close the application.

Changing DataRow Values

Changing the value of a DataColumn couldn't be simpler—you reference the column by using the Item property of the DataRow, and then assign the new value to it by using a simple assignment operator.

The Item property is overloaded, supporting the versions shown in Table 10-4. However, the three versions of the property that specify the DataRowVersion are read-only and cannot be used to change the values. The other three versions, which return the Current version of the value, can be used to change values.

Table 10-4   DataRow.Item Versions

Version	Description
Item(columnName)	Returns the value of the DataColumn with the specified name.
Item(dataColumn)	Returns the value of the specified DataColumn.
Item(columnIndex)	Returns of the value of the DataColumn at the specified zero-based columnIndex position in the DataRow's Columns collection.
Item(columnName, rowVersion)	Returns the value of the specified rowVersion of the DataColumn with the specified name.
Item(dataColumn, rowVersion)	Returns the value of the specified rowVersion of the DataColumn.

Table 10-4 DataRow.Item Versions

Version	Description
Item(columnIndex, rowVersion)	Returns of the value of the specified rowVersion of the DataColumn at the specified zero-based columnIndex position in the DataRow's Columns collection.

Edit a DataRow: Visual Basic

1. Add the following code to the btnEdit_Click event handler:

```
Dim drCurrent As DataRow

drCurrent = GetRow()
drCurrent.Item("FirstName") = "Changed"
UpdateDisplay()
```

Again, the GetRow and UpdateDisplay procedures are part of the exercise scaffolding, not intrinsic to the .NET Framework.

2. Press F5 to run the application.

3. Click Edit.

The application changes the Current version of the FirstName column to Changed and changes the RowStatus to Modified.

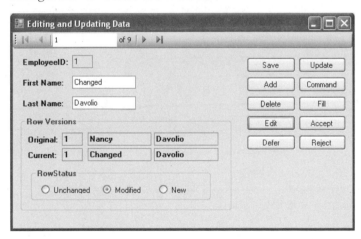

4. Close the application.

Edit a DataRow: Visual C#

1. Add the following code to the btnEdit_Click event handler:

```
DataRow drCurrent;

drCurrent = GetRow();
drCurrent["FirstName"] = "Changed";
UpdateDisplay();
```

Again, the GetRow and UpdateDisplay procedures are part of the exercise scaffolding, not intrinsic to the .NET Framework.

2. Press F5 to run the application.

3. Click Edit.

The application changes the Current version of the FirstName column to Changed and changes the RowStatus to Modified.

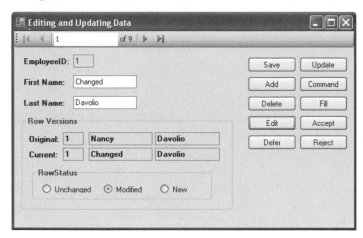

4. Close the application.

Deferring Changes to DataRow Values

Sometimes it's necessary to temporarily suspend validation of data until a series of edits have been completed, either for performance reasons or because rows will temporarily be in violation of business or integrity constraints.

The BeginEdit method of a DataRow does just that—it suspends the DataColumn and DataRow change events until either EndEdit or CancelEdit are called. During the editing process, assignments are made to the Proposed version of the DataRow instead of the Current version. This is the only time the Proposed version exists.

If the edit is completed by a call to EndEdit, the Proposed column values are copied to the Current version, and the Proposed version of the DataRow is removed from the DataSet. If the edit is completed by calling CancelEdit, the Proposed version of the DataRow is removed, leaving the Current versions unchanged. In effect, EndEdit and CancelEdit commit or roll-back changes, respectively.

Use BeginEdit to Defer Column Changes: Visual Basic

1. Add the following code to the btnDefer_Click event handler:

```
Dim drCurrent As DataRow

drCurrent = GetRow()
drCurrent.BeginEdit()
drCurrent.Item("FirstName") = "Proposed Name"
MessageBox.Show(drCurrent.Item("FirstName", DataRowVersion.Proposed))
drCurrent.CancelEdit()
```

2. Press F5 to run the application.

3. Click Defer.

   The application displays Proposed Name in a message box.

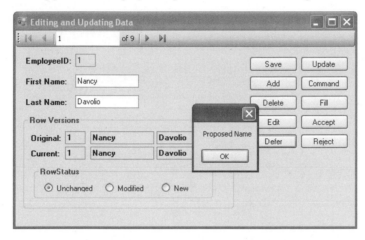

4. Click OK to close the message box.

   Because the edit was canceled, the Current value of the column and the RowStatus remain unchanged.

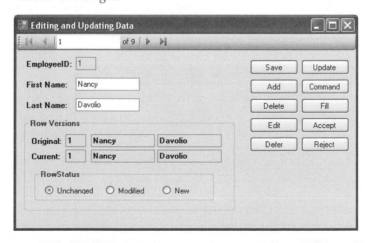

5. Close the application.

Use BeginEdit to Defer Column Changes: Visual C#

1. Add the following code to the btnDefer_Click event handler:

```
DataRow drCurrent;

drCurrent = GetRow();
drCurrent.BeginEdit();
drCurrent["FirstName"] = "Proposed Name";
MessageBox.Show(drCurrent["FirstName", DataRowVersion.Proposed].ToString());
drCurrent.CancelEdit();
```

2. Press F5 to run the application.

3. Click Defer.

   The application displays Proposed Name in a message box.

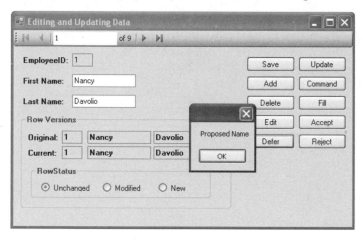

4. Click OK to close the message box.

   Because the edit was canceled, the Current value of the column and the RowStatus remain unchanged.

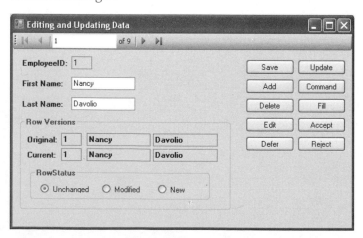

5. Close the application.

Updating Data Sources

After changes are made to the in-memory copy of the data represented by the DataSet, they can be persisted to the data source either by executing the appropriate Command objects against a Connection or by calling the Update method of the DataAdapter or TableAdapter.

Updating the Data Source by Using an Adapter

Both the TableAdapter and DataAdapter expose an Update method. The System.Data.Common.DbDataAdapter object, which is the DataAdapter class from which relational database Data Providers inherit their DataAdapters, supports a number of versions of the Update method, as shown in Table 10-5. All these methods are also exposed by the TableAdapter.

Table 10-5   DbDataAdapter Update Methods

Method	Description
Update(dataSet)	Updates the data source from a DataTable named Table in the DataSet.
Update(dataRows())	Updates the data source from the specified array of DataRows.
Update(dataTable)	Updates the data source from the specified DataTable.
Update(dataRows(), dataTableMapping)	Updates the data source from the specified array of DataRows by using the specified DataTableMapping.
Update(dataSet, dataTableName)	Updates the data source from the specified DataTableName string in the specified DataSet.

The Command object exposes a property called RowUpdated that controls whether the DataSet will be updated with any values that result from executing the SQL command on the data source. The possible values for the RowUpdated property are determined by the UpdateRowSource enumeration shown in Table 10-6.

Table 10-6   UpdateRowSource Enumeration

Value	Description
Both	Maps both the output parameters and the first returned row to the changed row in the DataSet.
FirstReturnedRecord	Maps the values in the first returned row to the changed row in the DataSet.
None	Ignores any output parameters or returned rows.
OutputParameters	Maps output parameters to the changed row in the DataSet.

By default, commands that are automatically generated for a DataAdapter or TableAdapter have their RowUpdated property set to None. Commands that are created by setting the CommandText property, either in code or by using the Query Builder, default to Both.

When the Update method of a DataAdapter is called, either directly or by means of a Table-Adapter, the following actions occur, in this order:

1. The DataAdapter examines the RowState of each row in the specified DataSet or Data-Table and then determines the appropriate Command to execute—InsertCommand, UpdateCommand or DeleteCommand.

2. The Parameters collection of the appropriate Command object is filled based on the SourceColumn and SourceVersion properties.

3. The RowUpdating event is raised.

4. The appropriate Command is executed.

5. Depending on the value of the OnRowUpdated property, which we'll discuss later in this section, the DataAdapter might update the row values in the DataSet.

6. The RowUpdated method is raised.

7. AcceptChanges is called on the DataSet or DataTable.

Update the Data Source by Using a DataAdapter: Visual Basic

1. Add the following code to the btnUpdate_Click event handler:

```
daEmployees.Update(dsAdoSbs.Employees)
UpdateDisplay()
```

2. Press F5 to run the application.

3. In the First Name text box, replace Nancy with **Changed**, and then click Save.

   The application sets the Current value of the column to Changed.

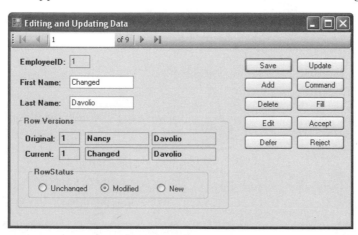

4. Click Update.

   The application updates the data source and then resets the contents of the DataSet.

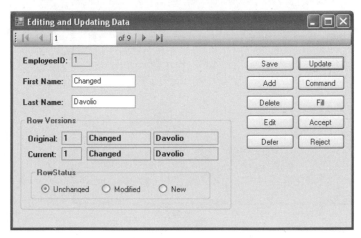

5. Close the application.

Update the Data Source by Using a DataAdapter: Visual C#

1. Add the following code to the btnUpdate_Click event handler:

```
daEmployees.Update(dsAdoSbs.Employees);
UpdateDisplay();
```

2. Press F5 to run the application.

3. In the First Name text box, replace Nancy with **Changed**, and then click Save.

   The application sets the Current value of the column to Changed.

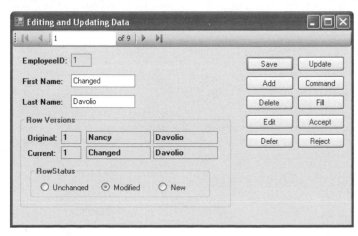

4. Click Update.

The application updates the data source and then resets the contents of the DataSet.

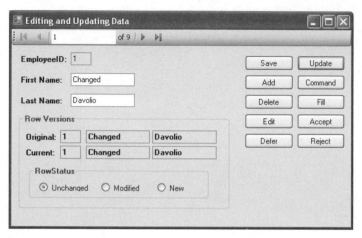

5. Close the application.

Updating the Data Source by Using a Data Command

The Update method, although convenient, isn't always the best choice for persisting changes to a data source. Sometimes, of course, you won't be using an adapter. Sometimes you'll be using a structure other than a DataSet to store the data. And sometimes, in order to maintain data integrity, you will need to perform operations in a particular order. In any of these situations, you can use Command objects to control the updates.

When the Update method is used to persist changes, it uses the SourceColumn and Source-Version properties to fill the Parameters collection. As we've seen, however, when executing a Command object directly, you must explicitly set the Parameter values.

Update the Data Source by Using a Data Command: Visual Basic

1. Add the following code to the btnCmd_Click event handler:

```vb
Dim drCurrent As DataRow

drCurrent = GetRow()

cmdUpdateEmployees.Parameters("@FirstName").Value = drCurrent("FirstName")
cmdUpdateEmployees.Parameters("@LastName").Value = drCurrent("LastName")
cmdUpdateEmployees.Parameters("@EmployeeID").Value = drCurrent("EmployeeID")

cnAdoSbs.Open()
cmdUpdateEmployees.ExecuteNonQuery()
cnAdoSbs.Close()
```

This code first creates two temporary variables, and then it sets them to the Update command of the daEmployees DataAdapter and to the row currently being displayed on the form, respectively. (Remember that GetRow is part of the exercise scaffolding.) The code then sets the three parameters in the Update command to the values of the row. Finally the connection is opened, the command is executed, and the connection is closed.

2. Add the following code to the btnFill_Click event handler:

```
dsAdoSbs.Employees.Clear()
daEmployees.Fill(dsAdoSbs.Employees)
UpdateDisplay()
```

This code reloads the data into the DataSet from the data source and then updates the version and status information of the form. (Remember that the UpdateDisplay method is part of the exercise scaffolding.)

3. Press F5 to run the application.

4. In the First Name text box, change Changed to **Nancy**, and then click Save.

The application updates the Current value of the DataRow.

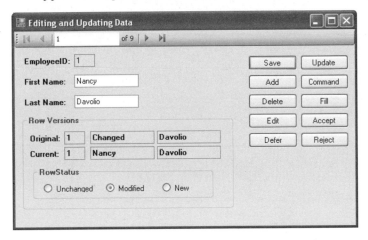

5. Click Command.

The application updates the data source, but because executing the command directly does not update the DataSet, the change isn't reflected in the form.

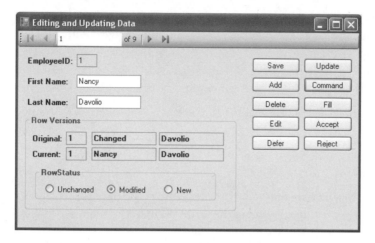

6. Click Fill.

The application reloads the data. Note that the First Name text has now been changed.

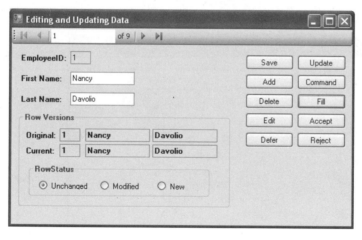

7. Close the application.

Update the Data Source by Using a Data Command: Visual C#

1. Add the following code to the btnCmd_Click event handler:

```
DataRow drCurrent;

drCurrent = GetRow();

cmdUpdateEmployees.Parameters["@FirstName"].Value = drCurrent["FirstName"];
cmdUpdateEmployees.Parameters["@LastName"].Value = drCurrent["LastName"];
cmdUpdateEmployees.Parameters["@EmployeeID"].Value = drCurrent["EmployeeID"];

cnAdoSbs.Open();
cmdUpdateEmployees.ExecuteNonQuery();
cnAdoSbs.Close();
```

This code first creates two temporary variables, and then it sets them to the Update command of the daEmployees DataAdapter and to the row currently being displayed on the form, respectively. (Remember that GetRow is part of the exercise scaffolding.) It then sets the three parameters in the Update command to the values of the row. Finally the connection is opened, the command is executed, and the connection is closed.

2. Add the following code to the btnFill_Click event handler:

```
dsAdoSbs.Employees.Clear();
daEmployees.Fill(dsAdoSbs.Employees);
UpdateDisplay();
```

This code reloads the data into the DataSet from the data source and then updates the version and status information of the form. (Remember that the UpdateDisplay method is part of the exercise scaffolding.)

3. Press F5 to run the application.

4. In the First Name text box, change Changed to **Nancy**, and then click Save.

The application updates the Current value of the DataRow.

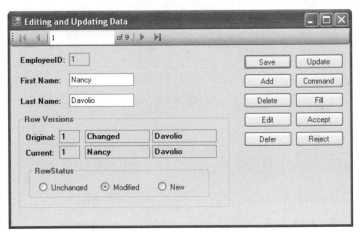

5. Click Command.

The application updates the data source, but because executing the command directly does not update the DataSet, the change isn't reflected in the form.

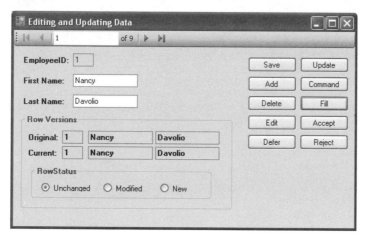

6.   Click Fill.

The application reloads the data. Note that the First Name text has now been changed.

7.   Close the application.

Accepting and Rejecting DataSet Changes

The final step in the process of updating data is to set a new baseline for the DataRows. This is done by using the AcceptChanges method. The DataAdapter's Update method calls AcceptChanges automatically. If you execute a command directly, you must call Accept-Changes to update the row state values.

If you want to discard instead of accept the changes made to the DataSet, you can call the RejectChanges method. RejectChanges returns the DataSet to the state it was in the last time AcceptChanges was called, discarding all new rows, restoring deleted rows, and returning all columns to their original values.

> **Important**   If you call AcceptChanges or RejectChanges prior to updating the data source,
> you lose the ability to persist the changes by using the Update method. The DataAdapter's
> Update method uses the RowStatus property to determine which rows to persist, and both
> AcceptChanges and RejectChanges set the RowStatus of every row to Unchanged.

The AcceptChanges Method

The AcceptChanges method is supported by the DataSet, DataTable and DataRow objects.
Under most circumstances, you need only call AcceptChanges on the DataSet because it calls
AcceptChanges for each DataTable that it contains, and the DataTable, in turn, calls Accept-
Changes for each DataRow.

When the AcceptChanges call reaches the DataRow, the Original values of each column in
rows with a RowStatus of either Added or Modified are changed to the Current values, and the
RowStatus is set to Unchanged. Deleted rows are removed from the Rows collection.

Accept Changes to a DataSet: Visual Basic

1. Add the following code to the end of the btnCmd_Click event handler created in the
previous exercise:

```
dsAdoSbs.AcceptChanges()
UpdateDisplay()
```

Your event handler should now be:

```
Dim drCurrent As DataRow

drCurrent = GetRow()

cmdUpdateEmployees.Parameters("@FirstName").Value = drCurrent("FirstName")
cmdUpdateEmployees.Parameters("@LastName").Value = drCurrent("LastName")
cmdUpdateEmployees.Parameters("@EmployeeID").Value = drCurrent("EmployeeID")

cnAdoSbs.Open()
cmdUpdateEmployees.ExecuteNonQuery()
cnAdoSbs.Close()

dsAdoSbs.AcceptChanges()
UpdateDisplay()
```

2. Add the same two lines to the btnAccept_Click event handler.

3. Press F5 to run the application.

4. In the Last Name text box, replace Davolio with **New**, and then click Save.

   The application updates the Current value.

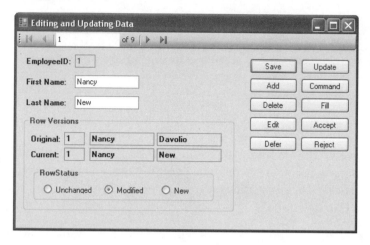

5. Click Command.

    Because the AcceptChanges method is called, the Version and RowStatus information is updated.

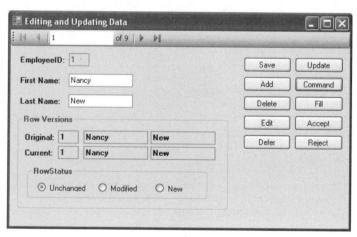

6. In the Last Name text box, change New back to **Davolio**, and then click Save.

    The application updates the Current value and Row Status.

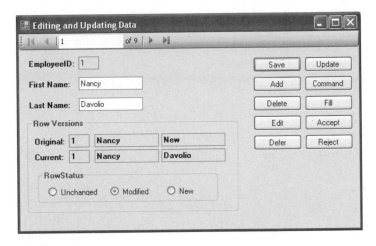

7. Click Accept.

   The application updates the Original value and Row Status.

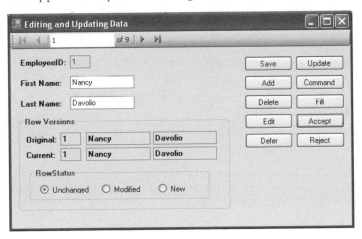

8. Click Update, and then click Fill.

   Because the RowStatus of the DataRow has been reset to Unchanged, no changes are persisted to the data source.

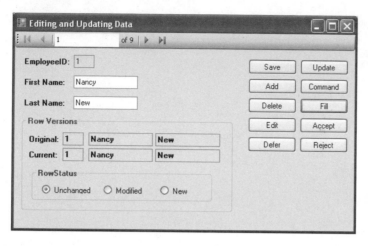

9. Close the application.

Accept Changes to a DataSet: Visual C#

1. Add the following code to the end of the btnCmd_Click event handler created in the previous exercise:

    ```
    dsAdoSbs.AcceptChanges();
    UpdateDisplay();
    ```

    Your event handler should now be:

    ```
    DataRow drCurrent;

    drCurrent = GetRow();

    cmdUpdateEmployees.Parameters["@FirstName"].Value = drCurrent["FirstName"];
    cmdUpdateEmployees.Parameters["@LastName"].Value = drCurrent["LastName"];
    cmdUpdateEmployees.Parameters["@EmployeeID"].Value = drCurrent["EmployeeID"];

    cnAdoSbs.Open();
    cmdUpdateEmployees.ExecuteNonQuery();
    cnAdoSbs.Close();

    dsAdoSbs.AcceptChanges();
    UpdateDisplay();
    ```

2. Add the same two lines to the btnAccept_Click event handler.

3. Press F5 to run the application.

4. In the Last Name text box, replace Davolio with **New**, and then click Save.

    The application updates the Current value.

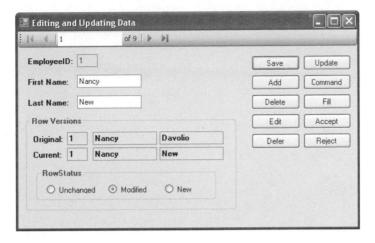

5. Click Command.

   Because the AcceptChanges method is called, the Version and RowStatus information is updated.

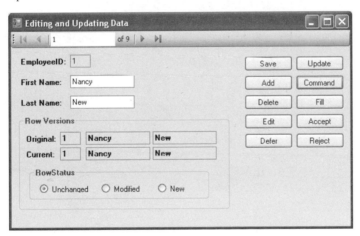

6. In the Last Name text box, change New back to **Davolio**, and then click Save.

   The application updates the Current value and Row Status.

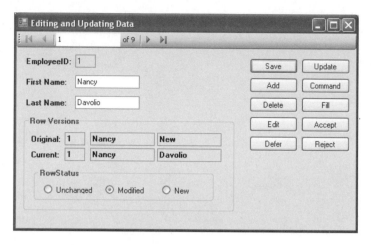

7. Click Accept.

   The application updates the Original value and Row Status.

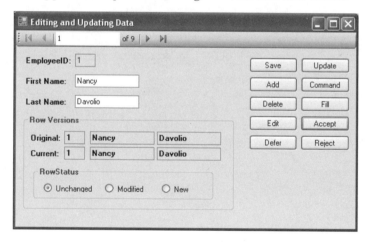

8. Click Update, and then click Fill.

   Because the RowStatus of the DataRow has been reset to Unchanged, no changes are persisted to the data source.

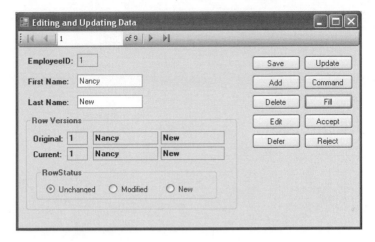

9. Close the application.

The RejectChanges Method

Like AcceptChanges, the RejectChanges method is supported by the DataSet, DataTable and DataRow objects, and each object cascades the call to the objects below it in the hierarchy.

When the RejectChanges call reaches the DataRow, the Current values of each column in rows with a RowStatus of either Deleted or Modified change to the Original values, and their RowStatus is set to Unchanged. Added rows are removed form the Rows collection.

Reject the Changes to a DataRow: Visual Basic

1. Add the following code to the btnReject_Click event handler:

```
dsAdoSbs.RejectChanges()
UpdateDisplay()
```

2. Press F5 to run the application.

3. In the First Name text box, change Nancy to **Reject**, and then click Save.

    The application updates the Current value and RowStatus.

4. Click Reject.

    The application returns the Current version of the row to its Original values and resets the RowStatus to Unchanged.

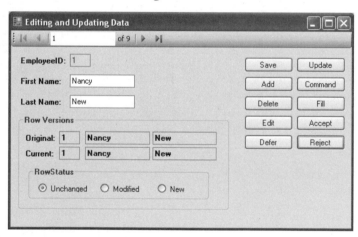

5. Close the application.

Reject the Changes to a DataRow: Visual C#

1. Add the following code to the btnReject_Click event handler:

    ```
    dsAdoSbs.RejectChanges();
    UpdateDisplay();
    ```

2. Press F5 to run the application.

3. In the First Name text box, change Nancy to **Reject**, and then click Save.

    The application updates the Current value and RowStatus.

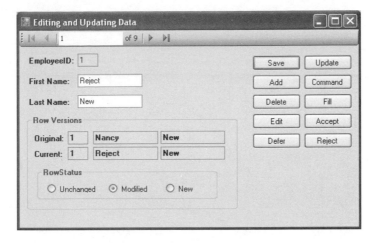

4. Click Reject.

    The application returns the Current version of the row to its Original values and resets the RowStatus to Unchanged.

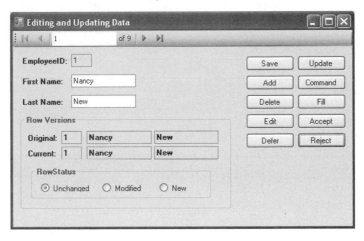

5. Close the application.

Summary

In this chapter we examined the four steps required to update a data source from a .NET Framework application: retrieving the data from the data source, modifying the in-memory copy, updating the data source and updating the DataSet.

We also examined the versions of the DataRow that are maintained by ADO.NET, and how the RowState property can be used to provide fine control over the editing process.

Chapter 11

Manual Data Binding in Windows Forms

After completing this chapter, you will be able to:

- Use various methods to simple-bind control properties.
- Use various methods to complex-bind control properties.
- Use CurrencyManager properties.
- Use the Binding object's properties.

In previous chapters we have bound data to controls on Windows Forms, but we haven't really looked at the process in any detail. We'll begin to do that in this chapter by examining the underlying mechanisms used to bind controls to Microsoft ADO.NET data sources. We'll continue our examination in Chapter 12, "Data Binding in Windows Forms by Using the BindingSource Component."

Understanding Data Binding in Windows Forms

The Microsoft .NET Framework provides an extremely powerful and flexible mechanism for binding data to control properties. Although in the majority of cases you will bind to the displayed value of a control—for example, the DisplayMember property of a ListBox control or the Text property of a TextBox control—you can bind any property of a control to a data source.

Because you can bind to any property, you can, for example, bind the background and foreground colors of a form and the font characteristics of its controls to a row in a database table. By using this technique, you could allow users to customize an application's user interface by simply updating a database without changing the code base, with all the maintenance issues that such a change would entail.

Data Sources

Windows Form controls can be bound to any data source, not just traditional database tables. Technically, to qualify as a data source, an object must implement the IList, IBindingList or IEditableObject interface.

The IList interface, the simplest of the three, is implemented by arrays and collections. This means that it's possible, for example, to bind the Text property of a Label control to the contents of a ListBox control's ObjectCollection (although it's difficult to think of a situation in which doing so might be useful). Any object that implements both the IList and the IComponent interfaces can be bound at design time as well as run time.

The IBindingList interface, which is implemented by the DataView and DataViewManager objects, supports change notification. Objects that implement this interface raise ListChanged events to notify the application when either an item in the list or the list itself has been changed.

Finally, the IEditableObject interface, which is implemented by the DataRowView object, exposes the BeginEdit, EndEdit and CancelEdit methods.

Fortunately, when you're working within ADO.NET, you can largely ignore the details of interface implementation. They're really only important if you're building your own data source objects.

Within the .NET Framework, the actual binding of data in a Windows Form is handled by a number of objects working in conjunction, as shown in the following graphic.

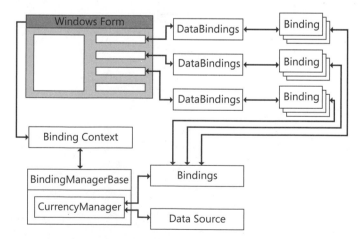

At the highest level in the logical architecture is the BindingContext object. The sole purpose of the BindingContext is to manage a collection of BindingManagerBase objects, one for each data source that is referenced by the form.

Any object that inherits from the Control class can contain a BindingContext. In most cases, you'll use the form's BindingContext, but if the form includes a container control, such as a Panel or a GroupBox that contains data-bound controls, it might be easier to create a separate BindingContext object for the contain control to avoid a level of indirection when referencing contained controls.

As stated, the BindingManagerBase is an abstract class, so instances of this object cannot be directly instantiated. Instead, the objects managed by the BindingContext object are actually instances of either the PropertyManager class or the CurrencyManager class.

If the data source can return only a single value, the BindingManagerBase object is an instance of the PropertyManager class. If the data source returns (or *can* return) a collection of objects, the BindingManagerBase object is an instance of the CurrencyManager class. ADO.NET objects always instantiate CurrencyManagers.

The CurrencyManager object keeps track of position in the list and manages the bindings to that data source. Note that the data source itself never knows which controls are bound to it or what item they display.

ADO

The CurrencyManager's Position property maintains the current row in a data set. ADO.NET data sources don't support cursors and therefore have no knowledge of the "current" row. This might seem awkward at first, but it is actually a more powerful architecture because it's now possible to maintain multiple "cursors" or pointers into a single data set.

There is a separate instance of the CurrencyManager object for each discrete data source. If all of the controls on a form bind to a single data source, there is a single CurrencyManager. For example, a form that contains text boxes displaying fields from a single table contains a single CurrencyManager object. However, if there are multiple data sources, as in a form that displays master/detail information, there is a separate CurrencyManager object for each data source.

Every Windows Form control contains a DataBinding collection that contains the Binding objects for that control. There will be one Binding for each data-bound property of the control. The Binding object, as we'll see, specifies the data source, the control that is being bound, and the property of the control that displays the data for simple-bound properties.

The CurrencyManager inherits a BindingsCollection property from the BindingManagerBase class. The BindingsCollection contains references to the Binding objects for each control.

Binding Controls to an ADO.NET Data Source

Windows Forms controls in the .NET Framework support two types of data binding:

- Control properties that contain a single value are simple-bound.
- Control properties that contain multiple values, such as the displayed contents of list boxes and data grids, are complex-bound.

Any given control can contain both simple-bound and complex-bound attributes. For example, the MonthCalendar control's MaxDate property, which determines the maximum allowable selected date, is a simple-bound property containing a single DateTime value, while its BoldedDates property, which contains an array of dates that are to be displayed in bold formatting, is a complex-bound property.

Simple-Binding Control Properties in Visual Studio

In the .NET Framework, any property of a control that contains a single value can be simple-bound to a single value in a data source.

Binding can take place either at design time or at run time. In either situation, you must specify three values:

- The name of the property to be bound
- The data source
- A navigation path within the data source that resolves to a single value

The navigation path consists of a period-delimited hierarchy of names. For example, to reference the ProductID column of the Products table in the dsAdoSbs DataSet, the navigation path would be Products.ProductID.

You can also include the TableName as part of the data source: dsAdoSbs.Products, in which case the navigation path is simply ProductID. As we'll see, while flexibility is a good thing, consistency is important.

The Visual Studio Properties window contains a DataBindings section that displays the properties that are most commonly data-bound. Other properties are available in the Formatting and Advanced Binding dialog box, which is displayed when you click the ellipsis button in the Advanced section of the Properties window. The Formatting and Advanced Binding dialog box provides design-time access to all the simple-bound properties of the selected control.

Bind a Property by Using the Properties Window

1. Open the Chapter 11 – Start project in Visual Studio, and if necessary, double-click Binding.vb (or Binding.cs if you're using C#) in the Solution Explorer.

    Visual Studio displays the form in the Form Designer.

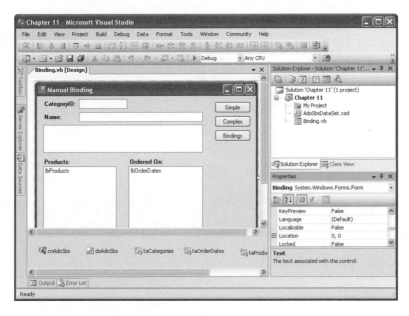

2. Select the tbCategoryID text box to the right of the CategoryID label.

3. In the Properties window, expand the DataBindings section, and then open the list for the Text property.

4. Expand the Other Data Sources node, expand the Binding List Instances node, expand dsAdoSbs, expand Categories, and then select CategoryID.

   Visual Studio binds the Text property to the CategoryID.

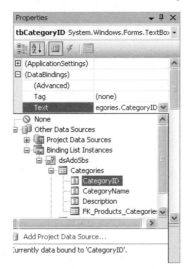

Bind a Property by Using the Formatting and Advanced Binding Dialog Box

1. In the Form Designer, select the tbCategoryName text box next to the Name label on the form.

2. In the Properties window, expand the DataBindings section (if necessary), select the Advanced field, and then click the ellipsis button after the Advanced property.

   Visual Studio opens the Formatting and Advanced Binding dialog box with the Text property selected.

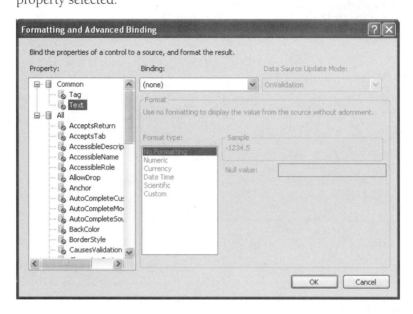

3. Open the Bindings list.

4. Expand the Other Data Sources node, expand the Binding List Instances node, expand dsAdoSbs, expand Categories, and then select CategoryName.

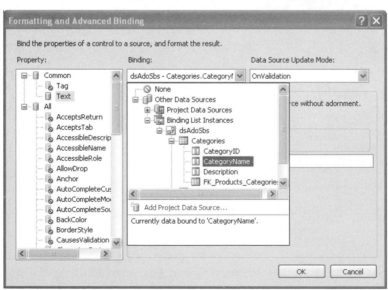

5. Click OK.

Visual Studio sets the data binding. Because Text is one of the default data-bound properties, its value is shown in the Properties window.

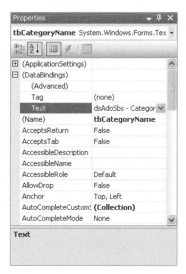

Simple-Binding Control Properties at Run Time

The .NET Framework provides a lot of flexibility in how you specify the data source and navigation path values when you create a binding at run time. For example, both of the following Binding objects will refer to the ProductID column of the Products table:

```
bndFirst = New System.Windows.Forms.Binding("Text", dsAdoSbs, _
   "Products.ProductsID")
bndSecond = New System.Windows.Forms.Binding("Text", _
   dsAdoSbs.Products, "ProductID")
```

However, because the data source properties are different, the .NET Framework creates different CurrencyManagers to manage them, and the controls on the form will not be synchronized.

This technique can be useful in some situations. For example, you might need to display two rows of a table on a single form, and this technique makes it easy to do so. However, in most cases, you'll want all the controls on a form to display information from the same row. To achieve that result you must be consistent in the way you specify the data source and navigation path values.

Tip   If you're creating a binding at run time that you want to synchronize with design-time bindings, specify only the top level of the hierarchy as the data source as follows:

```
bndFirst = New System.Windows.Forms.Binding("Text", _
   dsAdoSbs, "Products.ProductID")
```

As with many of the ADO.NET objects we've examined, to bind a control property at run time, you first create the Binding object and then add it to the control's DataBindings collection. The Binding object supports several versions of its constructor, as shown in Table 11-1.

Table 11-1   **Binding Constructor**

Method	Description
New(propertyName, dataSource, dataMember)	Creates a binding between the specified property and the specified data source and navigation path.
New(propertyName, dataSource, dataMember, formattingEnabled)	Creates a binding between the specified property and the specified data source and navigation path, displaying formatted data only if formattingEnabled is True.
New(propertyName, dataSource, dataMember, formattingEnabled, updateMode)	Creates a binding between the specified property and the specified data source and navigation path, displaying formatted data only if formattingEnabled is True, with the specified updateMode.
New(propertyName, dataSource, dataMember, formattingEnabled, updateMode, nullValue)	Creates a binding between the specified property and the specified data source and navigation path, displaying formatted data only if formattingEnabled is True, with the specified updateMode, displaying the object specified in nullValue if the value evaluates to dbNull.
New(propertyName, dataSource, dataMember, formattingEnabled, updateMode, nullValue, formatString)	Creates a binding between the specified property and the specified data source and navigation path, displaying formatted data only if formattingEnabled is True, with the specified updateMode and formatString, displaying the object specified in nullValue if the value evaluates to dbNull.
New(propertyName, dataSource, dataMember, formattingEnabled, updateMode, nullValue, formatString, formatInfo)	Creates a binding between the specified property and the specified data source and navigation path, displaying formatted data only if formattingEnabled is True, with the specified updateMode, formatString and formatInfo object, displaying the object specified in nullValue if the value evaluates to dbNull.

The versions of the constructor that specify an updateMode parameter accept one of the members of the DataSourceUpdateMode enumeration, which has the values shown in Table 11-2. The default setting for this property is OnPropertyChanged, and this is the setting you will use most often. However, if you use the Never setting, you can use the WriteValue method of the Binding to control when validation and formatting occur. We'll discuss WriteValue later in this chapter.

Table 11-2 DataSourceUpdateMode Enumeration

Value	Description
Never	The data source is never updated, and the values entered into the control are not parsed, validated or reformatted.
OnPropertyChanged	The data source is updated when the control property changes.
OnValidation	The data source is updated when the control property is validated, at which time the value is reformatted.

The last two versions of the constructor also take nullValue and formatString parameters. The nullValue object is used in the place of a dbNull value in the data source. Think of it as a kind of default value. The formatString object contains a series of special characters that are used to format the values in the data source. For details on format specifiers, see MSDN Help for the String class.

Bind a Property in Code: Visual Basic

1. Press F7 to display the Code Editor.

2. Add the following lines to the btnSimple_Click event handler:

```
Dim newBinding As System.Windows.Forms.Binding

newBinding = New System.Windows.Forms.Binding("Text", _
    dsAdoSbs, "Categories.Description")
tbCategoryDescription.DataBindings.Add(newBinding)
```

This code first declares a new Binding object and then instantiates it by passing the property name (Text), data source (dsAdoSbs) and navigation path (Categories.Description) to the constructor. Finally, the code adds the new Binding object to the DataBindings collection of the tbCategoryDescription control by using the Add method.

3. Press F5 to run the application.

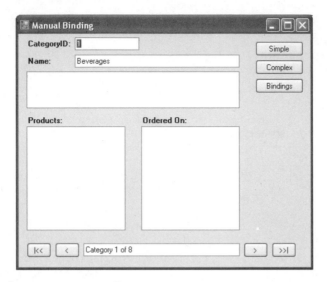

4. Click the Simple button.

   The application adds the binding and displays the value in the text box.

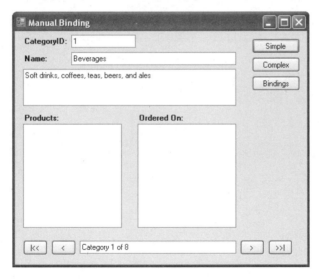

We'll examine the code that implements these buttons later in this chapter.

5. Click the Next Row button (>) at the bottom of the form.

   The application displays the next category, along with its description.

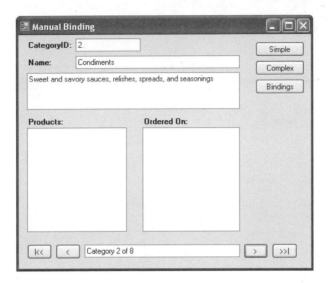

6. Close the application.

> **Important** If we had passed dsAdoSbs.Categories as the data source and Description as the navigation path to the Binding's constructor, the Description field would not display data from the current row because Visual Studio would have created a second CurrencyManager. When you create run-time bindings to be synchronized with design-time bindings, be sure to specify only the DataSet as the data source.

Bind a Property in Code: Visual C#

1. Press F7 to display the Code Editor.

2. Add the following lines to the btnSimple_Click event handler:

```
System.Windows.Forms.Binding newBinding;

newBinding = new System.Windows.Forms.Binding("Text",
    dsAdoSbs, "Categories.Description");
tbCategoryDescription.DataBindings.Add(newBinding);
```

This code first declares a new Binding object and then instantiates it by passing the property name (Text), data source (dsAdoSbs) and navigation path (Categories.Description) to the constructor. Finally, the code adds the new Binding object to the DataBindings collection of the tbCategoryDescription control by using the Add method.

3. Press F5 to run the application.

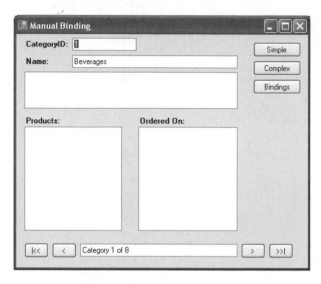

4. Click the Simple button.

   The application adds the binding and displays the value in the text box.

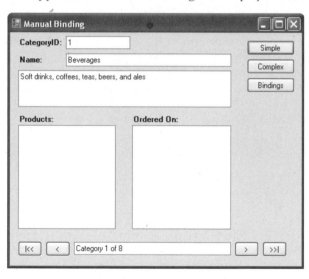

We'll examine the code that implements these buttons later in this chapter.

5. Click the Next Row button (>) at the bottom of the form.

   The application displays the next category, along with its description.

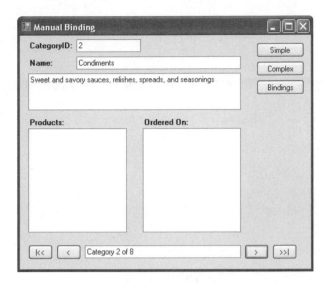

> **Important**   If we had passed dsAdoSbs.Categories as the data source and Description as the navigation path to the Binding's constructor, the Description field would not display data from the current row because Visual Studio would have created a second CurrencyManager. When you create run-time bindings to be synchronized with design-time bindings, be sure to specify only the DataSet as the data source.

    6. Close the application.

Complex-Binding Control Properties

Unlike simple-bound properties, which must be bound to a single value in the data source, complex-bound control properties can contain (and possibly display) multiple items. The most common examples of complex-bound control properties are, of course, the ListBox and ComboBox, but any control property that accepts multiple values can be complex-bound.

Although the techniques can vary somewhat depending on the specific control, most complex-bound controls are bound by setting the DataSource property directly rather than by adding a Binding object to the DataBindings collection.

The most common complex-bound controls, the ListBox and ComboBox, also expose a DisplayMember property that determines what the control displays. The DisplayMember property must resolve to a single value.

We'll examine the use of the ValueMember property to create look-up tables in Chapter 13.

In addition, the ListBox and ComboBox controls expose a ValueMember property, which allows the control to display a user-friendly value while also exposing a different value for programming purposes.

One particularly convenient possibility when using complex-bound controls is to bind to a relationship rather than a DataSet, which causes the items displayed in the control to be automatically filtered. We'll see an example of this technique in the following exercise.

Add a Complex Data Binding by Using the Properties Window

1. In the Form Designer, select the lbProducts list box.

2. In the Properties window, open the DataSource property, expand the Other Data Sources node, expand the Bindings List Instances node, and select dsAdoSbs.

3. Open the DisplayMember property, expand the Categories node, expand FK_Products_Categories, and then select the ProductName column.

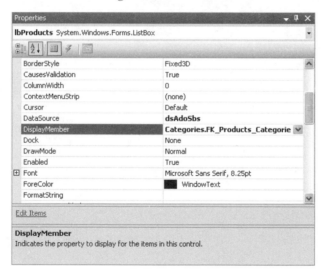

4. Press F5 to run the application.

Visual Studio displays the products in the current category.

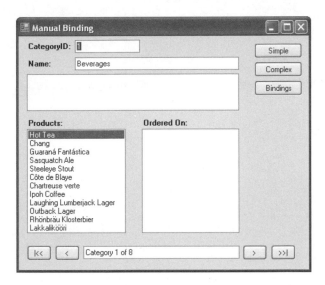

We'll examine the code that implements these buttons later in this chapter.

5. Click the Next button (>) at the bottom of the form.

   The application displays the next category, along with its products.

6. Close the application.

Add a Complex Data Binding in Code: Visual Basic

1. In the Code Editor, add the following code to the btnComplex_Click event handler:

   ```
   lbOrderDates.DataSource = dvOrderDates
   lbOrderDates.DisplayMember = "OrderDate"
   ```

   This code sets the DataSource to dvOrderDates and the DisplayMember property to the OrderDate column of the OrderDates DataTable.

2. Press F5 to run the application, and then click the Complex button.

   The OrderDates list box displays the dates for the product selected in the Products list box.

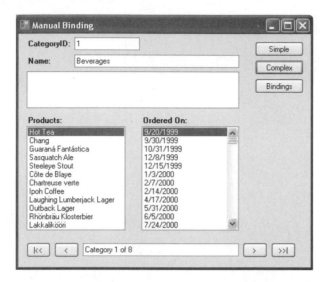

3. Select a different product to confirm that the dates displayed are changed.

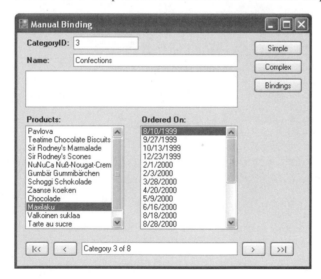

4. Close the application.

Add a Complex Data Binding in Code: Visual C#

1. In the Code Editor, add the following code to the btnComplex_Click event handler:

```
lbOrderDates.DataSource = dvOrderDates;
lbOrderDates.DisplayMember = "OrderDate";
```

This code sets the DataSource to dvOrderDates and the DisplayMember property to the OrderDate column of the OrderDates DataTable.

2. Press F5 to run the application, and then click the Complex button.

The OrderDates list box displays the dates for the product selected in the Products list box.

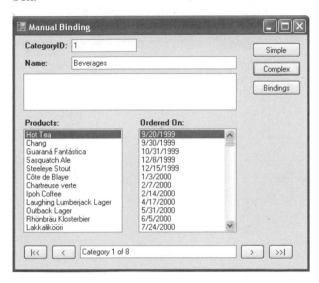

3. Select a different product to confirm that the dates displayed are changed.

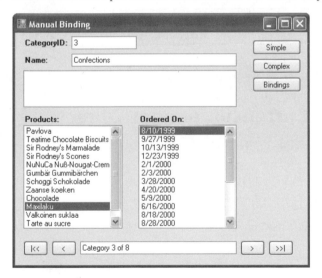

4. Close the application.

Understanding the BindingContext Object

As we've seen, the BindingContext object is the highest level object in the binding hierarchy. It manages the BindingManagerBase objects that control the interaction between a Data Source and the controls bound to it. The BindingContext object exposes no methods or events that are particularly useful, and only a single property, Item, that has two versions, which are shown in Table 11-3.

Table 11-3   BindingContext Item Versions

Version	Description
Item(dataSource)	Returns the BindingManagerBase object associated with the specified DataSource.
Item(dataSource, dataMember)	Returns the BindingManagerBase object associated with the DataSource and DataMember, where DataMember is either a DataTable or a Relation.

The first version of the Item property, which accepts only the data source as a parameter, is used if no navigation path is required. For example, if a DataTable is specified as the data source for a DataGridView, you can use the following syntax to retrieve the CurrencyManager that controls that binding:

```
myDGV.DataSource = myDataSet.myTable
myCurrencyMangager = BindingContext(myDataSet.myTable)
```

The second version of the Item property allows the specification of the navigation path. However, the navigation path provided here must resolve to a list, not a single property. For example, if a Text property is bound to the Description column of a DataTable, you can use the following syntax to retrieve the CurrencyManager that controls the binding:

```
myText.DataBindings.Add("Text", myDataSet, "myTable.Description")
myCurrencyManager = BindingContext(myDataSet, myTable)
```

Understanding the CurrencyManager Object

The CurrencyManager object is fundamental to the Windows Form data binding architecture. The CurrencyManager uses its properties, methods and events to manage the link between a data source and the controls that display data from that source.

The properties exposed by the CurrencyManager are shown in Table 11-4. With the exception of the Position property, they are all read-only.

Table 11-4   CurrencyManager Properties

Property	Description
Bindings	The collection of Binding objects managed by the CurrencyManager.
Count	The number of rows managed by the CurrencyManager.
Current	The value of the current object in the data source.
IsBindingSuspended	A value indicating whether binding is suspended.
List	The list managed by the CurrencyManager.
Position	Determines the current item in the list managed by the CurrencyManager.

The Bindings and List properties define the relationship between the data source and the controls bound to it. The Bindings property, which returns a BindingsCollection object, contains the Binding objects for each individual control that is bound to the data source. We'll examine the Binding object in detail later in this chapter.

The List property returns a reference to the data source that is managed by the Currency-Manager. The List property returns a reference to the IList interface. To treat the data source as its native type, such as a DataTable, in code, you must explicitly cast it to that type.

As might be expected, the Count property returns the number of rows in the list. Unlike some other environments, including ADO, the Count property is immediately available—it is not necessary to move to the end of the list before the Count property is set.

The Current property returns the value of the current row in the data source as an Object. As with the List property, if you want to treat the value returned by Current as its native type (typically a DataRowView), you must explicitly cast it.

The Position Property

Remember that the Current property is read-only. To change the current row in the data source, you must use the Position property, which is the only property exposed by the CurrencyManager that is not read-only. The Position property is an integer that represents the zero-based index into the List property.

The Position property is the key to navigating the List. Changing this property at run time will, as we've seen, change the Current row and update all data-bound controls.

Use the Position Property to Navigate a Data Source: Visual Basic

1. In the Code Editor, add the following code to the btnFirst_Click event handler:

```
BindingContext(dsAdoSbs, "Categories").Position = 0
UpdateDisplay()
```

This code sets the Position property of the CurrencyManager for the Categories Data-Table to the first row (remember that Position is a zero-based index) and then calls the UpdateDisplay function. UpdateDisplay, which is part of the exercise scaffolding, simply displays "Category x or y" in the text box at the bottom of the form.

2. Add the following code to the btnPrevious_Click event handler:

```
Dim bmb As BindingManagerBase
bmb = BindingContext(dsAdoSbs, "Categories")

If bmb.Position = 0 Then
   Beep()
Else
   bmb.Position -= 1
   UpdateDisplay()
End If
```

This code checks whether the Position property is already at 0 before decrementing it. The Position property does not throw an exception if it is set outside the bounds of the list, but the results are unpredictable.

3. The code for the remaining navigation buttons is already in place, so press F5 to run the application.

4. Use the navigation buttons to move through the display.

5. Close the application.

Use the Position Property to Navigate a Data Source: Visual C#

1. In the Code Editor, add the following code to the btnFirst_Click event handler:

```
BindingContext[dsAdoSbs, "Categories"].Position = 0;
UpdateDisplay();
```

This code sets the Position property of the CurrencyManager for the Categories Data-Table to the first row (remember that Position is a zero-based index) and then calls the UpdateDisplay function. UpdateDisplay, which is part of the exercise scaffolding, simply displays "Category x or y" in the text box at the bottom of the form.

2. Add the following code to the btnPrevious_Click event handler:

```
BindingManagerBase bmb;
bmb = BindingContext[dsAdoSbs, "Categories"];

if (bmb.Position == 0)
    Console.Beep();
else
{
    bmb.Position -= 1;
    UpdateDisplay();
}
```

This code checks whether the Position property is already at 0 before decrementing it. The Position property does not throw an exception if it is set outside the bounds of the list, but the results are unpredictable.

3. The code for the remaining navigation buttons is already in place, so press F5 to run the application.

4. Use the navigation buttons to move through the display.

5. Close the application.

CurrencyManager Methods

The commonly used public methods exposed by the CurrencyManager object are shown in Table 11-5.

Table 11-5   CurrencyManager Methods

Method	Description
AddNew	Adds a new item to the underlying list.
CancelCurrentEdit	Cancels the current edit operation.
EndCurrentEdit	Commits the current edit operation.
GetItemProperties	Returns the property descriptor collection for the data source.
Refresh	Redisplays the contents of bound controls.
RemoveAt(index)	Removes the item at the position specified by Index.
ResumeBinding	Resumes data binding and data validation after SuspendBinding has been called.
SuspendBinding	Temporarily suspends data binding and data validation.

The data editing methods AddNew and RemoveAt, which respectively add and remove items from the data source, along with the CancelCurrentEdit and EndCurrentEdit methods, are for use only within complex-bound controls. Unless you are creating a custom version of a complex-bound control, use the equivalent methods of the DataView or DataRowView.

We'll examine the Suspend-Binding and ResumeBinding methods in Chapter 13.

The SuspendBinding and ResumeBinding methods allow binding (and hence data validation) to be temporarily suspended. These methods are typically used when data validation requires that values be entered into multiple fields before they are validated.

The Refresh method is used only with data sources that don't support change notification, such as collections and arrays.

Responding to CurrencyManager Events

The events exposed by the CurrencyManager are shown in Table 11-6.

Table 11-6   CurrencyManager Events

Event	Description
BindingComplete	Occurs at the end of the binding process.
CurrentChanged	Occurs when the bound value changes.
CurrentItemChanged	Occurs when the state of the bound value changes.
DataError	Occurs when an error occurs.
ItemChanged	Occurs when the current item has changed.
ListChanged	Occurs when the list, or an item within the list, changes.
MetaDataChanged	Occurs when the metadata of the list changes.
PositionChanged	Occurs when the Position property is changed.

The CurrentChanged and PositionChanged events both occur whenever the current row in the CurrencyManager's list changes. The difference is the event arguments passed into the event: PositionChanged receives the standard System.EventArgs, while ItemChanged receives an argument of the type ItemChangedEventArgs, which includes an Index property.

The ItemChanged Event

The ItemChanged event occurs when the underlying data is changed. Under most circumstances, when working with ADO.NET objects, you use the Changed or Changing events of the DataRow or DataColumn because they provide greater flexibility. But there is nothing to prevent you from responding to the CurrencyManager's ItemChanged event if doing so is more convenient.

Respond to an ItemChanged Event: Visual Basic

1. In the Code Editor, add the following code to the Position_Changed event handler:

```vb
Dim strMsg As String

strMsg = "Row "
strMsg &= (BindingContext(dsAdoSbs, _
    "Categories").Position + 1).ToString()
MessageBox.Show(strMsg)
```

This code simply displays the current row number in a message box.

2. Press F5 to run the application, and then click the Next button (>).

The application displays a message box showing the new row number.

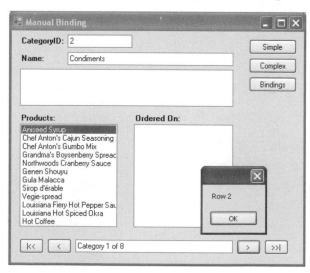

3. Close the message box and the application.

Respond to an ItemChanged Event: Visual C#

1. In the Code Editor, add the following code to the Position_Changed event handler:

```
string strMsg;

strMsg = "Row ";
strMsg += (BindingContext[dsAdoSbs,
   "Categories"].Position + 1).ToString();
MessageBox.Show(strMsg);
```

   This code simply displays the current row number in a message box.

2. Press F5 to run the application, and then click the Next button (>).

   The application displays a message box showing the new row number.

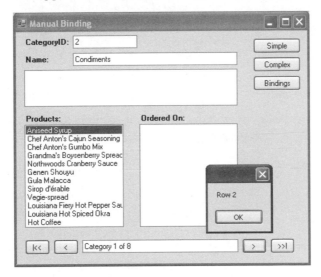

3. Close the application.

Understanding the Binding Object

The Binding object represents the link between simple-bound control properties and the CurrencyManager. As we've seen, the control's DataBindings collection contains a Binding object for each bound property.

Configuring the Binding Object

The properties exposed by the Binding object are shown in Table 11-7.

Table 11-7   Binding Properties

Property	Description
BindableComponent	The control with which the Binding is associated.
BindingManagerBase	The BindingManagerBase that manages this Binding object.
BindingMemberInfo	Returns information regarding this Binding object based on the DataMember specified in its constructor.
Control	The control to which the binding belongs.
ControlUpdateMode	Determines how changes to the data source are propagated to the bound property.
DataSource	The data source for the binding.
DataSourceNullValue	The value to be stored in the data source if the control value is null or empty.
DataSourceUpdateMode	Determines how changes in the bound property are propagated to the data source.
FormatInfo	The IFormatProvider used to format data before display.
FormatString	The format specifier characters used to format data before display.
FormattingEnabled	Determines whether formatting is applied to the data.
IsBinding	Indicates whether the binding is active.
NullValue	The object displayed if the value in the data source is dbNull.
PropertyName	The name of the bound property.

We've seen the majority of these properties in relation to the New constructor. Of the remaining properties, the BindingManagerBase property returns the CurrencyManager or Property-Manager that manages the Binding object, while the Control and PropertyName properties specify the control property bound to the data.

The IsBinding property indicates whether the binding is active. It returns True unless SuspendBinding has been evoked.

The BindingMemberInfo Property

The DataSource property returns the data source to which the property is bound as an object. Note that it returns the data source only, not the navigation path. To retrieve the Binding object's navigation path, you must use the BindingMemberInfo property. The fields of this complex object are shown in Table 11-8.

Table 11-8   BindingMemberInfo Properties

Property	Description
BindingField	The data source property specified by the Binding object's navigation path.
BindingMember	The complete navigation path of the Binding object.
BindingPath	The navigation path up to, but not including, the data source property.

The BindingMember property of the BindingMemberInfo property represents the entire navigation path of the binding, while the BindingField represents only the final field. The Binding-Path field represents everything up to the BindingField. For example, given the navigation path "Categories.CategoryProducts.ProductID," the BindingField is "ProductID" while the BindingPath is "Categories.CategoryProducts." Note that all three properties return a string value, not an object reference.

Examine the BindingMemberInfo Property: Visual Basic

1. In the Code Editor, add the following code to the btnBindings_Click event handler:

    ```
    Dim strMsg As String
    Dim bmo As System.Windows.Forms.BindingMemberInfo

    bmo = tbCategoryID.DataBindings(0).BindingMemberInfo
    strMsg = "BindingMember: " + bmo.BindingMember.ToString()
    strMsg += vbCrLf & "BindingPath:   " + bmo.BindingPath.ToString()
    strMsg += vbCrLf & "BindingField:  " + bmo.BindingField.ToString()
    MessageBox.Show(strMsg)
    ```

    The first two lines of code declare local variables to be used in the method. The third line assigns the BindingMemberInfo property of the first (and only) Binding object in the tbCategoryID.DataBindings collection to the bmo variable. The remaining lines display the properties of bmo in a message box.

2. Press F5 to run the application, and then click the Bindings button.

    The application displays the BindingMemberInfo properties in a dialog box.

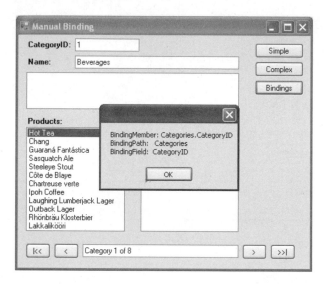

3. Close the application.

Examine the BindingMemberInfo Property: Visual C#

1. In the Code Editor, add the following code to the btnBindings_Click event handler:

```
string strMsg;
System.Windows.Forms.BindingMemberInfo bmo;

bmo = tbCategoryID.DataBindings[0].BindingMemberInfo;
strMsg = "BindingMember: " + bmo.BindingMember.ToString();
strMsg += "\nBindingPath:   " + bmo.BindingPath.ToString();
strMsg += "\nBindingField:  " + bmo.BindingField.ToString();
MessageBox.Show(strMsg);
```

The first two lines of code declare local variables to be used in the method. The third line assigns the BindingMemberInfo property of the first (and only) Binding object in the tbCategoryID.DataBindings collection to the bmo variable. The remaining lines display the properties of bmo in a message box.

2. Press F5 to run the application, and then click the Bindings button.

The application displays the BindingMemberInfo properties in a dialog box.

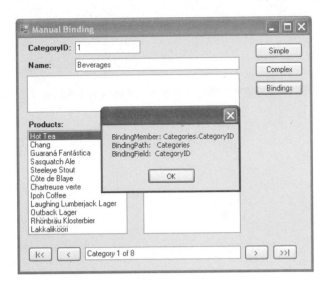

3. Close the application.

Using Binding Object Methods

The two most interesting methods exposed by the Binding object are shown in Table 11-9.

Table 11-9   Binding Methods

Method	Description
ReadValue	Sets the bound property to the value in the data source.
WriteValue	Sets the value in the data source to the value in the bound property.

These two methods are used to manually pull data from the data source to the bound property, and push it from the property to the data source, respectively. They are most often used when binding is suspended by using the SuspendBinding method.

Responding to Binding Object Events

We'll examine the Format and Parse events in Chapter 13.

The events exposed by the Binding object are shown in Table 11-10. These events are used to control the way data is displayed to the user.

Table 11-10   Binding Events

Event	Description
BindingComplete	Occurs when a binding operation is completed.
Format	Occurs when data is pushed from the data source to the control, or pulled from the control to the data source.
Parse	Occurs when data is pulled from the control to the data source.

Summary

In this chapter we examined the mechanics of data binding Windows Form control properties by using the low-level ADO.NET objects. We saw how to control properties at design time and run time, and examined the use of the CurrencyManager and the Binding object. In the next chapter we'll examine the BindingSource control, which automates much of this functionality, but at the cost of low-level control.

Chapter 12

Data Binding in Windows Forms by Using the BindingSource Component

After completing this chapter, you will be able to:

- Add a BindingSource to a form in Visual Studio.
- Create a BindingSource at run time.
- Bind a BindingSource component in Visual Studio.
- Bind a BindingSource component at run time.
- Set the Sort and Filter properties of a BindingSource.
- Add an item to an unbound BindingSource.
- Respond to BindingSource Events.

In Chapter 11, "Manual Data Binding in Windows Forms," we examined the low-level components that implement data binding on Windows Forms. As we've seen, the architecture is complex, and manipulating it can be, frankly, somewhat tedious.

The BindingSource class, new to Microsoft ADO.NET 2.0, acts as an intermediary between a data source and Windows Form controls, and both extends and simplifies the data-binding process.

Understanding the BindingSource

The BindingSource is a Windows Form component, implemented in the System.Windows.Forms namespace, and thus not technically part of ADO.NET. Although it performs much the same purpose as the BindingContext and CurrencyManager objects that we examined in Chapter 11, it can be usefully instantiated as an independent object. (The Binding-Context and CurrencyManager objects are most often used as encapsulated objects.)

The BindingSource encapsulates a CurrencyManager, and as we'll see, many of its properties and methods correspond directly to those of the CurrencyManager. However, the Binding-Source both simplifies and extends the data binding architecture based on the Currency-Manager in several important ways.

The BindingSource provides a level of indirection between the data source and the controls bound to it. This means, for example, that if the data source changes (as it does with distressing frequency), you need only change the DataSource and DataMember properties of the BindingSource and all the controls bound to it will draw their data from the new data source. This is much simpler than rebinding and reconfiguring all the controls on a form.

The BindingSource also extends the range of objects that can be used as a data source for bound controls. "Traditional" ADO.NET data binding requires that the data source support the IList interface. Objects that implement IList provide the means for individual items to be accessed by their index position. In reality, this functionality isn't sufficient for most applications, and you will most often use an object that implements a more powerful descendent of IList, usually IBindingList, which extends the basic IList functionality by supporting sorting and change notification.

Not only does the BindingSource extend the range of object types that can be used as data sources, but for those objects that don't support change notification, the BindingSource provides that functionality as well.

You can also use the BindingSource itself as a data source. Rather than setting the DataSource and DataMember properties of a BindingSource, you can manipulate its List property, which contains an instance of an IList object. The IList class exposes the normal complement of list manipulation commands—Add, Remove, Clear, and so on—that can be used to add and remove items that will be displayed by the controls bound to the BindingSource.

> **Note**   These two techniques are mutually exclusive. You cannot, for example, add temporary rows to a DataTable by manipulating the List property. Once the DataSource property of a BindingSource is set, calling the Add method generates a run-time error.

Not surprisingly, the methods and properties of the BindingSource correspond closely to the CurrencyManager. (Remember that the BindingSource component encapsulates a Currency-Manager object.)

The BindingSource is somewhat simpler to use than the CurrencyManager. It exposes properties of the CurrencyManager.List directly, for example, thereby saving a level of indirection. It also provides methods that perform common tasks. For example, we saw in Chapter 11 that to display the previous row of a DataSet by using a CurrencyManager, you use code like the following:

```
Dim bmb As BindingManagerBase
bmb = BindingContext(dsAdoSbs, "Categories")

bmb.Position -= 1
```

Compare those four lines with the following single-line method call, which uses a Binding-Source to accomplish the same thing:

```
myBindingSource.MovePrevious
```

We'll see other examples of this kind of simplification as we examine the properties and methods in detail in this chapter. For this reason, while it's always important to understand what's going on behind the scenes, the BindingSource is the recommended method for data binding Windows Forms in the Microsoft .NET Framework.

Creating BindingSource Components

BindingSource components can be created and configured at both design time and run time.

Creating BindingSource Components at Design Time

The BindingSource is included by default in the Data section of the Visual Studio Toolbox, and an instance of the control can be added to a form just like any other Toolbox control: by dragging it onto the form design surface.

Create a BindingSource in Visual Studio

1. Open the Chapter 12 – Start project in Visual Studio, and, if necessary, double-click BindingSources.vb (or BindingSources.cs if you're using C#) in the Solution Explorer.

   Visual Studio displays the form in the Form Designer.

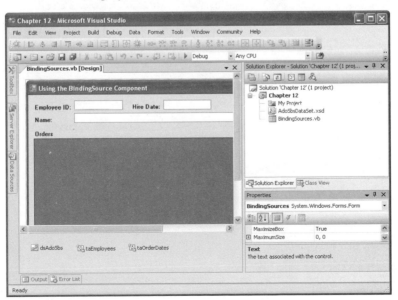

2. Drag a BindingSource Component from the Data section of the Toolbox onto the form design surface.

    Visual Studio adds the component to the component tray.

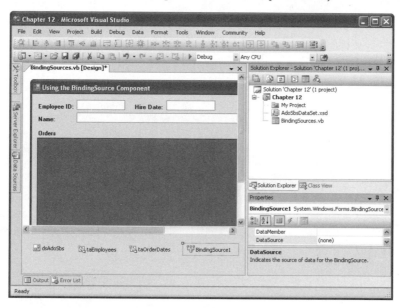

3. In the Properties window, change the name of the component to **bsOrders**.

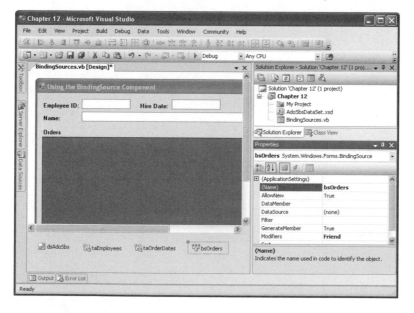

Creating BindingSource Components at Run Time

The BindingSource supports three versions of the New constructor, as shown in Table 12-1. Of these, the third version, which accepts DataSource and DataMember parameters, is the most commonly used.

Table 12-1   BindingSource Constructor

Method	Description
New()	Creates a new BindingSource with default property values.
New(IContainer)	Creates a new BindingSource with default property values and adds it to the specified Container.
New(dataSource, dataMember)	Creates a new BindingSource and sets its DataSource and DataMember properties to the values provided.

Create a BindingSource Component in Code Visual Basic

1. Press F7 to display the Code Editor.

2. Add the following line to the top of the class declaration, above the BindingSource_Load procedure:

```
Dim bsEmployees As BindingSource
```

The beginning of your class file should be:

```
Imports System.Data
Imports System.Data.SqlClient
Imports System.Windows.Forms
Public Class BindingSources

    Dim bsEmployees As BindingSource

    Private Sub BindingSources_Load(ByVal sender As System.Object, _
        ByVal e As System.EventArgs) Handles MyBase.Load

        taOrderTotals.Fill(dsAdoSbs.OrderTotals)
        taEmployees.Fill(dsAdoSbs.Employees)
    End Sub
```

3. Add the following code to the btnCreateEmployees_Click event handler:

```
bsEmployees = New BindingSource()
```

Create a BindingSource Component in Code: Visual C#

1. Press F7 to display the Code Editor.

2. Add the following line to the top of the class declaration, above the BindingSource constructor:

```
BindingSource bsEmployees;
```

The beginning of your class file should be:

```
using System;
using System.Collections.Generic;
using System.ComponentModel;
using System.Data;
using System.Data.SqlClient;
using System.Drawing;
using System.Text;
using System.Windows.Forms;

namespace Chapter_12
{
    public partial class BindingSources : Form
    {
        BindingSource bsEmployees;
        public BindingSources()
        {
            InitializeComponent();
        }

        private void BindingSources_Load(object sender, EventArgs e)
        {
            taOrderDates.Fill(dsAdoSbs.OrderDates);
            taEmployees.Fill(dsAdoSbs.Employees);
        }
    }
```

3. Add the following code to the btnCreateEmployees_Click event handler:

```
bsEmployees = new BindingSource();
```

Configuring BindingSource Components

Of the many properties exposed by the BindingSource component, the most commonly used are shown in Table 12-2.

Table 12-2   **BindingSource Properties**

Properties	Method	CurrencyManager	IList
AllowNew	Determines whether items can be added to the list managed by the BindingSource.		
Count	Returns the number of items in the list managed by the BindingSource.	X	
Current	Returns the current item in the list managed by the BindingSource.	X	
DataMember	Determines the list within the data source to which the BindingSource is bound.		
DataSource	Determines the data source to which the BindingSource is bound.		

Table 12-2   BindingSource Properties

Properties	Method	CurrencyManager	IList
Filter	Determines the expression that is used to filter items in the list managed by the BindingSource.		
IsBindingSuspended	Indicates whether binding is currently suspended.	X	
Item	Returns the element in the list managed by the BindingSource at the specified index position.		X
List	The list managed by the BindingSource.	X	
Position	Determines the current item in the list managed by the BindingSource.	X	
RaiseListChangedEvents	Determines whether the BindingSource raises ListChanged events.		
Sort	Determines the expression that is used to sort the items in the list managed by the BindingSource.		

Notice that the majority of these properties mirror the properties of the encapsulated CurrencyManager or IList objects. However, the properties are not one-to-one. The Currency-Manager exposes the Bindings property, which is not directly accessible from the Binding-Source. The IBindingList exposes the AllowEdit and AllowRemove properties, which are also not directly accessible.

On the other hand, the CurrencyManager doesn't expose the DataSource and DataMember properties of the BindingSource, which determine the source of the BindingSource data. The Sort and Filter properties, which in traditional ADO.NET data binding are exposed by the DataView, are supported directly by the BindingSource.

DataSource and DataMember Properties

As we've seen, the BindingSource can be used directly as a data source, without reference to any underlying data objects. If the DataSource property is null and an item is added to the BindingSource list by using the Add method, a new IBindingList is created, which contains the new item. Note that the list cannot be heterogeneous—all added items must be the same object type.

The unbound BindingSource as an independent data source can be useful in the following situations:

- The list is relatively small.
- Its members are all known at run time.
- There is no need to persist any changes.

However, the BindingSource component is most often used as an intermediary between a data source and bound controls—the component is bound to the data source, and the controls are bound to the component. The BindingSource is bound to a data source by setting the Data-Source property and, optionally, the DataMember property.

You can set the DataSource property to lists that implement a wide variety of list interfaces, including:

- IList objects, such as the Array
- IEnumerable objects, such as DataReaders
- IBindingList objects, such as the DataViewManager
- IBindingListView objects, such as the DataView
- IListSouce objects, such as the DataSet
- ITypedList objects

This range of interface classes is, in fact, far broader than the range that can be bound to controls directly. Notice, for example, that by using the BindingSource, you can bind a control to a DataReader. This technique avoids the overhead of a DataSet while still providing users with the ability to navigate through the data rows. This technique is most often useful when you need read-only access to the data.

In addition, the BindingSource provides change notification for objects that do not provide it themselves, such as Arrays, which implement only the IList interface. Although it was theoretically possible to bind controls to Arrays in earlier versions of ADO.NET, the technique was of limited use because changes to the underlying array were not reflected in the bound controls. The BindingSource provides an elegant solution to that problem.

The DataSource property of the BindingSource component need not even be bound to an instance of a class; you can bind it to a Type, or even to the results of a method call. This ability lies outside the scope of a book about ADO.NET, but it can be extraordinarily useful, and it represents a significant expansion of the Windows Form data-binding functionality.

Whatever the object, type or class to which your BindingSource is bound, if it contains more than one list item—as can be the case with an ADO.NET DataSet, for example—you must also set the DataMember property to the specific list from which the BindingSource will draw its data. As we saw in the Chapter 11, this behavior is typical of any complex-bound object.

Set the DataMember and DataSource Properties in Visual Studio

1. In the Form Designer, select the bsOrders control in the component tray.

2. In the Properties window, open the DataSource list, expand the Other Data Sources node, expand the BindingSources List Instances node, and then select dsAdoSbs.

3.   Open the DataMember list, and then select OrderTotals.

4.   Select the dgvOrders DataGridView.

5.   In the Properties window, open the DataSource list, and then select bsOrders.

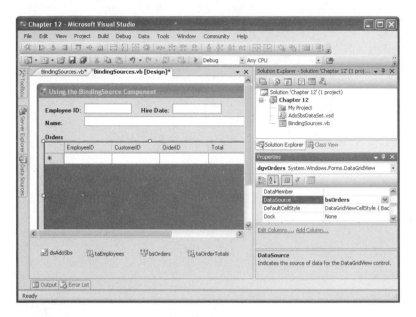

Set the DataMember and DataSource Properties in Code: Visual Basic

1. In the Code Editor, add the following lines to the end of the btnCreateEmployees_Click event handler, below the line you added earlier:

```
bsEmployees.DataSource = dsAdoSbs
bsEmployees.DataMember = "Employees"

tbEmployeeID.DataBindings.Add("Text", bsEmployees, "EmployeeID")
tbHireDate.DataBindings.Add("Text", bsEmployees, "HireDate")
tbFullName.DataBindings.Add("Text", bsEmployees, "FullName")
```

The first two lines set the DataSource and DataMember properties of the bsEmployees BindingSource that you created earlier. The last three lines bind the Textbox controls on the form to the new BindingSource. The body of your procedure should now be:

```
bsEmployees = New BindingSource()
bsEmployees.DataSource = dsAdoSbs
bsEmployees.DataMember = "Employees"

tbEmployeeID.DataBindings.Add("Text", bsEmployees, "EmployeeID")
tbHireDate.DataBindings.Add("Text", bsEmployees, "HireDate")
tbFullName.DataBindings.Add("Text", bsEmployees, "FullName")
```

2. Press F5 to run the application.

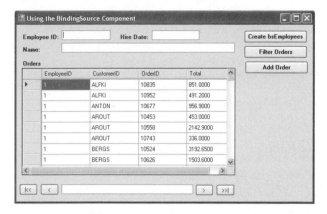

3. Click the Create bsEmployees button.

   The application displays the EmployeeID, HireDate and FullName data for the first employee.

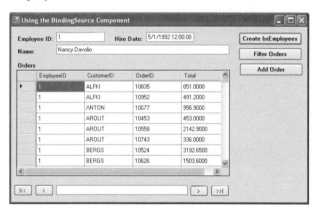

4. Close the application.

Set the DataMember and DataSource Properties in Code: Visual C#

1. In the Code Editor, add the following lines to the end of the btnCreateEmployees_Click event handler, below the line you added earlier:

```
bsEmployees.DataSource = dsAdoSbs;
bsEmployees.DataMember = "Employees";

tbEmployeeID.DataBindings.Add("Text", bsEmployees, "EmployeeID");
tbHireDate.DataBindings.Add("Text", bsEmployees, "HireDate");
tbFullName.DataBindings.Add("Text", bsEmployees, "FullName");
Your procedure should now be:
bsEmployees = new BindingSource();

bsEmployees.DataSource = dsAdoSbs;
bsEmployees.DataMember = "Employees";
```

```
tbEmployeeID.DataBindings.Add("Text", bsEmployees, "EmployeeID");
tbHireDate.DataBindings.Add("Text", bsEmployees, "HireDate");
tbFullName.DataBindings.Add("Text", bsEmployees, "FullName");
```

The first two lines set the DataSource and DataMember properties of the bsEmployees BindingSource that you created earlier. The last three lines bind the Textbox controls on the form to the new BindingSource.

2. Press F5 to run the application.

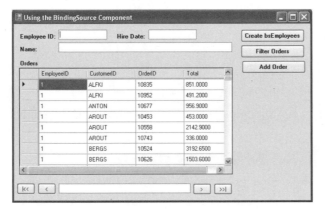

3. Click the Create bsEmployees button.

The application displays the EmployeeID, HireDate and FullName data for the first employee.

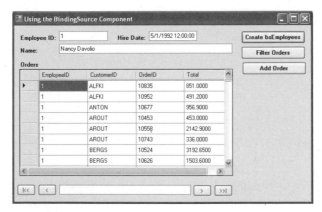

4. Close the application.

Sort and Filter Properties

The Sort and Filter properties of the BindingSource behave somewhat differently depending on the list managed by the BindingSource. If the underlying data source is an IBindingList, the Sort property accepts only a string representing the column name by which the list is sorted.

If the underlying data source is an IBindingListView, then you can use more complex sorting expressions because classes that implement this interface support advanced sorting.

The Filter property is only available if the underlying data source implements the IBindingListView interface. Note that this means that the Filter property is not available if the BindingSource is itself the data source.

Set the Sort Property in Visual Studio

1. In the Form Designer, select bsOrders.

2. In the Properties window, type **CustomerID** as the Sort property.

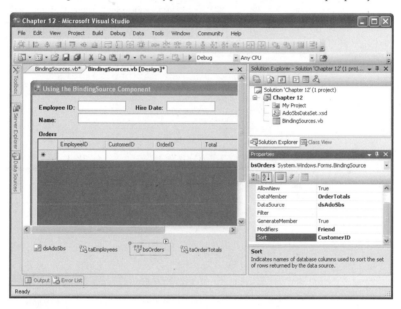

3. Press F5 to run the application.

   The orders are displayed in CustomerID order.

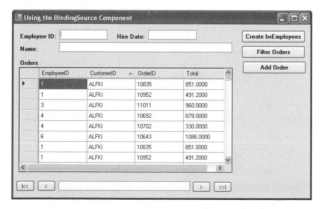

4. Close the application.

Set the Filter Property in Code: Visual Basic

1. In the Code Editor, add the following line to the btnFilterOrders_Click event handler:

```
bsOrders.Filter = "EmployeeID = " + tbEmployeeID.Text
```

2. Press F5 to run the application.

3. Click the Create bsEmployees button, and then click the Filter Orders button.

   The application displays only the orders for the first employee.

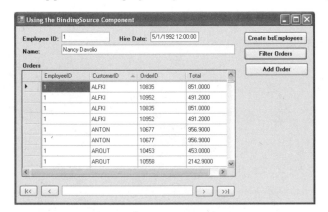

4. Close the application.

Set the Filter Property in Code: Visual C#

1. In the Code Editor, add the following line to the btnFilterOrders_Click event handler:

```
bsOrders.Filter = "EmployeeID = " + tbEmployeeID.Text;
```

2. Press F5 to run the application.

3. Click the Create bsEmployees button, and then click the Filter Orders button.

   The application displays only the orders for the first employee.

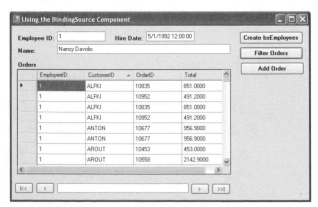

4. Close the application.

Using BindingSource Methods

The most frequently used methods exposed by the BindingSource component are shown in Table 12-3.

Table 12-3   BindingSource Methods

Method	Description	Currency Manager	IList	IBindingList
Add	Adds a new item to the internal list maintained by the BindingSource.			X
AddNew	Adds a new item to the list managed by the BindingSource.	X		X
CancelEdit	Cancels the current edit operation.	X		
Clear	Removes all elements from the list managed by the BindingSource.		X	
Contains	Determines whether an object exists in the list managed by the BindingSource.		X	
EndEdit	Applies pending changes to the list managed by the BindingSource.	X		
Find	Returns the index of the specified item.			X
IndexOf	Returns the index of the specified item.		X	
Insert	Inserts an item into the list managed by the BindingSource at the specified index.		X	
MoveFirst	Makes the first item in the list current.			
MoveLast	Makes the last item in the list current.			
MoveNext	Makes the next item in the list current.			
MovePrevious	Makes the previous item in the list current.			
Remove	Removes the specified item from the list managed by the BindingSource.		X	X
RemoveAt	Removes the item at the specified position from the list managed by the BindingSource.	X	X	
RemoveCurrent	Removes the current item from the list managed by the BindingSource.			
RemoveFilter	Removes any existing filter from the list managed by the BindingSource.			
RemoveSort	Removes any existing sort criteria from the list managed by the BindingSource.			X
ResetBindings	Notifies bound controls to refresh their values.			X

Table 12-3   BindingSource Methods

Method	Description	Currency Manager	IList	IBindingList
ResetCurrentItem	Notifies bound controls to refresh their values.			
ResumeBinding	Resumes data binding.	X		
SuspendBinding	Suspends data binding.	X		

Again, most of these correspond directly to the methods of the CurrencyManager, the IList interface, or the IBindingList interface. The remaining methods are specific to Currency-Manager and are simple encapsulations of existing functionality. So, for example, using RemoveFilter is equivalent to setting the Filter property to an empty string.

Be aware that the majority of these methods are passed directly to the underlying data source of a bound BindingSource. So, for example, the Find method of a BindingSource that is bound to a DataView simply calls the corresponding Find method of the DataView. This means that the exact functionality of the methods varies somewhat, depending on the functionality of the underlying data source.

Position Methods

The MoveFirst, MoveLast, MoveNext and MovePrevious methods are, of course, simple encapsulations of the CurrencyManager manipulation we saw in Chapter 11.

Use the Position Methods to Change the Current Row: Visual Basic

1. In the Code Editor, add the following code to the btnFirst_Click event handler:

   ```
   bsEmployees.MoveFirst()
   ```

2. Add the following code to the btnPrevious_Click event handler:

   ```
   bsEmployees.MovePrevious()
   ```

3. Add the following code to the btnNext_Click event handler:

   ```
   bsEmployees.MoveNext()
   ```

4. Add the following code to the btnLast_Click event handler:

   ```
   bsEmployees.MoveLast()
   ```

5. Press F5 to run the application.

6. Click the Create bsEmployees button, and then use the navigation buttons at the bottom of the form to move through the data.

   The application displays the details of employees.

> **Note** You must click the Filter Orders button for each employee because the Filter criteria set for the bsOrders BindingSource is static.

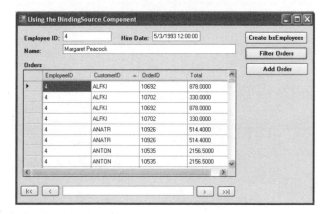

7. Close the application.

Use the Position Methods to Change the Current Row: Visual C#

1. In the Code Editor, add the following code to the btnFirst_Click event handler:

```
bsEmployees.MoveFirst();
```

2. Add the following code to the btnPrevious_Click event handler:

```
bsEmployees.MovePrevious();
```

3. Add the following code to the btnNext_Click event handler:

```
bsEmployees.MoveNext();
```

4. Add the following code to the btnLast_Click event handler:

```
bsEmployees.MoveLast();
```

5. Press F5 to run the application.

6. Click the Create bsEmployees button, and then use the navigation buttons at the bottom of the form to move through the data.

   The application displays the details of employees.

> **Note** You must click the Filter Orders button for each employee because the Filter criteria set for the bsOrders BindingSource is static.

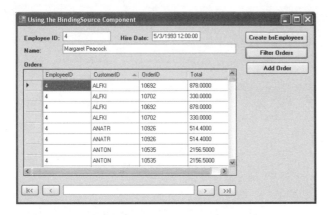

7. Close the application.

Add and AddNew Methods

Table 12-3 includes two methods, Add and AddNew, that appear to provide duplicate functionality, but this is deceptive. The Add method is used only with unbound BindingSource components, while the AddNew method is used only when the DataSource property has been set.

Add an Item to a BindingSource List: Visual Basic

1. In the Code Editor, add the following line to the btnAddOrder_Click event handler:

```
bsOrders.AddNew()
```

2. Press F5 to run the application.

3. Click the Create bsEmployees button, and then click the Filter Oders button.

4. Click the Add Order button.

    The application adds a new empty order to the underlying OrderTotals DataTable and makes that order current.

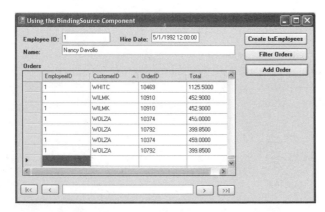

5. Close the application.

Add an Item to a BindingSource List: Visual C#

1. In the Code Editor, add the following line to the btnAddOrder_Click event handler:

```
bsOrders.AddNew();
```

2. Press F5 to run the application.

3. Click the Create bsEmployees button, and then click the Filter Oders button.

4. Click the Add Order button.

   The application adds a new empty order to the underlying OrderTotals DataTable and makes that order current.

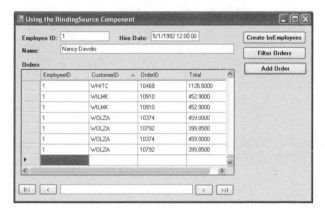

5. Close the application.

Responding to BindingSource Events

The events exposed by the BindingSource component are shown in Table 12-4. Again, the majority of these are in fact CurrencyManager events.

Table 12-4   BindingSource Events

Event	Description	CurrencyManager
AddingNew	Occurs after the AddNew method is called, but before an item is added to the BindingSource list.	
BindingComplete	Occurs after all the client controls have been bound to the BindingSource.	X
CurrentChanged	Occurs when the current item in the list managed by the BindingSource is changed.	X
CurrentItemChanged	Occurs when a property of the list managed by the BindingSource is changed.	X
DataError	Occurs when a currency error is handled by a BindingSource.	X

Table 12-4 **BindingSource Events**

Event	Description	CurrencyManager
DataMemberChanged	Occurs when the DataMember property of the BindingSource is changed.	
DataSourceChanged	Occurs when the DataSource property of the BindingSource is changed.	
ListChanged	Occurs when the underlying list or an item in the underlying list is changed.	X
PositionChanged	Occurs when the Position property of the Binding-Source is changed.	X

By responding to the AddingNew event, which occurs before an item is added to the list managed by the BindingSource, you can customize the way new items are added to an underlying data source. The event receives a parameter of the class AddinNewEventArgs, which contains a single property, NewObject. By setting this property to an object, you can circumvent the AddNew functionality implemented by the underlying data source.

As you might expect, the DataSourceChanged and DataMemberChanged properties are raised when the values of these properties are changed. You might respond to these events if, for example, you need to take some action based on the type of data source to which the Binding-Source is being bound.

The PositionChanged Event

The PositionChanged event, as we've seen, is inherited from the CurrencyManager. As you might expect, it is triggered whenever the Position property of the List is changed.

Respond to the PositionChanged Event: Visual Basic

1. In the Code Editor, add the following line to the end of the btnCreateEmployees_Click event handler that we created earlier.

```
AddHandler bsEmployees.PositionChanged, _
   AddressOf bsEmployees_PositionChanged
```

The body of the event handler should now be:

```
bsEmployees = New BindingSource()
bsEmployees.DataSource = dsAdoSbs
bsEmployees.DataMember = "Employees"

tbEmployeeID.DataBindings.Add("Text", bsEmployees, "EmployeeID")
tbHireDate.DataBindings.Add("Text", bsEmployees, "HireDate")
tbFullName.DataBindings.Add("Text", bsEmployees, "FullName")

AddHandler bsEmployees.PositionChanged, _
   AddressOf bsEmployees_PositionChanged
```

2. Add the following code to the bsEmployees_PositionChanged event handler:

```
txtPosition.Text = (bsEmployees.Position + 1).ToString() + " of " _
    + bsEmployees.Count.ToString()
```

3. Press F5 to run the application.

4. Click the Create bsEmployees button, and then click one of the navigation buttons.

   The application displays position information in the text box.

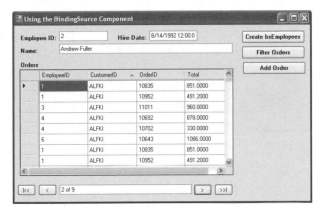

5. Close the application.

Respond to the PositionChanged Event: Visual C#

1. In the Code Editor, add the following lines to the end of the btnCreateEmployees_Click event handler that we created earlier:

```
bsEmployees.PositionChanged += new
    EventHandler(bsEmployees_PositionChanged);
```

   The body of the event handler should now be:

```
bsEmployees = new BindingSource();

bsEmployees.DataSource = dsAdoSbs;
bsEmployees.DataMember = "Employees";

tbEmployeeID.DataBindings.Add("Text", bsEmployees, "EmployeeID");
tbHireDate.DataBindings.Add("Text", bsEmployees, "HireDate");
tbFullName.DataBindings.Add("Text", bsEmployees, "FullName");

bsEmployees.PositionChanged += new EventHandler(bsEmployees_PositionChanged);
```

2. Place the following line in the bsEmployees_PositionChanged event handler:

```
txtPosition.Text = (bsEmployees.Position + 1).ToString() + " of "
    + bsEmployees.Count.ToString();
```

3. Press F5 to run the application.

4. Click the Create bsEmployees button, and then click one of the navigation buttons. The application displays position information in the text box.

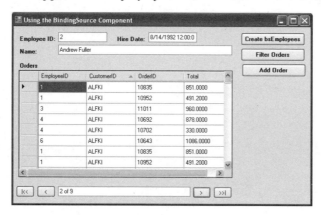

5. Close the application.

Summary

In this chapter we examined the BindingSource object, which, although not technically part of ADO.NET because it is declared in the System.Windows.Forms namespace, encapsulates ADO.NET CurrencyManager. The BindingSource simplifies access to the properties and data of the CurrencyManager, and expands the range of data sources for bound controls. As we've seen, you can even use it as an independent data source by manually adding items to the IList referenced by the CurrencyManager List property.

Chapter 13
Using ADO.NET in Windows Forms

After completing this chapter, you will be able to:

- Use the BindingNavigator control to navigate through a record set.
- Use specialized controls to simplify data entry.
- Use data relations to display related data.
- Format data by using the Format and Parse events.
- Find rows based on a DataSet's Sort column and other criteria.
- Work with data change events.
- Work with validation events.
- Use the ErrorProvider component.

In Chapter 11, "Manual Data Binding in Windows Forms," and Chapter 12, "Data Binding in Windows Forms by Using the BindingSource Component," we examined the objects that support Microsoft ADO.NET data binding. In this chapter, we'll explore using ADO.NET and Windows Forms to perform some common tasks.

Using the BindingNavigator to Navigate Through Data

In Chapters 11 and 12, we saw how to use button controls and either the CurrencyManager or BindingSource to provide users with a mechanism for navigating through a data set. The Microsoft .NET Framework 2.0 includes a new control, the BindingNavigator, which provides a standard interface for this very common task.

The BindingNavigator is a special type of ToolStrip control that works in conjunction with a BindingSource component. It is preconfigured to contain a set of ToolStripItem controls that correspond directly to BindingSource methods such as MoveFirst and Delete. Of course, because the BindingNavigator is a ToolStrip, you can easily add additional items to suit your application. You can find details about using the ToolStrip control in MSDN Help.

Add a BindingNavigator Control to a Form

1. In Microsoft Visual Studio 2005, open the Chapter 13 – Start project, and if necessary, double-click UsingADONet.vb (or UsingADONet.cs if you're using C#) in the Solution Explorer.

Visual Studio opens the form in the Form Designer.

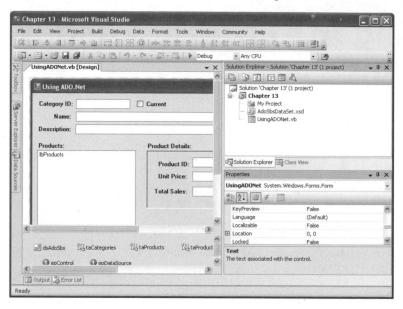

2. Drag a BindingNavigator control from the Data tab of the Toolbox to the form design surface.

Visual Studio adds the control to the form.

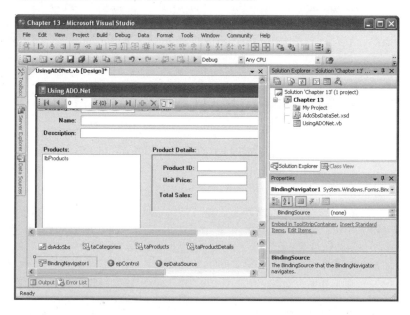

3. In the Properties window, change the name of the control to **bnCategories**.

4. Change the BindingSource property to bsCategories.

5. Change the Dock property of the control to Bottom.

6. Press F5 to run the application.

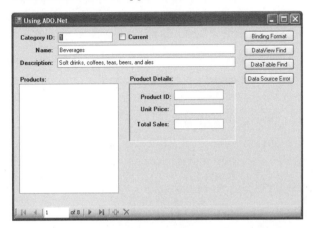

7. Use the BindingNavigator buttons to navigate through the Categories DataTable.

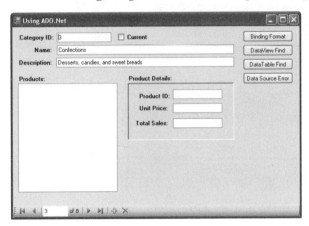

8. Close the application.

Displaying Data in Windows Controls

The .NET Framework supports a wide variety of controls for use on Windows Forms, and as we've seen, any form property can be bound directly or indirectly to an ADO.NET data source.

The details of each control are unfortunately outside the scope of this book, but in this section we'll examine a few common techniques for data-binding.

Simplifying Data Entry

One of the reasons that so many controls are provided by the .NET Framework, of course, is to make data entry simpler and more accurate. Textbox controls are always an easy choice, but the time spent choosing and implementing controls that more closely match the way the user thinks about the data will be richly rewarded.

To take a fairly simple example, it is certainly possible to use a combo box containing True and False or Yes and No to represent Boolean values, but in most circumstances, it's far more effective to use the CheckBox control provided by the .NET Framework.

The Checked property of the CheckBox control, which determines whether the box is selected, can be simple-bound at either design time or run time by using standard techniques.

Use the CheckBox Control to Display Boolean Values

1. In the Form Designer, select the cbCurrent CheckBox control.

2. In the Properties window, expand the Data Bindings node, and open the list box for the Checked property.

3. Expand the bsCategories node, and then select the Current column.

4. Press F5 to run the application.

   The application displays the Boolean value of the Current column in the check box.

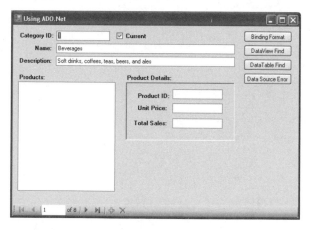

5. Close the application.

Displaying User-Comprehensible Values

To simplify the database schema, many designers use an artificial key of some type rather than a key derived from the entity's attributes. These artificial keys are usually assigned automatically by the database engine, typically as Identity columns (or whatever the database engine calls an automatically generated number value). These artificial keys are technologically efficient, but they don't typically have any meaning for users. The primary key can often be hidden from users or simply ignored by them when they are working with the primary table. However, this is rarely the case with foreign keys.

Fortunately, the .NET Framework controls that inherit from the ListControl class, including both the ListBox and the ComboBox, make it easy to bind the control to one column (even a column in a different table) while displaying another. This technique is reasonably straight-forward:

1. Set the DataSource and DisplayMember properties of the control to a user-friendly table and column. Under most circumstances, this isn't the table that the form is updating.

2. Then, to set the data-binding, set the ValueMember property to the key column in the table being updated.

3. Finally create a Binding object that links the SelectedValue property to the field to be updated.

For example, given the database schema shown in the following figure, if you create a form to update the Relatives table, you typically use a ComboBox control to represent the Relation-ship type rather than force the user to remember that Type 1 means Sister, Type 2 means Father, and so on.

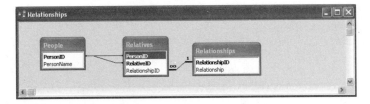

To implement this schema in the .NET Framework, you need to set the ComboBox control's DisplayMember property to Relationships.Relationship and then set its ValueMember property to Relationships.RelationshipID. Given these settings, the ComboBox displays Sister but returns a SelectedValue of 1.

After these properties are set, either in the Properties window or in code, you must then add a Binding object to the ComboBox control to link the SelectedValue to the RelationshipID column in the Relatives table. Because SelectedValue isn't available for data binding at design time, you must add the object in code:

```
Relationships.DataBindings.Add("SelectedValue", myDS, _
   "Relatives.Relationship")
```

Display Full Names in a ComboBox Control

1. In the Form Designer, select the bsProducts BindingSource.

2. In the Properties window, open the DataSource list box, and then choose bsCategories.

3. Expand the DataMember list box, and then choose Products_Categories (the name of the DataRelation that links the Categories and Products DataTables in the Typed DataSet).

4. Select the lbProducts list box.

5. In the Properties window, open the DataSource list, and select bsProducts.

6. Open the DisplayMember list, and select ProductName.

7. Open the ValueMember list, and select ProductID.

8. Press F5 to run the application, and then use the navigation keys to move through the DataSet.

    The application displays only the Products in the selected Category.

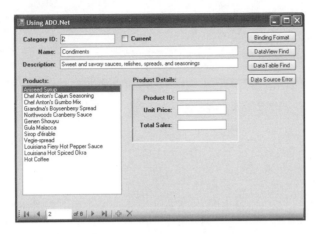

9. Close the application.

Working with DataRelations

The data model implemented by ADO.NET, with its ability to model complete relational schemas in a DataSet, makes it easy to represent relationships of arbitrary depth on a single form. By binding the control to a DataRelation rather than to a DataTable, the .NET Framework automatically handles synchronization of controls on a form.

In Visual Studio 2005 and ADO.NET 2.0, displaying related data is most easily achieved by using BindingSource components. First, you create DataRelations in a Typed DataSet. Then to display the related rows, you set the DataSource property of the BindingSource component to the DataTable on the one side of the relationship, and you set the DataMember property to the DataRelation (not to the DataTable) on the many side.

Bind Controls to a DataRelation

1. In the Form Designer, select the bsDetails BindingSource control and, in the Properties window, set the DataMember property to Products_ProductDetails.

2. In the Form Designer, select the Product ID text box.

3. In the Properties window, expand the Data Bindings section, expand the Text property list box, expand the bsDetails node, and then choose ProductID.

4. Select the Unit Price text box.

5. In the Properties window, expand the Data Bindings section, expand the Text property drop-down list box, expand the bsDetails node, and then choose UnitPrice.

6. Select the Total Sales text box.

7. In the Properties window, expand the Data Bindings section, expand the Text list box, expand the bsDetails node, and then choose TotalSales.

8. Press F5 to run the application, and select different Products in the Products list box.

   The application displays the details of the selected Product.

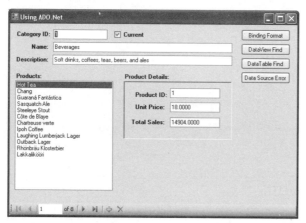

9. Close the application.

Formatting Data

It's an unfortunate fact of life in the world of database development that the raw data stored in your database is rarely completely suitable for display to your users. To facilitate data integrity, attributes that users think of as single values are split into multiple columns, and artificial codes are used for the sake of efficient storage. Sometimes you inherit something really weird, such as values being bit-packed or encoded according to some arcane or obsolete methodology.

Fortunately, the .NET Framework provides several powerful methods for interpreting raw data and displaying it in a format that is suitable for human consumption.

Custom Format Strings

New to the .NET Framework 2.0 are three properties of the Binding object: FormatString, FormatInfo and FormattingEnabled. These properties allow simple reformatting of raw numeric and DateTime values.

The FormatString property accepts a string code, called a *format specifier*, that indicates how the value should be formatted. The standard strings for numeric values are shown in Table 13-1, and those for DateTime values are shown in Table 13-2.

Table 13-1   Standard Numeric Format Specifiers

Specifier	Description
C or c	Currency
D or d	Decimal
E or e	Scientific notation
F or f	Fixed point
G or g	General, the most compact representation
N or n	Number, which is formatted with a thousands separator and decimal point
P or p	Percent
R or r	Round trip, which guarantees that the numeric string will be parsed to the same numeric value
X or x	Hexidecimal

Table 13-2   Standard DateTime Format Specifiers

Specifier	Description
d	Short date
D	Long date
t	Short time
T	Long time
f	Long date and short time
F	Long date and long time
g	Short date and short time
G	Short date and long time
M or m	Month day pattern
R or r	RFC1123 pattern
s	Sortable date and time
u	Universal sortable date and time
U	Sortable full date and time
Y or y	Year month pattern

All the standard format specifiers are culturally sensitive—the exact format returned is determined by the regional settings in the Control Panel. In addition, you can create custom format specifier strings by using codes such as "d" for day and "#" for a digit placeholder. For details about custom format specifiers, see MSDN Help.

The FormatInfo property allows you to specify an IFormatProvider that handles the formatting. If no value is supplied, the .NET Framework uses the IFormatProvider supplied by System.Windows.Forms.Application.CurrentCulture.

The IFormatProvider interface, part of the System namespace, allows you to create custom formatting functions. Custom format providers can be useful if you have complex formatting requirements, but they are, perhaps fortunately, outside the scope of this book. For implementation details, see MSDN Help.

Finally, the FormattingEnabled property, which defaults to False, determines whether the FormatString and FormatInfo properties are actually used. Unless you change the value of this property, any values you provide for the other two properties are ignored.

Format a Date Value by Using the FormatString Property: Visual Basic

1. Press F7 to display the Code Editor.

2. Add the following lines to the btnBindingFormat_Click event handler:

```vbnet
Dim myBinding As Binding
myBinding = tbUnitPrice.DataBindings("Text")
myBinding.FormatString = "C"
myBinding.FormattingEnabled = True
```

3. Press F5 to run the application.

4. Click the Binding Format button.

   The application displays the Unit Price formatted as a currency value.

5. Close the application.

Format a Date Value by Using the FormatString Property: Visual C#

1. Press F7 to display the Code Editor.

2. Add the following lines to the btnBindingFormat_Click event handler:

```
Binding myBinding;
myBinding = tbUnitPrice.DataBindings["Text"];
myBinding.FormatString = "C";
myBinding.FormattingEnabled = true;
```

3. Press F5 to run the application.

4. Click the Binding Format button.

   The application displays the Unit Price formatted as a currency value.

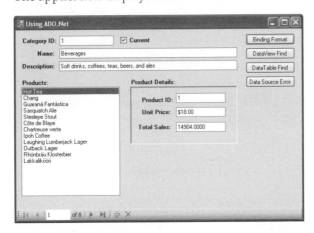

5. Close the application.

The Format and Parse Events

Although the FormatString and FormatInfo properties can be used for many common formatting tasks, their use is limited. These properties are intended to return a formatted string for display to users. Sometimes you need to perform more complicated operations, such as unpacking strings or even changing the data type of a value.

Fortunately, the ADO.NET Binding object exposes two events, Format and Parse, which support complex manipulation of data for an application. The Format event occurs whenever data is pushed from the data source to a control on a Windows Form, and when it is pulled from the control back to the data source, as shown in the following figure. The Parse event occurs only when data is pulled from the control back to the data source.

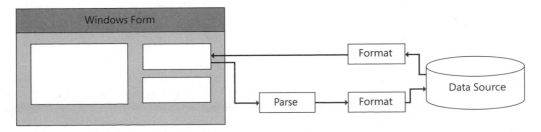

The Format event is used to translate the data from its native format to the format you want to display to the user, while the Parse event is used to translate it back to its original format.

Both events receive a ConvertEventArgs argument, which has the properties shown in Table 13-3.

Table 13-3   ConvertEventArgs Properties

Property	Description
DesiredType	The data type of the desired value
Value	The data value

The Value property contains the actual data. When the Format event is triggered, this property contains the original data in its original format. When the Parse event is fired, this property contains the formatted data. To change the formatting, you need to set this value to the new data or format within the event handler.

You use the DesiredType property when you are changing the data type of the value.

Using the Format Event

Because the Format event occurs both when the data is being pushed from the data source and when it is pulled from the control, you must be sure you know which event is taking place before performing any action. If you change the data type of the value, you can use the DesiredType property to perform this check. However, if the data type remains the same, you must use a method that is external to the event to determine the direction in which the data is being moved. Setting the Tag property of the control is an easy way to make this determination. If you're using the Tag property for another purpose, you can use a form-level variable instead or determine the direction from the value itself.

Change the Format of Data by Using the Format Event: Visual Basic

1. In the Code Editor, add the following lines to the FormatName event handler:

```
If tbName.Tag <> "PARSE" Then
    e.Value = CType(e.Value, String).ToUpper()
End If
tbName.Tag = "FORMAT"
```

This code first checks the tbName control's Tag property to determine whether the value is "PARSE". If it isn't, the body of the If statement translates the Value property of the e parameter, which contains the actual data value, to upper case.

> **Tip**   If you examine the form Load event handler, which is part of the exercise scaffolding, you will see that the Format event handler is added before the DataTables are filled. If you add it after they are filled, the handler does not affect the first row displayed.

2. Press F5 to run the application.

The application displays the content of the Name field in upper case.

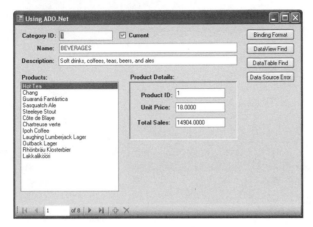

3. Close the application.

Change the Format of Data by Using the Format Event: Visual C#

1. In the Code Editor, add the following lines to the FormatName event handler:

```
if ((string)tbName.Tag != "PARSE")
{
    string eStr = (string) e.Value;
    e.Value = eStr.ToUpper();
}
tbName.Tag = "FORMAT";
```

This code first checks the tbName control's Tag property to determine whether the value is "PARSE". If it isn't, the body of the if statement translates the value property of the e parameter, which contains the actual data value, to upper case.

> **Tip** If you examine the form load event handler, which is part of the exercise scaffolding, you will see that the Format event handler is added before the DataTables are filled. If you add it after they are filled, the handler does not affect the first row displayed.

2. Press F5 to run the application.

The application displays the content of the Name field in upper case.

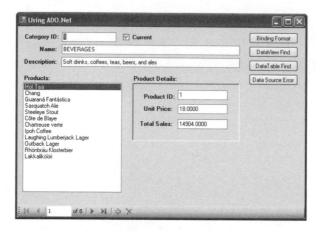

3. Close the application.

Using the Parse Event

As we've discussed, the Parse event occurs when data is pulled from a control back to the data source, and it is typically used to "unformat" data that has been customized for display by the Format event.

Because Parse is called only once, this "unformatting" operation should always happen, unlike the formatting operation, which should take place only when data is being pushed to the control, not when it is being pulled from it.

> **Important**   You need to be careful to set up any variables or properties required to make sure that the Format event, which is always called after Parse, doesn't reformat data before it is submitted to the data source.

Restore the Original Format of Data by Using the Parse Event: Visual Basic

1. In the Code Editor, add the following lines to the ParseName event handler:

```
tbName.Tag = "PARSE"
e.Value = CType(e.Value, String).ToLower()
MessageBox.Show(e.Value)
```

This code first changes the value of the Tag property to "PARSE". (Remember that we check this value in the Format event handler to avoid reformatting the value.) The code then converts the Value property of the e parameter to lower case and displays it in a message box.

2. Press F5 to run the application.

3. Change the Category Name from BEVERAGES to **DRINKS**, and then move to the next data row.

The Parse event handler changes the value to lower case and displays the new value, in lower case, in a message box.

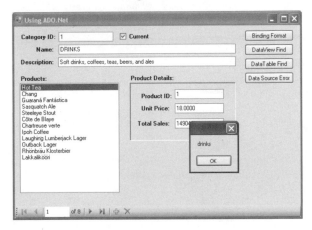

4. Close the message box and the application.

Restore the Original Format of Data by Using the Parse Event: Visual C#

1. In the Code Editor, add the following lines to the ParseName event handler:

```
tbName.Tag = "PARSE";
string eStr = (string)e.Value;
e.Value = eStr.ToLower();
MessageBox.Show(e.Value.ToString());
```

This code first changes the value of the Tag property to "PARSE". (Remember that we check the value in the Format event handler to avoid reformatting the value.) The code then converts the Value property of the e parameter to lower case and displays it in a message box.

2. Press F5 to run the application.

3. Change the Category Name from BEVERAGES to **DRINKS**, and then move to the next data row.

The Parse event handler changes the value to lower case and displays the new value in lower case.

4. Close the application.

Finding Data

Finding a specific row in a DataTable is a common application task, and Visual Studio 2005 has several methods for providing this functionality to users:

- The Form Designer in Visual Studio now supports a simple mechanism for adding this functionality to forms.

- The BindingSource component, which we examined in Chapter 12, supports a Find method.

- The low-level ADO.NET objects also support searching.

Finding Data by Using the Add Query Dialog Box

In Chapter 8, "Using TableAdapters," we saw that one advantage of TableAdapters is that they provide a mechanism for exposing parameterized queries as methods of the TableAdapter class. The Visual Studio Form Designer leverages this capability by providing a simple dialog-based mechanism for adding a search capability to any Windows Form.

By choosing Add Query from the Form Designer's Data menu, you can add a new query to a TableAdapter or select a pre-existing query. Either way, a ToolStrip control is added to the form. This standard ToolStrip includes, by default, text boxes for each of the query's parameters and a ToolStripButton control that executes the query.

Because these are standard controls, you can configure the ToolStrip to suit your application. One addition you might consider, from a usability standpoint, is a ToolStripButton that redisplays the entire record set by calling the standard Fill method of the TableAdapter.

Add a Search ToolStrip to a Windows Form

1. In the Form Designer, select the tbName TextBox, and then choose Add Query from the Data menu.

   Visual Studio displays the Search Criteria Builder dialog box.

2. Select the Existing Query Name option, and then choose FillByName(categoryName) from the list box.

   The FillByName(categoryName) query has already been added to the TableAdapter. The dialog box displays the text of the query.

3. Click OK.

   Visual Studio adds a search ToolStrip to the form.

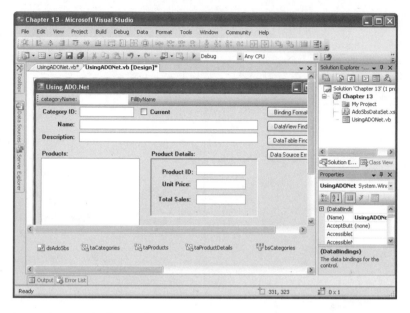

4. Press F5 to run the application.

5. Type **dairy products** in the CategoryName text box on the Toolstrip, and then click Fill-ByName.

   The application displays the Dairy Products Category row.

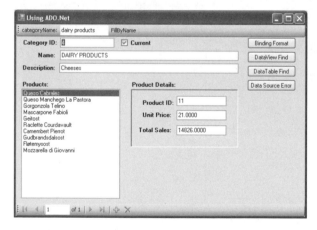

6. Close the application.

Finding Data by Using the BindingSource

Behind the scenes, the "execute query" button on the ToolStrip calls the corresponding query method of the TableAdapter to refill the DataTable. The effect of this method call is to filter the DataTable rather than simply display the appropriate DataRows. Because the code for the

ToolStripButton is in the code file for the form (not the designer file), displaying the DataRows is simple to do.

One way to display the DataRows is to use the Find method of the BindingSource component. As we saw in the Chapter 12, the BindingSource.Find method passes the method call directly to the underlying data source, so its exact behavior depends on the data class of that source. You can always perform simple searches on the column by which the data is sorted; more complex searches are only available if the underlying data source supports them.

Of course, altering the default code of a Visual Studio Search ToolStrip isn't the only way to implement a search mechanism that uses the Find method of the BindingSource. You can implement this functionality by using a button, a menu item, the exit event of a textbox control, or any user-interface widget that suits your application.

Find a Row by Using a BindingSource: Visual Basic

1. In the Code Editor, find the FillByNameToolStripButton_Click event handler that was added by the Search Criteria Builder dialog box.

2. Replace the existing code with the following:

```
Dim firstRow As Integer

firstRow = bsCategories.Find("CategoryName", _
    CategoryNameToolStripTextBox.Text)
If firstRow <> -1 Then
    bsCategories.Position = firstRow
End If
```

3. Press F5 to run the application.

4. Type **dairy products** in the CategoryName text box on the ToolStrip, and then click Fill-ByName.

   The application displays the Dairy Products category, but leaves the remaining rows available.

5.　Close the application.

Find a Row by Using a BindingSource: Visual C#

1.　In the Code Editor, find the fillByNameToolStripButton_Click event handler that was added by the Search Criteria Builder dialog box.

2.　Replace the existing code with the following:

```
int firstRow;

firstRow = bsCategories.Find("CategoryName",
    categoryNameToolStripTextBox.Text);
if (firstRow != - 1)
    bsCategories.Position = firstRow;
```

3.　Press F5 to run the application.

4.　Type **dairy products** in the CategoryName text box on the ToolStrip, and then click Fill-ByName.

The application displays the Dairy Products category, but leaves the remaining rows available.

5.　Close the application.

Finding a Row in a DataView

If you aren't using a BindingSource, you can use the Find method of a DataView to find rows based on the current sort key. (Remember that Windows Form controls are always bound to a DataTable's DefaultView, so you will most often be working with a DataView.)

There are two forms of the Find method: One selects a single object parameter, and the other accepts an array of parameters. You use the second version if your DataView is sorted on multiple columns.

Find a Row in a DataView: Visual Basic

1. In the Code Editor, add the following code to the btnDataView_Click event handler:

```
Dim firstRow As Integer
Dim dv As DataView

dv = dsAdoSbs.Categories.DefaultView
dv.Sort = "CategoryName"
firstRow = dv.Find(CategoryNameToolStripTextBox.Text)
If firstRow <> -1 Then
    bsCategories.Position = firstRow
End If
```

2. Press F5 to run the application.

3. Type **produce** in the CategoryName text box on the ToolStrip, and then click the Data-View Find button.

   The application displays the Produce category.

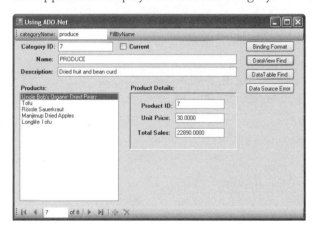

4. Close the application.

Find a Row in a DataView: Visual C#

1. In the Code Editor, add the following code to the btnDataView_Click event handler:

```
int firstRow;
DataView dv;

dv = dsAdoSbs.Categories.DefaultView;
dv.Sort = "CategoryName";
firstRow = dv.Find(categoryNameToolStripTextBox.Text);
if (firstRow != -1)
    bsCategories.Position = firstRow;
```

2. Press F5 to run the application.

3. Type **produce** in the CategoryName text box on the ToolStrip, and then click the Data-View Find button.

The application displays the Produce category.

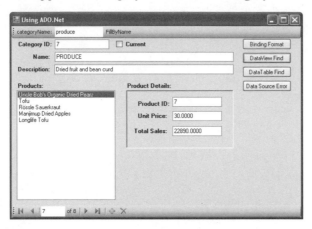

4. Close the application.

Finding a Row in a DataTable

The DataView's Find method is easy to use but limited in scope. If you need to find a row based on complex criteria, or based on a column other than the one by which the data is sorted, you must use the DataTable's Select method.

The Select method isn't difficult to use, but positioning the CurrencyManager to the correct row requires several steps. The process requires using both the DataView object and the DataTable object to perform the search, along with the BindingContext object to display the results.

First you must execute the Select method with the required criteria against the DataTable. After the correct row is found, you obtain the Sort column value from the array that is returned by the Select method and then use the array to perform a Find against the DataView. Finally, you use the Position property of the BindingContext or the CurrencyManager to display the result. In truth, the whole process is decidedly awkward, but you'll soon learn the steps by rote if you need to use this technique frequently.

Find a Row in a DataTable: Visual Basic

1. In the Code Editor, add the following lines to the btnDataTable_Click event handler:

```
Dim dr() As AdoSbsDataSet.CategoriesRow
Dim dv As DataView
Dim firstRow As Integer

dr = dsAdoSbs.Categories.Select("CategoryID = 5")
If dr.Length <> 0 Then
   dv = dsAdoSbs.Categories.DefaultView
   dv.Sort = "CategoryName"
   firstRow = dv.Find(dr(0).Item("CategoryName"))
   bsCategories.Position = firstRow
End If
```

After declaring some variables, this code uses the Select method of the Categories DataTable to find the DataRow with a CategoryID of 5. Because Select returns an array, the code checks that the length of the array is greater than 0 to ensure that a match was found. Assuming it was, the code uses the Find method of the DataTable's DefaultView to find the row in the DataView, and then positions the BindingSource to the result.

> **Note**   This example is for demonstration purposes only. For a simple search like this one, you would, in practice, use the DataView or BindingSource directly.

2. Press F5 to run the application, and then click the DataTable Find button.

The application displays the Grains/Cereals category.

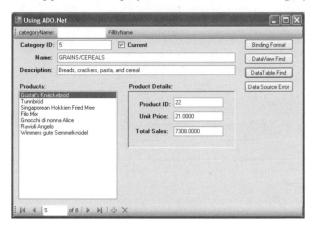

3. Close the application.

Find a Row in a DataTable: Visual C#

1. In the Code Editor, add the following lines to the btnDataTable_Click event handler:

```csharp
AdoSbsDataSet.CategoriesRow[] dr;
DataView dv;
int firstRow;

dr = (AdoSbsDataSet.CategoriesRow[])
    dsAdoSbs.Categories.Select("CategoryID = 5");
if (dr.Length != 0)
{
    dv = dsAdoSbs.Categories.DefaultView;
    dv.Sort = "CategoryName";
    firstRow = dv.Find(dr[0]["CategoryName"]);
    bsCategories.Position = firstRow;
}
```

After declaring some variables, this code uses the Select method of the Categories DataTable to find the DataRow with a CategoryID of 5. Because Select returns an array, the code checks that the length of the array is greater than 0 to ensure that a match was found. Assuming it was, the code then uses the Find method of the DataTable's Default-View to find the row in the DataView, and then positions the BindingSource to the result.

> **Note**   This example is for demonstration purposes only. For a simple search like this one, you would, in practice, use the DataView or BindingSource directly.

2. Press F5 to run the application, and then click the DataTable Find button.

The application displays the Grains/Cereals category.

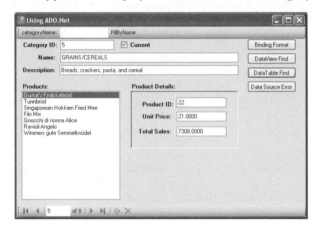

3. Close the application.

Validating Data in Windows Forms

The .NET Framework supports a number of techniques for validating data entry prior to submitting it to a data source. We've already seen some examples of the first of these techniques: the use of specific controls to constrain data entry to the appropriate values.

After the data has been entered, the .NET Framework exposes a series of events at both the control and data levels to allow you to trap and manage problems.

Data Change Events

Data validation is most often implemented at the data source level. This practice tends to be more efficient because the validation occurs regardless of which control or controls are used to change the data.

As we saw in Chapter 7, "Using DataTables," the DataTable object exposes six events that can be used for data validation. In order of occurrence, they are:

- ColumnChanging

- ColumnChanged

- RowChanging

- RowChanged

- RowDeleting

- RowDeleted

> **Note** If a row is being deleted, only the RowDeleting and RowDeleted events occur.

If you are using a Typed DataSet, you can create separate event handlers for each column in a DataTable. If you are using an Untyped DataSet, a single event handler must handle all the columns in a single DataRow. You can use the Column property of the DataColumnChangeArgs parameter that is passed to the event to determine which column is being changed.

Column Change Events

Two column change events are typically used for validating discrete values: ColumnChanging, which occurs before the value is updated, and ColumnChanged, which occurs after. For example, these events can be used to determine whether a value is within a specified range or has the correct format.

Respond to a ColumnChanging Event: Visual Basic

1. In the Code Editor, comment out the code in the ParseName event handler that we created earlier in this chapter.

2. Add the following lines to the Categories_ColumnChanging event handler:

   ```
   Dim str As String

   str = "Column:  " & e.Column.ColumnName.ToString()
   str += vbCrLf + "New Value:  " & e.ProposedValue
   MessageBox.Show(str, "Column Changing")
   ```

   This code simply displays the ProposedValue in a message box.

3. Press F5 to run the application.

4. Type **Beverages New** as the Category Name, and move to the next row.

   The application displays the new value in a message box.

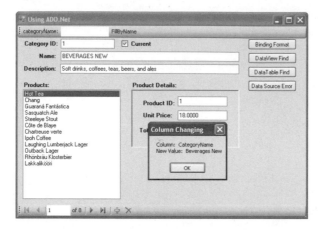

5. Close the application.

Respond to a ColumnChanging Event: Visual C#

1. In the Code Editor, comment out the code in the ParseName event handler that we created earlier in the chapter.

2. Add the following lines to the Categories_ColumnChanging event handler:

```
string str;

str = "Column:  " + e.Column.ColumnName.ToString();
str += "\nNew Value:  " + e.ProposedValue;
MessageBox.Show(str, "Column Changing");
```

This code simply displays the ProposedValue in a message box.

3. Press F5 to run the application.

4. Type **Beverages New** as the Category Name, and move to the next row.

The application displays the new value in a message box.

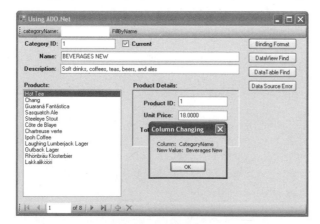

5. Close the message box and the application.

Control Validation Events

In addition to being triggered by DataTable events, data validation can be triggered by individual controls. Every control in the Windows.Forms namespace supports the following events, in the order shown:

- Enter
- GotFocus
- Leave
- Validating
- Validated
- LostFocus

For purposes of data validation, the Validating and Validated events roughly correspond to the ColumnChanging and ColumnChanged events. However, they have the advantage of occurring as soon as the user leaves the control rather than when the CurrencyManager object is repositioned, either directly or by means of a BindingSource.

The process of responding to these events is exactly the same as responding to data-change events, or indeed, to any .NET Framework class event: You simply create the event handler procedure and perform whatever operations are required within it.

Using the ErrorProvider Component

In the previous exercises, we've used MessageBox controls in response to data-validation events. This is a common technique, but it's not a very good one from a usability standpoint. MessageBox controls are disruptive, and after they are dismissed, the error information in them disappears.

Fortunately the .NET Framework provides the ErrorProvider component, a much better mechanism for displaying errors to the user. The ErrorProvider, which can be bound to either a specific control or a data source object, displays an error icon next to the appropriate control. When the user points to the icon, a ToolTip displays the specified error message.

Binding an ErrorProvider to a Form Control

When you attach an ErrorProvider to a form control, you typically set the error in the control's Validating event, which is triggered when the user exits the control. However, you can trigger the error checking in any event. For example, you can use the KeyPress event to check each character individually. But be aware that if you use the KeyPress event for complicated error checking, the responsiveness of your system might suffer.

Use an ErrorProvider with a Form Control: Visual Basic

1. In the Code Editor, comment out the Categories_ColumnChanging event handler that we added earlier in the chapter.

2. Add the following code to the tbName_Validating event handler:

```
If tbName.Text = "error" Then
    epControl.SetError(tbName, "Please re-enter the Category Name")
    e.Cancel = True
Else
    epControl.SetError(tbName, "")
End If
```

3. Press F5 to run the application.

4. Type **error** as the category name (remember that comparisons are case sensitive), and exit the field by pressing Tab.

   The application displays an error icon and returns focus to the Name text box.

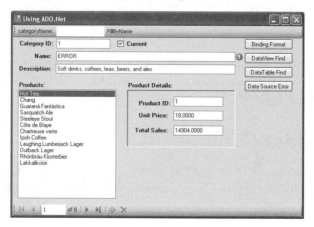

5. Close the application.

Use an ErrorProvider with a Form Control: Visual C#

1. In the Code Editor, comment out the Categories_ColumnChanging event handler that we added earlier in the chapter.

2. Add the following code to the tbName_Validating event handler:

```
if (tbName.Text == "error")
{
    epControl.SetError(tbName, "Please re-enter the Category Name");
    e.Cancel = true;
}
else
    epControl.SetError(tbName, "");
```

3. Press F5 to run the application.

4. Type **error** as the category name (remember that comparisons are case sensitive), and exit the field by pressing Tab.

The application displays a flashing error icon and returns focus to the Name text box.

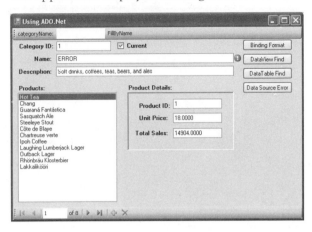

5. Close the application.

Binding an ErrorProvider to a Data Source

The previous exercise demonstrated the use of the ErrorProvider from within the Validating event of a control. But the ErrorProvider component can also be bound to a data source, and it can display an error icon for any column or row that contains an error. The ErrorProvider displays the error icon next to any control bound to the same source.

Binding an ErrorProvider to a data-source object has the advantage of allowing multiple errors to be displayed simultaneously—a significant improvement in system usability.

Use an ErrorProvider with a DataColumn: Visual Basic

1. In the Form Designer, select the epDataSource ErrorProvider control.

2. In the Properties window, open the DataSource property list box, and then select bsCategories.

3. In the Code Editor, comment out the tbName_Validating event handler that we created in the previous exercise.

4. Add the following lines to the btnDataError_Click event handler:

```
Dim dr As DataRow
dr = CType(bsCategories.Current, DataRowView).Row
dr.SetColumnError(1, "This is the error")
```

This code artificially creates an error condition for the Category Name column.

5.   Press F5 to run the application.

6.   Click the Data Source Error button.

The application displays an error icon next to the Name text box.

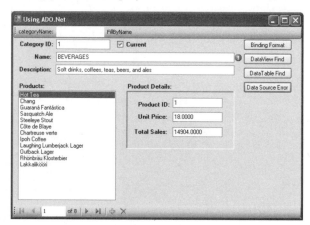

7.   Close the application.

Use an ErrorProvider with a DataColumn: Visual C#

1.   In the Form Designer, select the epDataSource ErrorProvider control.

2.   In the Properties window, select the DataSource property, expand its list box, and then
     select bsCategories.

3.   In the Code Editor, comment out the tbName_Validating event handler that we created
     in the previous exercise.

4.   Add the following lines to the btnDataError_Click event handler:

```
DataRow dr;
dr = ((DataRowView) bsCategories.Current).Row;
dr.SetColumnError(1, "This is the error");
```

This code artificially creates an error condition for the Category Name column.

5.   Press F5 to run the application.

6.   Click the Data Source Error button.

The application displays an error icon next to the Name text box.

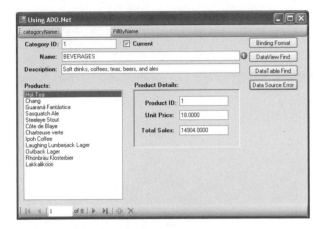

7. Close the application.

Summary

In this chapter we examined a number of techniques for working with ADO.NET data in Windows Forms. We took another look at simple and complex binding, which we first discussed in Chapter 10, and we explored the use of DataRelation objects to display data from related DataTables.

We also examined the Binding.Format property and the Format and Parse events that are used to format data. Finally, we examined various uses of the ErrorProvider control for data validation.

Chapter 14

Basic Data Binding in Web Forms

After completing this chapter, you will be able to:

- Simple-bind standard controls in various ways.
- Complex-bind data controls to ADO.NET objects.
- Maintain the state of ADO.NET objects at the server and on the page.
- Implement data navigation on an ASP.NET page.
- Update a data source from simple-bound controls.

In the previous chapters, we examined the Microsoft ADO.NET object model by using examples in Windows Forms. In this chapter we'll examine data binding in Microsoft ASP.NET and Web Forms.

Understanding Data Binding in Web Forms

As part of the Microsoft .NET Framework, ADO.NET is independent of any application in which it is deployed, whether it's a Windows Form, as in the exercises in the previous chapters, a Web Form, or a middle-level business object. But the way that data is pushed to and pulled from controls is a function of the control itself, not of ADO.NET, and the Web Form data-binding architecture is very different from anything we've seen so far.

The Web Form data-binding architecture is based on two assumptions: that the majority of data access is read-only, and that interactions between the Web server and the browser are one-way

First, the architecture assumes that data is displayed to users, but in most cases, it is not updated by them. As a result, with a few exceptions, Web Form data binding is one-way: Data is pushed from the data source to the control, but changes that the user makes to the control values are not propagated back to the data source.

As a simple example, if you have a Windows Form TextBox control that is bound to a column in a DataSet and the user changes the value of that TextBox control, the new value is automatically propagated to the DataSet by the .NET Framework, and the Item, DataColumn, and DataRow change events are triggered. If a TextBox control on a Web Form displays a column in a DataSet, however, you must add code to update the DataSet value.

We'll examine Data Source controls and the Web server controls designed to work with them in Chapter 15.ASP.NET 2.0 introduces the Data Source controls, a new set of Web server controls that are similar to the Windows Form BindingSource components, in that they encapsulate ADO.NET data objects to simplify data access and facilitate traditional two-way data binding. Along with the Data Source controls, ASP.NET 2.0 also includes a new set of data-bound controls that interact with the Data Source controls to implement two-way data binding.

Binding the standard Web server controls and HTML controls is possible, as we'll see in this chapter, but it's intrinsically one-way—when you bind one of these controls to a data source, the data is only pushed to the bound property; it is not pulled back from the control unless you take some action.

This doesn't mean that two-way binding is impossible when using standard Web server and HTML controls, or even that it's particularly difficult, but it has to be done manually. We'll examine the techniques for manually pushing, pulling and updating data by using these controls later in this chapter.

The second assumption underlying the .NET Framework Web Form data-binding architecture is that the Web server prepares and serves a page, and that the interaction ends there. In other words, the Internet is, by default, stateless—the state of the page is not maintained between round-trips to the server.

To continue our example, even after you add the code to update the DataSet, the user must explicitly submit any changes to the server, and you must write additional code to handle the submission and update the underlying data source, both on the client and the server. After the changes reach the DataSet, of course, the DataColumn and DataRow change events will still be triggered.

This behavior is only the default, however. ASP.NET, the part of the .NET Framework that supports Web development, supports a number of mechanisms for maintaining state, where appropriate, on both the client and server. We'll examine some of these mechanisms as they relate to data access later in this chapter.

Simple-Binding Web Controls to an ADO.NET Data Source

Like controls on Windows Forms, Web Form controls support simple-binding virtually any property to a single value in a data source and complex-binding control properties that display multiple values. However, the binding mechanisms for Web Forms are somewhat different from those we've seen and used with Windows Forms, and they vary depending on where the control lives in the .NET Framework class hierarchy.

We'll discuss data-bound controls in detail in Chapter 15.In terms of data binding, there are essentially three types of controls:

- Simple data-bound controls, such as the DetailsView.

- Complex data-bound controls, such as the GridView.

- Standard controls that must be data bound manually. These are all simple-bound.

Just as in the Windows Form environment, a simple-bound control property evaluates to a single value rather than a list. Unlike Windows Forms, standard simple-bound Web Form controls don't expose data-binding properties. Instead, the value is explicitly retrieved and assigned to the property at run time. There are three ways to do this:

- Set the property explicitly in code.

- Set the property in code by using the DataBinder.Eval method.

- Set the property in the HTML string by using a data-binding expression.

All three methods result in one-way binding: Data is pushed to the control property, but changes to the property values are not reflected in the DataSet. Given this, we're using the term "data-bound" somewhat loosely, but the result is that values from a data source are displayed in controls on a Web Form, so the term will do. We'll examine ways of pulling data from controls to the data source later in this chapter.

The ASP.NET Event Model

It might seem odd that in the examples in this chapter we add the data-binding code to the Page_PreRender event handler rather than to the Page_Load event handler. The reason has to do with the ASP.NET event model.

In ASP.NET, event handlers for control events are fired after the Page_Load event, but before the Page_PreRender event. In our examples, we implement navigation by using Button controls. As we'll see, the navigation buttons adjust the value of the Value property of the hfPosition hidden field control to change the Category row that is displayed by the page. For this to work, the Button event handlers must fire before the data binding occurs.

If your page doesn't support navigation, the data-binding code can just as well go in Page_Load. It's only when a control event must affect displayed data that the data binding needs to go in Page_PreRender.

Setting Control Properties Explicitly

The first technique for displaying data values in a control property is to explicitly set the property by using simple assignment. The technique (and the result) is identical to setting the property to a literal value.

Because Web Forms have no equivalent to a BindingContext, you must explicitly identify the DataRow from which the value is to be drawn. Many pages only display a single row (at least at the top level of the data hierarchy), and so the index into the Rows collection is 0. If, as in the examples in this chapter, you want users to be able to navigate through multiple Data-Rows, you must track the current row manually, typically by using a page-level variable or, as in our examples, a hidden field.

For Web pages that are rendered once and then discarded, there is no functional difference between using a page-level variable or a hidden field. In our examples, however, we will be implementing navigation and thus need to persist the row pointer between trips to the server. A hidden field is slightly easier to use here because its value is automatically persisted in the page's ViewState.

Set a Control Property: Visual Basic

1. Open the Chapter 14 – Start Web site in Microsoft Visual Studio 2005, and if necessary, double-click Default.aspx in the Solution Explorer to open the page in the designer.

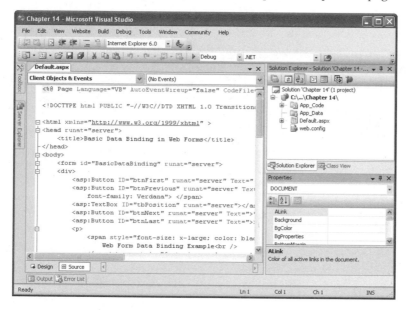

2. Press F7 to display the code-behind page.

3. Add the following lines to the top of the Page_PreRender event handler:

```
Dim pos As Integer
pos = CType(hfPosition.Value, Integer)
tbCategoryID.Text = _
    dsAdoSbs.Categories.Rows(pos).Item("CategoryID").ToString()
```

This code first obtains a numeric representation of the value stored in the hfPosition hidden field control, and then sets the value of the Text property of the tbCategoryID textbox control to the Categories DataRow at that position.

4. Press F5 to run the page.

The browser displays the CategoryID.

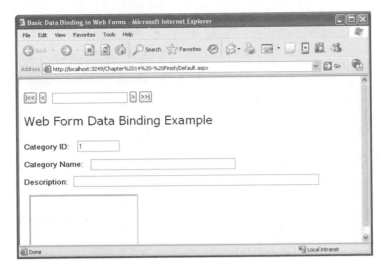

5. Close the browser.

Set a Control Property: Visual C#

1. Open the Chapter 14 – Start Web site in Visual Studio, and if necessary, double-click Default.aspx in the Solution Explorer to open the page in the designer.

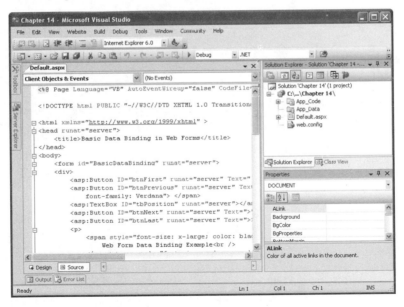

2. Press F7 to display the code-behind page.

3. Add the following lines to the top of the Page_PreRender event handler:

```
int pos;
pos = Convert.ToInt16(hfPosition.Value);

tbCategoryID.Text =
    dsAdoSbs.Categories.Rows[pos]["CategoryID"].ToString();
```

This code first obtains a numeric representation of the value stored in the hfPosition hidden field control, and then sets the value of the Text property of the tbCategoryID textbox control to the Categories DataRow at that position.

4. Press F5 to run the page.

The browser displays the CategoryID.

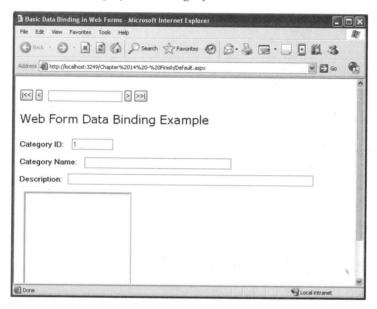

5. Close the browser.

Setting Control Properties by Using DataBinder.Eval

The second technique for displaying data values in a control property is to set the property in code by using the DataBinder.Eval method. The DataBinder class, which is part of the System.Web.UI namespace, exposes a static method, Eval, that evaluates data-binding expressions and optionally formats the result as a string.

The syntax of the Eval method is straightforward, and it can perform type conversion automatically, which greatly simplifies coding in some circumstances. This is particularly true when working with an ADO.NET object, where multiple castings are required and the syntax can be complex. However, the DataBinder is late-bound, and like all late-bound objects, it does incur a performance penalty.

Because the DataBinder is a static object, it can be used without instantiation. It can be called either from within the HTML for the page (surrounded by <%# and %> characters) or in code.

The Eval method is overloaded to accept an optional format string, as shown in Table 14-1.

Table 14-1   DataBinder.Eval Methods

Method	Description
Eval(dataSource, dataExpression)	Returns the value of dataExpression in the data source at run time.
Eval(dataSource, dataExpression, formatStr)	Returns the value of dataExpression in the data source at run time, and then formats it according to the formatStr.

The Eval method expects a data container object as the first parameter. When working with ADO.NET objects, this object is usually a DataSet, DataTable or DataView. It can also be the Container object if the expression runs from within a List control in a template, in which case the first parameter should always be Container.DataItem.

The second parameter of the Eval method is a string that represents the specific data item to be returned. When working with ADO.NET objects, this parameter is typically the name of a DataColumn, but it can be any valid data expression.

The final, optional, parameter is a format specifier that is identical in format to those used by the String.Format method. If this parameter is omitted, the return value of the Eval method is Object, and it must be explicitly cast to the correct type.

Use DataBinder.Eval: Visual Basic

1. Add the following line to the Page_PreRender event handler, after the assignment to tbCategoryID.Text that you added in the previous exercise:

```
tbCategoryName.Text = DataBinder.Eval(dsAdoSbs.Categories.Rows(pos), _
    "CategoryName").ToString()
```

This line assigns a value to the Text property of the tbCategoryName control by using the static Eval method of the DataBinder object.

Your Page_PreRender event should now be:

```
Protected Sub Page_PreRender(ByVal sender As Object, _
    ByVal e As System.EventArgs) Handles Me.PreRender

    Dim pos As Integer
    pos = CType(hfPosition.Value, Integer)
    tbCategoryID.Text = _
        dsAdoSbs.Categories.Rows(pos).Item("CategoryID").ToString()
    tbCategoryNameText = DataBinder.Eval(dsAdoSbs.Categories.Rows(pos), _
        "CategoryName").ToString()

End Sub
```

2. Press F5 to run the page.

   The browser displays the Category Name.

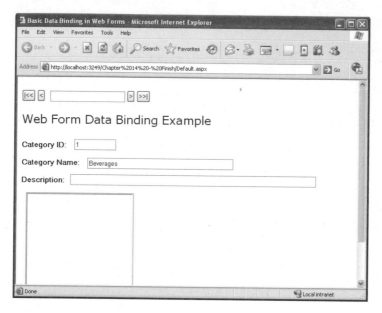

3. Close the browser.

Use DataBinder.Eval: Visual C#

1. Add the following line to the Page_PreRender event handler, after the assignment to tbCategoryID.Text that you added in the previous exercise:

   ```
   tbCategoryName.Text = DataBinder.Eval(dsAdoSbs.Categories.Rows[pos],
       "CategoryName").ToString();
   ```

   This line assigns a value to the Text property of the tbCategoryName control by using the static Eval method of the DataBinder object.

   Your Page_PreRender event should now be:

   ```
   protected void Page_PreRender(object sender, EventArgs e)
   {
      int pos;
      pos = Convert.ToInt16(hfPosition.Value);

      tbCategoryID.Text =
         dsAdoSbs.Categories.Rows[pos]["CategoryID"].ToString();
      tbCategoryName.Text = DataBinder.Eval(dsAdoSbs.Categories.Rows[pos],
         "CategoryName").ToString();

   }
   ```

2. Press F5 to run the page.

   The browser displays the Category Name.

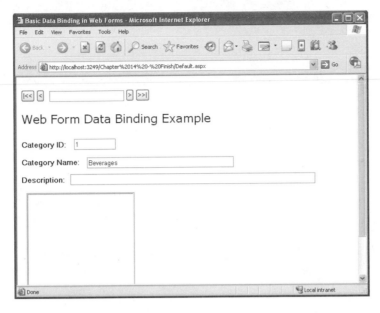

3. Close the browser.

Using Data-Binding Expressions

The final method for pushing data to a control property is a data-binding expression within the HTML stream. Data-binding expressions are surrounded by <%# and %> characters. They are placed within the HTML tag that defines the control.

Unlike the two explicit methods for setting a control property that we examined in the two preceding sections, data-binding expressions aren't implemented until the DataBind method is called. Because the DataBind method of a control calls the DataBind methods of all child controls, calling DataBind on the page is usually sufficient because the method call triggers the methods of all the controls on the page.

Use a Data-Binding Expression: Visual Basic

1. Add the following lines to the end of the Page_PreRender event handler:

```
tbPosition.Text = (pos + 1).ToString() + " of " + _
    dsAdoSbs.Categories.Count.ToString()
DataBind()
```

The first line displays position information in the tbPosition text box, while the second calls the DataBind method of the page, which in turn calls DataBind on all the controls on the page.

Your Page_PreRender event handler should be as shown on the next page.

```
Protected Sub Page_PreRender(ByVal sender As Object, _
    ByVal e As System.EventArgs) Handles Me.PreRender

    Dim pos As Integer = CType(hfPosition.Value, Integer)
    tbCategoryID.Text = _
        dsAdoSbs.Categories.Rows(pos).Item("CategoryID").ToString()
    tbCategoryNameText = DataBinder.Eval(dsAdoSbs.Categories.Rows(pos), _
        "CategoryName").ToString()

    tbPosition.Text = (pos + 1).ToString() + " of " + _
        dsAdoSbs.Categories.Count.ToString()
    DataBind()
End Sub
```

2. Select the Default.aspx tab of the designer, and if necessary, click the Source button. Visual Studio displays the HTML stream.

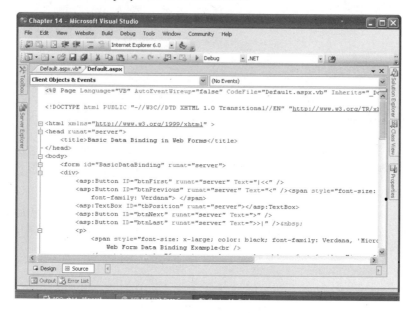

3. Add the following attribute to the tbDescription text box:

```
Text=<%#dsAdoSbs.Categories.Rows(hfPosition.Value).Item("Description")%>
```

This line uses a data-binding expression surrounded by <%# and %> characters to assign a value to the Text property of the tbDescription control.

The declaration of this control should now be:

```
<asp:TextBox ID="tbDescription"
    Text=<%#dsAdoSbs.Categories.Rows(hfPosition.Value).Item("Description")%>
    runat="server" Style="z-index: 103; left: 112px;
    position: absolute; top: 200px" Width="504px"></asp:TextBox>
```

4. Press F5 to run the page.

The browser displays the Description.

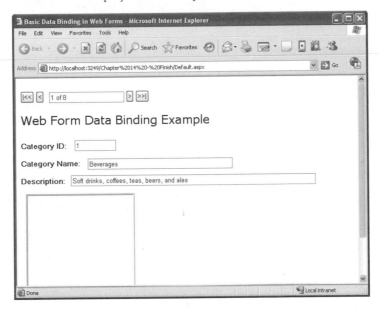

5. Close the browser.

Use a Data-Binding Expression: Visual C#

1. Add the following lines to the end of the Page_PreRender event handler:

```
tbPosition.Text = (pos + 1).ToString() + " of " +
    dsAdoSbs.Categories.Count.ToString();
DataBind();
```

The first line displays position information in the tbPosition text box, while the second calls the DataBind method of the page, which in turn calls DataBind on all the controls on the page.

Your Page_PreRender event handler should be:

```
protected void Page_PreRender(object sender, EventArgs e)
{
    int pos;
    pos = Convert.ToInt16(hfPosition.Value);

    tbCategoryID.Text =
        dsAdoSbs.Categories.Rows[pos]["CategoryID"].ToString();
    tbCategoryNaText = DataBinder.Eval(dsAdoSbs.Categories.Rows[pos],
        "CategoryName").ToString();

    tbPosition.Text = (pos + 1).ToString() + " of " +
        dsAdoSbs.Categories.Count.ToString();
    DataBind();
}
```

2. Select the Default.aspx tab of the designer, and if necessary, click the Source button. Visual Studio displays the HTML stream.

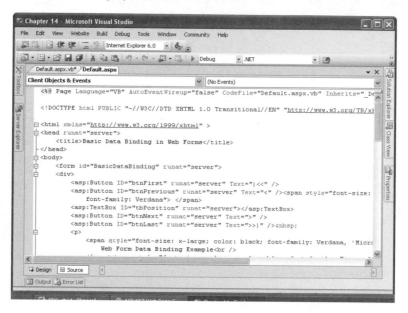

3. Add the following attribute to the tbDescription text box:

```
Text=<%#dsAdoSbs.Categories.Rows[Convert.ToInt16(hfPosition.Value)]
    ["Description"]%>
```

This line uses a data-binding expression surrounded by <%# and %> characters to assign a value to the Text property of the tbDescription control.

The declaration of this control should now be:

```
<asp:TextBox ID="tbDescription"
    Text=<%#dsAdoSbs.Categories.Rows[Convert.ToInt16(hfPosition.Value)]
    ["Description"]%>
    runat="server" Style="z-index: 103; left: 112px;
    position: absolute; top: 200px" Width="504px"></asp:TextBox>
```

4. Press F5 to run the page.

The browser displays the Description.

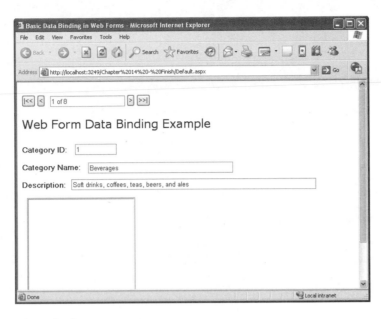

5. Close the browser.

Complex-Binding Web Controls

All complex-bound Web controls descend from either BaseDataBoundControl or BaseData-List, and are thus designed to work with the new Data Source controls. However, it is possible to bind them to ADO.NET objects by using techniques very similar to those used in the Windows Form environment.

All complex-bound controls expose DataSource and DataMember properties. Just as in the Windows Form environment, the DataSource property is set to the data container, which when you work with ADO.NET properties is typically a DataSet, DataTable or DataView. If the Data Source contains multiple lists, as in the case of a DataSet that contains multiple DataTables, the DataMember property is used to identify the list from which the control will draw its data. This is similar to the corresponding properties in the Windows Form environment, but the syntax is less flexible.

Finally, controls such as the ListBox that display a single value expose a DataTextField property that is used to identify the single column to be displayed.

Complex-Bind a ListBox Control: Visual Basic

1. Click the Default.aspx.vb tab, and add the following lines to the Page_PreRender event handler, before the call to DataBind that we added in the previous exercise:

```
dvProducts.Table = dsAdoSbs.Products
dvProducts.RowFilter = "CategoryID = " & tbCategoryID.Text

lbProducts.DataSource = dvProducts
lbProducts.DataMember = "Products"
lbProducts.DataTextField = "ProductName"
```

The first two lines filter the dvProducts DataView (declared and instantiated as part of the exercise scaffolding). The remaining lines assign the data-binding properties of the lbProducts ListBox control to the DataView.

Your Page_PreRender event handler should now be:

```
Protected Sub Page_PreRender(ByVal sender As Object, _
   ByVal e As System.EventArgs) Handles Me.PreRender

   Dim pos As Integer
   pos = CType(hfPosition.Value, Integer)
   tbCategoryID.Text = _
      dsAdoSbs.Categories.Rows(pos).Item("CategoryID").ToString()
   tbCategoryNaText = DataBinder.Eval(dsAdoSbs.Categories.Rows(pos), _
      "CategoryName").ToString()

   tbPosition.Text = (pos + 1).ToString() + " of " + _
      dsAdoSbs.Categories.Count.ToString()

   dvProducts.Table = dsAdoSbs.Products
   dvProducts.RowFilter = "CategoryID = " & tbCategoryID.Text

   lbProducts.DataSource = dvProducts
   lbProducts.DataMember = "Products"
   lbProducts.DataTextField = "ProductName"

   DataBind()
End Sub
```

2. Press F5 to run the page.

The browser fills the lbProducts list box with the names of products related to the current category.

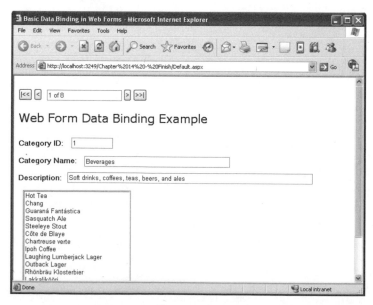

3. Close the browser.

Complex-Bind a ListBox Control: Visual C#

1. Click the Default.aspx.cs tab, and add the following lines to the Page_PreRender event handler, before the call to DataBind that we added in the previous exercise:

```
dvProducts.Table = dsAdoSbs.Products;
dvProducts.RowFilter = "CategoryID = " + tbCategoryID.Text;

lbProducts.DataSource = dvProducts;
lbProducts.DataMember = "Products";
lbProducts.DataTextField = "ProductName";
```

The first two lines filter the dvProducts DataView (declared and instantiated as part of the exercise scaffolding). The remaining lines assign the data-binding properties of the lbProducts ListBox control to the DataView.

Your Page_PreRender event handler should now be:

```
protected void Page_PreRender(object sender, EventArgs e)
{
    int pos;
    pos = Convert.ToInt16(hfPosition.Value);

    tbCategoryID.Text =
        dsAdoSbs.Categories.Rows[pos]["CategoryID"].ToString();
    tbCategoryNaText = DataBinder.Eval(dsAdoSbs.Categories.Rows[pos],
        "CategoryName").ToString();

    tbPosition.Text = (pos + 1).ToString() + " of " +
        dsAdoSbs.Categories.Count.ToString();

    dvProducts.Table = dsAdoSbs.Products;
    dvProducts.RowFilter = "CategoryID = " + tbCategoryID.Text;

    lbProducts.DataSource = dvProducts;
    lbProducts.DataMember = "Products";
    lbProducts.DataTextField = "ProductName";

    DataBind();
}
```

2. Press F5 to run the page.

The browser fills the lbProducts list box with the names of products related to the current category.

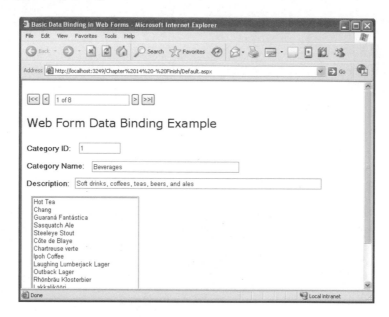

3. Close the browser.

Maintaining ADO.NET Object State

Because the Web Form doesn't maintain state between round-trips to the server, if you want to maintain a DataSet between the time that the page is first created and the time that it takes the user to send it back with changes, you must do so explicitly.

You can maintain a DataSet on the server by storing it in either the Application state or Session state, or you can maintain it on the page in the View state. You can also store the DataSet in a hidden field on the page, which is in fact what happens when you store it in the View state.

Whether you maintain the data on the server or the page, you must always be aware of concurrency issues. You can improve performance significantly by saving round-trips to the server, particularly if the data requires calculations. But changes to the underlying data source aren't reflected in the stored data. If the data is volatile, you must re-create the ADO.NET objects each time to ensure that they reflect the most recent changes.

Maintaining ADO.NET Objects on the Server

ASP.NET provides several mechanisms for maintaining state within an Internet application. On the server side, the Application state and Session state are the easiest to use. Both state structures are dictionaries that store data as name/value pairs. The value is stored and retrieved as an object, so you must cast it to the correct type when you restore it.

The Application state and Session state are used identically; the difference is scope. The Application state is global to all pages and all users within the application. The Session state is specific to a single browser session. (For additional information about the Application state and Session state, see the ASP.NET documentation.)

The IsPostBack property of the Page class, which is False the first time a page is loaded for a specific browser session and True thereafter, can be used in the Page_Load event to control when the data is created and loaded.

Store the DataSet in the Session State: Visual Basic

1. Add the following lines to the Page_Load event handler, inside the If block, where indicated:

```
dsAdoSbs = CType(Session("dsAdoSbs"), AdoSbsDataSet)
```

This line restores the DataSet, but only if the event handler is being called from a Postback event.

2. Add the following line to the Page_Load event handler, inside the Else block, where indicated:

```
Session("dsAdoSbs") = dsAdoSbs
```

This line stores the dsAdoSbs DataSet to the Session state with the key dsAdoSbs.

Your Page_Load event handler should now be:

```
Protected Sub Page_Load(ByVal sender As Object, _
    ByVal e As System.EventArgs) Handles Me.Load
    taCategories = New AdoSbsDataSetTableAdapters.CategoriesTableAdapter()
    taProducts = New AdoSbsDataSetTableAdapters.ProductsTableAdapter()
    dvProducts = New DataView()
    dsAdoSbs = New AdoSbsDataSet()

    If IsPostBack Then
        'Add exercise code here:
        dsAdoSbs = CType(Session("dsAdoSbs"), AdoSbsDataSet)
    Else
        taCategories.Fill(dsAdoSbs.Categories)
        taProducts.Fill(dsAdoSbs.Products)
        'Add exercise code here
        Session("dsAdoSbs") = dsAdoSbs
        hfPosition.Value = "0"
    End If
End Sub
```

Store the DataSet in the Session State: Visual C#

1. Add the following lines to the Page_Load event handler, inside the If block, where indicated:

```
dsAdoSbs = (AdoSbsDataSet)Session["dsAdoSbs"];
```

This line restores the DataSet, but only if the event handler is being called from a Post-back event.

2. Add the following line to the Page_Load event handler, inside the Else block, where indicated:

```
Session["dsAdoSbs"] = dsAdoSbs;
```

This line stores the dsAdoSbs DataSet to the Session state with the key dsAdoSbs.

Your Page_Load event handler should now be:

```
protected void Page_Load(object sender, EventArgs e)
{
    taCategories = new AdoSbsDataSetTableAdapters.CategoriesTableAdapter();
    taProducts = new AdoSbsDataSetTableAdapters.ProductsTableAdapter();
    dvProducts = new DataView();
    dsAdoSbs = new AdoSbsDataSet();

    if (IsPostBack)
    {
        //Add exercise code here:
        dsAdoSbs = (AdoSbsDataSet)Session["dsAdoSbs"];
    }
    else
    {
        taCategories.Fill(dsAdoSbs.Categories);
        taProducts.Fill(dsAdoSbs.Products);

        //Add exercise code here:
        Session["dsAdoSbs"] = dsAdoSbs;

        hfPosition.Value = "0";
    }
}
```

Maintaining ADO.NET Objects on the Page

Storing data on the server can be convenient, but it consumes server resources and can therefore negatively impact scalability. An alternative is to store the data on the page itself. This relieves the pressure on the server, but because the data is passed as part of the data stream, it can increase the time it requires to load and post the page.

Data is stored on the page either in a custom hidden field or in the ViewState property of a control. In theory, any ViewState property can be used, but the Page class's ViewState is the most common.

Store a DataSet in the ViewState Property: Visual Basic

1. Comment out the two lines that save and restore the DataSet to the Session state, which we added in the previous exercise.

2. Add the following lines to the Page_Load event handler, replacing the line that restored the DataSet from the Session state:

```
dsAdoSbs = CType(ViewState("dsAdoSbs"), AdoSbsDataSet)
```

This line restores the DataSet, but only if the event handler is being called from a Post-back event.

3. Add the following line to the Page_Load event handler, replacing the Session state assignment:

```
ViewState("dsAdoSbs") = dsAdoSbs
```

This line stores the dsAdoSbs DataSet to the ViewState with the key dsAdoSbs.

Your Page_Load event handler should now be:

```
Protected Sub Page_Load(ByVal sender As Object, _
    ByVal e As System.EventArgs) Handles Me.Load

    If IsPostBack Then
        'Add exercise code here:
        'dsAdoSbs = CType(Session("dsAdoSbs"), AdoSbsDataSet)
        dsAdoSbs = CType(ViewState("dsAdoSbs"), AdoSbsDataSet)

    Else
        taCategories.Fill(dsAdoSbs.Categories)
        taProducts.Fill(dsAdoSbs.Products)
        'Add exercise code here
        'Session("dsAdoSbs") = dsAdoSbs
        ViewState("dsAdoSbs") = dsAdoSbs
        hfPosition.Value = "0"
    End If
End Sub
```

Store a DataSet in the ViewState Property: Visual C#

1. Comment out the two lines that save and restore the DataSet to the Session state, which we added in the previous exercise.

2. Add the following lines to the Page_Load event handler, replacing the line that restored the DataSet from the Session state:

```
dsAdoSbs = (AdoSbsDataSet)ViewState["dsAdoSbs"];
```

This line restores the DataSet, but only if the event handler is being called from a Post-back event.

3. Add the following line to the Page_Load event handler, replacing the Session state assignment:

```
ViewState["dsAdoSbs"] = dsAdoSbs;
```

This line stores the dsAdoSbs DataSet to the ViewState with the key dsAdoSbs.

Your Page_Load event handler should now be:

```
protected void Page_Load(object sender, EventArgs e)
{
    taCategories = new AdoSbsDataSetTableAdapters.CategoriesTableAdapter();
    taProducts = new AdoSbsDataSetTableAdapters.ProductsTableAdapter();
    dvProducts = new DataView();
    dsAdoSbs = new AdoSbsDataSet();

    if (IsPostBack)
    {
        //Add exercise code here:
        //dsAdoSbs = (AdoSbsDataSet)Session["dsAdoSbs"];
        dsAdoSbs = (AdoSbsDataSet)ViewState["dsAdoSbs"];
    }
    else
    {
        taCategories.Fill(dsAdoSbs.Categories);
        taProducts.Fill(dsAdoSbs.Products);

        //Add exercise code here:
        //Session["dsAdoSbs"] = dsAdoSbs;
        ViewState["dsAdoSbs"] = dsAdoSbs;

        hfPosition.Value = "0";
    }
}
```

Implementing Navigation

When we examined navigation in Windows Forms in Chapter 11, "Manual Data Binding in Windows Forms," we saw that changing the Position property of the CurrencyManager changes the DataRow currently displayed on the form. The process is identical in the Web Form environment, but as with displaying data from ADO.NET objects, you have to handle the entire process manually.

In earlier exercises in this chapter, we used the Value property of the hfPosition hidden field control as an index into the Categories table. The hfPosition.Value property is initially set to 0 (the first row in the zero-based DataTable.Rows collection). To implement navigation, you manipulate this property by using code that is remarkably similar to navigation code for a Windows Form.

In Chapter 11, for example, the code for the btnNext_Click event handler was:

Visual Basic
```
Private Sub btnNext_Click(ByVal sender As System.Object, _
    ByVal e As System.EventArgs) Handles btnNext.Click

    Dim bmb As BindingManagerBase
    bmb = BindingContext(dsAdoSbs, "Categories")
```

```
      If bmb.Position = bmb.Count - 1 Then
         Console.Beep()
      Else
         bmb.Position += 1
      End If
   End Sub
```

Visual C#

```csharp
private void btnNext_Click(object sender, EventArgs e)
{
   BindingManagerBase bmb;
   bmb = BindingContext[dsAdoSbs, "Categories"];

   if (bmb.Position == bmb.Count - 1)
      Console.Beep();
   else
      bmb.Position += 1;
}
```

Compare this code with the equivalent procedures in the exercises for this chapter:

Visual Basic

```vbnet
Protected Sub btnNext_Click(ByVal sender As Object, _
   ByVal e As System.EventArgs) Handles btnNext.Click

   Dim pos As Integer = CType(hfPosition.Value, Integer)

   If pos < (dsAdoSbs.Categories.Count - 1) Then
      pos += 1
      hfPosition.Value = pos.ToString()
   End If
End Sub
```

Visual C#

```csharp
protected void btnNext_Click(object sender, EventArgs e)
{
   int pos = Convert.ToInt16(hfPosition.Value);
   if (pos < dsAdoSbs.Categories.Count - 1)
   {
      pos += 1;
      hfPosition.Value = pos.ToString();
   }
}
```

As you can see, the basic functionality is identical; if the position counter is less than the number of rows, decrement it. There are two trivial differences.

The first difference concerns the position counter. In the Web Form, the position counter is a hidden field, so there's no need to obtain a reference to the BindingManagerBase. But the Value property, a string, must be cast to a numeric value before the position is adjusted, and the count must be retrieved from the DataTable itself.

The other difference is environmental: Sounding a beep is problematic in the Web environment, so that part of the code is simply omitted.

Implement Move First Navigation: Visual Basic

1. Add the following line to the btnFirst_Click event handler:

   ```
   hfPosition.Value = "0"
   ```

   This line circumvents the casting required to translate the numeric row position to the string Value property by using the string representation of the digit 0.

2. Press F5 to run the page.

3. Use the navigation buttons to move through the Categories DataTable.

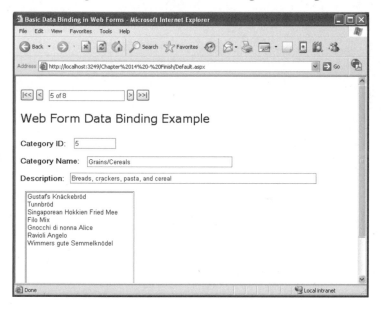

4. Close the browser.

Implement Move First Navigation: Visual C#

1. Add the following line to the btnFirst_Click event handler:

   ```
   hfPosition.Value = "0";
   ```

   This line circumvents the casting required to translate the numeric row position to the string Value property by using the string representation of the digit 0.

2. Press F5 to run the page.

3. Use the navigation buttons to move through the Categories DataTable.

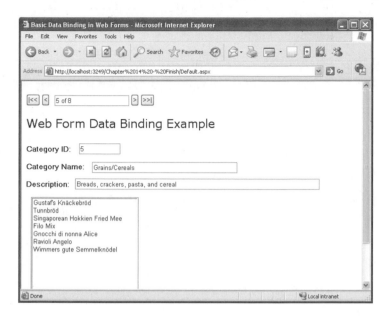

4. Close the browser.

> **Note** In a real-world Web application, you would include code to disable the navigation controls, but that bit of code is omitted from this example for simplicity. Another omission: Passing the entire DataSet back and forth between the browser and server works perfectly well in the example because both DataTables are quite small, but in a real-world application, you would typically include code to filter the data, passing only a single Category DataRow and its related Product DataRows. You would typically do this using a standard SQL SELECT...WHERE statement.

Updating an Underlying Data Source

Remember that ADO.NET objects behave in exactly the same manner when they're instantiated in a Web Form as when they're used in a Windows Form. In theory, identical behavior should mean that the processes of updating a data source are identical.

On one level, they are. The actual update is performed by directly running a Data command or by calling the Update method of an Adapter. But remember that the Web data-binding architecture is one-way. Because of this, you must explicitly push the values returned by the page into the appropriate data object.

On a Windows Form, after a control property has been bound to a column in a DataTable, any changes that the user makes to the value are immediately and automatically reflected in the DataTable. On a Web Form, on the other hand, you must explicitly retrieve the value from the control and update the ADO.NET object. You might, for example, use the control values to set the parameters of a Data command or update a row in a DataTable.

Using a Command Object

Perhaps the most straightforward way to update an underlying data source is to use a Data Command, which performs the update directly and efficiently. The drawback of this technique is that a Data Command updates the data source, but not the DataTable.

To reflect the changes in the DataTable and the Page that are sent to the browser after the postback, you must either update the DataTable as a separate step or refill the DataTable from the underlying data source. The latter approach incurs a performance penalty because you're making a round-trip to the database server, but it does ensure concurrency.

Update a Data Source by Using a Command Object: Visual Basic

1. Add the following code to the btnUpdateCmd_Click event handler:

```
Dim cn As New SqlConnection()
cn.ConnectionString = "Data Source=(local)\SQLEXPRESS;" + _
    "Initial Catalog=AdoStepByStep;Integrated Security=True"

Dim cmdUpdate As New SqlCommand()
cmdUpdate.Connection = cn
cmdUpdate.CommandText = "UPDATE Categories " + _
    "SET CategoryName = @name, Description = @description WHERE (CategoryID = @ID)"
cmdUpdate.Parameters.AddWithValue("@name", tbCategoryName.Text)
cmdUpdate.Parameters.AddWithValue("@description", tbDescription.Text)
cmdUpdate.Parameters.AddWithValue("@ID", tbCategoryID.Text)

cn.Open()
cmdUpdate.ExecuteNonQuery()
cn.Close()

taCategories.Fill(dsAdoSbs.Categories)
```

This code first creates and instantiates a new SqlConnection object. It then declares a new SqlCommand and sets its ConnectionString, Connection and CommandText properties.

It then adds three Parameters to the Command by using the AddWithValue method to assign them the values of the Text properties of TextBox controls. The next block of code uses the ExecuteNonQuery method of the Command object to update the underlying data source. Finally, the code updates the Categories DataTable by using the Fill method of the TableAdapter.

2. Press F5 to run the page.

3. Type **XXX** at the end of the Description.

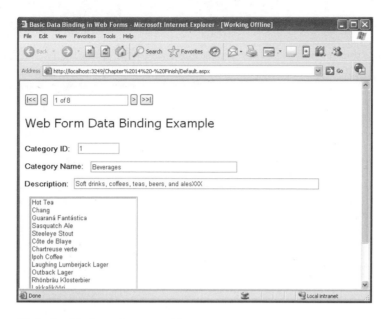

4. Click the Update Command button.

5. Close the browser, press F5 to re-open the browser, and then confirm that the change has been persisted to the underlying data source.

6. Close the browser.

Update a Data Source by Using a Command Object: Visual C#

1. Add the following code to the btnUpdateCmd_Click event handler:

```
SqlConnection cn - new SqlConnection();
cn.ConnectionString = "Data Source=(local)\\SQLEXPRESS;" +
    "Initial Catalog=AdoStepByStep;Integrated Security=True";

SqlCommand cmdUpdate = new SqlCommand();
cmdUpdate.Connection = cn;
cmdUpdate.CommandText = "UPDATE Categories " +
    "SET CategoryName = @name, Description = @description WHERE (CategoryID = @ID)";

cmdUpdate.Parameters.AddWithValue("@name", tbCategoryName.Text);
cmdUpdate.Parameters.AddWithValue("@description", tbDescription.Text);
cmdUpdate.Parameters.AddWithValue("@ID", tbCategoryID.Text);

cn.Open();
cmdUpdate.ExecuteNonQuery();
cn.Close();

taCategories.Fill(dsAdoSbs.Categories);
```

This code first creates and instantiates a new SqlConnection object. It then declares a new SqlCommand and sets its ConnectionString, Connection and CommandText properties.

It then adds three Parameters to the Command by using the AddWithValue method to assign them the values of the Text properties of TextBox controls. The next block of code uses the ExecuteNonQuery method of the Command object to update the underlying data source. Finally, the code updates the Categories DataTable by using the Fill method of the TableAdapter.

2. Press F5 to run the page.

3. Type **XXX** at the end of the Description.

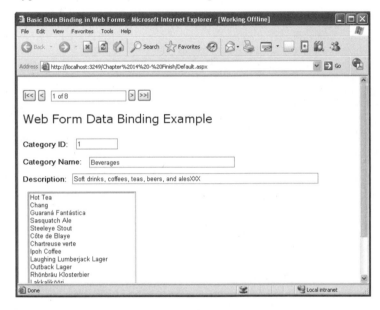

4. Click the Update Command button.

5. Close the browser, press F5 to re-open the browser, and then confirm that the change has been persisted to the underlying data source.

6. Close the browser.

Using an Adapter

In the previous exercise, we updated the underlying data source directly by using a Data Command. As we saw, this is an efficient technique, but it doesn't update the DataSet persisted in the ViewState property.

An alternative approach is to first update the DataSet, and then use either a TableAdapter or DataAdapter to update the underlying data source through the DataSet. This approach ensures that the data returned to users reflects any changes they make, and it allows you to leverage the adapter functionality. In most cases you will already have instantiated an instance of either a TableAdapter or a DataAdapter to fill the DataTable.

Update a Data Source by Using a TableAdapter: Visual Basic

1. Add the following code to the btnUpdateAdapter_Click event handler:

```
Dim dr As DataRow
dr = dsAdoSbs.Categories.Rows(CType(hfPosition.Value, Integer))

dr("CategoryName") = tbCategoryName.Text
dr("Description") = tbDescription.Text

taCategories.Update(dsAdoSbs.Categories)
```

This code first declares a new DataRow, setting it to the current row of the Categories DataTable. This isn't strictly necessary, but it makes the remaining code easier to read.

The second block updates two columns of the DataRow based on the Text values of TextBox controls on the page, while the final line updates the Categories table in the underlying data source by using the Update method of the TableAdapter.

2. Press F5 to run the page.

3. Change the Description back to its original value by removing the XXX.

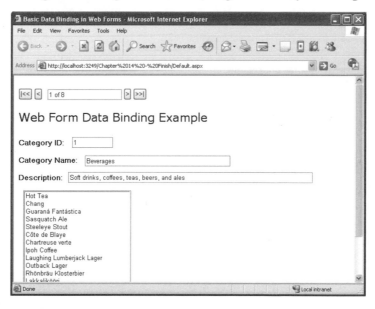

4. Click the Update TableAdapter button.

5. Close the browser, press F5 to re-open the browser, and then confirm that the change has been persisted to the underlying data source.

6. Close the browser.

Update a Data Source by Using a TableAdapter: Visual C#

1. Add the code on the next page to the btnUpdateAdapter_Click event handler.

```
DataRow dr;
dr = dsAdoSbs.Categories.Rows[Convert.ToInt16(hfPosition.Value)];

dr["CategoryName"] = tbCategoryName.Text;
dr["Description"] = tbDescription.Text;

taCategories.Update(dsAdoSbs.Categories);
```

This code first declares a new DataRow, setting it to the current row of the Categories DataTable. This isn't strictly necessary, but it makes the remaining code easier to read.

The second block updates two columns of the DataRow based on the Text values of TextBox controls on the page, while the final line updates the Categories table in the underlying data source by using the Update method of the TableAdapter.

2.   Press F5 to run the page.

3.   Change the Description back to its original value by removing the XXX.

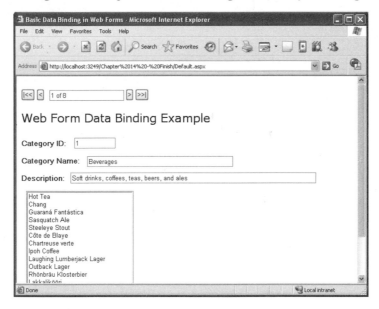

4.   Click the Update TableAdapter button.

5.   Close the browser, press F5 to re-open the browser, confirm that the change has been persisted to the underlying data source, and then close the browser again.

Summary

In this chapter we began our examination of data binding in the Web Form environment by examining manual binding with low-level ADO.NET objects. We saw that unlike Windows Form data binding, Web Form data binding is one-way: Changes made to the values displayed on the page will not be reflected in the underlying DataTable unless some action is taken in code.

Chapter 15

Data Binding in Web Forms by Using the Data Source Component

After completing this chapter, you will be able to:

- Create a data source in the Visual Web Designer.
- Create a data source at run time.
- Configure Data Source controls.
- Enable Data Source caching.
- Use Data Source methods.
- Respond to Data Source events.

In Chapter 14, "Basic Data Binding in Web Forms," we examined the techniques for binding Web Form controls to Microsoft ADO.NET objects. In this chapter, we'll examine the Data Source controls that are new to Microsoft .NET Framework 2.0.

Understanding the Data Source Component

New to the .NET Framework 2.0, the Data Source component is roughly equivalent to the Windows Form BindingSource component, in that it serves as an intermediary between ADO.NET and bound controls displayed on a form, but there are several important differences.

The most obvious difference is that, unlike the BindingSource, the Data Source is not data-provider independent. There are several versions customized for different providers, as shown in Table 15-1.

Table 15-1   Data Source Controls

Control	Description
SqlDataSource	Communicates with data sources that use SQL for retrieving and updating data.
AccessDataSource	A descendant of the SqlDataSource customized for OleDb databases.
ObjectDataSource	Communicates with middle-tier data objects.
XmlDataSource	Communicates with Extensible Markup Language (XML) data.
SiteMapDataSource	Communicates with site-map providers.

You'll notice that the categories of Data Source controls don't correspond to ADO.NET Data Providers. In fact, all of the Data Providers defined in the System.Data namespace can be accessed using the SqlDataSource. The "Sql" prefix, in this case, refers to the SQL language, not the Microsoft SQL Server database engine.

The AccessDataSource is a direct descendant of the SqlDataSource control. The functionality of the two classes is identical. The only difference is the connection properties. The Access-DataSource replaces the ConnectionString property with a DataFile property, which is simpler to specify at run time.

All of the Data Source controls descend from the System.Web.UI.DataSourceControl, and as such, are not technically part of ADO.NET, which is defined in the System.Data namespace. However, the SqlDataSource and AccessDataSource controls that talk to relational data presumably do encapsulate ADO.NET objects. These are the only two versions of the Data Source controls that we'll be discussing.

The second difference between the BindingSource and the SqlDataSource control is that the latter's functionality is somewhat less extensive. The CurrencyManager still isn't present in the Web Form environment, so using a SqlDataSource doesn't provide navigation. If you want to support navigation on your form, you'll need to use the techniques we examined in Chapter 14.

Surprisingly, the SqlDataSource also doesn't provide access to the data it manages. The List or Item properties exposed by the BindingSource control have no SqlDataSource equivalent.

In essence, the SqlDataSource functionality is limited to connecting to data and implementing Select, Insert, Delete and Update commands, and controlling data caching. But this component isn't just a simple encapsulation of objects. It also supports the data-bound controls that we'll examine in Chapter 16, "Data-Bound and Validation Controls," and provides a mechanism for implementing two-way data binding with standard Web controls.

Creating Data Source Components

Unlike ADO.NET objects, Data Source controls can be created both at design time and at run time in the Visual Web Developer by using the usual techniques.

Creating Data Source Components at Design Time

All Data Source controls are included on the Data tab of the Visual Web Designer toolbox that is available in the designer. To create a design-time Data Source, simply drag the correct control onto the design surface.

Create a Data Source in the Visual Web Designer

1. Open the Chapter 15 – Start Web site in Microsoft Visual Studio 2005, and if necessary, double-click Default.aspx in the Solution Explorer, and then click the Design button to display the page in form view.

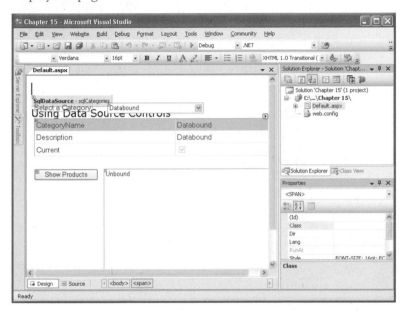

2. From the Toolbox, drag an instance of the SqlDataSource control onto the design surface.

3. In the Properties window, change the ID of the control to **sqlCategoryDetails**.

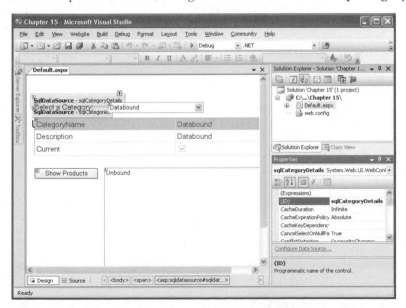

Creating Data Source Components at Run Time

Any Web Form control can be instantiated and configured in the HTML stream, but HTML lies outside the scope of this book. You can, of course, also instantiate the controls by using your chosen CLR-compliant language and standard programming techniques. The only requirement is that you must add the control, once it has been instantiated, to the Controls collection of the page or a container control on the page.

Create a Data Source in Code: Visual Basic

1. Press F7 to display the code-behind file for the page.

2. Add the following line to the top of the class declaration, before the Page_PreInit event handler:

    ```
    Dim WithEvents sqlProducts As SqlDataSource
    ```

3. Add the following line to the Page_PreInit event handler:

    ```
    sqlProducts = New SqlDataSource()
    sqlProducts.ID = "sqlProducts"
    Me.Controls.Add(sqlProducts)
    ```

    The first two lines instantiate the Data Source control and set its ID property. The final line adds the control to the Controls collection of the page. The beginning of your class file should now be:

    ```
    Imports System.Data
    Imports System.Data.SqlClient
    Imports System.Web.UI

    Partial Class _Default
        Inherits System.Web.UI.Page

        Dim sqlProducts As SqlDataSource
        Protected Sub Page_PreInit(ByVal sender As Object, _
            ByVal e As System.EventArgs) Handles Me.PreInit

            sqlProducts = New SqlDataSource()
            sqlProducts.ID = "sqlProducts"
            Me.Controls.Add(sqlProducts)
        End Sub
    ```

Create a Data Source in Code: Visual C#

1. Press F7 to display the code-behind file for the page.

2. Add the following line to the top of the class declaration, before the Page_PreInit event handler:

    ```
    SqlDataSource sqlProducts;
    ```

3. Add the following line to the Page_PreInit event handler:

```
sqlProducts = new SqlDataSource();
sqlProducts.ID = "sqlProducts";
this.Controls.Add(sqlProducts);
```

The beginning of your class file should now be:

```
using System;
using System.Data;
using System.Data.SqlClient;
using System.Configuration;
using System.Web;
using System.Web.Security;
using System.Web.UI;
using System.Web.UI.WebControls;
using System.Web.UI.WebControls.WebParts;
using System.Web.UI.HtmlControls;

public partial class _Default : System.Web.UI.Page
{
    SqlDataSource sqlProducts;
    protected void Page_PreInit(object sender, EventArgs e)
    {
        sqlProducts = new SqlDataSource();
        sqlProducts.ID = "sqlProducts";
        this.Controls.Add(sqlProducts);
    }
```

Configuring Data Source Controls

The properties exposed by the Data Source control fall neatly into four categories:

- Connection properties, which determine how the Data Source control connects to the underlying data source.
- Command properties, which specify the SQL statements used by the Data Source control, along with the command behavior.
- Configuration properties, which determine the behavior of the Data Source control.
- Caching properties, which determine whether the Data Source control caches data, and if so, how.

With the exception of the Connection properties, the SqlDataSource and AccessDataSource expose the same properties, and we'll examine each set of properties in this section.

Connection Properties

The first set of properties exposed by the Data Source controls are the Connection properties, which, as you'd expect, determine how the control connects to the underlying data source.

These are the only properties that work differently for the SqlDataSource and AccessData-
Source, as shown in Tables 15-2 and 15-3.

Table 15-2   SqlDataSource Connection Properties

Property	Description
ConnectionString	The string that is used to connect to the underlying data source.
ProviderName	The name of the Data Provider that is used to connect to the underlying data source.

Table 15-3   AccessDataSource Connection Properties

Property	Description
ConnectionString	The string that is used to connect to the underlying data source.
DataFile	The location of the database file.
ProviderName	The name of the Data Provider that is used to connect to the underlying data source.

In the SqlDataSource, the ConnectionString completely specifies the provider, data table and
access mechanism, while the ProviderName determines the ADO.NET Data Provider used
for access.

In the AccessDataSource, the DataFile is used to specify the location and file name of the .mdb
file from which the AccessDataSource draws its data, while the ConnectionString is created at
run time, and the ProviderName is always OleDb. The later two properties are read-only in
this Data Source control.

Set Connection Properties: Visual Basic

1. In the Code Editor, add the following line to the bottom of the Page_PreInit event
    handler:

```
sqlProducts.ConnectionString = _
    "Data Source=(local)\SQLEXPRESS;Initial Catalog=AdoStepByStep;" + _
    "Integrated Security=True"
```

The body of the event handler event handler should now be:

```
sqlProducts = New SqlDataSource()
sqlProducts.ID = "sqlProducts"
Me.Controls.Add(sqlProducts)

sqlProducts.ConnectionString = _
    "Data Source=(local)\SQLEXPRESS;Initial Catalog=AdoStepByStep;" + _
    "Integrated Security=True"
```

Set Connection Properties: Visual C#

1. In the Code Editor, add the following line to the bottom of the Page_PreInit event handler:

```
sqlProducts.ConnectionString =
    "Data Source=(local)\\SQLEXPRESS;Initial Catalog=AdoStepByStep;" +
    "Integrated Security=True";
```

The body of the event handler should now be:

```
sqlProducts = new SqlDataSource();
sqlProducts.ID = "sqlProducts";
this.Controls.Add(sqlProducts);

sqlProducts.ConnectionString =
    "Data Source=(local)\\SQLEXPRESS;Initial Catalog = AdoStepByStep;" +
    "Integrated Security=True";
```

Command Properties

The next set of properties define the SQL commands used by the Data Source control to retrieve, update, insert and delete rows in the underlying data source. There is a set of commands for each action, and each command set has three separate properties, as shown in Table 15-4.

Table 15-4   Data Source Command Properties

Property	Description
DeleteCommand	The SQL statement or stored procedure that is used to delete rows from the underlying data source.
DeleteCommandType	Determines whether the string contained in DeleteCommand should be interpreted as a SQL statement or stored procedure.
DeleteParameters	The ParameterCollection used by the Delete command.
InsertCommand	The SQL statement or stored procedure that is used to insert rows into the underlying data source.
InsertCommandType	Determines whether the InsertCommand string is interpreted as a SQL statement or stored procedure.
InsertParameters	The ParameterCollection used by the Insert command.
SelectCommand	The SQL statement or stored procedure that is used to retrieve data from the underlying data source.
SelectCommandType	Determines whether the SelectCommand string is interpreted as a SQL statement or stored procedure.
SelectParameters	The ParameterCollection used by the Select command.
UpdateCommand	The SQL statement or stored procedure that is used to update data in the underlying data source.
UpdateCommandType	Determines whether the UpdateCommand string is interpreted as a SQL statement or stored procedure.
UpdateParameters	The ParameterCollection used by the Update command.

The <action>Command properties, where <action> is either Select, Update, Insert or Delete, correspond to the CommandText property of the ADO.NET Data Command classes. These properties contain the SQL statement or stored procedure to be executed.

As with the DataColumn classes, the <action>CommandType properties specify how the string contained in the <action>Command property is to be interpreted. For both the SqlData-Source and AccessDataSource, the <action>CommandType property accepts a member of the SqlDataSourceCommandType enumeration, which has the values StoredProcedure and Text.

Each type of command also exposes an <action>Parameters collection, which we'll discuss in the next section.

The Data Source controls also expose three properties, shown in Table 15-5, that determine how commands behave.

Table 15-5   Command Configuration Properties

Property	Description
CancelSelectOnNullParameter	Determines whether data retrieval is cancelled if any parameter in the SelectParameters collection is Null.
ConflictDetection	Determines how the Data Source control handles concurrency conflicts.
OldValuesParameterFormatString	The format string applied to the names of parameters passed to the Delete or Update methods.

The CancelSelectOnNullParameter property, which accepts a Boolean value, does just what its name implies: If the property is True (the default), the Select operation is cancelled if any of the parameters evaluates to Null.

The ConflictDetection property determines how concurrency is handled for Update and Delete operations. It is set to a member of the ConflictOptions enumeration, which has the values OverwriteChanges and CompareAllValues.

OverwriteChanges, the default, causes these operations to simply overwrite any changes that might have been made to the underlying data source since the data was initially read. This option is efficient, but dangerous in a multi-user environment.

The name of the CompareAllValues option is somewhat misleading. It doesn't actually cause the Update or Delete to compare the old and new values; it simply passes the old values to a procedure that you must write to perform the comparison and take the appropriate action.

The OldValuesParamterFormatString is only used when the ConflictDetection property is set to CompareAllValues. It contains a format string that uses the syntax of the String.Format method. This string is used to format the names of parameters passed to the Delete and Update methods.

Set the SelectCommand Property: Visual Basic

1. In the Code Editor, add the following lines to the end of the Page_PreInit event handler:

```
sqlProducts.SelectCommand = "SELECT [CategoryID], [ProductID], " + _
    "[ProductName], [SupplierID] FROM [Products] " + _
    "WHERE ([CategoryID] = @CategoryID)"
```

The body of the event handler should now be:

```
sqlProducts = New SqlDataSource()
sqlProducts.ID = "sqlProducts"
Me.Controls.Add(sqlProducts)

sqlProducts.ConnectionString = _
    "Data Source=(local)\SQLEXPRESS;Initial Catalog=AdoStepByStep;" + _
    "Integrated Security=True"
sqlProducts.SelectCommand = "SELECT [CategoryID], [ProductID], " + _
    "[ProductName], [SupplierID] FROM [Products] " + _
    "WHERE ([CategoryID] = @CategoryID)"
```

Set the SelectCommand Property: Visual C#

1. In the Code Editor, add the following lines to the end of the Page_PreInit event handler:

```
sqlProducts.SelectCommand = "SELECT [CategoryID], [ProductID], " +
    "[ProductName], [SupplierID] FROM [Products] " +
    "WHERE ([CategoryID] = @CategoryID)";
```

The body of the event handler should now be:

```
sqlProducts = new SqlDataSource();
sqlProducts.ID = "sqlProducts";
this.Controls.Add(sqlProducts);

sqlProducts.ConnectionString =
    "Data Source=(local)\\SQLEXPRESS;Initial Catalog = AdoStepByStep;" +
    "Integrated Security=True";
sqlProducts.SelectCommand = "SELECT [CategoryID], [ProductID], " +
    "[ProductName], [SupplierID] FROM [Products] " +
    "WHERE ([CategoryID] = @CategoryID)";
```

Command Parameters

While the <action>Command and <action>CommandType properties of the Data Source control correspond directly to properties of the ADO.NET DataAdapter, the <action> Parameters properties of the Data Source controls are significantly different. Both the Data-Adapter properties and the Data Source properties represent collections, but in the case of the Data Source, the collections contain descendants of the Parameter class defined in the

System.Web.UI.WebControls namespace, not the parameter class defined by a specific Data Provider. The Parameter classes are shown in Table 15-6.

Table 15-6 Data Source Parameter Classes

Parameter Class	Description
ControlParameter	Retrieves a value from the property of a control on the page.
QueryStringParameter	Retrieves a value from a key-value combination in the current query string.
SessionParameter	Retrieves a value from a Session variable.
CookieParameter	Retrieves a value from the specified cookie.
FormParameter	Retrieves a value from a property exposed in the current Request object.

Most of the Parameter classes are designed to take advantage of the Web Form environment. We discussed the Session variable briefly in Chapter 14. The other types, with the exception of the ControlParameter, are outside the scope of our discussion.

The ControlParameter is used to implement two-way binding. For example, a ControlParameter that has its ControlID and PropertyName properties set to the Text property of a TextBox control pulls the data from the control when the statement is executed.

You must still write code that uses one of the techniques we examined in Chapter 14 to push the data into the control when the page is initially displayed, ,but updating the underlying data source with run-time changes is completed without additional code.

As we've seen, all of the parameter classes descend from the Parameter base class, which exposes the properties shown in Table 15-7.

Table 15-7 Parameter Properties

Property	Description
ConvertEmptyStringToNull	Determines whether the Parameter should return a Null if it contains an empty string.
DefaultValue	Determines the default value of the Parameter.
Direction	Determines whether the Parameter is used to bind a value to the control, or the control can be used to change the value.
Name	The name of the property in the Parameters collection.
Size	The size of the Parameter.
Type	The system data type of the Parameter.

The properties of the Parameter class are self-explanatory. Notice, however, that the Type property accepts a .NET Framework system data type. This differs from Data Command parameters, which accept a DbType specific to the Data Provider.

Add a Command Parameter: Visual Basic

1. In the Code Editor, add the following lines to the end of the Page_PreInit event handler:

```
Dim theParam As ControlParameter
theParam = New ControlParameter("CategoryID", "lbCategories", "SelectedValue")
sqlProducts.SelectParameters.Add(theParam)
```

The body of the event handler should now be:

```
sqlProducts = New SqlDataSource()
sqlProducts.ID = "sqlProducts"
Me.Controls.Add(sqlProducts)

sqlProducts.ConnectionString = _
    "Data Source=(local)\SQLEXPRESS;Initial Catalog=AdoStepByStep;" + _
    "Integrated Security=True"
sqlProducts.SelectCommand = "SELECT [CategoryID], [ProductID], " + _
    "[ProductName], [SupplierID] FROM [Products] " + _
    "WHERE ([CategoryID] = @CategoryID)"

Dim theParam As ControlParameter
theParam = New ControlParameter("CategoryID", "lbCategories", "SelectedValue")
sqlProducts.SelectParameters.Add(theParam)
```

Add a Command Parameter: Visual C#

1. In the Code Editor, add the following lines to the end of the Page_PreInit event handler:

```
ControlParameter theParam;
theParam = new ControlParameter("CategoryID", "lbCategories", "SelectedValue");
sqlProducts.SelectParameters.Add(theParam);
```

Your event handler should now be:

```
sqlProducts = new SqlDataSource();
sqlProducts.ID = "sqlProducts";
this.Controls.Add(sqlProducts);

sqlProducts.ConnectionString =
    "Data Source=(local)\\SQLEXPRESS;Initial Catalog=AdoStepByStep;" +
    "Integrated Security=True";
sqlProducts.SelectCommand = "SELECT [CategoryID], [ProductID], " +
    "[ProductName], [SupplierID] FROM [Products] " +
    "WHERE ([CategoryID] = @CategoryID)";

ControlParameter theParam;
theParam = new ControlParameter("CategoryID", "lbCategories", "SelectedValue");
sqlProducts.SelectParameters.Add(theParam);
```

Setting Connection and Command Properties at Design Time

In the Visual Web Designer, the connection and command properties of Data Source controls are defined in a single step by using the Configure Data Source Wizard.

Configure a Data Source in the Visual Web Designer

1. Click the Default.aspx tab, and if necessary, click Design to display the page in form view.

2. Display the sqlCategoryDetails Smart Tag menu, and then choose Configure Data Source.

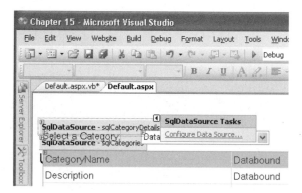

The Visual Web Designer starts the Configure Data Source Wizard.

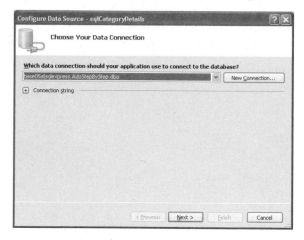

3. Select the connection that points to the AdoStepByStep sample database. If the connection doesn't exist, click the New Connection button, and create a new connection as described in Chapter 1, "Getting Started with ADO.NET." When you are finished, click Next.

4. Clear the check box that will save the connection string in the application configuration file, and then click Next.

5. On the Configure The Select Statement page, select Specify Columns From A Table Or View, and then select Categories in the Name list box.

6. Select the all columns (*) check box.

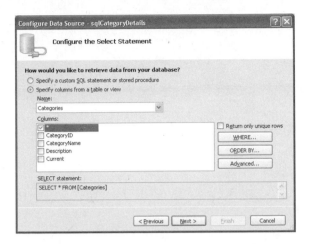

7. Click WHERE.

   The Configure Data Source Wizard displays the Add WHERE Clause dialog box.

8. Select CategoryID in the Column list box and Control in the Source list box.

9. Select lbCategories in the Control ID list box, and then click Add.

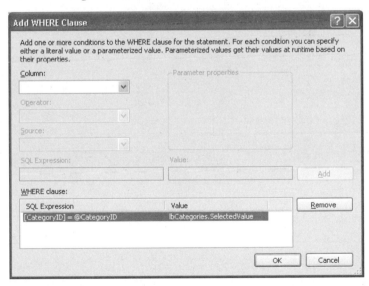

10. Click OK, and then click Next.

    The Configure Data Source Wizard displays the Test Query page.

11. Click Finish.

12. If the Visual Web Designer displays a message box confirming the regeneration of fields and data keys, click No.

13. Press F5 to display the page in the default browser.

Microsoft ASP.NET populates the SqlDataSource controls and displays the results in the bound controls.

14. Close the browser.

Configuration Properties

The next set of properties exposed by the SqlDataSource and AccessDataSource controls are the configuration properties shown in Table 15-8. These properties determine the general behavior of the Data Source.

Table 15-8   Data Source Configuration Properties

Property	Description
DataSourceMode	Determines the ADO.NET object that is used to retrieve data.
FilterExpression	A filtering expression applied to the results of a Select method call.
FilterParameters	The ParameterCollection used by the filter expression.
SortParameterName	Determines the name of a stored procedure parameter that is used to sort the data retrieved using a stored procedure.

The DataSourceMode property of both the SqlDataSource and the AccessDataSource accepts a member of the SqlDataSourceMode enumeration, which contains two values: DataReader and DataSet. The default is DataSet.

The FilterExpression property specifies a string that is applied to the results of the Select method. Rather than using SQL syntax, the FilterString property uses String.Format syntax. It draws its parameter values from the FilterParameters collection, which like the <action>Parameters properties, accepts parameters of the types shown earlier in Table 15-6.

Finally, the SortParameterName property is used only if the SelectCommandText property evaluates to the name of a stored procedure. In this case, the result set returned by the stored procedure is sorted by the member of the SelectParameters collection that has the name specified in this property.

Caching Properties

The final set of Data Source properties control if and how the Data Source caches data. This set of properties is shown in Table 15-9. Caching is only possible if the DataSourceMode is DataSet. If DataSourceMode is set to DataReader, setting any of these properties throws a NotSupportedException.

Table 15-9   Data Source Cache Properties

Property	Description
CacheDuration	The number of seconds for which the Data Source control caches data.
CacheExpirationPolicy	Determines the caching behavior of the control.
CacheKeyDependency	Determines the user-defined key that is used to control expiration of cached objects.
EnableCaching	Determines whether the Data Source control caches data.
SqlCacheDependency	The SQL databases and tables used for cache dependency.

The CacheDuration property determines how long data is cached by the Data Source control. The length of time is specified in seconds.

CacheDuration is interpreted according to the setting of the CacheExpirationPolicy, which can be set to either Absolute or Sliding. When CacheExpirationPolicy is set to Absolute (the default), cached data is discarded CacheDuration seconds after it was retrieved. When CacheExpirationPolicy is set to Sliding, cached data is discarded CacheDuration seconds after it was last accessed.

The CacheKeyDependency and SqlCacheDependency properties provide finer control over caching. The CacheKeyDependency property allows you to set a key value for multiple cache items. Expiring the key expires all the linked items. SqlCacheDependency uses the cache dependency feature of SQL Server if it is available. This property accepts pairs of tables specified as ConnectionString;TableName. The cache expires when the database engine notifies ASP.NET of a change to the table.

All these properties are ignored unless EnableCaching is set to True. (The default is False.)

Enable Simple Caching: Visual Basic

1.   Click the Default.aspx.vb tab, and add the following lines to the end of the Page_PreInit event handler:

```
sqlProducts.EnableCaching = True
sqlProducts.CacheDuration = 120
```

The body of the event handler should now be:

```
sqlProducts = New SqlDataSource()
sqlProducts.ID = "sqlProducts"
Me.Controls.Add(sqlProducts)

sqlProducts.ConnectionString = _
    "Data Source=(local)\SQLEXPRESS;Initial Catalog=AdoStepByStep;" + _
    "Integrated Security=True"
sqlProducts.SelectCommand = "SELECT [CategoryID], [ProductID], " + _
    "[ProductName], [SupplierID] FROM [Products] " + _
    "WHERE ([CategoryID] = @CategoryID)"

Dim theParam As ControlParameter
theParam = New ControlParameter("CategoryID", "lbCategories", "SelectedValue")
sqlProducts.SelectParameters.Add(theParam)

sqlProducts.EnableCaching = True
sqlProducts.CacheDuration = 120
```

Enable Simple Caching: Visual C#

1. Click the Default.aspx.cs tab, and add the following lines to the end of the Page_PreInit event handler:

```
sqlProducts.EnableCaching = true;
sqlProducts.CacheDuration = 120;
```

The body of the event handler should now be:

```
sqlProducts = new SqlDataSource();
sqlProducts.ID = "sqlProducts";
this.Controls.Add(sqlProducts);

sqlProducts.ConnectionString =
    "Data Source=(local)\\SQLEXPRESS;Initial Catalog=AdoStepByStep;" +
    "Integrated Security=True";
sqlProducts.SelectCommand = "SELECT [CategoryID], [ProductID], " +
    "[ProductName], [SupplierID] FROM [Products] " +
    "WHERE ([CategoryID] = @CategoryID)";

ControlParameter theParam;
theParam = new ControlParameter("CategoryID", "lbCategories", "SelectedValue");
sqlProducts.SelectParameters.Add(theParam);

sqlProducts.EnableCaching = true;
sqlProducts.CacheDuration = 120;
```

Using Data Source Methods

The methods exposed by the SqlDataSource and AccessDataSource controls are shown in Table 15-10. The methods correspond directly to the command properties for each type of action; in other words, each method simply executes the SQL statement or stored procedure contained in the corresponding <action>Command property.

Table 15-10   SqlDataSource Methods

Method	Description
Delete	Executes the SQL command or stored procedure contained in the DeleteCommand property.
Insert	Executes the SQL command or stored procedure contained in the InsertCommand property.
Select	Executes the SQL command or stored procedure contained in the SelectCommand property.
Update	Executes the SQL command or stored procedure contained in the UpdateCommand property.

The Update, Insert and Delete methods use the Parameters specified in their corresponding <action>Parameters collection to perform their operations. The Select method has a required argument, an instance of the DataSourceSelectArguments class. The properties of this class are shown in Table 15-11.

Table 15-11   DataSourceSelectArguments Properties

Property	Description
Empty	Returns an empty instance of the DataSourceSelectArguments class.
MaximumRows	Determines the maximum number of rows to be returned.
RetrieveTotalRowCount	Determines whether the total number of rows should be returned.
SortExpression	A string that the data source view uses to sort data retrieved by the DataSourceView.Select method.
StartRowIndex	Determines the starting row to be returned.
TotalRowCount	The total number of rows.

The Empty property is used when none of the special capabilities of the DataSource-SelectArguments are required. Because the property is static, you can pass DataSourceSelect-Arguments.Empty without instantiating the class, as in:

```
myDataSource.Select(DataSourceSelectArguments.Empty)
```

The RetrieveTotalRowCount and TotalRowCount properties are used together. When RetrieveTotalRowCount is True, the total number of rows that satisfy the selection criteria in the underlying data source is returned in the TotalRowCount property after the Select method returns. As we'll see in the next section, you can interrogate this property in an event handler for the Selected event.

The StartRowIndex and MaximumRows properties are used for data paging. The Select method retrieves MaximumRows rows starting at StartRowIndex. This makes it possible, for example, to retrieve rows 11 through 16 from the underlying data source by setting StartRowIndex to 11 and MaximumRows to 5.

The DataSourceSelectArguments exposes one additional property, SortExpression, that is used only by the Select method of the DataSourceView. Because the GetView method of the DataSet is a protected method, you cannot manipulate the Data SourceView directly except in derived controls.

Load Data by Using the Select Method: Visual Basic

1. Add the following lines to the btnProducts_Click event handler:

```
Dim dv As DataView
dv = sqlProducts.Select(DataSourceSelectArguments.Empty)
lbProducts.DataSource = dv
lbProducts.DataTextField = "ProductName"
lbProducts.DataBind()
```

This code first declares a DataView variable, dv, and then sets it to the DataView returned by the Select method of the SqlDataSource. Notice that the Select method receives an instance of the static Empty DataSourceSelectedArguments.

The next three lines set the DataSource and DataTextField properties of the lbProduct list box to the ProductName column of the DataView. The final line binds the list box, causing the values to be displayed.

2. Press F5 to display the page in the default browser.

3. Select a Category, and then click Show Products.

ASP.NET displays the selected products in the list box.

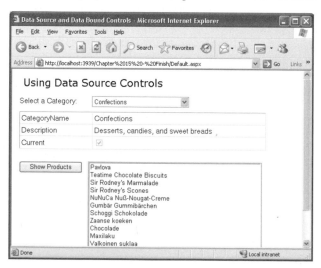

4.   Close the browser.

Load Data by Using the Select Method: Visual C#

1.   Add the following lines to the btnProducts_Click event handler:

```
DataView dv;
dv = (DataView)sqlProducts.Select(DataSourceSelectArguments.Empty);
lbProducts.DataSource = dv;
lbProducts.DataTextField = "ProductName";
lbProducts.DataBind();
```

This code first declares a DataView variable, dv, and then sets it to the DataView returned by the Select method of the SqlDataSource. Notice that the Select method receives an instance of the static Empty DataSourceSelectedArguments.

The next three lines set the DataSource and DataTextField properties of the lbProduct list box to the ProductName column of the DataView. The final line binds the list box, causing the values to be displayed.

2.   Press F5 to display the page in the default browser.

3.   Select a Category, and then click Show Products.

ASP.NET displays the selected products in the list box.

4.   Close the browser.

Responding to Data Source Events

The data source-related events exposed by the SqlDataSource and AccessDataSource controls are shown in Table 15-12. With the exception of the Filtering event, all Data Source events bracket one of the methods we examined in the last section.

Table 15-12   Data Source Events

Event	Description
Deleted	Occurs after the Delete operation has completed.
Deleting	Occurs before the Delete operation is executed.
Filtering	Occurs before a Filter is applied.
Inserted	Occurs after the Insert operation has completed.
Inserting	Occurs before the Insert operation is executed.
Selected	Occurs after the Select operation has completed.
Selecting	Occurs before the Select operation is executed.
Updated	Occurs after the Update operation has completed.
Updating	Occurs before the Update operation is completed.

Respond to a Selected Event: Visual Basic

1. Add the following lines to the sqlProducts_Selected event handler:

```
txtSelectedRows.Text = "This product has " + e.AffectedRows.ToString() + _
    " associated products."
txtSelectedRows.Visible = True
```

This code simply displays the number of rows returned by the Select method in a label control on the page.

2. Press F5 to display the page in the browser.

3. Select a Category, and then click Show Products.

ASP.NET displays the related products and the number of products selected.

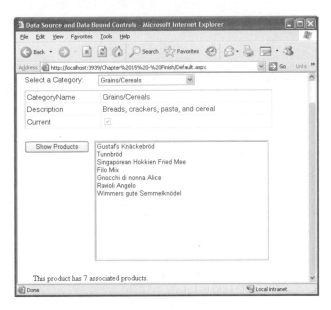

4. Close the browser.

Respond to a Selected Event: Visual C#

1. Add the following line to the end of the Page_PreInit event handler:

```
sqlProducts.Selected += new
    SqlDataSourceStatusEventHandler(sqlProducts_Selected);
```

2. Add the following lines to the sqlProducts_Selected event handler:

```
txtSelectedRows.Text = "This product has " + e.AffectedRows.ToString() +
    " associated products.";
txtSelectedRows.Visible = true;
```

This code simply displays the number of rows returned by the Select method in a label control on the page.

3. Press F5 to display the page in the browser.

4. Select a Category, and then click Show Products.

ASP.NET displays the related products and the number of products selected.

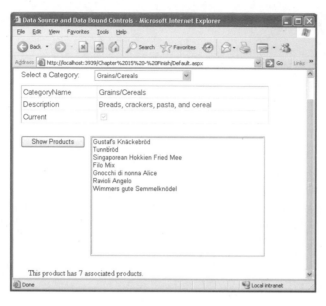

5. Close the browser.

Summary

In this chapter we examined the Data Source controls, focusing on SqlDataSource, which handles two-way binding between a SQL-based data source (not necessarily SQL Server) and Web Form controls. We saw that the SqlDataSource controls can be created at design time or run time, and that they are bound to Web Form controls by adding a Parameter to the appropriate <action>Parameters property. Finally, we briefly examined caching and the simple methods and events exposed by the component. In the next chapter, we'll turn to the controls that are designed to work closely with Data Source controls.

Chapter 16

Data-Bound and Validation Controls

After completing this chapter, you will be able to:

- Create and configure List controls.
- Use List control methods.
- Respond to List control events.
- Add templates to template-based controls.
- Bind Template controls to a data source.
- Add DataControlFields to DetailView and DataGrid controls.
- Add validation controls to Web Form pages.

In Chapter 14, "Basic Data Binding in Web Forms," we examined the use of ADO.NET objects in a Web Form. In Chapter 15, "Data Binding in Web Forms by Using the Data Source Component," we examined the Data Source controls that simplify data binding in a Web Form and make it possible to bind to data with very little code.

In this chapter, we'll examine the data-bound Web Form controls that are designed to work with Data Source controls and can also be used with ADO.NET objects. We'll also examine the ASP.NET validation controls that, like their Windows Form counterparts, provide an elegant solution to handling data entry errors.

Understanding Data-Bound Controls

With the exception of the Repeater control, which descends directly from System.Web.UI.-Controls, the data-bound controls descend either from BaseDataBoundControl or BaseDataList, which define their basic functionality. The hierarchy of data-bound controls is shown in the figure on the following page.

The Repeater control is the most flexible of the data-bound controls. You can use any combination of ASP.NET Web server controls and HTML within an <ItemTemplate> </ItemTemplate> block.

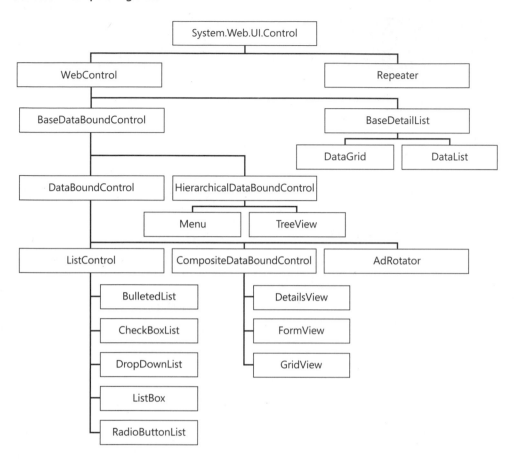

The Repeater control repeats the block for each row in the underlying data source. Data is pushed to controls by using the data-binding syntax we examined in Chapter 14. (Remember that this is one-way data binding—data is pushed to the control but not pulled from it.) Because the Repeater is defined exclusively in the HTML stream, we won't discuss it here.

The Data List controls, DataGrid and DataList, descend from the BaseDataList class. Like the Repeater control, these controls display multiple rows of data in the underlying data source, but unlike the Repeater, they can be configured at design time and are available programmatically.

The DataGrid control, while still supported in Microsoft ASP.NET 2.0, has been supplanted by the GridView control. We won't be discussing it here. The DataList control is like the Repeater in that it doesn't impose any structure on the data. Instead, it displays multiple rows from the data source in a layout defined by templates.

The ListControl class defines the functionality of a group of classes that appear to be different but have very similar properties and behavior. This set of controls displays values from a single column of all the rows in the data source.

A composite data-bound control acts as a container for other server controls that are, in turn, bound to the actual data items in the BindingSource. ASP.NET 2.0 defines three data controls: DetailsView, FormView and GridView.

The DetailsView and FormView controls both display single rows from the data source, while the GridView control, which is the successor to the earlier DataGrid, displays multiple rows. Like the DataList, the layout of data in these controls is defined by templates.

Finally, the hierarchical data-bound controls, as you might expect, display data in a hierarchy. ASP.NET defines two hierarchical controls: Menu and TreeView. Both can be bound to either an XmlDataSource or a SiteMapDataSource. We won't be discussing hierarchical data-bound controls in this book.

Like most Microsoft .NET Framework objects, you can create data-bound controls at design time or run time, but run-time creation, particularly of the template-based controls, can be tedious. In this chapter, we'll concentrate on creating and configuring the controls at design time. Calling methods and responding to events, of course, are always performed at run time.

Data-Binding Properties

All data-bound controls expose DataSource and DataSourceID properties, which provide basic data-binding functionality. It's these properties more than their position in the class hierarchy that identifies them as data-bound controls.

The DataSource property accepts any object that implements the IEnumerable or IListSource interface. This includes, of course, ADO.NET objects such as DataTable and DataView, but also ArrayLists and Hashtables. However, if you set the DataSource property directly, you must implement data binding manually by using the techniques we examined in Chapter 14. The examples in this chapter all use the DataSourceID property.

The DataSourceID property accepts the ID string of a Data Source control. All of the data-bound controls pull data from the data source when this property is set, without additional coding. In addition, the DetailsView, FormView and GridView controls support two-way binding—they pull changes from the controls back to the data source, without additional code.

Understanding List Controls

The ListControl itself is an abstract class and therefore can't be directly instantiated, but ASP.NET defines five controls that descend from this base class, and you can also define your own controls that descend from this class. The controls defined in the .NET Framework are:

- BulletedList
- CheckBoxList
- DropDownList

- ListBox

- RadioButtonList

Each of these controls extends the basic ListControl, but their additional properties, methods and events are related to the display and standard behavior of the specific control. So, for example, the BulletedList class exposes a BulletStyle property that you can use to define the glyph displayed next to each item, while the ListBox class exposes a SelectionMode property that determines whether the control supports multiple selections.

Creating List Controls

As with any .NET Framework control class, you can create List controls at design time or run time by using standard techniques: At design time, simply drag the control onto the page design surface; at run time, declare a variable and instantiate the class.

Change the Positioning Option for Controls in the Toolbox

1. Open the Chapter 16 – Start Web site in Microsoft Visual Studio 2005.

2. If necessary, double-click Default.aspx in the Solution Explorer, and then click the Design button.

    The Visual Web Designer displays the form in design view.

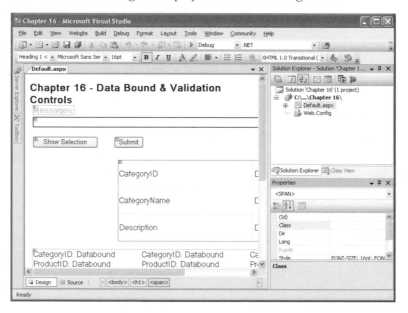

3. Select Options from the Tools menu, expand the HTML Designer node, and select CSS Positioning.

    To control the position of the controls on the page, you must set the CSS Positioning option to absolute.

4. If it is not already selected, select the check box labeled "Change positioning to the following for controls added using the Toolbox, paste, or drag and drop." Make sure the list box selection is Absolutely Positioned, which is the default.

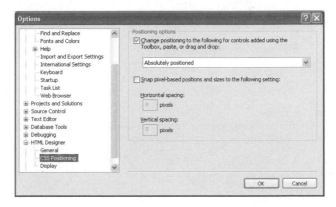

5. Click OK.

Create a ListBox Control in the Visual Web Designer

1. Drag a ListBox control from the Standard tab of the Toolbox onto the page.

    The Visual Web Designer adds the control to the upper-left corner of the page.

2. Drag the control to the left of the existing DetailsView, and adjust the size as shown in the following figure.

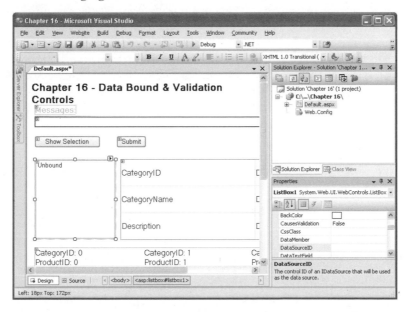

3. In the Properties window, change the (ID) of the control to **lbCategories**. If a Verification Results dialog box appears, click OK.

Configuring List Controls

As we've seen, the basic functionality of all List controls is defined by their abstract base class, ListControl. In addition to the DataSource, DataSourceID and DataMember data-binding properties, the base class exposes the configuration properties shown in Table 16-1.

Table 16-1   ListControl Configuration Properties

Properties	Description
AppendDataBoundItems	Determines whether items from the data source are appended to static items added to the Items collection.
DataTextField	Determines the column in the underlying data source that will be displayed in the list.
DataTextFormatString	The formatting string used to format the DataTextField values before they are displayed.
DataValueField	Determines the column in the underlying data source that is returned by the SelectedValue property.
Items	The collection of ListItem objects displayed by the control.
SelectedIndex	The zero-based index of the item selected in the control.
SelectedItem	The selected ListItem.
SelectedValue	The value of the DataValueField of the selected ListItem.

The AppendDataBoundItems property allows you to combine items from an underlying data source with static items that you add to the Items collection manually. This property, which defaults to False, is particularly useful when you want to add generic values such as All to the list retrieved from the data source.

The DataTextField property accepts a string that identifies the column in the underlying data source that is to be displayed in the control. The values in this column can optionally be formatted by setting the DataTextFormatString property to a format string that complies with the syntax of the String.Format method. The DataValueField allows you to specify a value column other than that displayed to the user. This property is useful when you need to manipulate a field other than the one displayed to the user.

The most important property of any List control is, of course, Items, which contains a collection of the ListItem objects that will be displayed by the control. If the List control is data-bound, ListItems are created based on the rows of the underlying data source. They can also be added manually to the collection. As we've seen, the two techniques are not necessarily mutually exclusive, depending on the value of the AppendDataBoundItems property.

The SelectedIndex property of the List control determines the zero-based index of the currently selected ListItem in the Items Collection, while SelectedItem is the selected ListItem itself. SelectedValue returns only the Value property of the selected ListItem.

The ListItem class that represents the items displayed in the List control exposes four main properties: Enabled, Selected, Text and Value. The Enabled and Selected properties are self-explanatory. The Text property contains the formatted string that will be displayed in the List control, while the Value property contains the value of the column defined by DataValue-Field property.

Configure a ListBox in the Visual Web Designer

1. In the Form Designer, click the lbCategories ListBox, click the Smart Tag to display its menu, and then select Choose Data Source.

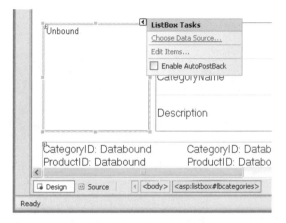

The Visual Web Designer displays the Data Source Configuration Wizard.

2. Expand the Select A Data Source list box, and select sqlCategories.

3. If displayed, click the Refresh Schema link.

> **Tip** Clicking Refresh Schema ensures the field names are available.

4. Expand the Select A Data Field To Display In The ListBox list box, and select Category-Name. Leave the Select A Data Field For The Value Of The ListBox list box with its default value.

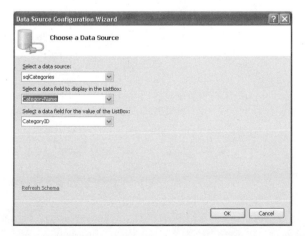

5. Click OK.

6. In the Properties window for the lbCategories list box, change the AutoPostBack property to True.

7. Press F5 to display the page in your default browser.

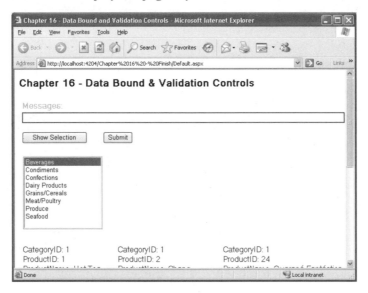

8. Close the browser.

Using List Control Methods

The base ListControl class exposes only a single method, ClearSelection, which sets the Selected property of all the ListItems contained in the control's Items collection to False. Of the concrete classes that descend from ListControl, only the ListBox control defines an additional method, GetSelectedIndices. As you might expect, GetSelectedIndices returns an array of Integer values representing the indices of each selected item in the ListBox.

Retrieve the Selected ListItems in a ListBox: Visual Basic

1. Press F7 to display the code behind page in the Code Editor.

2. Add the following lines to the btnShowSelection_Click event handler:

```
Dim currSelection As Int32()
currSelection = lbCategories.GetSelectedIndices()
tbMessages.Text = currSelection(0).ToString()
```

This code block declares an integer array and then sets it to the value returned by the GetSelectedIndices method. The last line displays the first (and only) member of the array in the Messages text box.

3. Press F5 to display the page in the default browser.

4.   Select an item in the Categories list box, and then click Show Selection.

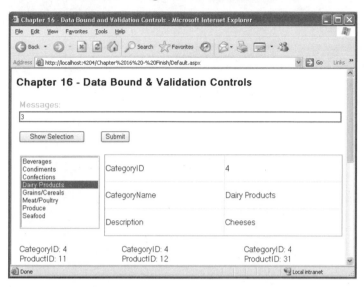

ASP.NET displays the index of the selected item in the Messages text box.

5.   Close the browser.

Retrieve the Selected ListItems in a ListBox: Visual C#

1.   Press F7 to display the code behind page in the Code Editor.

2.   Add the following lines to the btnShowSelection_Click event handler:

```
Int32[] currSelection;
currSelection = lbCategories.GetSelectedIndices();
tbMessages.Text = currSelection[0].ToString();
```

This code block declares an integer array and then sets it to the value returned by the GetSelectedIndices method. The last line displays the first (and only) member of the array in the Messages text box.

3.   Press F5 to display the page in the default browser.

4.   Select an item in the Categories list box, and then click Show Selection.

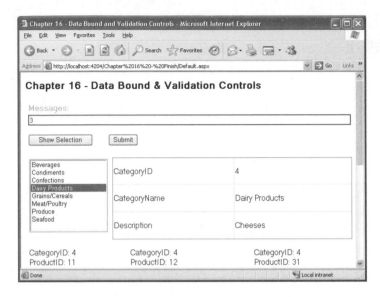

ASP.NET displays the index of the selected item in the Messages text box.

5. Close the browser.

Responding to List Control Events

The base ListControl class exposes two events, shown in Table 16-2. The BulletedList class exposes an additional event, Click, which occurs when a link button in the list is clicked. The remaining List controls do not extend the basic functionality.

Table 16-2   ListControl Events

Event	Description
SelectedIndexChanged	Occurs when the selected index changes between trips to the server.
TextChanged	Occurs when the Text property changes between trips to the server.

Notice that the events are triggered only when the page is posted back to the server. For either of the ListControl events to be triggered, the EnableViewState property of the control must be set to True. This is the default value.

Respond to a SelectedIndexChanged Event: Visual Basic

1. In the Code Editor, add the following line to the lbCategories_SelectedIndexChanged event handler:

    ```
    tbMessages.Text = lbCategories.SelectedItem.Text
    ```

2. Press F5 to display the page in the default browser.

3.   Select an item in the Categories list box.

ASP.NET displays the name of the selected item in the Messages text box.

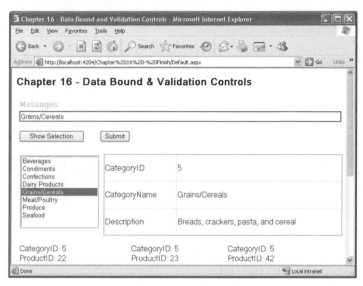

4.   Close the browser.

Respond to a SelectedIndexChanged Event: Visual C#

1.   In the Form Designer, double-click the lbCategories list box.

The Visual Web Designer adds an lbCategories_SelectedIndexChanged event handler and displays the Code Editor.

2.   In the Code Editor, add the following line to the lbCategories_SelectedIndexChanged event handler:

```
tbMessages.Text = lbCategories.SelectedItem.Text;
```

3.   Press F5 to display the page in the default browser.

4.   Select an item in the Categories list box.

ASP.NET displays the name of the selected item in the Messages text box.

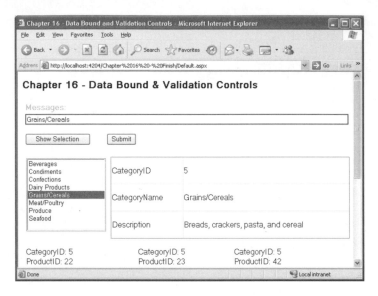

5. Close the browser.

Understanding Template-Based Controls

The DataList, DetailsView, FormView and GridView controls are all composite in that they are containers for other controls. (This is true of the DataList control even though it doesn't descend from the CompositeDataBoundControl base class.) The contents and layout of the controls that these composite controls contain is defined by templates.

A *template* is simply a set of HTML elements and Web server controls that will be displayed within the composite control. Some template-based controls, such as the FormView, are completely defined by their templates, while others, such as the DetailsView, impose a basic structure on their contents and use templates only for some sections of their contents.

Template Types

Each template-based control exposes a different set of templates, as shown in Table 16-3.

Table 16-3   Template-Based Controls

Control	Templates
DataList	HeaderTemplate
	FooterTemplate
	ItemTemplate
	AlternatingItemTemplate
	SelectedItemTemplate
	EditItemTemplate
	SeparatorTemplate

Table 16-3   **Template-Based Controls**

Control	Templates
DetailsView	HeaderTemplate
	FooterTemplate
	PagerTemplate
	EmptyDataTemplate
FormView	HeaderTemplate
	FooterTemplate
	PagerTemplate
	ItemTemplate
	EmptyDataTemplate
	EditItemTemplate
	InsertItemTemplate
GridView	EmptyDataTemplate
	PagerTemplate

As you can see from the table, although each of the template-based controls exposes a slightly different set of templates, there is quite a bit of overlap. And despite some minor differences, each type of template performs the same basic function in each control, as shown in Table 16-4.

Table 16-4   **Types of Templates**

Template	Description
HeaderTemplate	Defines the header section.
FooterTemplate	Defines the footer section.
PagerTemplate	Defines the section containing navigation controls in a paged control.
ItemTemplate	Defines the row displayed for unselected data.
AlternatingItemTemplate	Defines the row displayed for alternating unselected data.
EmptyDataTemplate	Defines the row displayed when the data source contains no data.
SelectedItemTemplate	Defines the row displayed for selected data.
EditItemTemplate	Defines the row displayed for data being edited.
InsertItemTemplate	Defines the row displayed for data being inserted.
SeparatorTemplate	Defines the section displayed between data rows.

Adding Templates to Template-Based Controls

Not all of the template-based controls require templates. The DetailsView and GridView controls, for example, have default structures that can be used without creating templates to define them. Other controls, like the FormView, are completely defined by their templates, and you must, at the very least, define an ItemTemplate before this control can display data.

The process of creating and editing templates at design time is straightforward. You simply right-click the control, select Edit Templates from the context menu, and choose the template with which you wish to work. The Visual Web Designer then displays a labeled box within the control. Any Web server controls or HTML elements that you add to the box will be included in the template.

Although we won't be examining the technique here, you can also create templates in the HTML stream by declaring the controls and elements within template elements. Any controls declared within an <ItemTemplate></ItemTemplate> element, for example, becomes part of the ItemTemplate displayed for unselected data items.

Edit an ItemTemplate in a DataList Control

1. Click the Default.aspx tab to display the page designer, display the Smart Tag menu for dlProducts DataList, and then select Edit Templates.

    The Visual Web Designer displays the ItemTemplate in the control.

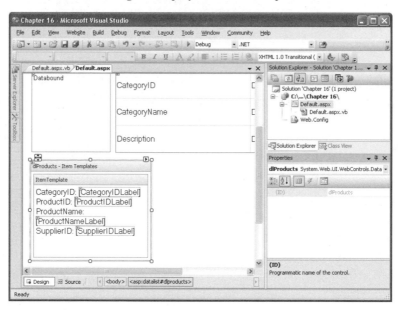

2. Delete the CategoryID caption and label.

3. Display the Smart Tag menu for the DataList (not the template), and then select End Template Editing.

   The Visual Web Designer updates the display.

Binding Controls Within a Template

Unlike controls that are automatically generated, when you add a control to a template, you must establish the data bindings explicitly. In the Visual Web Designer, this is done by using the Fields dialog box that is displayed when you choose Edit Data Bindings from the control's context menu.

In the Fields dialog box, you can bind any property of the control either directly to a field in the data source or by using a custom data-binding expression that uses the syntax we examined in Chapter 14.

Bind a Template Control to a Data Source

1. Display the Smart Tag menu for dlProducts DataList, and then select Edit Templates.

2. Display the Smart Tag menu for the label control following the SupplierID caption, and then select Edit DataBindings.

   The Visual Web Designer displays the DataBindings dialog box.

3. If displayed, click the Refresh Schema link. If a Refresh Data Source Schema dialog box appears, click OK.

4. Expand the Bound To list box, and select SupplierID.

   The Visual Web Designer creates a Custom Binding expression.

5. Click OK.

6. Display the Smart Tag menu for the dlProducts DataList, and then select End Template Editing.

7. Press F5 to display the page in the default browser.

   ASP.NET displays the Supplier ID in the DataList.

8. Close the browser.

Understanding DataControlFields

Neither the DetailsView nor the GridView support any of the item templates that define how data rows are displayed in various situations. Instead, both controls impose a grid structure on the data and use controls derived from the DataControlField class to display the actual data.

The classes derived from the DataControlField are shown in Table 16-5. You can, of course, derive your own custom control field types from the DataControlField if necessary.

Table 16-5   DataControlField Derived Classes

Class	Description
BoundField	Displays text.
ButtonField	Displays a button.

Table 16-5   **DataControlField Derived Classes**

Class	Description
CheckBoxField	Displays a check box.
CommandField	Displays buttons that perform basic data manipulation—selecting, editing, inserting and deleting.
HyperLinkField	Displays a hyperlink.
ImageField	Displays an image.
TemplateField	Displays custom content.

Configuring DataControlFields

Each type of the derived control field types implements its own set of properties, methods and events that pertain to the type of interface element displayed to the user. The ButtonField, for example, exposes a ButtonType property that you use to define the type of button to display. The possible values are Button, Image and Link. Most of these properties are quite straightforward and correspond to the properties of the standard control of the same type. So, for example, the properties of the CheckBoxField are almost the same as those of the CheckBox.

> **Note**   DataControlField classes are used by both the DetailsView control and the DataGrid control, but because of the different interfaces presented by the controls, they don't support the same properties. Properties that are not applicable to the control that contains the Data-ControlField are simply ignored.

The two exceptions are the CommandField and TemplateField class, neither of which corresponds to standard Web server controls.

The CommandField DataControlField

The CommandField class exposes a set of properties that you can use to control which data commands are displayed. The properties that are specific to the CommandField class are shown in Table 16-6.

Table 16-6   **CommandField Properties**

Property	Description
ButtonType	The type of buttons to display.
CancelImageUrl	The URL to an image to display for the cancel button.
CancelText	The cancel button caption.
DeleteImageUrl	The URL to an image to display for the delete button.
DeleteText	The delete button caption.
EditImageUrl	The URL to an image to display for the edit button.
EditText	The edit button caption.

Table 16-6   CommandField Properties

Property	Description
InsertImageUrl	The URL to an image to display for the insert button.
InsertText	The insert button caption.
NewImageUrl	The URL to an image to display for the new button.
NewText	The new button caption.
SelectImageUrl	The URL to an image to display for the select button.
SelectText	The select button caption.
ShowCancelButton	Determines whether the cancel button is displayed.
ShowDeleteButton	Determines whether the delete button is displayed.
ShowEditButton	Determines whether the edit button is displayed.
ShowInsertButton	Determines whether the insert button is displayed.
ShowSelectButton	Determines whether the select button is displayed.
UpdateImageUrl	The URL to an image to display for the update button.
UpdateText	The update button caption.

As you can see, the properties fall into two groups: those that determine how an action button is displayed, and those that determine whether an action button is displayed. The <action>ImageUrl and <action>Text buttons specify the URL to an image or a caption, respectively.

The display property used is determined by the setting of the ButtonType property. If Button-Type is Image, the <action>ImageUrl property is used. If ButtonType is Button or Link, the text contained in the <action>Text property is used as the button caption.

The other set of properties, Show<action>Button, accept Boolean values that, not surprisingly, determine whether the corresponding action button is displayed. Notice that there is no ShowUpdateButton property. The Update button is only displayed after the user has chosen one of the other operations, and it is the only way to complete the operation.

For example, if the user chooses Edit, they must choose Update to commit their changes. Because Update is only displayed if one or more of the other buttons is displayed (and their operations are therefore enabled), and it *must* be displayed during the operation, a Show-UpdateButton property is unnecessary.

Add a Button Field to a DetailsView Control

1. Display the Smart Tag menu of the dvCategoryDetails control, and then select Add New Field.

    The Visual Web Designer displays the Add Field dialog box.

2. Select CommandField in the Choose A Field Type list box, and select the Edit/Update check box.

3. Click OK.

   The Visual Web Designer adds an Edit button to the DataView.

4. Press F5 to display the page in the default browser.

5. Click an item in the list box and then click the Edit button.

   ASP.NET displays the Category Details in edit mode.

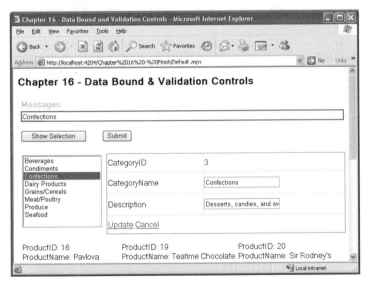

6. Click Cancel, and then close the browser.

The TemplateField DataControlField

The other DataControlField that doesn't correspond to a standard control type is the TemplateField. The TemplateField class is designed to display custom content. The contents of the TemplateField are defined, as you might expect, by templates. The TemplateField supports the following template types:

- AlternatingItemTemplate
- EditItemTemplate
- FooterTemplate
- HeaderTemplate
- InsertItemTemplate
- ItemTemplate

Templates for the TemplateField are created and configured at design time by using standard template-editing techniques. At run time, any of the control field types can be instantiated and added to the Fields collection.

Add a TemplateField to a DetailsView Control

1. Display the Smart Tag menu for dvCategoryDetails, and select Add New Field.

   The Visual Web Designer displays the Add Field dialog box.

2. Select TemplateField in the Choose A Field list box, and set the Header Text field to **Sample Template Field**.

3. Click OK.

   The Visual Web Designer adds the row to the DetailsView.

4. Display the Smart Tag menu for dvCategoryDetails again, and select Edit Templates.

   The Visual Web Designer displays the ItemTemplate of the new template control.

5. Click in the ItemTemplate, and add the text **Sample** to the template.

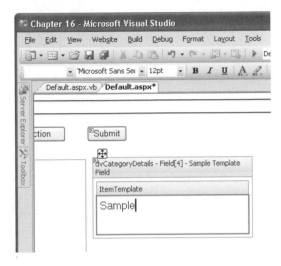

6. Display the Smart Tag menu for dvCategoryDetails again, and select End Template Editing.

   The Visual Web Designer displays the text in the template control row.

Understanding Validation Controls

The .NET Framework supports a number of validation controls that can be used to validate data. The Web Form validation controls, shown in Table 16-7, are more sophisticated than their Windows Form equivalent, the ErrorProvider control, which only displays error messages. The Web Form controls perform the validation checks and display any resulting error messages.

Table 16-7 Validation Controls

Control	Description
CompareValidator	Compares the contents of the input control to a constant value or the contents of another control.
CustomValidator	Checks the contents of the input control based on custom logic.
RangeValidator	Checks that the contents of the input control are between the specified upper and lower bounds, which may be characters, numbers, or dates.
RegularExpressionValidator	Checks that the contents of the input control match the pattern specified by a regular expression.
RequiredFieldValidator	Ensures that the input control contains a value.
ValidationSummary	Summarizes errors.

Each validation control checks for a single condition in a single control, known as the *input control*. To check for multiple conditions, multiple validation controls can be assigned to a single input control. This is frequently the case, particularly because all the controls except the RequiredFieldValidator consider an empty control to be valid.

The conditions specified by the validation controls assigned to a given input control are combined with a logical AND—all of the conditions must be met, or the control is considered invalid. If you need to combine validation conditions with a logical OR, you can use a CustomValidator control to manually check the value.

If the browser supports DHTML, validation first takes place on the client, and the Web Form is not submitted until all conditions are met. Whether or not validation has occurred on the client, it always occurs on the server when a Click event is processed. Additionally, you can manually call a control's Validate method to validate its contents from code.

When the page is validated, the contents of the input control are passed to the validation control (or controls), which tests the contents and sets the control's IsValid property to False. If any control on the page is invalid, the Page object's IsValid property is also set to False. You can check for these conditions in code and take whatever action is required.

Add a RequiredFieldValidator Control to a Page

1. Drag a RequiredFieldValidator control from the Validation tab of the Toolbox onto the page design surface.

2. Drag the control above the right corner of the Messages text box.

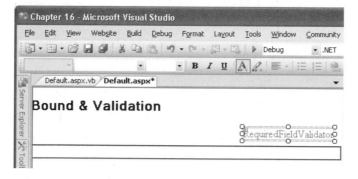

3. In the Properties window, set the ErrorMessage property to **Missing Value**, the ControlToValidate property to **tbMessages**, and the ID property to **IsMissing**.

4. Press F5 to display the page in the default browser.

5. Click the Submit button.

   ASP.NET displays the error message.

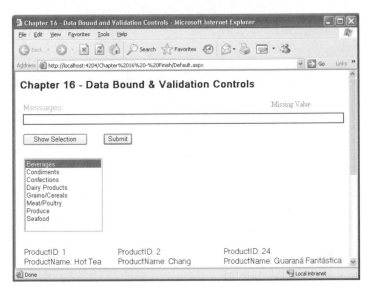

6. Close the browser.

> **Note**   We set the CSS Positioning options to Absolute for the purpose of this chapter.
> If this doesn't suit your development style, you can reset the value now by selecting
> Options from the Tools menu, expanding the HTML Designer node, selecting CSS
> Positioning, and clearing the Change Positioning check box.

Summary

In this chapter we examined the ASP.NET Web server controls that are specifically designed to
be data-bound. We created and bound a ListBox control, edited the templates of a DataList
and DataView, and added new data-bound fields. We also took a quick look at the validation
controls supported by ASP.NET, and saw an example of a RequiredFieldValidator, which
prohibits users from submitting empty fields.

Part V
ADO.NET and Other Types of Data

In this part:

Chapter 17

Reading and Writing XML

After completing this chapter, you will be able to:

- Retrieve an XML schema from a DataSet.

- Create a DataSet schema by using ReadXmlSchema.

- Infer the schema of an XML document.

- Load XML data by using ReadXml.

- Create an XML schema by using WriteXmlSchema.

- Write data to an XML document.

In this chapter, we'll begin our examination of the interaction between Microsoft ADO.NET and Extensible Markup Language (XML) by looking at the structure of an XML schema and the DataSet methods that support reading and writing data from an XML data stream.

Note The Microsoft .NET Framework provides extensive support for manipulating XML, most of which is outside the scope of this book. In this chapter, we'll examine only the interface between XML and the ADO.NET DataSet.

Understanding XML Schemas

An XML schema is a document that defines the structure of XML data. Much like a database schema, an XML schema can also be used to validate the contents and structure of an XML file.

An XML schema is defined by using the XML Schema Definition Language (XSD). XSD is similar in structure to HTML, but whereas HTML defines the layout of a document, XSD defines the structure and content of the data.

Note XML schemas in the .NET Framework conform to the World Wide Web Consortium (W3C) recommendation, as defined at *http://www.w3.org/2001/XMLSchema*. Additional schema elements that are used to support .NET Framework objects, such as DataSet and DataRelations, conform to the schema defined at *urn:schemas-microsoft-com:xml-msdata*. (These extentions conform to the W3C recommendation and are simply ignored by XML parsers that do not support them.)

XML schemas are defined in terms of elements and attributes. Elements and attributes are very similar and can often be used interchangeably, although there are some distinctions:

- Elements can contain other items; attributes are always atomic, meaning that they cannot contain other items.

- Elements can occur multiple times in the data; attributes can occur only once.

- By using the <xs:sequence> tag, a schema can stipulate that elements must occur in the specified order; attributes can occur in any order.

- Only elements can be nested within <xs:choice> tags, which specify mutually-exclusive elements (that is, one and only one element can occur).

- Elements can be defined using user-defined types; attributes are restricted to built-in data types

By convention, elements are used for raw data, while attributes are used for metadata. However, you can use whichever best suits your purposes.

Both elements and attributes define items in terms of a type, which in turn defines the data that the element or attribute can validly contain. XML schemas support two types:

- Simple, which are atomic values such as string or Boolean.

- Complex, which are composed of other elements and attributes in any combination.

Optionally, elements and attributes can define a name that identifies the element that is being defined. XML element names cannot begin with a number or the letters XML, nor can they contain spaces. Note that XML is case sensitive, so the names MyName and myName are considered distinct.

XML schemas are stored in text files with an XSD extension. Microsoft Visual Studio 2005 provides a visual user interface for creating XML schemas, the XML Schema Editor. In this chapter, however, we'll concentrate on manipulating XML schemas in code. For information on the XML Schema editor, refer to MSDN Help.

Understanding ADO.NET and XML

The .NET Framework provides a complete set of documents and data for manipulating XML. The XmlReader and XmlWriter objects, and the classes that descend from them, provide the ability to read and optionally validate XML. The XmlDocument and XmlSchema objects and their related classes represent the XML itself, while the XslTransformation class supports Extensible Stylesheet Language (XSL) Transformations (XSLT) and the XPathNavigator class applies XML Path Language (XPath) queries.

In addition to providing the ability to manipulate XML data, the XML standard is fundamental to data transfer and serialization in the .NET Framework. For the most part, this happens behind the scenes, but we've already seen that ADO.NET Typed DataSets are represented using XML schemas.

We'll examine the XmlData-Document in Chapter 18. The ADO.NET DataSet class also provides direct support for reading and writing XML data and schemas. The XmlDataDocument provides the ability to synchronize XML data and a relational ADO.NET DataSet, allowing you to manipulate a single set of data by using both XML and relational tools. We'll explore some of these techniques in this chapter.

Using the DataSet XML Methods

The .NET Framework exposes a set of classes that allow you to manipulate XML data directly. However, if you need to perform relational operations such as sorting, filtering or retrieving related rows, the DataSet provides an easier mechanism. Furthermore, the XML classes don't support data binding in Windows Forms, so if you intend to display the data to users, you must use the DataSet XML methods.

Fortunately, the choices of treating any given set of data as an XML hierarchy and treating it as a relational DataSet aren't mutually exclusive. As we'll see later in this chapter, the XmlData-Document allows you to manipulate a single set of data by using either or both sets of tools.

The GetXml and GetXmlSchema Methods

Perhaps the most straightforward of the XML methods supported by the DataSet are GetXml and GetXmlSchema, which simply return XML data or an XSD schema as a string value.

Retrieve a DataSet Schema by Using GetXmlSchema: Visual Basic

1. Open the Chapter 17 – Start project in an instance of Visual Studio, and if necessary, double-click XmlForm.vb in the Solution Explorer.

   Visual Studio opens the form in the Form Designer.

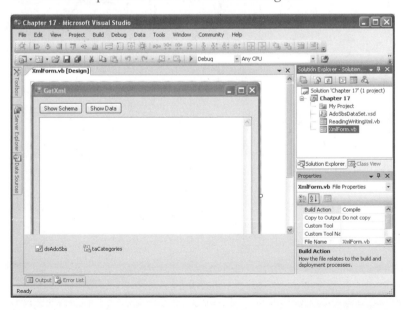

2. Press F7 to display the Code Editor.

3. Add the following lines to the btnShowSchema_Click event handler:

```
Dim xmlStr As String

xmlStr = dsAdoSbs.GetXmlSchema()
tbResults.Text = xmlStr
```

4. Press F5 to run the application.

Visual Studio displays the main application window.

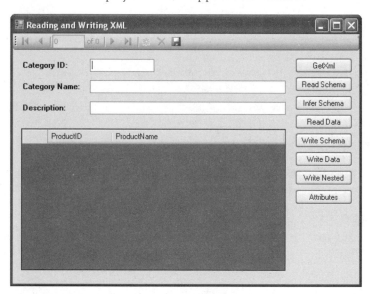

5. Click GetXml.

The application displays the GetXml form.

6. Click Show Schema.

The application displays the DataSet schema in the text box.

7. Close the GetXml form and the application.

Retrieve a DataSet Schema by Using GetXmlSchema: Visual C#

1. Open the Chapter 17 – Start project in an instance of Visual Studio, and if necessary, double-click XmlForm.cs in the Solution Explorer.

Visual Studio opens the form in the Form Designer.

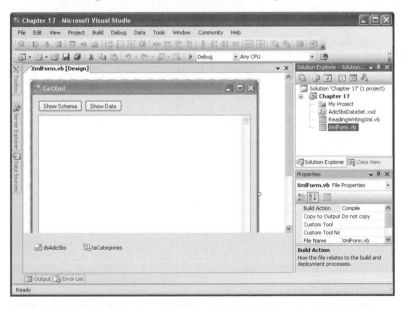

2. Press F7 to display the Code Editor.

3. Add the following lines to the btnShowSchema_Click event handler:

```
string xmlStr;

xmlStr = dsAdoSbs.GetXmlSchema();
tbResults.Text = xmlStr;
```

4. Press F5 to run the application.

   Visual Studio displays the main application window.

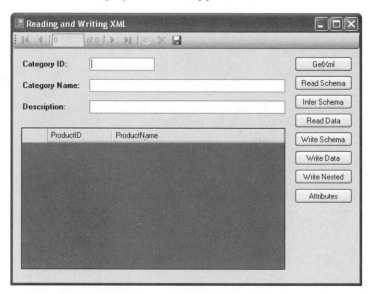

5. Click GetXml.

   The application displays the GetXml form.

6. Click Show Schema.

   The application displays the DataSet schema in the text box.

7. Close the GetXml form and the application.

Retrieve DataSet Data by Using GetXml: Visual Basic

1. In the Code Editor, add the following lines to the btnShowData_Click event handler:

```
Dim xmlStr As String

taCategories.Fill(dsAdoSbs.Categories)
xmlStr = dsAdoSbs.GetXml()
tbResults.Text = xmlStr
```

2. Press F5 to run the application.

3. Click GetXml.

   The application displays the GetXml form.

4. Click Show Data.

   The application displays the XML data in the text box.

5. Close the form and the application.

6. Close the GetXml Form Designer and the Code Editor window.

Retrieve DataSet Data by Using GetXml: Visual C#

1. In the Code Editor, add the following lines to the btnShowData_Click event handler:

```
string xmlStr;

taCategories.Fill(dsAdoSbs.Categories);
xmlStr = dsAdoSbs.GetXml();
tbResults.Text = xmlStr;
```

2. Press F5 to run the application.

3. Click GetXml.

   The application displays the GetXml form.

4. Click Show Data.

   The application displays the XML data in the text box.

5. Close the form and the application.

6. Close the GetXml Form Designer and the Code Editor window.

The ReadXmlSchema Method

The ReadXmlSchema method loads a DataSet schema definition either from the XSD schema definition or from XML. ReadXmlSchema supports four versions, as shown in Table 17-1. You can pass the method a stream, a string identifying a file name, a TextReader or an XmlReader object.

Table 17-1   ReadXmlSchema Method

Method	Description
ReadXmlSchema(stream)	Reads an XML schema from the specified Stream object.
ReadXmlSchema(string)	Reads an XML schema from the file specified in the string parameter.
ReadXmlSchema(textReader)	Reads an XML schema from the specified TextReader.
ReadXmlSchema(xmlReader)	Reads an XML schema from the specified XmlReader.

ReadXmlSchema does not load any data; it loads only tables, columns and constraints (keys and relations). If the DataSet already contains schema information, new tables, columns and constraints are added to the existing schema as necessary. If an object defined in the schema being read conflicts with the existing DataSet schema, the ReadXmlSchema method throws an exception.

> **Note**   If the ReadXmlSchema method is passed XML that does not contain inline schema information, the method infers the schema according to the rules discussed in the following section.

Create a DataSet Schema by Using ReadXmlSchema: Visual Basic

1. In the Solution Explorer, double-click ReadingWritingXML.vb.

   Visual Studio displays the form in the Form Designer.

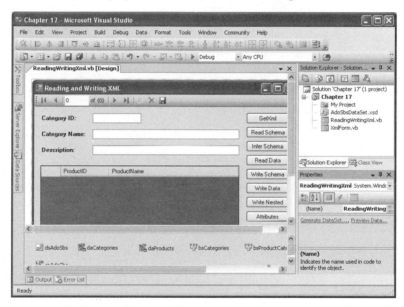

2. Press F7 to display the Code Editor.

3. Add the following lines to the btnReadSchema_Click event handler:

```
Dim newDS As DataSet

newDS = New DataSet()
newDS.ReadXmlSchema("masterSchema.xsd")
daCategories.Fill(newDS.Tables("Categories"))
daProducts.Fill(newDS.Tables("Products"))
SetBindings(newDS)
```

   This block first declares and creates a new Untyped DataSet, and then establishes its schema with a call to ReadXmlSchema based on the XSD schema that is defined in the masterSchema file. This file is in the bin\Debug folder of the project directory. The procedure then uses existing data adapters to load data into the DataSet and calls the SetBindings scaffolding method to bind the controls on the form to the new DataSet.

4. Press F5 to run the application.

5. Click Read Schema.

The application displays the data from the new DataSet in the form's controls.

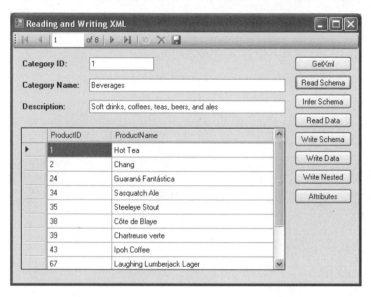

6. Close the application.

Create a DataSet Schema by Using ReadXmlSchema: Visual C#

1. In the Solution Explorer, double-click ReadingWritingXml.cs.

Visual Studio displays the form in the Form Designer.

2. Press F7 to display the Code Editor.

3. Add the following lines to the btnReadSchema_Click event handler:

```
DataSet newDS;

newDS = new DataSet();
newDS.ReadXmlSchema("masterSchema.xsd");
daCategories.Fill(newDS.Tables["Categories"]);
daProducts.Fill(newDS.Tables["Products"]);
SetBindings(newDS);
```

This block first declares and creates a new Untyped DataSet, and then establishes its schema with a call to ReadXmlSchema based on the XSD schema that is defined in the masterSchema file. This file is in the bin\Debug folder of the project directory. The procedure then uses existing data adapters to load data into the DataSet and calls the Set-Bindings scaffolding method to bind the controls on the form to the new DataSet.

4. Press F5 to run the application.

5. Click Read Schema.

The application displays the data from the new DataSet in the form's controls.

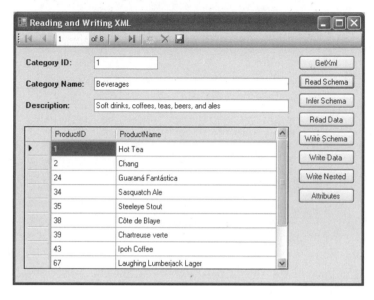

6. Close the application.

The InferXmlSchema Method

The InferXmlSchema method of the DataSet class derives a DataSet schema from the structure of the XML data passed to it. As shown in Table 17-2, InferXmlSchema has the same input sources as the ReadXmlSchema method we examined in the previous section, but it also accepts an array of strings representing the namespaces that should be ignored when generating the DataSet schema.

Table 17-2   InferXmlSchema Method

Method	Description
InferXmlSchema(stream, nsArray)	Reads a schema from the specified Stream, ignoring the namespaces identified in the nsArray string array.
InferXmlSchema(file, nsArray)	Reads a schema from the file specified in the file string, ignoring the namespaces identified in the nsArray string array.
InferXmlSchema(textReader, nsArray)	Reads a schema from the specified TextReader, ignoring the namespaces identified in the nsArray string array.
InferXmlSchema(xmlReader, nsArray)	Reads a schema from the specified XmlReader, ignoring the namespaces identified in the nsArray string array.

InferXmlSchema follows a fixed set of rules when generating a DataSet schema:

- If the root element in the XML has no attributes and no child elements that would otherwise be inferred as columns, it is inferred as a DataSet. Otherwise, the root element is inferred as a table.

- Elements that have attributes are inferred as tables.

- Elements that have child elements are inferred as tables.

- Elements that repeat are inferred as a single table.

- Attributes are inferred as columns.

- Elements that have no attributes or child elements and do not repeat are inferred as columns.

- If elements that are inferred as tables are nested within other elements also inferred as tables, a DataRelation is created between the two tables. A new primary key column named "TableName_Id" is added to both tables and is used by the DataRelation. A ForeignKeyConstraint is created between the two tables by using the "TableName_Id" column as the foreign key.

- If elements that are inferred as tables contain text but have no child elements, a new column named "TableName_Text" is created for the text of each of the elements.

- If elements that inferred as tables contain text but also have child elements, the text is ignored.

> **Note**   Only nested (hierarchical) data results in the creation of a DataRelation. By default, the XML that is created by the WriteXml method of the DataSet doesn't create nested data, so a round-trip won't result in the same DataSet schema. As we'll see, however, this behavior can be controlled by setting the Nested property of the DataRelation object.

Infer the Schema of an XML Document: Visual Basic

1. In the Code Editor, add the following lines to the btnInferSchema_Click event handler:

```
Dim newDS As DataSet
Dim nsStr() As String

newDS = New DataSet()
newDS.InferXmlSchema("dataOnly.xml", nsStr)

daCategories.Fill(newDS.Tables("Categories"))
daProducts.Fill(newDS.Tables("Products"))
newDS.Relations.Add("CategoryProducts", _
    newDS.Tables("Categories").Columns("CategoryID"), _
    newDS.Tables("Products").Columns("CategoryID"))
SetBindings(newDS)
```

The first two lines declare DataSet and String array variables, while the next two instantiate the DataSet and pass both variables to the InferXmlSchema method. The remaining code adds a new DataRelation to the new DataSet, fills it, and then calls the SetBindings utility function that binds the form controls to the DataSet.

2. Press F5 to run the application

3. Click Infer Schema.

    The application displays the data in the form controls.

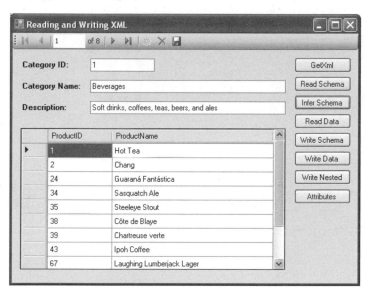

4. Close the application.

Infer the Schema of an XML Document: Visual C#

1. In the Code Editor, add the following lines to the btnInferSchema_Click event handler:

```csharp
DataSet newDS;
string[] nsStr = new string[0];

newDS = new DataSet();
newDS.InferXmlSchema("dataOnly.xml", nsStr);

daCategories.Fill(newDS.Tables["Categories"]);
daProducts.Fill(newDS.Tables["Products"]);
newDS.Relations.Add("CategoryProducts",
    newDS.Tables["Categories"].Columns["CategoryID"],
    newDS.Tables["Products"].Columns["CategoryID"]);

SetBindings(newDS);
```

The first two lines declare DataSet and String array variables, while the next two instantiate the DataSet and pass both variables to the InferXmlSchema method. The remaining code adds a new DataRelation to the new DataSet, fills it, and then calls the SetBindings utility function that binds the form controls to the DataSet.

2. Press F5 to run the application

3. Click Infer Schema.

The application displays the data in the form controls.

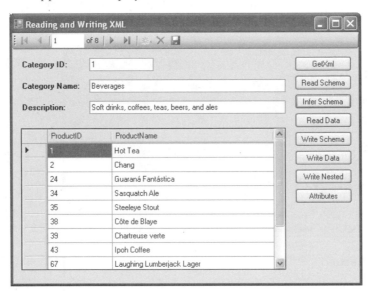

4. Close the application.

The ReadXml Method

The ReadXml method of the DataSet class reads XML data into a DataSet. Optionally, it might also create or modify the DataSet schema. As shown in Table 17-3, the ReadXml method supports the same input sources as the other DataSet XML methods we've examined.

Table 17-3   **ReadXml Method**

Method	Description
ReadXml(stream)	Reads an XML schema and data from the specified Stream object.
ReadXml(string)	Reads an XML schema and data from the file specified in the string parameter.
ReadXml(textReader)	Reads an XML schema and data from the specified TextReader object.
ReadXml(xmlReader)	Reads an XML schema and data from the specified XmlReader object.
ReadXml(stream, xmlRead-Mode)	Reads an XML schema and data from the specified Stream object, as determined by the XmlReadMode.
ReadXml(file, xmlRead-Mode)	Reads an XML schema and data from the file specified by the File string parameter, as determined by the XmlReadMode.

Table 17-3 ReadXml Method

Method	Description
ReadXml(textReader, xml-ReadMode)	Reads an XML schema and data from the specified TextReader object, as determined by the XmlReadMode.
ReadXml(xmlReader, xml-ReadMode)	Reads an XML schema and data from the specified XmlReader object, as determined by the XmlReadMode.

The ReadXml method exposes an optional XmlReadMode parameter that determines how the XML is interpreted. The possible values for XmlReadMode are shown in Table 17-4.

Table 17-4 XmlReadMode Enumeration

Value	Description
Auto	Chooses a ReadMode based on the contents of the XML.
ReadSchema	Reads an inline schema and then loads the data, adding DataTables as necessary.
InferSchema	Ignores any inline schema, infers a schema from the data, and loads the data.
InferTypedSchema	Ignores any inline schema, infers a strongly typed schema from the data, and loads the data.
IgnoreSchema	Loads data into an existing DataSet, ignoring any inline schema information.
DiffGram	Reads DiffGram information into an existing DataSet.
Fragment	Adds XML fragments that match the existing DataSet schema to the DataSet, ignoring those that do not match.

Unless the ReadXml method is passed an XmlReadMode parameter of DiffGram, it does not merge the data that it reads with existing rows in the DataSet. If it reads a row with the same primary key as an existing row, the method throws an exception.

A DiffGram is an XML format that encapsulates the current and original versions of an element, along with any DataRow errors. The nominal structure of a DiffGram is shown here:

```
<diffgr:diffgram
      xmlns:msdata="urn:schemas-microsoft-com:xml-msdata"
      xmlns:diffgr="urn:schemas-microsoft-com:XML-diffgram-v1"
      xmlns:xsd="http://www.w3.org/2001/XMLSchema">

  <ElementName>
  </ElementName>

  <diffgr:before>
  </diffgr:before>

  <diffgr:errors>
  </diffgr:errors>
</diffgr:diffgram>
```

In the real DiffGram, the first section (shown as <ElementName></ElementName> in the example) has the name of the complexType defining the DataRow. This section contains the current version of the contents of the DataRow. The <diffgr:before> section contains the original versions, while the <diffgr:errors> section contains error information for the row.

For DiffGram to be passed as the XmlReadMode parameter, the data must be in DiffGram format. If you need to merge XML that is written in standard XML format with existing data, you must create a new DataSet and then call the Merge method of the DataSet to merge the two sets of data.

Load XML Data by Using ReadXml: Visual Basic

1. In the Code Editor, add the following lines to the btnReadData_Click event handler:

```
Dim newDS As DataSet

newDS = New DataSet()
newDS.ReadXml("data.xml", XmlReadMode.ReadSchema)

SetBindings(newDS)
```

The data.xml file contains an inline schema definition, so by passing XmlRead-Mode.ReadSchema parameter to the ReadXml method, this code block instructs the DataSet to first create the DataSet schema and then load the data.

2. Press F5 to run the application.

3. Click Read Data.

The application displays the data retrieved from the file.

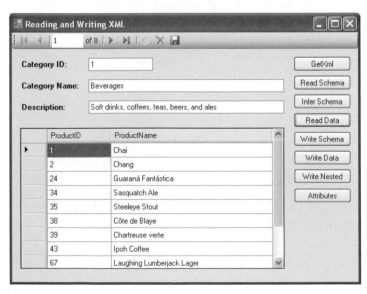

4. Close the application.

Load XML Data by Using ReadXml: Visual C#

1. In the Code Editor, add the following lines to the btnReadData_Click event handler:

    ```
    DataSet newDS;

    newDS = new DataSet();
    newDS.ReadXml("data.xml", XmlReadMode.ReadSchema);

    SetBindings(newDS);
    ```

    The data.xml file contains an inline schema definition, so by passing XmlRead-Mode.ReadSchema parameter to the ReadXml method, this code block instructs the DataSet to first create the DataSet schema and then load the data.

2. Press F5 to run the application.

3. Click Read Data.

    The application displays the data retrieved from the file.

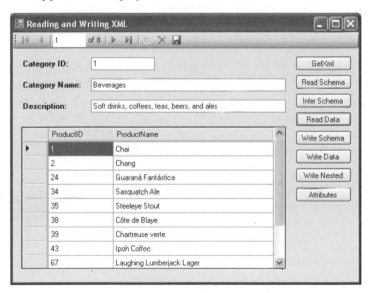

4. Close the application.

The WriteXmlSchema Method

As might be expected, the WriteXmlSchema method writes the schema of the DataSet, including tables, columns and constraints, to the specified output. The versions of the method, which accept the same output parameters as the other XML methods, are shown in Table 17-5.

Table 17-5   WriteXmlSchema Method

Method	Description
WriteXmlSchema(stream)	Writes an XML schema to the specified Stream object.
WriteXmlSchema(string)	Writes an XML schema to the file specified in the string parameter.
WriteXmlSchema(textWriter)	Writes an XML schema to the specified TextWriter object.
WriteXmlSchema(xmlWriter)	Writes an XML schema to the specified XmlWriter object.

Create an XML Schema by Using WriteXmlSchema: Visual Basic

1. In the Code Editor, add the following lines to the btnWriteSchema_Click event handler:

    ```
    dsAdoSbs.WriteXmlSchema("testSchema.xsd")
    MessageBox.Show("Finished", "WriteXmlSchema")
    ```

    Because no path is passed to the method, the file will be written to the \bin subfolder of the project folder.

2. Press F5 to run the application.

3. Click Write Schema.

    The application displays a message box after the file has been written.

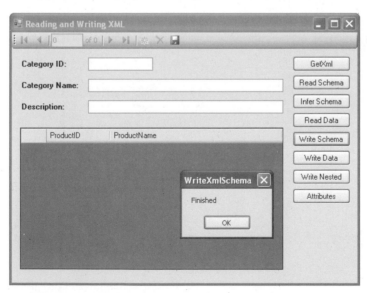

4. Close the message box, and then close the application.

5. Open Windows Explorer, navigate to the Chapter 17 – Start\bin\Debug project folder, right-click the testSchema.xsd file, select Open With, and then select Notepad.

    Windows displays the schema file.

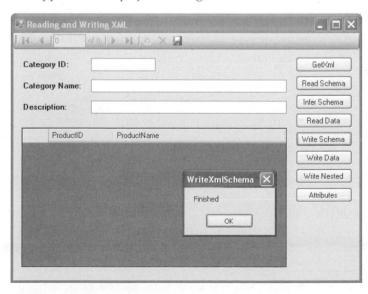

6. Close Microsoft Notepad, and return to Visual Studio.

Create an XML Schema by Using WriteXmlSchema: Visual C#

1. In the Code Editor, add the following lines to the btnWriteSchema_Click event handler:

```
dsAdoSbs.WriteXmlSchema("testSchema.xsd");
MessageBox.Show("Finished", "WriteXmlSchema");
```

Because no path is passed to the method, the file will be written to the bin\Debug sub-folder of the project folder.

2. Press F5 to run the application.

3. Click Write Schema.

The application displays a message box after the file has been written.

4. Close the message box, and then close the application.

5. Open Windows Explorer, navigate to the Chapter 17 – Start\bin\Debug project folder, right-click the testSchema.xsd file, select Open With, and then select Notepad.

Windows displays the schema file.

6. Close Notepad, and return to Visual Studio.

The WriteXml Method

The WriteXml method of the DataSet class writes XML and, optionally, DataSet schema information to a specified output, as shown in Table 17-6. As we'll see in the following section, the structure of the XML resulting from the WriteXml method is controlled by DataSet property settings.

Table 17-6   The WriteXml Method

Method	Description
WriteXml(stream)	Writes an XML schema and data to the specified Stream object.
WriteXml(string)	Writes an XML schema and data to the file specified by the file string parameter.
WriteXml(textWriter)	Writes an XML schema and data to the specified TextWriter object.
WriteXml(xmlWriter)	Writes an XML schema and data to the specified XmlWriter object.
WriteXml(stream, xmlWriteMode)	Writes an XML schema, data or both to the specified Stream object as specified by the XmlWriteMode parameter.
WriteXml(string, xmlWriteMode)	Writes an XML schema, data or both to the file specified by the file string parameter as specified by the XmlWriteMode parameter.
WriteXml(textWriter, xmlWriteMode)	Writes an XML schema, data or both to the specified TextWriter object as specified by the XmlWriteMode parameter.
WriteXml(xmlWriter, xmlWriteMode)	Writes an XML schema, data or both to the specified XmlWriter object as specified by the XmlWriteMode parameter.

The valid XmlWriteMode parameters are shown in Table 17-7. The DiffGram parameter causes the output to be written in DiffGram format. If no XmlWriteMode parameter is specified, WriteSchema is assumed.

Table 17-7   XmlWriteMode Enumeration

Value	Description
IgnoreSchema	Writes data only.
WriteSchema	Writes data and an inline schema.
DiffGram	Writes the entire DataSet in DiffGram format.

Write Data to a File in XML Format: Visual Basic

1. In the Code Editor, add the following lines to the btnWriteData_Click event handler:

```
daCategories.Fill(dsAdoSbs.Categories)
daProducts.Fill(dsAdoSbs.Products)

dsAdoSbs.WriteXml("newData.xml", XmlWriteMode.IgnoreSchema)
MessageBox.Show("Finished", "WriteXml")
```

Because no path is passed to the method, the file will be written to the \bin subfolder of the project folder.

2. Press F5 to run the application.

3. Click Write Data.

The application displays a message box after the file has been written.

4. Close the message box, and then close the application.

5. In Windows Explorer, navigate to the Chapter 17 – Start\bin\Debug project folder if necessary, and double-click the data.xml file.

   The XML file opens in the default browser.

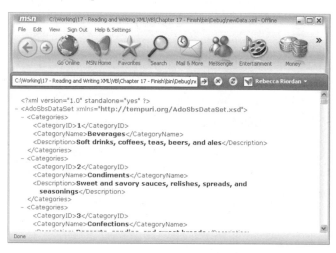

6. Close the browser, and return to Visual Studio.

Write Data to a File in XML Format: Visual C#

1. In the Code Editor, add the following lines to the btnWriteData_Click event handler:

```
daCategories.Fill(dsAdoSbs.Categories);
daProducts.Fill(dsAdoSbs.Products);

dsAdoSbs.WriteXml("newData.xml", XmlWriteMode.IgnoreSchema);
MessageBox.Show("Finished", "WriteXml");
```

   Because no path is passed to the method, the file will be written to the \bin\Debug sub-folder of the project folder.

2. Press F5 to run the application.

3. Click Write Data.

   The application displays a message box after the file has been written.

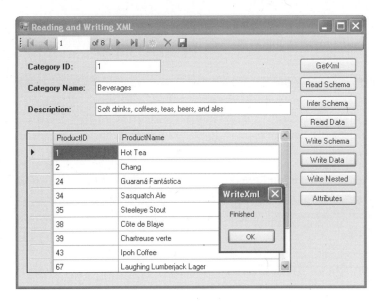

4. Close the message box, and then close the application.

5. Open Windows Explorer, navigate to the Chapter 17 – Start\bin\Debug project folder, and double-click the data.xml file.

   The XML file opens in the default browser.

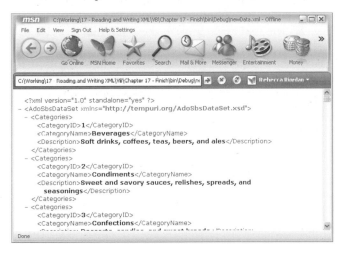

6. Close the browser, and return to Visual Studio.

Controlling How XML Is Written

By default, the WriteXml method generates XML with DataTables structured as complex-Types and DataColumns structured as elements within them. This isn't necessarily what you want the output to be.

If, for example, you want to read the data back into a DataSet, ADO.NET won't create relationships correctly unless the schema is present—an unnecessary overhead in many situations—or the related data is nested hierarchically in the XML.

In other situations, you might need to control whether individual columns are written as elements, attributes or simple text, or you might even need to prevent some columns from being written at all. This might be the case, for example, if you're interchanging data with another application.

The Nested Property of the DataRelation

The ADO.NET DataRelation class exposes a Nested property that overrides the default WriteXml behavior, causing child DataRows to be written within their parents and creating the hierarchical structure that ReadXml requires. The Nested property can be set at run time or in the DataSet Designer. In the DataSet Designer, this property is exposed in the Data-Relations dialog box.

Use the Nested Property of the DataRelation: Visual Basic

1. In the Code Editor, add the following lines to the btnWriteNested_Click event handler:

```
daCategories.Fill(dsAdoSbs.Categories)
daProducts.Fill(dsAdoSbs.Products)

dsAdoSbs.Relations("CategoryProducts").Nested = True
dsAdoSbs.WriteXml("nestedData.xml", XmlWriteMode.IgnoreSchema)
MessageBox.Show("Finished", "WriteXml Nested")
```

This code sets the Nested property to True before writing it to the file.

2. Press F5 to save and run the application.

3. Click Write Nested.

The application displays a message box after the file has been written.

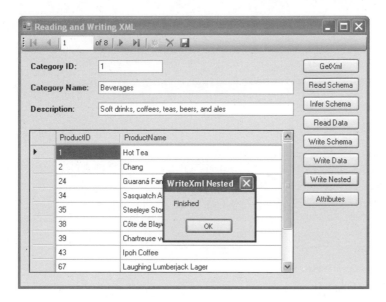

4. Close the message box, and then close the application.

5. Open Windows Explorer, navigate to the Chapter 17 – Start\bin\Debug project folder, and double-click the nestedData.xml file.

   The XML file opens in the default browser.

6. Close the browser, and return to Visual Studio.

Use the Nested Property of the DataRelation: Visual C#

1. In the Code Editor, add the following lines to the btnWriteNested_Click event handler:

```
daCategories.Fill(dsAdoSbs.Categories);
daProducts.Fill(dsAdoSbs.Products);

dsAdoSbs.Relations["CategoryProducts"].Nested = true;
```

```
dsAdoSbs.WriteXml("nestedData.xml", XmlWriteMode.IgnoreSchema);
MessageBox.Show("Finished", "WriteXml Nested");
```

This code sets the Nested property to True before writing it to the file.

2. Press F5 to save and run the application.

3. Click Write Nested.

The application displays a message box after the file has been written.

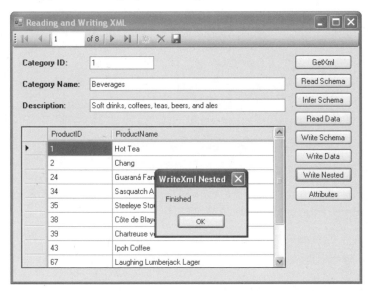

4. Close the message box, and then close the application.

5. Open Windows Explorer, navigate to the Chapter 17 – Start\bin\Debug project folder, and double-click the nestedData.xml file.

The XML file opens in the default browser.

6. Close the browser, and return to Visual Studio.

Controlling Column Mapping

The ColumnMapping property of the DataColumn class controls how the column is written by the WriteXml method. The possible values of the ColumnMapping are shown in Table 17-8.

Table 17-8   ColumnMapping Property Values

Value	Description
Element	The column is written as an XML element.
Attribute	The column is written as an XML attribute.
SimpleContent	The contents of the column are written as text.
Hidden	The column will not be included in the XML output.

Element, the default value, writes the column as a nested element within the complexType representing the DataTable, while Attribute writes the column as one of its attributes. The Hidden value prevents the column from being written at all. These three values can be freely mixed within a single DataTable.

SimpleContent, which writes the column as a simple text value, cannot be combined with columns that are written as elements or attributes, nor can it be used if the Nested property of a DataRelation referencing the table has its Nested property set to True.

Write Columns as Attributes: Visual Basic

1. In the Code Editor, add the following lines to the btnAttributes_Click event handler:

```
daCategories.Fill(dsAdoSbs.Categories)

With dsAdoSbs.Categories
   .Columns("CategoryID").ColumnMapping = MappingType.Attribute
   .Columns("CategoryName").ColumnMapping = MappingType.Attribute
   .Columns("Description").ColumnMapping = MappingType.Attribute
End With

dsAdoSbs.WriteXml("attributes.xml", XmlWriteMode.IgnoreSchema)
MessageBox.Show("Finished", "Write Attributes")
```

2. Press F5 to save and run the program.

3. Click Attributes.

The application displays a message box after the file has been written.

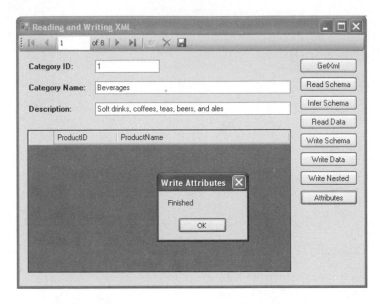

4. Close the message box, and then close the application.

5. In Windows Explorer, navigate to the Chapter 17 – Start\bin\Debug project folder, and double-click the attributes.xml file.

   The XML file opens in the default browser.

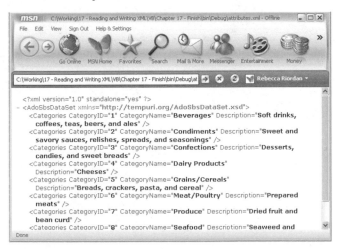

6. Close the browser, and return to Visual Studio.

Write Columns as Attributes: Visual C#

1. In the Code Editor, add the following lines to the btnAttributes_Click event handler:

```
daCategories.Fill(dsAdoSbs.Categories);

dsAdoSbs.Categories. Columns["CategoryID"].ColumnMapping =
    MappingType.Attribute;
dsAdoSbs.Categories.Columns["CategoryName"].ColumnMapping =
    MappingType.Attribute;
dsAdoSbs.Categories.Columns["Description"].ColumnMapping =
    MappingType.Attribute;

dsAdoSbs.WriteXml("attributes.xml", XmlWriteMode.IgnoreSchema);
MessageBox.Show("Finished", "Write Attributes");
```

2. Press F5 to save and run the program.

3. Click Attributes.

    The application displays a message box after the file has been written.

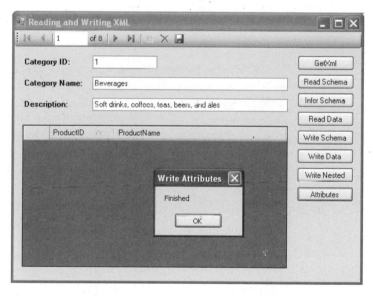

4. Close the message box, and then close the application.

5. Open Windows Explorer, navigate to the Chapter 17 – Start\bin\Debug project folder, and double-click the attributes.xml file.

    The XML file opens in the default browser.

6.   Close the browser, and return to Visual Studio.

Summary

In this chapter, we briefly examined the structure of an XML schema file and then looked at the methods that the DataSet class exposes for returning, reading and writing XML data and XML schemas. We saw how the GetXml and GetXmlSchema methods return XML representations of a DataSet. (GetXml returns just the data, while GetXmlSchema returns an XML schema.) The corresponding reading methods are ReadXml and ReadXmlSchema, which create a DataSet or load it with data from an XML data stream or schema. The DataSet also exposes an InferXmlSchema, which derives a DataSet schema based on the structure of XML data. Finally the WriteXml and WriteXmlSchema methods return XML data or an XML schema from a DataSet. Unlike the GetXml and GetXmlSchema methods, these methods persist their data to a Stream, TextReader, File or XmlReader.

We also examined two methods for controlling the way that XML is produced from the DataSet: the Nested property, which nests child DataRows within their parent element declarations; and the ColumnMapping property, which provides a fine degree of control over how individual DataColumns are represented.

In the next chapter, we'll examine the XmlDataDocument, which allows you to treat XML data as a DataSet and a DataSet as XML data, giving you the best of both worlds.

Chapter 18

The XmlDataDocument

After completing this chapter, you will be able to:

- Create an XmlDataDocument from a DataSet.

- Create a DataSet from an XmlDataDocument.

- Navigate an XmlDataDocument by using the XML Document Object Model (DOM).

- Execute XPath queries against an XmlDataDocument.

- Create nodes in an XmlDataDocument.

- Retrieve a DataRow from an XmlDataDocument node.

- Retrieve an XmlDataDocument node from a DataRow.

In this chapter, we'll examine the XmlDataDocument, a descendant of the XmlDocument that provides an XML view of the relational data contained in a DataSet.

Understanding the XmlDataDocument

Although the relational data model is efficient, there are times when it is convenient to manipulate data by using the tools that XML provides—the Extensible Stylesheet Language (XSL), XSL Transformations (XSLT), and XPath. On the other hand, as convenient and universal as XML is, there are other times when it is convenient to manipulate XML data by using the relational data model. Sorting and filtering tend to be simpler, and modeling complex relationships is, as a general rule, simpler when you use the relational model. Even updating individual DataColumns can be simpler when you use a DataSet rather than XML.

The Microsoft .NET Framework's XmlDataDocument makes it possible to have the best of both worlds. The XmlDataDocument is a descendant of the XmlDocument, which, as the name implies, is the .NET Framework in-memory representation of an XML document tree. Using an XmlDataDocument, you can manipulate a single set of data relationally as a DataSet and hierarchically by using XML.

The XmlDataDocument doesn't create a new set of data, but rather it creates a DataSet that references all or part of the XML data. Because there's only one set of data, changes made in one view are automatically reflected in the other view, and of course, memory resources are conserved because only one copy of the data is being manipulated, as shown in the figure on the next page.

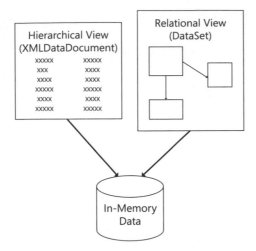

> **Important**   It's important to note that an XmlDataDocument only mirrors the data of a DataSet, not the schema. Schema changes made to one object are not propagated to the other object.

Creating XmlDataDocuments

Depending on the initial source of your data, you can create an XmlDataDocument based on the schema and contents of the DataSet, or you can create a DataSet based on the contents of the XmlDataDocument.

To create an XmlDataDocument based on an existing DataSet, you pass the DataSet to the XmlDataDocument constructor, as follows:

```
myXdd = New XmlDataDocument(myDS)
```

You can also begin with an XML document and create a DataSet. To do so, you use the default XmlDataDocument constructor and then reference its DataSet property, as shown here:

```
myDS = New DataSet()
'Create DataSet Schema
myDS = myXDD.DataSet
```

If you use this method, you must create the DataSet schema manually. For the data in the Xml-DataDocument to be available through the DataSet, the DataTable and DataColumn names must match those in the XmlDataDocument. The matching is case-sensitive.

The DataSet schema can be set by manually adding DataTables and DataColumns, or it can be read from an XSD schema by using the ReadXmlSchema method.

If you want the DataSet to match an existing DataSet, you can use the schema returned by the GetXmlSchema method. (Unfortunately, you can't use the DataSet.Clone method, because the XmlDataDocument DataSet is read-only.) Using GetXmlSchema isn't difficult, but the syntax is somewhat complicated. You must pass the string returned by GetXmlSchema to a StringReader that is then passed as the parameter of the ReadXmlSchema, as follows:

```
myXdd.DataSet.ReadXmlSchema(New StringReader(myDataSet.GetXmlSchema()))
```

Although this third method requires slightly more code, it provides a mechanism for creating a partial relational view of the XML data. It isn't necessary to duplicate the entire XML schema in the DataSet. Any DataTables or DataColumns that are not in the DataSet are simply ignored during DataSet operations.

Data can be loaded into either the DataSet or the XmlDataDocument at any time, before or after synchronization. Any data changes made to one object, including adding, deleting or changing values, are automatically reflected in the other object.

Create a Synchronized XML View of a DataSet: Visual Basic

1. Open the Chapter 18 – Start project in an instance of Microsoft Visual Studio 2005 and, if necessary, double-click XDD.vb in the Solution Explorer.

    Visual Studio displays the form in the Form Designer.

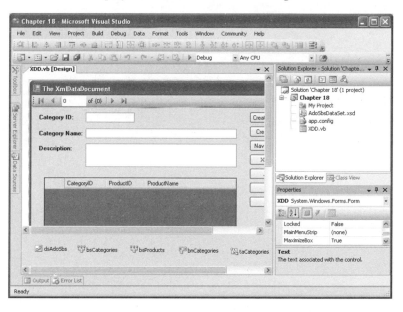

2. Press F7 to display the Code Editor.

3. Add the following lines to the btnCreateFromDataSet_Click event handler:

```
Dim xddFromDataSet As XmlDataDocument

xddFromDataSet = New XmlDataDocument(dsAdoSbs)
xddFromDataSet.Load("AdoSbs.xml")
```

This code block declares and instantiates an XmlDataDocument, passing the dsAdoSbs DataSet to the constructor. It then loads data from the AdoSbs.xml file located in the bin\Debug project folder.

4. Press F5 to run the application.

5. Click Create From DataSet.

The application loads the data and displays it in the form.

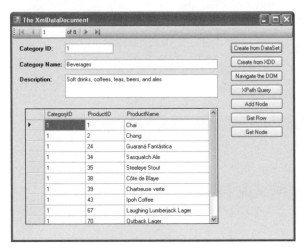

6. Close the application.

Create a Synchronized XML View of a DataSet: Visual C#

1. Open the Chapter 18 – Start project in an instance of Visual Studio and, if necessary, double-click XDD.cs in the Solution Explorer.

Visual Studio displays the form in the Form Designer.

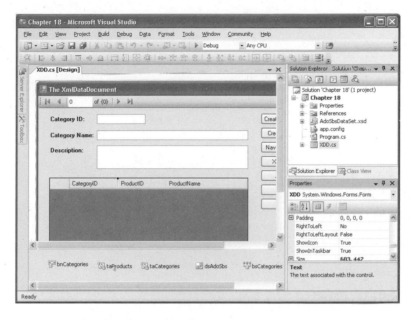

2. Press F7 to display the Code Editor.

3. Add the following lines to the btnCreateFromDataSet_Click event handler:

```
XmlDataDocument xddFromDataSet;

xddFromDataSet = new XmlDataDocument(dsAdoSbs);
xddFromDataSet.Load("AdoSbs.xml");
```

This code block declares and instantiates an XmlDataDocument, passing the dsAdoSbs DataSet to the constructor. It then loads data from the AdoSbs.xml file located in the bin\Debug project folder.

4. Press F5 to run the application.

5. Click Create From DataSet.

The application loads the data and displays it in the form.

6. Close the application.

Create a DataSet based on XML Data: Visual Basic

1. In the Code Editor, add the following lines to the btnCreateFromXdd_Click event handler:

```
Dim xddCreateDataSet As XmlDataDocument

xddCreateDataSet = New XmlDataDocument()

xddCreateDataSet.DataSet.ReadXmlSchema(New _
    System.IO.StringReader(dsAdoSbs.GetXmlSchema()))
xddCreateDataSet.Load("AdoSbs.xml")

SetBindings(xddCreateDataSet.DataSet)
```

This code block declares and instantiates an XmlDataDocument, passing the dsAdoSbs DataSet to the constructor. It then sets the schema of the XmlDataDocument DataSet by passing the string returned by the GetXmlSchema method of the dsAdoSbs DataSet to a StringReader that is, in turn, passed to the ReadXMLSchema method.

After the XmlDataDocument is created and the DataSet schema is established, the code block loads data from the AdoSbs.xml file located in the bin\Debug project folder, and then calls the SetBindings scaffolding procedure to bind the form controls to the dsAdoSbs DataSet.

2. Press F5 to run the application.

3. Click Create From XDD.

The application loads the data and displays it in the form. Notice that it isn't necessary to load the data into dsAdoSbs because the data is shared with the XmlDataDocument.

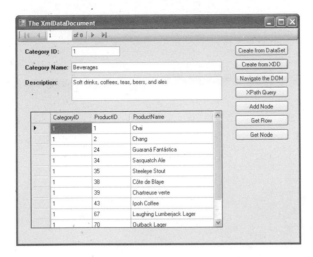

4. Close the application.

Create a DataSet based on XML Data: Visual C#

1. In the Code Editor, add the following lines to the btnCreateFromXdd_Click event handler:

```
XmlDataDocument xddCreateDataSet;

xddCreateDataSet = new XmlDataDocument();

xddCreateDataSet.DataSet.ReadXmlSchema(new
    System.IO.StringReader(dsAdoSbs.GetXmlSchema()));
xddCreateDataSet.Load("AdoSbs.xml");

SetBindings(xddCreateDataSet.DataSet);
```

This code block declares and instantiates an XmlDataDocument, passing the dsAdoSbs DataSet to the constructor. It then sets the schema of the XmlDataDocument DataSet by passing the string returned by the GetXmlSchema method of the dsAdoSbs DataSet to a StringReader that is, in turn, passed to the ReadXMLSchema method.

After the XmlDataDocument is created and the DataSet schema is established, the code block loads data from the AdoSbs.xml file located in the bin\Debug project folder, and then calls the SetBindings scaffolding procedure to bind the form controls to the dsAdoSbs DataSet.

2. Press F5 to run the application.

3. Click Create From XDD.

The application loads the data and displays it in the form. Notice that it isn't necessary to load the data into dsAdoSbs because the data is shared with the XmlDataDocument.

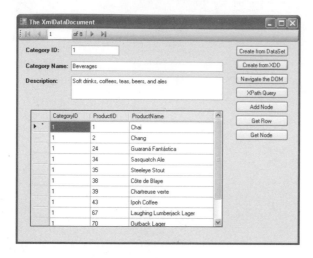

4. Close the application.

Navigating an XML Document

The in-memory representation of XML in the .NET Framework complies with the W3C Document Object Model (DOM) Core Levels 1 and 2. Using the XmlDataDocument and the properties and methods of the DOM, it's possible to navigate a DataSet.

> **Note**   A detailed discussion of the XML DOM is outside the scope of this book. For details, see Visual Studio Help or the World Wide Web Consortium (W3C) Web site.

Within the DOM, the basic object is the node. Nodes are arranged in a hierarchical tree as shown in the figure on the facing page, which illustrates the node structure of an XmlData-Document based on the AdoSbsDataSet.

As you can see, the top of the tree is the Document, represented in the .NET Framework by the XmlDocument object, from which the XmlDataDocument directly descends. When the Document models a DataSet, the first child is named xml, and it contains the XML text that precedes the DataSet declaration. The second child represents the DataSet itself—AdoSbsDataSet in this case.

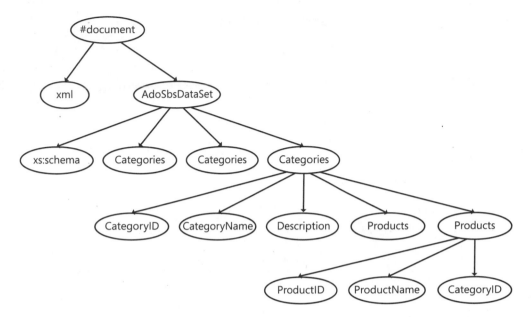

The first child of the DataSet node is xs:schema, which contains the raw XSD schema text. The remaining child nodes represent the table objects at the top of the hierarchy. In this case, the DataSet contains only two tables, Categories and Products, which have a one-to-many relationship, so Categories is at the top of the hierarchy. There is a Categories node for each DataRow in the Categories DataTable.

The child nodes of each Categories node represent the DataColumns of the Categories DataTable and also the Products that are related to that Category DataRow. Again, there is a Products node for each Product related to the Category.

Because the example in the preceding figure contains only two DataTables, the Categories nodes contain only the DataColumns in the DataTable. If there were other DataTables in the chain of relationships, they would be represented by nodes at this level.

Notice that only a single hierarchy can be represented by a DOM tree. If a DataSet has DataTables that are related in a network, with any given DataTable being related to multiple other DataTables, the DataSet cannot easily be represented with this model.

Navigating a DataSet by Using the DOM

The .NET Framework XmlNode class exposes properties that make it possible to navigate its node tree, as shown in Table 18-1. Because the XmlDataDocument descends from the Xml-Document, which in turn descends from XmlNode, these properties are available within the XmlDataDocument for navigating a DataSet.

Table 18-1   XmlNode Navigation Properties

Property	Description
ChildNodes	Returns the collection of child nodes.
FirstChild	Returns the first child node.
HasChildNodes	Indicates whether the node contains child nodes.
Item(childNodeName)	Returns the child node that has the Name property specified by the childNodeName string.
LastChild	Returns the last child node.
NextSibling	Returns the next node at the same level in the node tree.
ParentNode	Returns the parent node.
PreviousSibling	Returns the previous node at the same level in the node tree.

Navigate a DataSet by Using the XML DOM: Visual Basic

1. In the Code Editor, add the following lines to the btnDOM_Click event handler:

```
Dim xdd As XmlDataDocument
Dim str As String
Dim catNode As XmlNode
Dim prodNode As XmlNode

xdd = New XmlDataDocument(dsAdoSbs)
xdd.Load("AdoSbs.xml")


catNode = xdd.Item("AdoSbsDataSet").LastChild
str = "Category ID:  " + catNode.Item("CategoryID").InnerText + vbCrLf

For Each prodNode In catNode.ChildNodes
    If prodNode.Name = "Products" Then
        str += vbCrLf + "Product Name:  " + _
            prodNode.Item("ProductName").InnerText
    End If
Next

MessageBox.Show(str, "Navigating the DOM")
```

After declaring some local variables, this code block creates an XmlDataDocument from the dsAdoSbs DataSet and loads data from the AdoSbs.xml file located in the bin\Debug project folder. It then sets the catNode variable to the last child of the AdoSbsDataSet node, and sets the str String variable to the value of the CategoryID node.

The For…Each block iterates through the child nodes of the catNode and, if the node represents one of the Products DataRows, adds the ProductName to the str variable, which is displayed in a message box in the last line of the procedure.

2. Press F5 to run the application.

3. Click Navigate The DOM.

    The application displays the Category ID and related products of the last Category node.

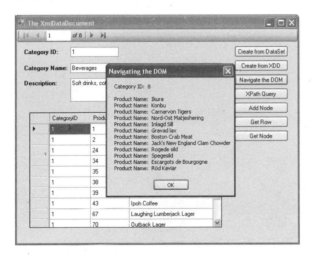

4. Close the message box, and then close the application.

Navigate a DataSet by Using the XML DOM: Visual C#

1. In the Code Editor, add the following lines to the btnDOM_Click event handler:

```csharp
XmlDataDocument xdd;
string str;
XmlNode catNode;

xdd = new XmlDataDocument(dsAdoSbs);
xdd.Load("AdoSbs.xml");

catNode = xdd["AdoSbsDataSet"].LastChild;
str = "Category ID:   " + catNode["CategoryID"].InnerText + "\n";

foreach(XmlNode prodNode in catNode.ChildNodes)
{
    if (prodNode.Name == "Products")
    {
        str += "\nProduct Name:   " +
            prodNode["ProductName"].InnerText;
    }
}

MessageBox.Show(str, "Navigating the DOM");
```

After declaring some local variables, this code block creates an XmlDataDocument from the dsAdoSbs DataSet and loads data from the AdoSbs.xml file located in the bin\Debug project folder. It then sets the catNode variable to the last child of the AdoSbsDataSet node, and sets the str String variable to the value of the CategoryID node.

The For...Each block iterates through the child nodes of the catNode and, if the node represents one of the Products DataRows, adds the ProductName to the str variable, which is displayed in a message box in the last line of the procedure.

2. Press F5 to run the application.

3. Click Navigate The DOM.

The application displays the Category ID and related products of the last Category node.

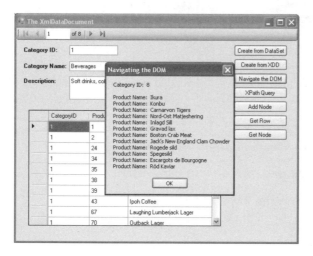

4. Close the message box, and then close the application.

Navigating a DataSet by Using XPath

The navigation properties of the XmlNode are functional, but performing anything other than simple navigation can be clumsy and tedious. Fortunately, the .NET Framework implementation of XML also supports XPath queries.

XPath is a query language defined by the W3C that is designed for navigating XML hierarchies. Functionally, it is similar to the SQL language, although its syntax is entirely different.

> **Note** XPath, like the details of the DOM, is outside the scope of this book. For details, see Visual Studio Help or the W3C Web site.

The XmlNode exposes two methods, SelectNodes and SelectSingleNode, which accept an XPath expression as a string and, optionally, an XmlNamespaceManager that is used to resolve namespaces within the XPath expression. The SelectNodes method returns an XmlNodeSet, while the SelectSingleNode method returns only the first node that matches the specified expression.

> **Note** The XmlDocument also exposes a CreateNavigator method that returns an instance of the XPathNavigator class. The XPathNavigator can be used for performing multiple XPath queries against the XmlDocument, as well as for more complex XPath navigation.

XPath expression syntax is very similar to that used to navigate a folder hierarchy, except that levels of the hierarchy are indicated with the forward slash (/) rather than the backslash (\). All navigation in the node list is relative to the current node. (In the case of the SelectNodes and SelectSingleNodes methods, the Document node is always the current node.)

So, for example, C:\Microsoft Press\ADO.NET 2.0 Step by Step\SampleDBs is the path to the default installation of the sample databases for this chapter, and /AdoSbsDataSet/Categories is the path to the level of the node tree containing the Categories elements.

We're using only simple expressions in this chapter, and as we've seen, simple navigation can be performed by using the XML DOM. So even though the following example uses a simple expression, bear in mind that the true strength of XPath lies in its ability to perform sophisticated node selection based on multiple criteria and the relationships of nodes.

Select DataRows by Using XPath: Visual Basic

1. In the Code Editor, add the following lines to the btnXPath_Click event handler:

```vb
Dim xdd As XmlDataDocument
Dim qry, msg As String
Dim selectedNodes As XmlNodeList
Dim theNode As XmlNode

taCategories.Fill(dsAdoSbs.Categories)
taProducts.Fill(dsAdoSbs.Products)
xdd = New XmlDataDocument(dsAdoSbs)

qry = "*"
selectedNodes = xdd.FirstChild.SelectNodes(qry)

msg = ""
For Each theNode In selectedNodes
    msg += vbCrLf + theNode.ChildNodes(1).InnerText
Next

MessageBox.Show(msg)
```

The first few lines of this code block declare local variables and instantiate an XmlData-Document based on the dsAdoSbs DataSet. Then the SelectNodes method is called by using an XPath expression that returns all of the nodes at the first level of the hierarchy. Finally the name of the returned Category is displayed in a message box.

2. Press F5 to run the application.

3. Click XPath Query.

    The application displays the Category names.

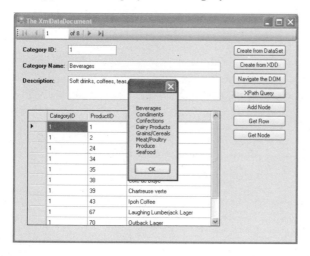

4. Close the message box, and then the application.

Select DataRows by Using XPath: Visual C#

1. In the Code Editor, add the following lines to the btnXPath_Click event handler:

```
XmlDataDocument xdd;
String qry;
String msg;
XmlNodeList selectedNodes;

taCategories.Fill(dsAdoSbs.Categories);
taProducts.Fill(dsAdoSbs.Products);
xdd = new XmlDataDocument(dsAdoSbs);

qry = "*";
selectedNodes = xdd.FirstChild.SelectNodes(qry);

msg = "";
foreach(XmlNode theNode in selectedNodes)
    msg += "\n" + theNode.ChildNodes[1].InnerText;

MessageBox.Show(msg);
```

The first few lines of this code block declare local variables and instantiate an XmlData-Document based on the dsAdoSbs DataSet. Then the SelectedNodes method is called by using an XPath expression that returns all of the nodes at the first level of the hierarchy. Finally the name of the returned Category is displayed in a message box.

2. Press F5 to run the application.

3. Click XPath Query.

   The application displays the Category names.

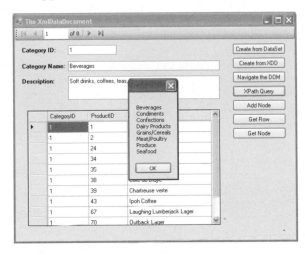

4. Close the application.

Using XmlDataDocument Methods

The methods of the XmlDataDocument, most of which are inherited from the XmlDocument or the XmlNode class, fall into two primary categories: those that are used to manipulate the XmlNode objects, and those that are used to coordinate the nodes of the XmlDataDocument with the DataRows of the DataSet.

Manipulating DataRows by Using XML

The most important of the XmlDataDocument methods that create, add and remove XmlNodes from the XmlDataDocument are shown in Table 18-2.

Table 18-2   XmlNode Creation and Manipulation Methods of XmlDataDocument

Method	Description
AppendChild(childNode)	Appends the childNode to the end of the list of child nodes of the current node.
Clone	Creates a duplicate of the current node.

Table 18-2   XmlNode Creation and Manipulation Methods of XmlDataDocument

Method	Description
CloneNode(cloneDeep)	Creates a duplicate of the current node and, if the cloneDeep Boolean parameter is True, of the child nodes of the current node.
CreateAttribute(name)	Creates an XmlAttribute that has the specified name.
CreateElement(name)	Creates an XmlElement that has the specified name.
CreateNode(name)	Creates an XmlNode that has the specified name.
CreateTextNode(text)	Creates an XmlText that has the specified text.
InsertAfter(node)	Inserts the specified node immediately after the current node.
InsertBefore(node)	Inserts the specified node immediately before the current node.
PrependChild(node)	Adds the specified node to the beginning of the list of child nodes of the current node.
RemoveAll	Removes all the child nodes.
RemoveChild(node)	Removes the specified child node.
ReplaceChild(newNode, oldNode)	Replaces the specified existing child node with the specified new child node.

Most of the methods are self-explanatory, but it's important to remember that the nodes of an XmlDataDocument are an ordered list. Unlike the relational table, which is set of rows without inherent order, XML elements are inherently ordered, and in the XML world, that order is frequently important.

The other thing to be careful about when manipulating a DataSet through an XmlData-Document is that you must set the EnforceConstraints property of the DataSet to False before the operations. You'll almost always want to set this property to True when the operations are complete.

Add a Category by Using XML: Visual Basic

1. In the Code Editor, add the following lines to the btnAddNode_Click event handler:

```vb
Dim xdd As XmlDataDocument
Dim newNode As XmlElement
Dim childNode As XmlNode
Dim x As Integer

xdd = New XmlDataDocument(dsAdoSbs)
xdd.Load("AdoSbs.xml")

dsAdoSbs.EnforceConstraints = False

newNode = xdd.LastChild.LastChild.CloneNode(True)
For x = newNode.ChildNodes.Count - 1 To 0 Step -1
    childNode = newNode.ChildNodes(x)
    If childNode.Name = "Products" Then
```

```
        newNode.RemoveChild(childNode)
    End If
Next
```

```
newNode.ChildNodes(0).InnerText = 999
newNode.ChildNodes(1).InnerText = "New Category"
```

```
xdd.LastChild.AppendChild(newNode)
```

```
dsAdoSbs.EnforceConstraints = True
```

This code first declares some local variables and instantiates an XmlDataDocument, and then sets the EnforceConstraints property of the DataSet to False. It then clones the last Category and all of that node's child nodes, assigning the result to newNode.

The For...Next loop removes the subsidiary Products nodes, sets the attributes of the new Category node, and then adds the new Category node to the XmlDataDocument. Finally, the EnforceConstraints property of the DataSet is set to True.

2. Press F5 to run the application.

3. Click Add Node.

    The application adds the new Category to the DataSet.

4. Click the Move Last button on the BindingNavigator to display the new row.

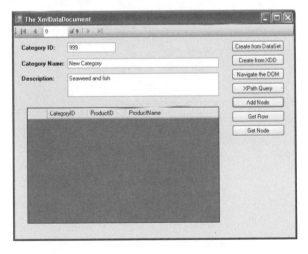

5. Close the application.

Add a Category by Using XML: Visual C#

1. In the Code Editor, add the following lines to the btnAddNode_Click event handler:

```
XmlDataDocument xdd;
XmlNode newNode;
XmlNode childNode;
```

```
xdd = new XmlDataDocument(dsAdoSbs);
xdd.Load("AdoSbs.xml");

dsAdoSbs.EnforceConstraints = false;

newNode = xdd.LastChild.LastChild.CloneNode(true);
for (int x = newNode.ChildNodes.Count - 1; x > 0; x--)
{
    childNode = newNode.ChildNodes[x];
    if (childNode.Name == "Products")
        newNode.RemoveChild(childNode);
}

newNode.ChildNodes[0].InnerText = "999";
newNode.ChildNodes[1].InnerText = "New Category";

xdd.LastChild.AppendChild(newNode);

dsAdoSbs.EnforceConstraints = true;
```

This code first declares some local variables and instantiates an XmlDataDocument, and then sets the EnforceConstraints property of the DataSet to False. It then clones the last Category and all of that node's child nodes, assigning the result to newNode.

The For...Next loop removes the subsidiary Products nodes, sets the attributes of the new Category node, and then adds the new Category node to the XmlDataDocument. Finally the EnforceConstraints property of the DataSet is set to True.

2. Press F5 to run the application.

3. Click Add Node.

    The application adds the new Category to the DataSet.

4. Click the Move Last button on the BindingNavigator to display the new row.

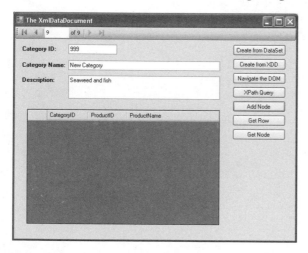

5. Close the application.

Coordinating DataRows and XmlDataDocument Elements

The XmlDataDocument exposes two properties, GetNodeFromRow and GetRowFromNode, which are used to convert XML nodes to DataRows and vice versa.

Retrieve a Node from a DataRow: Visual Basic

1. In the Code Editor, add the following code to the btnGetRow_Click event handler:

```
Dim xdd As XmlDataDocument
Dim theNode As XmlElement
Dim theRow As DataRow
Dim theCatRow As AdoSbsDataSet.CategoriesRow

taCategories.Fill(dsAdoSbs.Categories)
taProducts.Fill(dsAdoSbs.Products)
xdd = New XmlDataDocument(dsAdoSbs)

theNode = CType(xdd.DocumentElement.FirstChild, XmlElement)
theRow = xdd.GetRowFromElement(theNode)
theCatRow = CType(theRow, AdoSbsDataSet.CategoriesRow)

MessageBox.Show("Category Name:  " + theCatRow.CategoryName, _
    "Get Row From Node")
```

2. Press F5 to run the application.

3. Click Get Row.

   The application displays the Category Name in a message box.

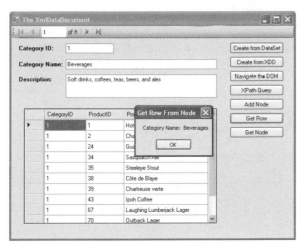

4. Close the application.

Retrieve a Node from a DataRow: Visual C#

1. In the Code Editor, add the following code to the btnGetRow_Click event handler:

```
XmlDataDocument xdd;
XmlElement theNode;
DataRow theRow;
AdoSbsDataSet.CategoriesRow theCatRow;

taCategories.Fill(dsAdoSbs.Categories);
taProducts.Fill(dsAdoSbs.Products);
xdd = new XmlDataDocument(dsAdoSbs);

theNode = (XmlElement)xdd.DocumentElement.FirstChild;
theRow = xdd.GetRowFromElement(theNode);
theCatRow = (AdoSbsDataSet.CategoriesRow)theRow;

MessageBox.Show("Category Name:  " + theCatRow.CategoryName,
    "Get Row From Node");
```

2. Press F5 to run the application.

3. Click Get Row.

   The application displays the Category Name in a message box.

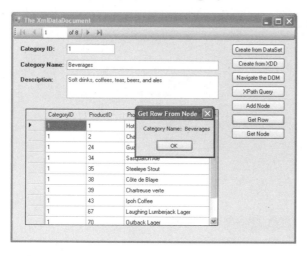

4. Close the application.

Retrieve a DataRow from a Node: Visual Basic

1. In the Code Editor, add the following code to the btnGetNode_Click event handler:

```
Dim xdd As XmlDataDocument
Dim theNode As XmlElement
Dim theRow As AdoSbsDataSet.CategoriesRow

taProducts.Fill(Me.dsAdoSbs.Products)
taCategories.Fill(Me.dsAdoSbs.Categories)
```

```
xdd = New XmlDataDocument(dsAdoSbs)

theRow = dsAdoSbs.Categories.Rows(3)
theNode = xdd.GetElementFromRow(theRow)

MessageBox.Show("Category Name: " + theNode.ChildNodes(2).InnerText)
```

2. Press F5 to run the application.

3. Click Get Node.

   The application displays the Category Name in a message box.

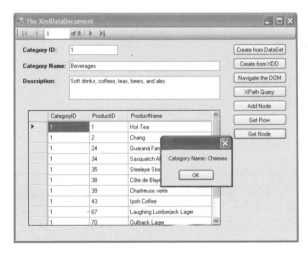

4. Close the application.

Retrieve a DataRow from a Node: Visual C#

1. In the Code Editor, add the following code to the btnGetNode_Click event handler:

```
XmlDataDocument xdd;
XmlElement theNode;
AdoSbsDataSet.CategoriesRow theRow;

taProducts.Fill(dsAdoSbs.Products);
taCategories.Fill(dsAdoSbs.Categories);
xdd = new XmlDataDocument(dsAdoSbs);

theRow = (AdoSbsDataSet.CategoriesRow)dsAdoSbs.Categories.Rows[3];
theNode = xdd.GetElementFromRow(theRow);

MessageBox.Show("Category Name: " + theNode.ChildNodes[2].InnerText);
```

2. Press F5 to run the application.

3. Click Get Node.

   The application displays the Category Name in a message box.

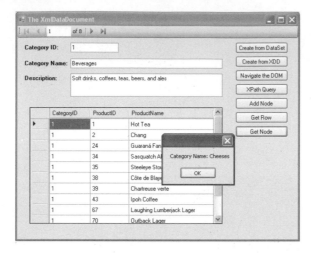

4. Close the application.

Summary

In this chapter we discussed the XmlDataDocument, which provides a mechanism for manipulating relational data by using XML. You can create an XmlDataDocument from a DataSet by passing the DataSet to the XmlDataDocument constructor, and you can create a DataSet from an XmlDataDocument by referencing its DataSet property.

We then briefly examined the XML DOM and the properties of the XmlDataDocument that allow you to navigate the DOM hierarchy. We also saw how to perform XPath queries that provide a more efficient and powerful mechanism for navigating and selecting XmlDataDocument nodes.

We also explored the XmlDataDocument methods that you can use to create rows in the DataSet by adding nodes to the XmlDataDocument. Finally, we examined the GetRowFromNode and GetNodeFromRow methods that you can use to translate XmlDataDocument nodes to DataSet DataRows and vice versa.

Chapter 19

Using ADO and ADOX in the .NET Framework

After completing this chapter, you will be able to:

- Establish a reference to the ADO and ADOX COM libraries.
- Create an ADO Connection.
- Retrieve data from an ADO Recordset.
- Update an ADO Recordset.
- Create a database by using ADOX.
- Add a table to a database by using ADOX.

In the previous two chapters, we examined using XML data with Microsoft ADO.NET objects. In this chapter, we'll look at the interface to another type of data: data objects created using previous versions of ADO.

We'll also examine the Microsoft ADO Extensions for DDL and Security (ADOX) library, which provides the ability to create database objects under programmatic control. This functionality is not available in ADO.NET, although you can execute Data Definition Language (DDL) statements such as CREATE TABLE on servers that support them.

Understanding COM Interoperability

Maintaining interoperability with Component Object Model (COM) components was a design goal of the Microsoft .NET Framework. By using the COM Interop functions provided by the .NET Framework, you can gain access to all the objects, methods and events that are exposed by any COM object simply by establishing a reference to it. This extends to previous versions of ADO and to COM objects developed with those versions.

After the reference has been established, the COM objects behave just as though they were .NET Framework classes. What happens behind the scenes, of course, is more complicated. When a reference to any COM object, including ADO or ADOX, is declared, the .NET Framework creates an interop assembly that handles communication between the .NET Framework and COM.

The interop assembly handles a number of tasks, but the most important is translating between COM and .NET Framework data types, a process known as *data type marshalling*. Table 19-1 shows the type conversion performed by the interop assembly for standard COM value types.

Table 19-1   COM Data Type Marshalling

COM Data Type	.NET Framework Type
bool	Int32
char, small	SByte
short	Int16
long, int	Int32
hyper	Int64
unsigned char, byte	Byte
wchar_t, unsigned short	UInt16
unsigned long, unsigned int	UInt32
unsigned hyper	UInt64
float	Single
double	Double
VARIANT_BOOL	Boolean
void *	IntPtr
HRESULT	Int16 or IntPtr
SCODE	Int32
BSTR	String
LPSTR	String
LPWSTR	String
VARIANT	Object
DECIMAL	Decimal
DATE	DateTime
GUID	Guid
CURRENCY	Decimal
IUnknown *	Object
IDispatch *	Object
SAFEARRAY(type)	type[]

Understanding ADO in the .NET Framework

In addition to the generic COM interoperability and data type marshalling provided by the .NET Framework for all COM objects, the .NET Framework provides specific support for the ADO and ADOX libraries and COM objects by using them.

This additional support includes data type marshalling for core ADO data types. The .NET Framework equivalents for core ADO data types are shown in Table 19-2. Of course, after a reference to ADO is established, complex types such as Recordset and ADO Connection become available through the ADO component.

Table 19-2   **ADO Data Type Marshalling**

ADO Data Type	.NET Framework Type
adEmpty	null
adBoolean	Int16
adTinyInt	SByte
adSmallInt	Int16
adInteger	Int32
adBigInt	Int64
adUnsignedTinyInt	promoted to Int16
adUnsignedSmallInt	promoted to Int32
adUnsignedInt	promoted to Int64
adUnsignedBigInt	promoted to Decimal
adSingle	Single
adDouble	Double
adCurrency	Decimal
adDecimal	Decimal
adNumeric	Decimal
adDate	DateTime
adDBDate	DateTime
adDBTime	DateTime
adDBTimeStamp	DateTime
adFileTime	DateTime
adGUID	Guid
adError	ExternalException
adIUnknown	object
adIDispatch	object
adVariant	object
adPropVariant	object
adBinary	byte[]
adChar	string
adWChar	string
adBSTR	string
adChapter	not supported
adUserDefined	not supported
adVarNumeric	not supported

Establishing a Reference to ADO

The first step in using a previous version of ADO, or a COM component that references a previous version, is to set a reference to the component. There are several methods for exposing the ADO component, but the most convenient is simply to add the reference within Microsoft Visual Studio 2005.

Add References to the ADO and ADOX Libraries: Visual Basic

1. In an instance of Visual Studio, open the Chapter 19 – Start project, and if necessary, double-click ADOInterop.vb in the Solution Explorer.

   Visual Studio displays the form in the Form Designer.

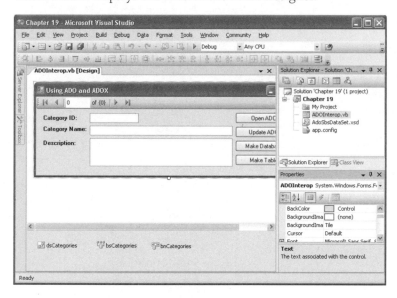

2. In the Solution Explorer, double-click My Project to display the My Projects window, and then click the References tab.

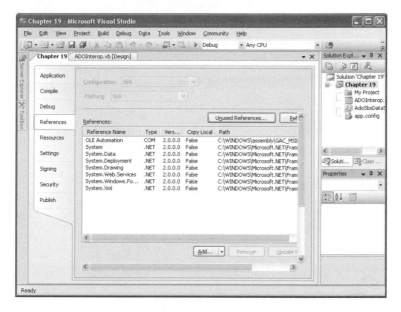

3. Click the Add button.

   Visual Studio displays the Add References dialog box.

4. Click the COM tab, and select the component named Microsoft ActiveX Data Objects 2.8 Library.

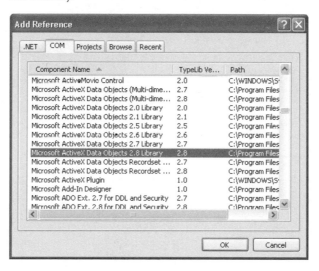

5. Click OK.

   Visual Studio adds the component to the list of references.

6. Click the Add button.

   Visual Studio displays the Add References dialog box.

7. On the COM tab, select the component named Microsoft ADO Ext. 2.8 For DDL And Security.

8. Click OK.

   Visual Studio adds the component ADOX to the list of references.

9. Close the My Project window.

Add References to the ADO and ADOX Libraries: Visual C#

1. In an instance of Visual Studio, open the Chapter 19 – Start project, and if necessary, double-click ADOInterop.cs in the Solution Explorer.

   Visual Studio displays the form in the Form Designer.

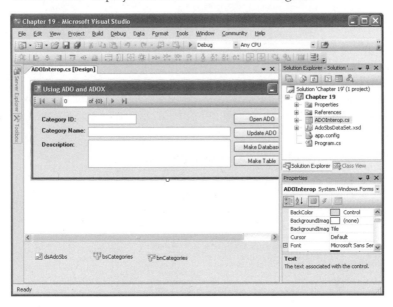

2. In the Solution Explorer, right-click the References node, and select Add Reference.

   Visual Studio displays the Add References dialog box.

3. Click the COM tab, select the component named Microsoft ActiveX Data Objects 2.8.

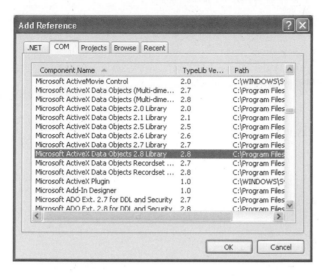

4. Click OK.

    Visual Studio adds the component to the list of references.

5. In the Solution Explorer, right-click the References node, and select Add Reference.

    Visual Studio displays the Add References dialog box.

6. On the COM tab, select the component named Microsoft ADO Ext. 2.8 For DDL And Security.

7. Click OK.

    Visual Studio adds the component ADOX to the list of references.

Creating ADO Objects

After the references to the ADO components have been added, you can create ADO objects and set their properties set just like any object exposed by the .NET Framework class library.

The ADO Connection Object

Like ADO.NET, ADO uses a Connection object to represent a unique session with a data source. The most important property of an ADO Connection, just like an ADO.NET Connection, is the ConnectionString that establishes the Data Provider, the database information, and if appropriate, the user information.

Create an ADO Connection: Visual Basic

1. Press F7 to display the Code Editor.

2. Add the following lines to the CreateConnection procedure, modifying the path of the dsStr text value as necessary if you have not installed the practice files in their default location:

```
Dim dsStr As String
Dim dsCn As String
Dim cn As ADODB.Connection

cn = New ADODB.Connection
dsStr = "C:\Microsoft Press\ADO.NET 2.0 Step by Step\" + _
    "SampleDBs\AdoStepByStep.mdb"
dsCn = "Provider=Microsoft.Jet.OLEDB.4.0;Data Source=" + dsStr + ";"
cn.ConnectionString = dsCn

Return cn
```

Create an ADO Connection: Visual C#

1. Press F7 to display the Code Editor.

2. Add the following lines to the CreateConnection procedure, modifying the path of the dsStr text value as necessary if you have not installed the practice files in their default location:

```
string dsStr;
string dsCn;
ADODB.Connection cn;

cn = new ADODB.Connection();
dsStr = "C:\\Microsoft Press\\ADO.NET 2.0 Step by Step\\" +
  "SampleDBs\\AdoStepByStep.mdb";
dsCn = "Provider=Microsoft.Jet.OLEDB.4.0;Data Source=" + dsStr + ";";
cn.ConnectionString = dsCn;

return cn;
```

Using ADO Recordsets

ADO has no direct equivalent for a DataSet. The ADO Recordset object is roughly equivalent to an ADO.NET DataTable and is the primary data object in the ADO model.

Filling ADO Recordsets

In addition to support for ADO data types, the OleDbDataAdapter provides direct support for ADO Recordsets by exposing a version of the Fill method that accepts an ADO Recordset as a parameter. There are two versions of the Fill method, as shown in Table 19-3.

Table 19-3   OleDbDataAdapter Recordset Fill Methods

Method	Description
Fill(dataTable, recordset)	Adds or refreshes rows in the specified DataTable to match those in the specified Recordset.
Fill(dataSet, recordset, dataTable)	Adds or refreshes rows in the specified DataTable in the specified DataSet to match those in the specified Recordset.

If the DataTable passed to the Fill method doesn't exist in the DataSet, it is created based on the schema of the ADO Recordset. If primary key information does not exist, the rows in the ADO Recordset are simply added to the DataTable. If primary key information does exist, the rows in the ADO Recordset that match rows in the DataTable are merged.

Retrieve Data from an ADO Recordset: Visual Basic

1. In the Code Editor, add the following lines to the btnOpen_Click event handler:

```
Dim rs As ADODB.Recordset
Dim cnADO As ADODB.Connection
Dim daTemp As New OleDbDataAdapter()

rs = New ADODB.Recordset()
cnADO = CreateConnection()

cnADO.Open()

rs.Open("SELECT * FROM CategoriesByName", cnADO)
daTemp.Fill(dsCategories.CategoriesByName, rs)

cnADO.Close()

SetBindings(dsCategories)
```

The first thee lines declare an ADO Recordset, an ADO Connection and an OleDbData-Adapter. The next two lines call the CreateConnection function that we added in the previous exercise to create the ADO Connection object, and then open the connection.

The next three lines open the ADO Recordset, load the rows by using the DataAdapter, and then close the ADO Recordset. The final line calls a scaffolding function that binds the form's text boxes to the specified DataSet.

2. Press F5 to run the application.

3. Click Open ADO.

The application loads the data from ADO and displays it in the form's text boxes.

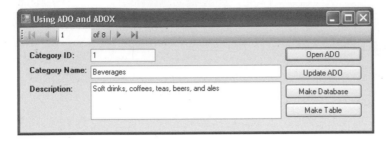

4. Close the application.

Retrieve Data from an ADO Recordset: Visual C#

1. In the Code Editor, add the following lines to the btnOpen_Click event handler:

```
ADODB.Recordset rs;
ADODB.Connection cnADO;
OleDbDataAdapter daTemp;

rs = new ADODB.Recordset();
cnADO = CreateConnection();
daTemp = new OleDbDataAdapter();

cnADO.Open("", "", "",0);
rs.Open("SELECT * FROM CategoriesByName", cnADO,
    ADODB.CursorTypeEnum.adOpenForwardOnly, ADODB.LockTypeEnum.adLockReadOnly, 0);
daTemp.Fill(dsCategories.CategoriesByName, rs);

cnADO.Close();

SetBindings(dsCategories);
```

The first thee lines declare an ADO Recordset, an ADO Connection, and an OleDbData-Adapter. The next two lines call the CreateConnection function that we added in the previous exercise to create the ADO Connection object, and then open the connection. The next three lines open the ADO Recordset, load the rows by using the DataAdapter, and then close the ADO Recordset. The final line calls a scaffolding function that binds the form's text boxes to the specified DataSet.

2. Press F5 to run the application.

3. Click Open ADO. The application loads the data from ADO and displays it in the form's text boxes.

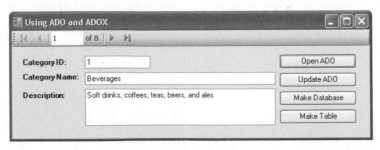

4. Close the application.

Updating ADO Recordsets

The Fill method of the OleDbDataAdapter provides a convenient mechanism for loading data from an ADO Recordset into a .NET Framework DataTable. Unfortunately the communication is one-way. The .NET Framework doesn't provide a direct method for updating an ADO Recordset based on ADO.NET data.

Fortunately, it isn't difficult to update an ADO data source from within the .NET Framework: You simply copy the data values from the appropriate sources and then use intrinsic ADO functions to do the update.

Update an ADO Recordset: Visual Basic

1. In the Code Editor, add the following lines to the btnUpdate_Click event handler:

```
Dim rsADO As ADODB.Recordset
Dim cnADO As ADODB.Connection

rsADO = New ADODB.Recordset()
cnADO = CreateConnection()

cnADO.Open()

rsADO.ActiveConnection = cnADO
rsADO.Open("SELECT * FROM CategoriesByName", cnADO, _
    ADODB.CursorTypeEnum.adOpenDynamic, _
    ADODB.LockTypeEnum.adLockOptimistic)

rsADO.AddNew()
rsADO.Fields("CategoryName").Value = "Test"
rsADO.Fields("Description").Value = "Description"
rsADO.Update()

MessageBox.Show("Finished", "ADO Update")

rsADO.Delete(ADODB.AffectEnum.adAffectCurrent)
rsADO.Close()
cnADO.Close()
```

The first few lines declare some local variables and then instantiate and configure an ADO Recordset and an ADO Connection. The code block then uses the ADO AddNew and Update methods to create a new row and set its values. A message box is displayed when the update is complete. Next the new row is deleted in case you want to run this code multiple times. Finally, the Recordset and ADO Connection are closed.

2. Press F5 to run the application.

3. Click Update ADO.

The application adds the row to the Recordset and then displays a message box showing completion.

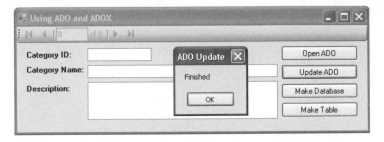

4. Close the message box, and then close the application.

Update an ADO Recordset: Visual C#

1. In the Code Editor, add the following lines to the btnUpdate_Click event handler:

```
ADODB.Recordset rsADO;
ADODB.Connection cnADO;

rsADO = new ADODB.Recordset();
cnADO = CreateConnection();

cnADO.Open("", "", "", 0);

rsADO.ActiveConnection = cnADO;
rsADO.Open("Select * From CategoriesByName", cnADO,
    ADODB.CursorTypeEnum.adOpenDynamic,
    ADODB.LockTypeEnum.adLockOptimistic, 0);

rsADO.AddNew(Type.Missing, Type.Missing);
rsADO.Fields["CategoryName"].Value = "Test";
rsADO.Fields["Description"].Value = "Description";
rsADO.Update(Type.Missing, Type.Missing);

MessageBox.Show("Finished", "ADO Update");

rsADO.Delete(ADODB.AffectEnum.adAffectCurrent);
rsADO.Close();
cnADO.Close();
```

The first few lines declare some local variables and then instantiate and configure an ADO Recordset and an ADO Connection. The code block then uses the ADO AddNew and Update methods to create a new row and set its values. A message box is displayed when the update is complete. Next the new row is deleted in case you want to run this code multiple times. Finally, the Recordset and ADO Connection are closed.

2. Press F5 to run the application.

3. Click Update ADO.

The application adds the row to the Recordset and then displays a message box showing completion.

4.   Close the message box, and then close the application.

Understanding ADOX in the .NET Framework

ADOX exposes an object model that allows data source objects to be created and manipulated. The ADOX object model is shown in the following figure. Note that not all data sources support all the objects in the model; this is determined by the specific Data Provider.

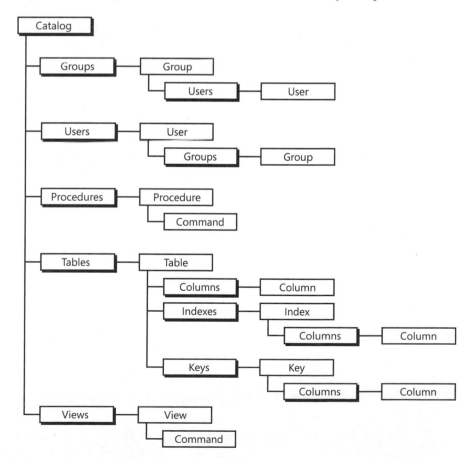

The top-level object, Catalog, equates to a specific data source. This data source is almost always a database, but specific OLE DB Data Providers might expose different objects. The Groups and Users collections control access security for the data sources that implement this type of security.

The Tables object represents the tables within the database. Each table contains a Columns collection, which represents the following:

- Individual fields in the table

- An Indexes collection, which represents physical indexes

- A Keys collection, which is used to define unique primary and foreign keys.

The Procedures collection represents stored procedures on the data source, and the Views collection represents views or queries. This model doesn't always match the object model of the data source. For example, Microsoft Jet, the underlying data source for Microsoft Access, represents both Views and Procedures as Query objects. When mapped to an ADOX Catalog, any query that updates or inserts rows, along with any query that contains parameters, is mapped to a Procedure object. Queries that consist solely of SELECT statements are mapped to views.

Creating Database Objects by Using ADOX

As we've seen, ADOX provides a mechanism for creating data source objects programmatically. ADO.NET doesn't support this functionality. You can, of course, execute a CREATE <object> SQL statement by using an ADO.NET Data Command, but data definition syntax varies wildly between data sources, so it is often more convenient to use ADOX and let the OLE DB Data Provider handle the operation.

The Catalog object supports a Create method that you can use to create a new database, while the Tables and Columns collections support Append methods that you can use to create new schema objects.

Create a Database by Using ADOX: Visual Basic

1. In the Code Editor, add the following lines to the btnMakeDB_Click event handler, modifying the file location as necessary:

```
Dim dsStr As String
Dim dsCn As String
Dim mdb As ADOX.Catalog

mdb = New ADOX.Catalog()

dsStr = "C:\Microsoft Press\ADO.NET 2.0 Step by Step\SampleDBs\Test.mdb"
If File.Exists(dsStr) Then
    File.Delete(dsStr)
End If
```

```
dsCn = "Provider=Microsoft.Jet.OLEDB.4.0;Data Source=" + dsStr + ";"

mdb.Create(dsCn)
mdb.ActiveConnection.Close()

MessageBox.Show("Finished","Make DB")
```

2. Press F5 to run the application.

3. Click Make Database.

    The application creates a Jet database named Test.mdb and then displays the message box.

4. Close the message box, and then close the application.

5. Use Windows Explorer to verify that the new Test.mdb database has been created.

Create a Database by Using ADOX: Visual C#

1. In the Code Editor, add the following lines to the btnMakeDB_Click event handler, modifying the file location as necessary:

```
string dsStr;
string dsCn;
ADOX.Catalog mdb;

mdb = new ADOX.Catalog();

dsStr = "C:\\Microsoft Press\\ADO.NET 2.0 Step by Step\\" +
    "SampleDBs\\Test.mdb";
if (File.Exists(dsStr))
{
    File.Delete(dsStr);
}
dsCn = "Provider=Microsoft.Jet.OLEDB.4.0;Data Source=" + dsStr + ";";

mdb.Create(dsCn);
((ADODB.Connection)mdb.ActiveConnection).Close();

MessageBox.Show("Finished","Make DB");
```

2. Press F5 to run the application.

3. Click Make Database.

The application creates a Jet database named Test.mdb and then displays the message box.

4. Close the message box, and then close the application.

5. Use Windows Explorer to verify that the new Test.mdb database has been created.

Add a Table to a Database by Using ADOX: Visual Basic

1. In the Code Editor, add the following lines to the btnMakeTable_Click event handler:

```vb
Dim dsStr As String
Dim dsCn As String
Dim cnADO As ADODB.Connection
Dim mdb As ADOX.Catalog
Dim dt As ADOX.Table

mdb = New ADOX.Catalog()
cnADO = New ADODB.Connection()
dsStr = "C:\Microsoft Press\ADO.NET 2.0 Step by Step\SampleDBs\Test.mdb"
dsCn = "Provider=Microsoft.Jet.OLEDB.4.0;Data Source=" + dsStr + ";"
cnADO.ConnectionString = dsCn

cnADO.Open()
mdb.ActiveConnection = cnADO

dt = New ADOX.Table()
dt.Name = "New Table"
dt.Columns.Append("TableID", ADOX.DataTypeEnum.adWChar, 5)
dt.Columns.Append("Value", ADOX.DataTypeEnum.adWChar, 20)
dt.Keys.Append("PK_NewTable", ADOX.KeyTypeEnum.adKeyPrimary, _
    "TableID")
mdb.Tables.Append(dt)

cnADO.Close()

MessageBox.Show("Finished", "Make Table")
```

2. Press F5 to run the application.

3. Click Make Table. The application adds the table to the Test.mdb database and displays the message box.

4. Close the message box, and then close the application.

5. If you have Microsoft Access installed on your computer, open the Test.mdb database, and confirm that the table named New Table has been added.

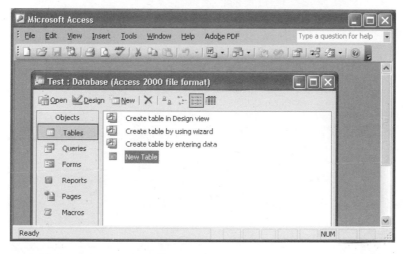

Add a Table to a Database by Using ADOX: Visual C#

1. In the Code Editor, add the following lines to the btnMakeTable_Click event handler:

```
string dsStr;
string dsCn;
ADODB.Connection cnADO;
ADOX.Catalog mdb;
ADOX.Table dt;

mdb = new ADOX.Catalog();
cnADO = new ADODB.Connection();
dsStr = "C:\\Microsoft Press\\ADO.NET 2.0 Step by Step\\" +
    "SampleDBs\\Test.mdb";
dsCn = "Provider=Microsoft.Jet.OLEDB.4.0;Data Source=" + dsStr + ";";
cnADO.ConnectionString = dsCn;

cnADO.Open("", "", "", 0);
mdb.ActiveConnection = cnADO;

dt = new ADOX.Table();
dt.Name = "New Table";
dt.Columns.Append("TableID", ADOX.DataTypeEnum.adWChar, 5);
```

```
dt.Columns.Append("Value", ADOX.DataTypeEnum.adWChar, 20);
dt.Keys.Append("PK_NewTable", ADOX.KeyTypeEnum.adKeyPrimary,
    "TableID","","");
mdb.Tables.Append(dt);

cnADO.Close();

MessageBox.Show("Finished", "Make Table");
```

2. Press F5 to run the application.

3. Click Make Table.

4. Close the message box, and then close the application.

5. If you have Microsoft Access installed on your computer, open the Test.mdb database, and confirm that the table named New Table has been added.

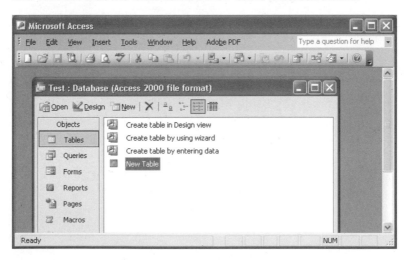

Summary

In this final chapter, we examined the use of the ADO and ADOX COM libraries from within the .NET Framework. We examined COM interoperability with the .NET Framework, looking at data type marshalling for COM objects in general and for ADO data types in particular. We then turned to using the ADO and ADOX libraries. We saw the method for creating an ADO Connection—which is similar to creating an ADO.NET Connection—and a way to retrieve and update data by using an ADO Recordset. Finally we examined using the ADOX library to create databases, tables and columns.

Index

Symbols

@ character, SqlCommand object and, 61

A

AcceptChanges methods, 139, 176, 180, 248, 249
  AcceptChangesDuring properties and, 90–91
accepting changes
  to DataSets (Visual Basic), 249–252
  to DataSets (Visual C#), 252–255
AcceptRejectRule property, 168
  Access databases, ConnectionString property, setting to connect to, 30
AccessDataSource control, 369, 370. 374
Action Rule values, table, 168
Add methods, 61, 154, 301
  adding data to DataTables with form of, 173
  adding parameters with, 63
  BindingSource lists and, 304
  types of, 154–155
AddingNew event, 305
addition (+) operator, 217
AddNew method, 222, 279, 301, 304
ADO
  .NET Framework and, data type marshalling, 471
  adding references to libraries (Visual Basic), 472
  adding references to libraries (Visual C#), 474
  Connection objects, creating (Visual Basic, Visual C#), 476
  objects, creating, 475
  Recordsets, filling, 477
  Recordsets, retrieving data from (Visual Basic), 477
  Recordsets, retrieving data from (Visual C#), 478
  Recordsets, updating (Visual Basic), 479
  Recordsets, updating (Visual C#), 480
ADO.NET, xiii, 3
  adapters. *See* DataAdapter objects; TableAdapter objects
  BindingSources. *See* BindingSources
  book support links, xviii
  book's intended audience, xiii
  classes, division of, 4. *See also* Data Providers (.NET Framework), 4
  code samples, xvii

Commit method, 113
concurrency, 228
conventions, features of book, xiv
CurrencyManagers. *See* CurrencyManagers
Data Command, 48
data model, 315
DataSets, 125
finding starting point in book, xiv
installing code samples, xvi
multiple transactions and, 113
object model, primary object view, 4
objects, maintaining state, 356
online companion content page, xviii
organization of book, xiii
Rollback method, 113
sample code, 51
supported DataSets, 124
system requirements for practice exercises, xv
transactions, 107
uninstalling code samples, xvii
Web forms and, 341
AdoStepByStep database, attaching, xvi
ADOX, 481
  adding tables to databases by using (Visual Basic), 484
  adding tables to databases by using (Visual C#), 485
  creating databases by using (Visual Basic), 482
  creating databases by using (Visual C#), 483
  libraries, adding references to (Visual Basic), 472
  libraries, adding references to (Visual C#), 474
  Tables object, 482
aggregate functions, 216
AllowDbNull property, 164
AllowDelete property, 214
AllowEdit property, 214
AllowNew property, 214, 292
AlternatingItemTemplates, 403
AND operator, 216
AppendChild(childNode) method, 461
AppendDataBoundItems property, 396
Application Configuration file, storing ConnectionString property in, 31
Application state, storing data on servers, 356, 357
ApplyDefaultSort property, 214
arithmetic operators, table, 217

artificial keys, 312
ASP.NET
  data controls, 393
  event handlers. *See* navigation button controls
  hierarchical controls, 393
  ListControl class, 393
  maintaining object state within Internet applications, 356
assignment statements (Visual Basic, Visual C#), 113
attributes, 418
  InferXmlSchemas and, 428
  writing columns as (Visual Basic), 443
  writing columns as (Visual C#), 445
AutoIncrement property, 164
AutoIncrementSeed property, 164
AutoIncrementStep property, 164
Avg function, 216

B

BaseClass property, 193, 194
BeginEdit method, 180, 238
  deferring column changes by using (Visual Basic), 238
  deferring column changes by using (Visual C#), 240
BeginInit method, 176, 222
BeginLoadData method, 176
BeginTransaction methods, 37, 108
  IsolationLevel parameters, table, 109
BindableComponent property, 282
binding. *See also* data binding
  complex data, adding in code (Visual Basic), 273
  complex data, adding in code (Visual C#), 274
  complex data, by using Properties window, 272
  complex, ListBox controls (Visual Basic), 353–355
  complex, ListBox controls (Visual C#), 355–356
  connection properties to form controls (Visual Basic), 35
  connection properties to form controls (Visual C#), 36
  control properties, at run time, 266
  controls, 294
  controls within templates, 405
  controls, to DataRelations, 315

About the Author

Rebecca M. Riordan has more than 15 years' experience designing and developing databases and other applications. She is a Microsoft MVP and a frequent speaker at conferences, including Microsoft TechEd. She is the author of many books, including *Microsoft SQL Server 2000 Programming Step by Step* (Microsoft Press, 2000), *Seeing Data: Designing User Interfaces for Database Systems Using .NET* (Addison-Wesley, 2005), and *Designing Effective Database Systems* (Addison-Wesley, 2005).

What do you think of this book? We want to hear from you!

Do you have a few minutes to participate in a brief online survey? Microsoft is interested in hearing your feedback about this publication so that we can continually improve our books and learning resources for you.

To participate in our survey, please visit:

www.microsoft.com/learning/booksurvey

And enter this book's ISBN, 0-7356-2164-0. As a thank-you to survey participants in the United States and Canada, each month we'll randomly select five respondents to win one of five $100 gift certificates from a leading online merchant.* At the conclusion of the survey, you can enter the drawing by providing your e-mail address, which will be used for prize notification *only*.

Thanks in advance for your input. Your opinion counts!

Sincerely,

Microsoft Learning

Learn More. Go Further.